religion

THE PROPHETIC CLERGY

THE PROPHETIC CLERGY
Social Activism Among Protestant Ministers

HAROLD E. QUINLEY

A WILEY-INTERSCIENCE PUBLICATION

JOHN WILEY & SONS, New York · London · Sydney · Toronto

Library of Congress Cataloging in Publication Data:

Quinley, Harold E.
  The prophetic clergy.

  "A Wiley-Interscience publication."
  Includes bibliographical references.
  1. Protestant churches—United States—Clergy.
2. Church and social problems—United States.
I. Title.

BR517.Q56   253'.2   74–5175
ISBN 0–471–70265–X

Printed in the United States of America

10 9 8 7 6 5 4 3 2 1

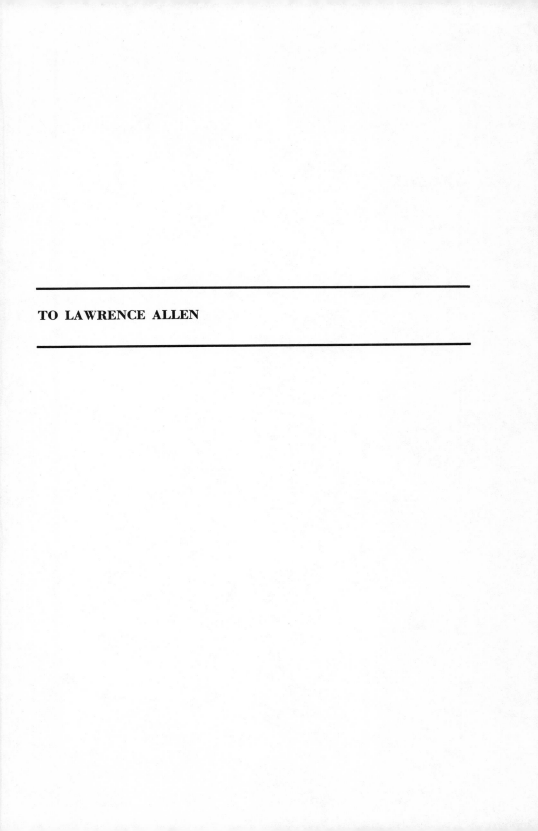

TO LAWRENCE ALLEN

ACKNOWLEDGMENTS

The research reported here was begun in 1968 at the Institute of Political Studies, Stanford University, as one of several efforts to investigate linkages between professionals and politics. The author is grateful to the supervisor of this project and his teacher at Stanford, Heinz Eulau. Professor Eulau provided encouragement and patient guidance throughout the research and demanded standards of professionalism and objectivity which greatly improved the final product.

This study benefited greatly as well from the assistance of Charles Y. Glock and Rodney Stark of the Survey Research Center, University of California, Berkeley. Both shared with the author their knowledge of the problems facing organized religion and suggested many of the formulations that eventually found their way into the study. The research design and the questionnaire itself drew heavily from their published work in the field of religion.

Also making a major contribution to the study was Stuart McLean, who enlightened the author on many of the practical problems of the ministry—particularly those involved in developing a more ethically oriented church. Professor McLean likewise had a direct hand in a number of considerations that were brought into the study and offered valuable comments on the changes that have taken place in liberal churches over the last several years.

Others offering their expertise and advice at an early stage in the research project were Jeffrey K. Hadden, who kindly allowed the author to borrow questions from his own survey of Protestant clergymen, William Clebsch, Robert MacAfee Brown, and Rev. James Siefkes. Mrs. Sheila Babbie provided much needed and appreciated assistance in the study's design and execution and played a major role in assuring its success.

Alexander George contributed insightful comments on an early draft of the manuscript. William G. McLoughlin and Wendell S. Dietrich offered a number of useful suggestons for the first chapter. Elizabeth K. Beardsley improved the final product immeasurably through her astute criticisms of the manuscript. Rev. George Wilson was especially helpful in his suggestions on the follow-up study reported in the preface. Many thanks are also due to Elaine Casey, Mrs. Elaine Ugolnik, Barbara Pool, and Mrs. Mary Thayer for patiently typing the final manuscript and its many tables.

A special note of gratitude, finally, must be extended to the California ministers who took the time to complete the lengthy questionnaire. Without their cooperation, this research would most certainly have been impossible.

Support to conduct this study was obtained through grants from the National Science Foundation and the Anti-Defamation League. A post-doctoral Fellowship from the Social Science Research Council was invaluable in providing the author the opportunity for further study of the professions and of Protestant religion. As always, such support is greatly appreciated.

HAROLD E. QUINLEY

February 1974
Stanford University
Stanford, California

CONTENTS

THE PROPHETIC CLERGY

PROLOGUE

This study was conducted in 1968, when social activism in Protestant churches was near its peak. Based on a survey of 1580 parish ministers in California, it shows that prophetic leadership was strong even among those clergymen who were most directly exposed to the constraints of a predominantly conservative Protestant laity. A large majority of the California ministers, for example, actively campaigned against a controversial anti-fair housing initiative in the state (popularly known as Proposition 14); about one-third openly opposed the war in Vietnam while it still had overwhelming public support; and from 10 to 15 percent actively supported efforts to organize migratory farm workers in California's fertile San Joaquin Valley. Such statistics, moreover, are based on a sample that included such highly conservative denominations as the Southern Baptist Convention and the Missouri Synod-Lutheran Church; among the state's predominantly liberal Protestant churches, the proportion of ministers involved in public issues was considerably higher. One crude indicator of the extent of so-called new breed activism in California is the percentage of clergymen who reported that they had engaged in protest marches or acts of civil disobedience. Such actions—highly controversial during the sixties—had come to be associated with the new mood in the churches. In total, a quarter of the California ministers reported that they had participated in such activities, this figure reaching almost 40 percent in the more liberal denominations surveyed.[1]

1

There is no doubt that the situation has changed radically since 1968, both within the churches and outside them. Among the public in general, there exist greater feelings of resignation and apathy, as well as withdrawal from matters of public concern. Americans seem to be no more happy with the state of affairs than they were in the 1960s, but far less heavily involved in politics and more uncertain about what is to be done; in various ways, they are turning inward for answers and self-understanding. More importantly, the institutions that should be providing moral and intellectual leadership on public issues have been beset by major problems of their own. Most are suffering from the effects of financial difficulties, internal discord, and public distrust and are now attempting retrenchment and reorganization.

Protestant churches, most particularly liberal ones, exhibit many of these problems; indeed, they appear to be among the hardest hit by the new public mood and the worsening economic situation. Much of the optimism and sense of purpose that characterized the ministry during the 1960s has disappeared. Clergymen are less certain of their ethical roles today, and feelings of fatigue and frustration are not uncommon among former activists. Conservative sentiment and influence have also risen in Protestant churches. Laymen are more vocal in expressing their dissatisfaction with their churches' liberal policies, and they are demanding a stronger voice in church affairs and a return to more traditional religious concerns. The decline in membership and financial contributions, which has plagued liberal denominations for several years, appears finally to have reached crisis proportions. Large-scale cutbacks have recently been made in the staff personnel and expenditures of all the liberal churches—the major casualties being activist-oriented officials and programs.

Discussions with clergymen and others familiar with the situation in California churches confirm that substantial changes have occurred in the ethical behavior of Protestant ministers since the heyday of social activism in the 1960s.[2] Clergymen are not as socially active as they once were, and the churches have shifted their priorities away from ethical concerns. We examine some of the major causes for these changes in a moment, seeking to understand them in terms of some of the findings from our earlier study. First, however, we should note that the more spectacular and well-publicized recent changes have occurred on the denominational level, not within parish churches. Denominational officials were more insulated from conservative lay pressures during the 1960s and were freer to speak out on controversial issues; for them, the backlash has been later in coming and, as a result of the present financial crisis, more severe. On the parish level, the situation has worsened in the past several years for the activists, but not nearly as much. Employment is tight, and the more ethically committed clergy are feeling the squeeze the most. But being socially active has always been difficult for parish clergymen, and in this respect the situation today is not a great deal different from five years ago.

Moreover, the recent retrenchment in liberal churches should not block our recognition that with few exceptions, liberal church leaders remain committed to an ethically involved church. As our study clearly shows, the modernist clergy (as we call them) possess a highly integrated set of beliefs about theological, ethical, and political issues. They are not likely to change such views for more expediency, "going back" to an other worldly, conservative conception of the role of religion in society. They may indeed temper their activism in the face of strong lay pressures, or they may adopt new forms of church prophecy as a result of changing conditions or past failures. But their religion is ethically involved, and it would be a mistake to regard the present lull as a permanent retreat from social activism.

With these comments in mind, it is useful to review some of the changes that have taken place in Protestant churches since the 1960s and some of the factors that have contributed to these changes.

Politics in the 70s. Most recent discussions of the churches' role in public affairs have emphasized the current internal problems, especially those involving finances, of Protestant denominations. In a more fundamental sense, however, the changing nature of clergy activism can be traced to the generally conservative mood of the past several years. The early 1970s have not favored liberals and left-leaning partisans, whose combined forces have largely failed to implement either their domestic or their foreign policy goals. They were ineffectual in bringing the war in Vietnam to a quick end, and they have had little success in advancing any of the social causes that were prominent in the sixties. Moreover, except for the presidential campaign of George McGovern, the ability of these groups to command large followings or to mobilize public opinion has had no triumphs—indeed, it has greatly diminished in recent years. The "movement" (already an antiquated term) is dead; student activism is largely a thing of the past; and liberals generally are on the defensive. The set of events known collectively as Watergate may bring about some changes, but the years since 1968 have most certainly belonged to those conservatives and moderates who would maintain the status quo.

Activism in the Churches. Like many other activists of the sixties, liberal clergymen have been more restrained in their political actions since the time of our study. They have come to question many of their previous assumptions about politics and the political process and have grown weary of the continued conflict and frenzy of active political life. Many of these feelings of doubt and resignation are shared with other liberals; however, the recent changes in the political environment have had some peculiar effects on organized religion, as well. Many of the issues that first aroused the clergy have been redefined in a way that delimits the areas of clerical involvement in public affairs or makes clergy leadership much more difficult. In addition, the shift in political tactics from public protest to electoral politics has served to devalue the type of symbolic and moral leadership that ministers are best able to provide and to emphasize activities that are held to be less legitimate for men of the cloth.

The field of race relations provides perhaps the best example of the changing role of clergymen in political issues. Civil rights was the major issue through which the churches first became embroiled in public affairs during the sixties, and in retrospect it is not difficult to see why this was true. The early civil rights movement was relatively clear-cut in the moral values it espoused and the choices it presented the church. The existence of discrimination and racial hatred was obvious to all, and it was also clear that organized religion itself had been more than a tacit partner in this process. If the churches were to have any claim of social relevance, it seemed to be necessary for them to become actively involved in efforts to improve relations between the races. Furthermore, the solution advanced by the civil rights movement—the bringing together of the races—was a moderate one, reading as if it had come from the pages of the Scriptures, as indeed it often had. Clergymen might choose to ignore the issue, but it was difficult for them as Christian spokesmen to oppose the call for racial equality.

In addition, the tactics of the early civil rights movement placed a premium on the type of leadership that is best provided by religious leaders. In its early phase, the civil rights movement concentrated on revealing the discrepancies between American values and actions with respect to racial practices; once Americans were made aware of such inconsistencies, it was believed, they would support integrationist goals. Clergymen were well suited to serve as moral spokesmen on such matters and to participate in the symbolic acts of protest that became a major tactic of the movement. For the participants themselves, finally, it might be argued that such tactics were of particular appeal. Feelings of personal empathy and involvement were aroused when the white clergyman locked hands with his black brothers and marched for peace and brotherhood.

For reasons such as these, clerical support for the civil rights movement was strong during the 1960s. For example, in our investigation of the issues surrounding a 1964 initiative proposal to repeal California's fair housing laws, we found that an extraordinarily large number of parish ministers actively campaigned against repeal. Opposition to the initiative proposal

(Proposition 14) was almost unanimous in the liberal denominations and was strong in most of the conservative churches as well.

Racial issues have, of course, changed considerably since the 1960s. Indeed, the situation was changing at the time of our survey, and our respondents reported very mixed feelings about the emerging black power movement. The current emphasis on black identity and self-determination— and the decline in civil rights (or strictly integrationist) goals—has subsequently limited the role that can be played by white clergymen in racial matters. All the major Protestant denominations remain strongly committed to racial equality and have designed programs for advancing this purpose. By and large, however, their efforts are confined to two major thrusts: to support black-initiated and black-run causes or to deal directly with white racism (and thus racism within the church itself). Neither alternative is particularly comfortable for churches that rely on a predominantly white, conservative clientele for organizational support and financial security. The first option, tried several years ago in the form of "reparation" payments to black groups, was abandoned after strong lay resistance. At present, the emphasis is on supporting black organizations within the churches themselves in the form of black caucuses and all-black churches. Such policies, however, have created divisions within the liberal ranks of many denominations; not all white church leaders are willing to abandon their integrationist views and to accept the notion that whites should be excluded from black congregations. The second tactic with regard to racial issues—concentrating on white racism within the church—is likely to be even more controversial. Tentative efforts are being made in this direction by some denominations, but without a long-term commitment and willingness to accept risks, such programs are likely to have little success.

Many of the same points can be made with regard to the clergy's involvement in the antiwar movement. Peace, like brotherhood, would seem to be an issue of special concern to Christians, and one that the churches cannot easily avoid. Moreover, the tactics of the early antiwar movement were similar to those practiced by the proponents of civil rights, giving emphasis to expressions of moral outrage and symbolic protest. As of 1968, when our survey was conducted, Protestant clergymen in California were highly divided in their views toward the war. They were split about equally into hawkish and dovish groups—with about the same number favoring the bombing of North Vietnam (or harsher military measures) as favoring an end to the bombing or military withdrawal. Such views, however, were far more dovish than those held at the time by the American public. More importantly, we found that a significant minority of our respondents were active in expressing their opposition to the United States involvment in Southeast Asia.

As the Vietnam war became more unpopular with the American public in the early 1970s, the war issue consequently became a less divisive one for the churches. At the same time, liberal clergymen were not particularly successful in mobilizing their congregations to express their antiwar views or in generalizing this issue to other questions of American foreign policy. Although active peace organizations still exist among Protestant ministers, they seem to have relatively few clerical members now, and have gained little apparent support among laymen. There has been a great deal of discussion in religious publications of the need to develop a "post-Vietnam" perspective on and commitment to public issues. But liberal churches have not yet found a "cause" as compelling as civil rights or the war in Vietnam or a strategy of ethical leadership that is geared to the politics of the seventies.

Somewhat analogous developments have taken place with respect to other public issues that mobilized churchmen during the sixties. The issues seem less clear-cut than they once did, and less amenable to easy solution. The weaknesses of the liberal position have been exposed, and many former (and present) activists are questioning its assumptions. In California, the political issue that seems to have attracted the most widespread clerical attention in recent years is the continuing struggle of Cesar Chavez and the members of the United Farm Workers' Organizing Committee to organize the state's farm workers. Even in this area, however, Protestant churches appear to be pursuing a more cautious and restrained social policy. Support for the farm workers' cause remains high in liberal denominations, but the assistance given by churches is less direct and less concrete than formerly.

From Confrontation to Electoral Politics. The shifts that have occurred in the goals and tactics of liberal activists are in many respects as consequential for organized religion as these more substantive changes in the issues themselves. During the 1960s a major tactic of church activists was to confront private or public authorities directly through the use of sit-ins, protest marches, or acts of civil disobedience. Such actions came to symbolize the new mood in the churches, and a large part of our 1968 study was concerned with the involvement of clergymen in these acts and the resulting controversies. Such tactics are much less common within the churches today. In part, this turn away from direct confrontations reflects the desire of many church leaders to avoid unnecessary or overly disruptive conflicts with Protestant laymen. In part, however, it also represents a reassessment by many activists—outside as well as within the church—of the usefulness of confrontation tactics. Public acts of protest may draw attention to one's cause, but they do not necessarily contribute to the long-term solution of public problems and indeed may worsen the situation by the anger they arouse.

How much of the notion of counter productivity is a rationalization for the churches' present conservatism is hard to say. But it seems likely that a poll of Protestant clergymen in 1974 would find far less support for protest marches and civil disobedience than our survey conducted in 1968.

More importantly, the shift away from confrontation politics has been accompanied by renewed emphasis on the use of the electoral process as a means to bring about political change. Whereas many activists of the sixties scorned elections as a meaningless exercise, liberals of the seventies have concentrated much of their energy on campaigning for the "right" candidates or party. The high point of such activities was the 1972 McGovern campaign, but numerous efforts have been made at the state and local level as well.

Emphasis on electoral politics presents obvious difficulties for those clergymen who wish to remain active in the liberal reform movement. It appears that clerical participation in the formal political process is becoming more common and acceptable today; at least the norm against clergymen running for office seems to have been relaxed. But a strong belief in the separation of church and state still exists in this country, and direct clerical involvement in political campaigns remains a taboo. Thus as more attention is paid to elections and campaigns as a means to effect social change, we are likely to see clerical leadership in liberal politics diminishing. The moral prestige that can be used to focus attention on social injustices is one of the chief resources of clerical leadership. The clergy's special standing with the public was distinctly advantageous with respect to civil rights and peace issues, but it places limitations on the role they can play in partisan politics.

The Mood Within the Churches.   Thus in recent years the issues, tactics, and ideology of politics have changed in a way that affects the activism of liberals in general and of clergymen in particular. Liberal ministers have not turned away from the prophetic role; but they are less certain of the course of action they should pursue in public affairs. Neither the issues nor the tactics of political change are as compelling to them as they were in the sixties.

At the same time, it is apparent that the mood within Protestant churches has also changed in a number of important respects. Conservative churches are growing, liberal denominations are in the midst of a severe financial crisis, and Protestant laymen continue to resist the notion of a critical, action-oriented church. In such a situation, it is not surprising to find liberal church leaders and denominations adopting a more cautious, conservative policy. Large cutbacks have been made in appropriations for social action personnel and programs, and the feeling is widespread that the church should pay more attention to its own internal problems.

The Continuing Lay Backlash.   Most of the rank-and-file members of the liberal Protestant denominations have never supported the idea that the church should become critically involved in public affairs. They have accepted neither their leaders' liberal views on public issues nor the belief that it is the churches' moral mission to provide leadership on such issues as race, poverty, and peace. As long as church officials limited themselves to debating general propositions, these differences between the lay public and the clerical leadership of liberal denominations were of little importance. The resolutions passed at annual church conventions may have been extremely liberal or progressive, but most laymen cared little about politics and, in any case, had no idea what stand their church was taking on public questions. All this changed during the 1960s, when large numbers of ministers first began to speak out on public issues. As the study reported here shows, the resulting conflicts within liberal churches were great, and the costs of social activism high. Virtually all the "new breed" activists in California reported that they had lost members and finances as a result of their ethical activities, and many had the issue taken up before their church boards or faced losing their parish position for their outspoken views.

The prevailing sentiment among Protestant laymen toward social activism continues to be extremely negative, and such lay conservatism is a primary factor in the recent retreat of liberal churches from a more active role in social issues. In a recent survey of Episcopal dioceses, for example, public affairs was ranked twenty-fourth in terms of priority of the denomination's 25 programs. The same survey found that dissatisfaction within the Episcopal Church was widespread and that a major redirection in the church's basic policies was desired by a large majority of the respondents.[3]

A second example—one more closely related to the information reported here—comes from a poll completed during the summer of 1973 by the Northern California Conference of the United Methodist Church.[4] This survey is particularly interesting because our earlier study had shown that Methodist ministers in California were more socially active than those in any of the other eight Protestant denominations examined. In one of the questions included in the 1973 survey, the respondents were asked how the church's stand on social issues "such as race, poverty, or peace" should be made. The large differences that remain between the clergy and laity with respect to ethical issues are obvious in the responses to this inquiry:

	Clergy	Laity
Be decided by General Conference	46%	14%
Be decided by the California–Nevada Annual Conference	8%	5%
Be referred to the local church by the conference or district for a vote	29%	25%
Not be made. The individual should decide for himself.	18%	56%

The percentage of laymen saying that such stands should not be made at all was surprising even to those who sponsored the survey. In the past, the passage of official church resolutions has been far less controversial than many of the other actions taken by ethically oriented clerics.

Recent conversations with California ministers and church officials serve to confirm these reports of negative lay attitudes toward social activism. None of the officials with whom we discussed the matter felt that laymen were any more receptive to church activism today than they had been during the 1960s. Most laymen—whatever they think about public issues—do not feel that the church should involve itself directly and forcefully in public affairs. If anything, it appears that the rank-and-file membership of liberal churches are more hostile to clerical activism now than they were in the 1960s and are less hesitant to voice their disapproval of their leaders' actions.[5]

A Spiritual Revival.   The lay reaction against social activism has received an added dimension in the 1970s—namely, a revival of lay interest in the so-called spiritual side of religion—in Biblical study, evangelism, and re-affirmation of the Christian faith. Most Protestant laymen, of course, place primary emphasis on the churchly as opposed to worldly functions of religion. They attend church to be "comforted" rather than to be "challenged": to feel better about themselves and the world around them; not to be lectured about societal wrongs, and not to be urged to move to correct them. In the past several years, however, there has been renewed lay interest in the more traditional teachings of Christianity and in the personal aspects of religion. Bible study groups have become popular, and the fastest-growing churches have been those which most emphasize orthodox and evangelistic approaches to religion. Like other such "revivals" in American religion, this one has roots in general societal shifts, as well as parallels in trends outside the church. The rapid upheavals in social values—and apparent failures of contemporary institutions and leaders—have caused many Americans to turn inward in an attempt to gain personal strength and to find meaning in an increasingly unfathomable world.

As with the backlash against social activism, it is not difficult to document recent lay interest in spiritual concerns. In the previously mentioned survey of Episcopal laymen, for example, the highest priority was attached to the need for more education and evangelism. The authors of the report summarize their findings this way:

> A clear pattern emerges from the diocesan statements. With few exceptions, there is almost total agreement that a major change in emphasis is desired in the General Church Program. . . . Ap-

parent throughout the statements is a consciousness of spiritual
awakening, both in and out of the church, which has evoked a
strong individual and corporate desire for growth in the life of
faith, education in Christian thought and viewpoint, and guides
to involvement with the world. There is a deep desire to know
Christ and to be involved with others. There is an expressed need
for training in the skills and disciplines that nuture us in Christ
and that enable us to make Him known to others by both word
and life style. Believer and nonbeliever need nurture and con-
version.[6]

A similar emphasis emerges from the survey of Methodist laymen in northern
California. Asked to select those "needs" which they felt ought to be given
more attention by their church, laymen most often chose "spiritual needs,"
"loneliness/not needed," "youth and student needs," "parent–child relationships," and "marriage relationships." Much lower on the list were the social
issues that were more frequently mentioned by the clergy—"unresolved conflict," "rapid social change," "racism," and "war."

There is no need to belabor the point. The demand of laymen that greater
attention be given to the personal meaning of their religious commitments
is widely recognized within the church; it is the theme of much recent religious writing and was a frequent topic in our conversations with California
church officials. The practical effects of this renewed interest in religious
spirituality, however, is to move liberal churches even further away from
active involvement in public issues. To a large degree, a personal, inward
orientation is antithetical to a broadly focused concern with social conditions
and the problems of others. Under such conditions, the church is likely to
serve more as a haven of escape from worldly problems than as a spring-
board for social activism. In addition, limited time and resources are available for commitment to church programs. If major changes in emphases are
undertaken in liberal churches, cutbacks must be made someplace. Given
the problems that ethical programs have caused in the past, it is not surprising to find these changes being made at the expense of ethical commitments.

Finally, the lay call for greater spiritual emphasis provides weary church
leaders with a strong rationale for pursuing more cautious and limited ethical
objectives. What might be perceived as a retreat under pressure can be
viewed more in positive terms; after all, it is the business of the church to
teach about the Bible and to show the personal relevance of religious truths
and values. The reasoning of church liberals in this respect is not always
very different from the traditional conservative view that the church must
attend to men's spiritual needs before it can hope to influence their social
values and conduct; once individuals truly understand the Christian message,

they will find it in their hearts to correct social wrongs. Unfortunately, however, there are many different Christian "messages," and men are more likely to use religion to justify their secular conduct than the other way around.

Liberal Losses.   Thus the 1970s have been marked by a continuing lay backlash against the challenging or prophetic functions of religion and by a revived interest in the comforting or spiritual aspects of Christianity. The existence of such sentiments among a large portion of the Protestant laity, well recognized within liberal churches, has been a major factor in the recent reformulations in church policy. However, such a review of religious priorities has been made imperative for religious leaders by the severe organizational problems experienced by liberal churches over the past decade. Since the mid-sixties all the major liberal denominations have reported losses in members and financial support. In the past several years, as already noted, these losses have become so serious that large reductions in staff personnel and in scope of church programs have become necessary. While liberal denominations have been on the decline, furthermore, conservative churches have been growing and prospering, maintaining a high level of commitment among their own members, acquiring at least some new affiliates among those who have become disenchanted with liberal churches, and being especially adept at attracting young people to their congregations.

The relative fortunes of conservative and liberal churches have been the focus of a number of recent analyses of Protestant religion; our interviews with California officials and clergymen serve to identify unequivocally the problems that liberal churches are experiencing with their lay members. Fundamentalist churches, religious revivals, the Jesus movement, Eastern mysticism, meditation societies, and assorted other religious groups are flourishing in the state. Virtually all the parish ministers with whom we discussed the matter reported that these movements were growing in their areas and that they had lost members to one or another of them. The situation for liberal churches now appears to be most serious among youth and young adults. Sunday school enrollments have been dropping in liberal churches for several years, and the number of confirmations is substantially lower. A rise in religious consciousness is certainly taking place among the young, at least in California, but to date it has not involved liberal religion. Young people reportedly view liberal churches as a part of the "establishment" and are repelled by their formal worship services.

Perhaps the situation is most striking on the college campuses. The campus ministry in many California schools had an active student following in the sixties and was closely involved in the radical student movement of the time. In the early seventies, however, one campus minister reported, "There are virtually no students who are politically committed to change and who are searching for meaning in liberal Christian theology. Most of the young people who are concerned about change are finding secular channels for this purpose. They are impatient with liberal churches, which they see being concerned with perpetuating themselves." However, at the same time that liberal religion is gaining few student adherents, conservative church groups are thriving on many college campuses. They have attracted large memberships and have reportedly succeeded in providing students with a needed sense of friendship, fellowship, and belonging.

Thus the campus ministry—only recently a center of radicalism within many churches—is dying as a result of denominational neglect and the absence of student interest. Ironically, one of the major rationales for the churches' turn to activism in the sixties was the need to become socially relevant to attract the concerned youth of the day. In the seventies, however, there are very few politically concerned youth, and those who are interested in social change seek their ideology and the means of their activism mainly from secular organizations.

Retrenchment and Decentralization.   Liberal churches thus are faring poorly in attracting new members and, to a lesser extent, in retaining their old ones. The lay backlash and financial pinch have had their most direct impact on church policies and personnel at the national and regional levels. Many local congregations have failed to meet their annual pledges to the national church or have refused to provide funding for certain programs; conservative laymen and ministers, at the same time, have become better organized in liberal churches and have grown more vocal in their opposition to liberal social policies. Because of such actions—and because of the discontent among laymen generally—all the major liberal Protestant denominations have recently introduced major policy and structural reforms. The net results of these changes, thus far, have been the reduction (in some cases quite substantial) of the number of clergymen serving in denominational staff positions, special ministries, and the campus ministry; the reordering of priorities and the withdrawal from certain areas of social action; and the placing of greater authority in the hands of laymen and basically conservative elements within the churches.

It is too soon to judge the overall effects of such changes on the social policies of liberal denominations, but it is apparent that they have contributed to a more cautious and conservative ethical stance and that this trend is likely to continue. Most of the recent reductions in staff personnel have been made at the expense of church liberals. Clergymen who serve in such nonparish positions are removed from direct lay supervision or control and are able to engage in actions that would be extremely difficult at the parish level. In the past, such positions served as an important source of employment for ministers who wished to engage in social action activities, but now many of these clergymen face the difficult task of finding new positions, presumably (if they are to stay in the church) in local parishes. The employment situation is poor in many liberal denominations, however, and activist-oriented ministers are likely to experience an especially difficult time being called by a local congregation. Furthermore, not only will many of these clergymen be lost to the church—or be forced to assume a less controversial profile—but many will also leave behind a vacuum in liberal leadership. Clergymen serving in special roles on campuses or in urban areas have often been successful in mobilizing others to support social causes. Thus the indirect effects of such reductions in personnel may be as important as the more direct ones.

Liberal denominations have also been reducing their financial allocations for social purposes. To some extent, such reductions in spending must be viewed as an economic necessity, and budgets for programs in other areas have been trimmed as well. Nevertheless, there appears to be a broad move from programs of a social nature to programs with a more traditional, churchly focus (evangelism, Bible education, etc.). This shift in priorities may prove to be temporary, as many of our respondents seem to think. If so, it might allow liberal church leaders time to regroup and to educate their religious constituents in the need for a socially involved church. Alternatively, this trend may be seen as evidence of a major retrenchment within liberal denominations. Whatever course is followed in the future, these are lean and uncertain times for the social action divisions of Protestant churches.

The structural changes that are taking place in liberal denominations may have an important effect on the churches' ethical role as well. During the past several years, liberal denominations have tried to decentralize authority and decision making within the churches. At the national level, these actions have been analogous to the recently enacted revenue-sharing programs of the federal government. Funds collected through pledges to the national church are being returned to regional or local church associations for expenditure, under the assumption that since conditions vary in different parts of the country, the lower-level organizations are best able to decide what local projects should be supported. Similar efforts, moreover, are currently being undertaken at the regional level. Responsibility for various programs is being delegated to the churches' smallest decision-making units (associations, presbyteries, synods, etc.), and ad hoc committees that include laymen are being formed to advise officials on such important church matters as hiring.

The impetus behind the structural reforms, of course, is the widespread lay disenchantment with their liberal leadership, particularly at the national level. It is hoped that bringing more laymen into the organizational structure

of the church and opening new lines of communication with local parishes
will help create greater harmony and mutual understanding between the
different levels of constituencies within the churches. Whatever the motive,
it seems likely that such decentralization will move liberal denominations
even further in the conservative direction. Laymen, as a group, are far more
conservative than the clergy, and in the past the more conservative laity
have tended to be most active in church affairs. Thus if authority passes
from the generally liberal leadership of Protestant denominations to local
church bodies—where laymen have greater representation and a greater
chance of having their views favorably responded to—the conservative, antiactivist position probably will be strengthened. As our study shows, the
authority structure in liberal denominations is quite important in shaping
the clergy's response to public issues. Parish ministers in the more hierarchically organized denominations were more outspoken in their social behavior than other clerical liberals and were more likely to feel that their
church leaders had given them strong support in their ethical activities.

The current structural reforms in liberal denominations may be of long-
term importance to the churches' role in public affairs, although of course
the exact effects of such decentralized decision making will vary according
to local circumstances. Most of the California clergymen and church officials
with whom we discussed the matter, in fact, felt that the changes would
make little difference to them; some even believed that these modifications
would allow the churches to become more involved in local political issues,
since their (geographical) area is highly liberal. One may seriously question
such an assertion, especially after reviewing the ethical views of supposedly
liberal Methodist laymen in supposedly liberal northern California. Certainly
the effects of these structural changes will vary according to the attitudes
of the local church constituency and the skill of the local church leadership.

Rethinking the Activist Role. Along with the foregoing structural changes in
church policy, many liberal clergymen have been rethinking the activist role
itself. Although not necessarily abandoning their commitment to an ethically
oriented church, they feel that for the time being the church should pay
more attention to its traditional functions and to healing the wounds left by
the activist sixties. The result is a more cautious mood in liberal churches
and a reluctance to engage in activities that would further alienate large
numbers of laymen.

Numerous critical assessments have been made of the churches' role in
the political controversies of the decade just past. Among other things, the
activists of the sixties have been charged with being too far ahead of the
laity, ignoring the spiritual needs of their parishioners, failing to stay in
communication with rank-and-file church members, making naïve political

assumptions, adopting the protest tactics of more successful political groups, and, more sweepingly, with being bored, upper-middle-class Christian intellectuals. Probably the most widely read and discussed of these critiques is that of Dean Kelley, himself a social action specialist with the National Council of Churches. In *Why Conservative Churches Are Growing*,[7] Kelley argues that the basic function of religion is to provide meaning to the ultimate questions of life. From this perspective, conservative churches are growing because they fulfill this need for many churchgoers through their strict, demanding, and absolutist teachings. Kelley admits that such a religious orientation may lead to religious intolerance and fanaticism and that, in any case, this course of action could not be adopted by liberal churches. However, he says that liberal church leaders must realize that people attend church to be nurtured and comforted, not to be told what they should think about social issues or to be led to the barricades; other organizations exist for these purposes, and those who wish to become politically active will join them, not the church. Liberal churches need not avoid politics altogether— indeed, they should not—but they must remember that their basic reason for existence is to provide meaning to men's lives, and this essential function should not be jeopardized over a temporary political cause. Thus liberal church leaders must pay primary attention to those functions which are concerned with the meaning and celebration of religion. If they attend to such activities—and are careful to maintain close communication with the laity—they will have a more committed lay membership and will be better able to pursue their social goals.

It should be apparent that such admonitions are inherently conservative, as indeed Kelley views the functions of religion to be. Such themes, however, were repeatedly expressed during our interviewing. Like Kelley, almost all our respondents thought that the growth in fundamentalist churches and movements could be explained in terms of the certainty of their religious message and the expressivity of their religious services. The times were such, it was felt, that many Americans were looking for concrete answers and were turning to conservative religion[8] for this purpose. Unlike Kelley, however, none of our liberal respondents thought that the trend toward religious conservatism was permanent or irreversible; rather, they felt that it was a product of temporary social conditions and that the "pendulum" would soon swing back in a liberal direction. Such views were particularly common with respect to the attractiveness that fundamentalist religion currently has among the young.

As for the churches' ethical role, the most widely taken position was similar to the argument advanced in Kelley's book. Most of those interviewed felt that liberal churches had indeed pushed too far too fast during the 1960s and that they had given inadequate attention to communicating with their lay members or explaining the need for a prophetic church. It was widely believed that liberal churches at least for the present should devote more effort to internal organization and communication. In practical terms, this means paying more attention to the traditional, theological foundations of religion and to showing the relevance of religion to contemporary life. It is assumed that once laymen have a better understanding of Christianity and Christian teachings, they will be more likely to go along with their leaders on ethical matters. The retreat from social activism, then, is viewed as temporary—a development strategically necessary in the face of present conditions and past failures.

Given the limited scope of our interviewing, it is difficult to know how widespread such feelings are among Protestant ministers; the attitudes cited, however, do seem to represent the dominant thinking of those most directly responsible for making policy decisions within the liberal denominations. Thus the present mood within liberal churches is cautious and conservative. Much the same arguments were made during the 1960s by those who opposed the trend toward social activism but received less attention because of pressing political problems. Now that political passions have cooled—and liberal churches are having difficulties of their own—the need to attend to internal organizational problems has become more important.

Fatigue and Frustration.   Again none of the foregoing discussion should be taken to mean that large numbers of liberal clergymen have rejected the prophetic role or that Protestant churches are likely to return to the political passivity that marked the 1950s. One of the most frequently mentioned reasons for the present quiescence in Protestant churches, in fact, had nothing to do with these structural reforms or strategic considerations. Many of the parish ministers who were most actively involved in the political controversies of the sixties report that feelings of fatigue, frustration, and uncertainty are among the most immediate factors affecting their ethical behavior and that of their colleagues. This is certainly not surprising. It is difficult to maintain for long the hyperactive lives that many of these clergymen and other activists led at the peak of the civil rights and antiwar movements. Unsurprisingly, the frustrations due to the repeated failures (or "partial successes") of these efforts can be great. No clear-cut victories were won by the clergy and their liberal allies during the 1960s, and most of the social problems they so strongly attacked are no nearer solution today. Even with respect to Vietnam, the signing of the Paris peace agreements did not take place until well after the influence of antiwar forces had waned. In such a situation, political indignation can easily give way to cynicism, and moral fervor to feelings of doubt and uncertainty. Much of the exuberance and optimism with which many clergymen entered the political struggles of the sixties has faded, and those who push for social action in the churches are on the defensive.

Public leadership can also inflict personal costs on those involved. Families must be attended to, the years of conflict and rancor can be wearing, and the desire for a more stable and relaxed environment increases. All this is especially true in a profession such as the ministry, in which human inter-action and social skills are central. It is not easy or particularly satisfying to serve a congregation that is continually polarized over social issues.

Finally, the Protestant ministry now appears to be characterized by an unusually high degree of personal and occupational unrest. Personal prob-lems, particularly divorce, are reported to have increased sharply over the past several years among California ministers, and a significant number of clergymen are leaving their chosen profession or are contemplating doing so.[9] Such phenomena are by no means unique to liberal clergymen or to the ministry itself, but in a number of reported instances they have diverted clerical attention from social issues.

A Tightening Job Market. The currently prevalent feelings of fatigue and frustration are said by the activist clergy themselves to be a primary reason for their retreat from a rather active role in public affairs. The recent finan-cial problems of liberal denominations have also had an impact on activism at the local level, although denominational leaders and policies have been much more drastically affected. Parish ministers have never found it easy to engage in controversial political issues, and partly for this reason they have been less socially active than clergymen who are more insulated from lay pressure or control. A large part of the study reported here was concerned with the activists' difficulties with their congregational members at the parish level and the reported effects of such conflicts on their careers. Not surpris-ingly, we found that their problems were great and that most felt that their careers had suffered because of their social actions.

Not only does the same situation hold in the early 1970s, but a tight job market is beginning to develop within the liberal denominations as well, particularly in the choice areas of California, where the activists tend to be located. The many reasons for this situation are not entirely related to social activism. Churches have stopped expanding as the number of potential con-verts has been exhausted; the financial situation has obliged many of the larger churches to reduce the size of their ministerial staffs; and rising mi-nority demands have led to decreasing job opportunities for white males.[10] Not least important, many clergymen want to live and practice in California, especially in the San Francisco Bay area. Finally, the cutbacks that have been made in nonparish positions—denominational personnel, special ministries, and the campus ministry—have reduced the number of such traditional job outlets for liberal ministers. Presumably, the clergymen who have occupied such positions (predominantly liberals) will also be looking for jobs at the parish level, thus putting a further strain on an already overcrowded market.

The effects of the employment situation, just now being felt on the parish level, are likely to increase in the future. It seems apparent that the scarcity of jobs can only have a chilling effect on activism at the parish level. As in any "buyers' market," deviation from the norm is likely to be penalized, and individuals who are controversial will have the most trouble finding employment. Speaking out on public issues is one act (although not the only one) that gives clergymen a reputation for being controversial. At present, a number of activists are without employment in the church, and others are rewriting their dossiers to play down their past involvement in social issues. Moreover, among those who have resigned from the ministry in recent years, it is reported that some have been "forced" to do so by inability to overcome their activist reputations and find employment.

Under such conditions, we should point out, the organizational structure and policies of liberal churches are likely to increase in importance to local activists. If the parish minister can be assured of obtaining employment, he could be expected to be more outspoken in his ethical conduct than would otherwise be the case. Methodist ministers in particular are favored by a hierarchical polity structure and the guarantee of employment (once ordained). Such characteristics, which encouraged activism among Methodist clergymen in the sixties, may be even more important in the future.

Liberals and the Political Future. The dynamics of church activism thus have changed in many important respects since the late sixties—the period examined in the study to follow. The political assumptions and tactics of the sixties have been brought into question, liberal denominations have encountered difficult times, and priorities have been shifted away from the social action field. Some of these changes are shared with other liberal or professional groups; others are unique to the ministry itself.

If our account here is accurate, however, the current situation in liberal churches is not very different in fundamental respects from that which existed during the 1960s. Strong divisions remain between a predominantly liberal clerical leadership and a predominantly conservative lay membership, and the authority exerted by Protestant laymen over church affairs continues to inhibit the development of a more action-oriented church. How such factors contributed to clergy activism and inactivism during the sixties is the major focus of this study.

Periods of intense political passions and social unrest present organized religion with a difficult dilemma. On the one hand, if the churches do not speak out on public issues that are important to others, they risk being charged with moral hypocrisy and social irrelevance. They will be seen as ignoring their own moral teachings and principles and, through their inaction, giving tacit support to the status quo. On the other hand, if the churches become too involved in such issues, they risk alienating church members who disagree with their positions or who feel the church should stay out of politics altogether. In this case, they will create dissent within their own ranks and drive members away from the church.

For Protestant churches the temptation has been particularly strong to avoid controversial issues or to support the status quo, since most of their members belong to the more privileged classes of American society. As our study shows, conservative churches largely managed to avoid the political controversies of the sixties. They maintained that such issues as civil rights, the war on poverty, and the fighting in Vietnam were not "moral" issues, thus were no business of the institutional church. Matters were made easier because a relative (conservative) consensus existed within these churches over most such issues.[11] Liberal churches could not so easily escape this dilemma. The ethical and political views of their rank-and-file members are very similar to those typifying the mainline conservative denominations; but the leaders possess a more liberal social ethic, and many believe that the church should participate in efforts to reform secular society. Conflict is thus inevitable within liberal churches whenever political passions run high and polarizations over social issues develop within the greater society. Such a pattern has been repeated within liberal denominations during periods of political strife ever since the emergence of theological liberalism in the late nineteenth century.

Both our study of activism in the sixties and the discussion here have emphasized the costs—surely severe—of ethical leadership to liberal churches. Much religious writing, however, has tended to accentuate the weaknesses of liberal churches while ignoring their strengths. Since our stress has been in this direction as well, let us conclude this introduction in a more positive vein. The years following a period of intense political activism are frequently troublesome for individuals and institutions caught up in them. They often produce feelings of doubt and dissillusion among those activists whose social goals remain unfulfilled, and retrenchment in organizations that have become politicized over public issues. Although both these developments have taken place in liberal churches, they have not been carried as far as in other professions involved in the politics of the sixties. The retrenchment in universities was earlier in coming and appears to be more severe, at least financially.[12] Activist doctors and lawyers have been frustrated in their attempts to establish radical practices and have largely returned to more traditional means of livelihood.[13] In contrast with these other professional groups, it appears that the commitment of liberal clergymen to social activism is more firmly based in an integrated worldview and that the church as an organization is more supportive of those who engaged in controversial political actions. From a political perspective, then, the ministerial profession remains one of the more hospitable occupations for individuals who wish to commit themselves to social change.

Much has also been made of the contrasting fortunes of conservative and liberal churches in recent years. It is true that conservative-oriented churches have grown more rapidly over the past decade and appear to be more successful in eliciting a strong commitment by their members and from the young. Past religious "revivals" have generally proved to be temporary phenomena, however, and youth as a group is especially prone to temporary behavior changes. Liberal churches for their part are by no means fading from the scene. They may be faring poorly in a relative sense, but they continue to command the loyalty and support of several million members. Moreover, their membership is drawn disproportionately from the upper income strata of American society—from those who are most powerful in economic, political, and cultural affairs. In this respect, the potential of liberal religion to have far-reaching secular effects is much greater than that of conservative churches.

Finally, the liberal theological perspective—as ambiguous and adaptable as it has been—represents an attempt by church leaders to come to grips with secular society and to create a religious perspective that is relevant to modern conditions. To the extent that religion can offer insights into man's social existence, such perceptions are likely to come from liberal theologians and practitioners. More orthodox or fundamentalist religious concepts may have a strong appeal to many churchgoers, but their social relevance lies more in the escape they provide from worldly concerns than in their contributions to political thinking or problem solving. Conservative churches may be growing, but their otherworldly emphasis and narrowly defined ethical concerns make it unlikely that they will have a large, positive effect on public affairs.

In short, despite the well-known and well-exposed problems of liberal religion, the political future is likely to be influenced more by liberal clergymen than by conservatives. Given this probability, liberal churches are an important subject of study for those who wish to understand more about the causes and effects of political change.

NOTES AND REFERENCES

1. Parish ministers were most socially active in the United Methodist Church, the United Church of Christ, the Episcopal Church, the Presbyterian Church, and the Lutheran Church in America.

2.   The information that follows is based in part on interviews conducted during the summer of 1973 with about 25 church officials and parish ministers in California. Most of the interviews were with clergymen in the San Francisco Bay area and may to some extent reflect the unique characteristics of this region.

3.   A summary of the Episcopal survey is found in "What We Learned from What you Said," a report of the Office of Development of the Episcopal Church, February 1973.

4.   The results of this survey were made available to the author by Arthur Hammer, who compiled the information for the United Methodist Church.

5.   As we discuss in Chapter 8, the conflicts of the sixties often had the effect of polarizing local congregations further along conservative or liberal lines. Conservative laymen left congregations served by activist clergymen, and vice versa, with the result that many congregations became more homogeneous in the ethical orientations of their members. We found a few congregations in which support for social activism was reported to be more solid at present because of such conservative attritions. There are many more conservative than liberal laymen, however, and as an overall strategy it would obviously be disastrous for liberal churches to alienate their conservative members to build up a liberal constituency.

6.   "What We Learned from What You Said," p. 6.

7.   New York: Harper & Row, 1972.

8.   To follow Kelley's terminology, we are being somewhat inconsistent in our use of the word "conservative" to describe churches that have been growing. The mainline conservative denominations have expanded only slightly in recent years, the more fundamentalist-oriented churches having grown the most rapidly.

9.   The satisfaction of our 1968 respondents with the ministerial profession is reported in Chapter 11. A nationwide Gallup poll conducted in 1971 found that 33 percent of Protestant ministers reported that they had seriously considered leaving the religious life. See "Religion in America," *The Gallup Opinion Index,* April 1971.

10.   The job opportunities of white males in Protestant churches are likely to become even more restricted in the future. A number of factors are involved in this development. First, liberal clerics have strongly backed efforts to bring minority groups into the church, even though many are likely to lose job or advancement opportunities in the process. Given their general ideological commitments, we would expect such clergymen to continue to push for greater minority representation in the church. Second, as the percentage of blacks in urban areas increases—along with demands that black congregations be served only by black ministers—the need for white clergymen to serve urban parishes will decrease. Thus many liberal denominations now find themselves with a shortage of black clergymen and a surplus of whites. (Much the same phenomenon, on a smaller scale, is occurring with respect to other minority groups.) Finally, women are becoming better organized within the liberal denominations and are beginning to push for more representation in church councils and in the pulpit. Since women are disproportionately active in local churches, this development may be highly significant in the future.

11.   There is some evidence that the conservative churches are beginning to be affected by the ethical and political issues that divided liberal churches during the 1960s. By and large, however, this conservative consensus seems to remain today within these churches—particularly at the local level.

12.   See Earl F. Cheit, *The New Depression in Higher Education* (New York: McGraw-Hill, 1971): and *The New Depression in Higher Education—Two Years Later* (Berkeley, Calif.: The Carnegie Foundation for the Advancement of Teaching, 1973). Both reports were sponsored by the Carnegie Commission on Higher Education.

13.   The situation varies from area to area, but neither profession has institutional outlets for their radicals as well-established as those within the Protestant ministry. In the 1970s, as a result, radical lawyers and doctors have lost much of their previous clientele and following and have had to earn a living through more traditional means of employment. For an examination of these groups, see Ruth Ann Becker, "Potential Groups: An Examination of the Conditions and Processes of Group Formation Among Doctors and Lawyers," doctoral dissertation, Stanford University, 1974. From this perspective, the reduction of such nonparish outlets for activist clergymen may be one of the most significant developments for the churches' future role in public affairs.

PROTESTANT RELIGION AND POLITICAL LEADERSHIP

1.

For many Americans the 1960s were a period of social awakening and deepening moral crisis. One social problem seemed to follow on the heels of another: racial antagonisms accelerated and began to spread out of control; pockets of grinding poverty came to light in the nation whose affluence had gone unquestioned; American troops became mired in an unlikely and unpopular war in Southeast Asia; cities became increasingly unpleasant places; even the country's natural resources—its land, its air, and its waters—were fouled by the apparent shortsightedness and greediness of men.

Faced with such realities, a growing number of Americans shed their complacency and sought to redirect the course of public actions. They challenged the nation's priorities and called attention to its injustices. They condemned established institutions and procedures and developed new insights into political problems. In their quest for social change, furthermore, these dissenters often went beyond conventional means of seeking political redress. Increasingly, their protests became more direct, militant, and disruptive. Political lobbying gave way to civil disobedience; peaceful protest to massive demonstrations and acts of political violence.

As the decade wore on, this attack on the status quo created deep and obvious fissures within American society. It polarized much of the public and served to politicize those institutions most directly involved in the "new politics" of the period. Severe social conflicts thus accompanied this increasing concern with political issues. Individuals who were the most socially active often found it difficult to find or to maintain normal employment, and the institutions that housed such political dissidents frequently lost public backing and financial support. By the decade's end, the number of political activists in the country appeared to dwindle, and the institutions affected

24

by the surge in activism struggled to survive. A period of uneasy calm and reassessment dominated American politics, and new forms were sought to pursue the still unrealized political goals of the 1960s.

As has often been the case in the past, religious leaders were among the most active participants in the political protests of the 1960s, and the church was among the most seriously disrupted of established institutions. Men of the cloth marched for civil rights, joined in the disheveled and irreverent antiwar protests of the young, and picketed in the hot and hostile vineyards of California. Increasingly, they involved themselves in unpopular political causes within their own communities and brought the troublesome issues of the day into their own sanctuaries. Many such activists, in turn, paid a personal price for their ethical convictions. Clergymen were caricatured, vilified, and spat on for some of their efforts to forge a new moral conscience; jailed, assaulted, and martyred for others. The activities of these "new breed" activists, as they have sometimes been called, also created deep and bitter conflicts within Christian churches. They set conservative church leaders against liberals and antagonized large numbers of laymen. This politicization of organized religion was particularly severe within Protestant churches— organizations that have generally been identified with the status quo and are closely governed by conservative laymen. In such a situation, the most outspoken of the activist clergy often lost members, contributions, even their jobs, because of their involvement in controversial social issues.

By the 1970s it appeared that many church denominations had suffered for the social activism of their leaders. Membership figures remained stagnant or declined in liberal denominations while they increased in more conservative or fundamentalist ones. Such statistics prompted a number of post-1960 analysts to argue that Protestant churches should stay out of controversial social issues—or they would further alienate loyal churchgoers and exacerbate the problems presently encountered by liberal religion. In *Religion and the New Majority*, for example, Lowell D. Streiker and Gerald Strober maintain that the nation's center—its celebrated middle America—remained loyal to the theological and political positions of Billy Graham and Richard Nixon. They assert that Americans go to church to be comforted in their daily problems, not to hear about social ills, and termed the activism of the 1960s a "disaster" for liberal churches.[1] In *Why Conservative Churches Are Growing*, Dean Kelley, an executive with the National Council of Churches, gives an even bleaker assessment of the future of liberal religion. Citing as evidence a wide range of statistics, Kelley argues that liberal churches are dying because of their failure to pursue strict, meaningful, and inspiring goals.[2] He too feels that the activists' cause is doomed, despite his own leanings in this direction:

> The churches and synagogues are not social-action barracks where the
> troops of militant reform are kept in readiness to charge forth at the
> alarums and excursions of social change. Rather, they are the con-
> servatories where the hurts of life are healed, where new spiritual
> strength is nourished, and where the virtues and verities of human
> experience are celebrated.[3]

Membership statistics are notoriously unreliable, and no evidence exists
to show that large numbers of laymen have left the church as a direct result
of the ethical actions of their leaders. Furthermore, it appears that the problems facing contemporary religion are much broader and more deep-
seated than those arising from the activist controversy alone (see below).
Nevertheless, the political events of the 1960s did bring Protestant churches
face to face with the "institutional dilemma" experienced in times of social
unrest by any religion purporting to be the repository of universal ideals and
truths.[4] On the one hand, if organized religion does not speak out on the
secular issues that raise moral questions, it undermines its own meaning and
purpose in society. It becomes irrelevant to the issues that trouble the greater
society and denies its own claim for truth and preeminence. On the other
hand, if churches press their moral positions too diligently and come to be
identified with particular political causes, they risk collision with the powerful forces that support the status quo. In this case, organized religion en-
dangers its unique position of power and prestige within society and exposes
itself to external and internal sources of discord. This dilemma would seem
to be particularly acute in such a large, heterogeneous, and essentially
secular society as that of the United States.

This book is an empirical inquiry into the clergy activism of the 1960s and
the conflicts it produced within Protestant churches. It focuses on activism
among parish ministers—since most Protestant clergymen work within parish
churches, and it is at this level that the conflict between laymen and the
activist clergy is the most direct and acrimonious. In the first part of the book,
we are concerned with clerical attitudes toward religious, ethical, and political issues and with the involvement of parish ministers in controversial
social questions. We find that a relatively large number of clergymen at the
parish level did speak out on important public issues, and their activism in
this respect was closely related to the ministerial belief system. In the second
part of the study, we examine the conflicts within Protestant churches over
social activism and the impact of occupationally related factors on the ethical
beliefs and actions of the parish clergy. Here we pay a great deal of attention
to what parish ministers have to say about the ethical and political beliefs of
their parishioners, how laymen reportedly respond to activism at the parish
level, and how they serve to constrain or to encourage the development of a

more critical, action-oriented church. We also investigate the distribution of authority within Protestant denominations and the role played by local denominational leaders with respect to aqtivism at the parish level.

The data for this study were obtained by means of a mail questionnaire sent to a two-thirds randomly selected sample of parish ministers in California during the spring and early summer of 1968. The denominations chosen for analysis were the nine largest mainline Protestant denominations in the state and represented both conservative and liberal church groups: the American Baptist Convention, the American Lutheran Church, the Episcopal Church, the Lutheran Church in America, the United Methodist Church, the Missouri Synod-Lutheran Church, the United Presbyterian Church, the Southern Baptist Convention, and the United Church of Christ. A total of 1580 parish clergymen completed and returned usable questionnaires, for a response rate of 63 percent. A detailed description of the procedures used to collect the data is presented in Appendix A; the questionnaire itself is reproduced in Appendix C.

Before turning to our findings in this study, let us review the prophetic potential of Protestant churches from historical, theological, and organizational perspectives. Such considerations place the social actions of church leaders within a broader context and serve as a theoretical guide for our subsequent analysis.

American Protestantism in Historical Perspective. The recent upsurge in clergy activism can hardly have surprised those familiar with church history and the development of Protestant theology during the past century. Indeed, it would have been more surprising if Protestant church leaders had remained silent while the public debated such critical, at least partly moral issues as civil rights, poverty, and the war in Vietnam. Historically, we find that Protestant church leaders have often exhibited a great deal of concern and involvement in societal affairs. They have not attempted to flee into monastic enclaves from the sins of temporal society; nor have they so isolated themselves from secular issues that they became superfluous to social problems. Protestant religion, as a result, has had wide-ranging effects on the nation's values and institutions. In the realm of politics, it has had much to do with the shaping of American beliefs and with the attention (or inattention) given to various public problems.

At the same time, important ethical and political divisions have developed within Protestant churches. During the early part of the nineteenth century —when. Protestantism grew tremendously in membership and influence— the religious impulse to reform secular society tended to be largely individualistic and moralistic. It inspired clerical leadership in opposing such practices as prostitution, drinking, and gambling, rather than in combating social injustices and inequities. A small number of Protestant leaders were involved in social issues during this period, but it was not until the end of the century that a tradition of critical Protestant leadership was established in the "social gospel" movement. Since then, an active concern in public issues seems to have grown within at least one major segment of Protestantism. The unprecedented component of the 1960s, then, was not the social concern exhibited by religious leaders, but rather the scope and breadth of their ethical actions. Never before, it appears, were so many Protestant ministers willing to risk the wrath of a reluctant laity and speak out forcefully on controversial public issues.

To understand the recent eruption of prophetic leadership by religious leaders, therefore, we must become familiar with the historical development of American Protestantism and the present divisions within Protestant ranks. Briefly, Protestant churches grew steadily in strength and influence during the nineteenth century; they blended comfortably with the secular environment during this period; and (with some major exceptions) they emphasized an individualistic, moralistic ethic. This consensus within Protestantism broke down toward the end of the century as a result of changes in American society and the challenge created by historical and scientific criticisms of the Bible. Out of this conflict emerged two opposing schools of Protestant theology —one that continued the nineteenth-century tradition of an orthodox, individualistic church; another that was more politically liberal and more responsive to social problems. This division still exists within Protestantism and is directly related to the response of church leaders to events such as those of the 1960s.

Nineteenth-Century Protestantism.[5]   The nineteenth century marks the heyday of Protestant influence and hegemony and the beginning of a pattern of ethical conduct which predominates in most churches today. At the time of the Revolution, the vast majority of Americans did not belong to an organized church. Many of the founding fathers, although nominally church members, were Deists, and organized religion had made a few inroads into the frontiers. During the first part of the nineteenth century, however, church membership rose sharply in the United States at the same time that it was declining in Europe. Church historians often name the disestablishment of state religion as a primary cause for this so-called second great awakening among Americans. In freeing organized religion from civil control or sponsorship, it is argued, Protestant churches were given license to compete with one another on equal terms for new converts. They did so within a general consensus over religious issues and without threat to civil libertarians, who might otherwise have been mobilized to resist the influence of a state-sponsored church.[6]

Perhaps equally important to the early growth of Protestantism, however, is the stance it took with regard to its secular surroundings. Early church leaders openly identified the destiny of the new nation with Divine Providence. They saw in their expanding country the promised land of the Biblical Scriptures and Americans as the new chosen people. A major theological interpretation of the time even held that an act of God had delayed the discovery of the New World until the Protestant Reformation had had a chance to establish itself. The new nation was thus to be a Protestant nation —a land established by Providence with a destiny guided by God Himself.[7]

Divisions did exist among the early Protestant groups in the United States. Episcopalians and Congregationalists tended to align themselves with the conservative Federalists, and members of the Baptist, Methodist, and Presbyterian churches with the more liberal Jeffersonians.[8] With some prominent exceptions, however, most contemporary Protestant groups shared a Calvinistic orientation toward theological issues. Their religious perspective was literal, supernatural, individualistic, and moralistic; in important respects, it was otherworldly as well. The dominant theology of these American Protestants was first of all a revealed one. It maintained a strict separation between the natural and the supernatural—between heaven and earth and between an all-knowing God and a fallen, sinful man. Salvation was possible only through God's grace and the redemptive act of His Son, Jesus Christ. Primary concern was thus given to the miraculous, "soul-saving" aspects of Christianity. It was the role of the Christian minister to bring the Word of God to others so that they might be forgiven for their sins and obtain the blessing of eternal salvation.

Such an "otherworldly" orientation—along with this embrace of the American way of life—served generally to deter Protestants from playing a critical role in social and political affairs. Protestantism developed an early evangelistic impulse to reform its secular surroundings, and the first half of the nineteenth century witnessed the creation of various religious-sponsored reform movements.[9] The ethics of the period, however, were defined largely in individualistic and moralistic terms. Protestant church leaders wanted to change society not by attacking existing social conditions but by attempting to change the individual. They did not challenge existing social arrangements or public authorities, but tried instead to save individuals and to educate the young. Once enough individuals were brought to Christ, it was believed, right-minded Christians would find it in their hearts to make the necessary changes in society. The reform societies that sprung up during the period reflected this individualistic conception of public problems—and the pattern was to dominate American thinking toward the poor and disadvantaged at least until the New Deal period. "In an optimistic age of equal and seemingly unlimited opportunity," William G. McLoughlin writes, "poverty increasingly assumed the character of sin, essentially private sin, for which the errant individual alone was to blame."[10] The distinction commonly made by Americans between the deserving and undeserving poor thus came to be defined mainly in terms of the Christian character of the individual.[11]

The reforms urged by most nineteenth-century religious leaders, furthermore, dealt not with social problems but with the moral conduct of individuals. Attention was directed toward such vices as prostitution, drinking, card-playing, and disrespect for the Sabbath; broader social conditions or reforms were regarded as outside the proper sphere of religious concern. Indeed, many of these religious norms were highly functional for the rural frontier life of most Americans during the early part of the nineteenth century. As William Clebsch notes, sobriety avoided economic waste and ineptitude in work, the rejection of gambling made the frontiersman more careful with his meager assets and less susceptible to the appeals of frontier sharpies, and sexual fidelity helped keep the family unit intact. The observance of the Sabbath itself provided a much-needed day of rest and served to bring families together in a common, symbolic observance.[12]

Thus the individualistic, moralistic ethics of nineteenth-century Protestantism were not irrelevant to the needs of churchgoers. America during this period was peopled largely by rural, small property owners who were involved in the expansion of the frontier. The social problems brought about by industrialization and mass immigration did not emerge in a major way until after the Civil War, although these developments spawned some early Protestant–Catholic conflicts in the Know-Nothing movement.

Nineteenty-century Protestant ethics failed most dismally in its treatment of those not of white, European stock—namely, native Americans and the country's black population—yet in neither respect is the record of Protestant churches one of total neglect. From 1817 onward, a widespread missionary movement existed among Indians, and Protestant churches provided an important institutional base for abolitionist sentiment in the North. As a whole, however, Protestant church leaders offered little dissent from prevailing norms and practices. After early attempts to Christianize the Indians had floundered, most church leaders considered them to be unreachable heathens and supported the country's policies of removing them to reservations.[13] Similarly, Protestant churches never accorded the Negro equal status within Christianity. Instead, blacks were assigned to separate churches at an early date, and Protestants were generally no more receptive of free blacks in the North than they were of slaves in the South. (Most abolitionists, in fact, agreed with southerners that the Negro race was inferior.[14]) During the Civil War and the years preceding it, Protestant church leaders in both sections of the country confidently proclaimed that God was on their side, and the three major Protestant denominations with roots in the South broke apart over the slavery issue. These early patterns of discrimination, moreover, have continued to influence Protestantism. Despite some recent changes, there is little doubt that Protestant churches remain one of the most segregated institutions in American society.

The Emerging Split. Many of the foregoing aspects of nineteenth-century Protestantism continue to influence the ethical conduct of church leaders. A number of major factors in the late nineteenth century, however, combined to challenge the place of Protestant churches in American society and to create deep divisions within Protestant ranks: the massive influx of immigrants that began just before the Civil War, the plight of workers in the new industrial order, the corruption of urban politics, and the acceptance of scientific and historical criticisms of the Bible.

The immigrants were not easily assimilated into their new surroundings. They were set off from Anglo-Saxon Protestants not only by their customs and (except for the Irish) their language but also by their religion. Most remained loyal Catholics, and for the first time in American history a strong competitive theology and religious organization confronted Protestantism. It was during this period that anti-Catholicism reemerged in force, and Protestant political loyalties in the North coalesced around the Republican party. (The South at this time, of course, became solidly Democratic.) The realignment in the North following the Civil War had obvious class and geographical bases. Most of the immigrants settled in the cities, went to work in the factories, and continued to practice their native customs. For predominantly rural, middle-class Protestants, the customs and behavior of these new Americans were frightening and incomprehensible. The cities came to be viewed as hostile territories—as centers of sin, wickedness, and loose living.

The influx of immigrants into the cities in the middle and late nineteenth century thus broke the dream of a Protestant empire in the New World and created social conditions that linked Protestantism even closer to the status quo. Church leaders who had earlier praised the initiative of businessmen found it easy to support the industrial giants who appeared toward the end of the century. Many became beholden to them for financial support, and the main body of Protestantism entered its gilded age, becoming a chief spokesman for the new industrial order and an opponent of the unionization of workers.

At the same time, some Protestant leaders sought to cope with these new developments and began to call for a more socially concerned church. More importantly, they faced the challenge to orthodox Protestantism brought about by historical criticisms of the Bible and by the new theory of evolution. The spread of such scientific thinking clearly undermined literal interpretations of the Bible and the separation between the natural and supernatural maintained by Protestant traditionalists. For many, religious truths could no longer be considered as divine revelation of objective fact, but were seen as purely symbolic—as a fallible product of man's understanding and interpretation of what is sacred and divine. "Modern theologians," as Langdon Gilkey puts it," ... have regarded theology as reflection on religion, and thus as the very human and fallible *result* of religious faith or experience rather than as the sacred *object* of religious faith, that is, as an authoritative exposition of divinely revealed truth."[15]

Such a perspective, which obviously takes from religion much of its claim for authority and unique status, was inimical to the literalism and supernaturalism of nineteenth-century Protestantism (although not necessarily to its economic and political conservatism). As a result, many church leaders at the turn of the century sought to accommodate Protestant theology with science by demythologizing religion and looking to God's immanence in the world as the source of religious understanding. They abandoned much of the supernaturalism and literalism of traditional Protestantism and replaced these doctrines with a theology centering on man's experience of God's presence in the world around him.

The term "liberalism" is associated with this position within Protestantism; "modernism" relates to the more general theological effort to come to terms with secular culture.[16] Historically, religious modernism (the expression we use in this study) slowly gained dominance in most of the more established Protestant denominations; its formal date of recognition is often set at 1908, the year of the organization of the Federal Council of Churches (now the National Council of Churches). Most of the more modernist denominations, however, contained a large minority of orthodox clergymen—a pattern that continues today.

This new theological movement was politically significant because it contained a sizable number of Protestant church leaders who wanted to involve organized religion in the social and political problems of the period. The "social gospel" movement aligned itself generally with the reformist politics of progressivism, although its adherents ranged from mild reformists to doctrinaire Marxists. Many of these church officials assumed major positions of leadership during this period and developed an important theological justification for their actions. Such activists, however, remained in the minority even within the modernist wing of Protestantism, and prophetic leadership was limited largely to persons occupying nonparish positions within the church.[17]

This early attempt at social reform virtually died following World War I, along with most other liberal reformist movements of the period. From 1890 to the 1920s, Protestant demoninations were split by a bitter struggle between traditionalists and modernists over institutional control of the church—a struggle that hardened theological differences between the two sides. During this period the term "fundamentalism" was coined as a call for a return to "the fundamentals," and in many quarters literalism became the true test of faith.[18] This struggle further weakened the influence of organized religion and, together with the Protestant enthusiam over Prohibition,[19] deterred church leaders from speaking out on social issues.

The last major theological movement within Protestantism prior to the 1960s was known as "neoorthodoxy." Like early modernism (or liberalism), it too was influenced by the secular events of the period: the horror of world war, the pallor of the Depression, and the stark immorality of one of the most "civilized" (and Protestant) European countries. Its common point of departure was an attack on the liberals' optimism about man's rational capabilities and the inevitability of human progress. Neoorthodox churchmen called for a recognition of the tragic sense of human life and of the finitade of man's existence. Doctrinally, this theological movement was rather diverse —emphasizing the transcendent elements of Christian faith and the sovereignty and majesty of God. As such, it reintroduced at least some of the Biblical questions swept aside by early liberal leaders. With respect to social issues, however, neoorthodoxy continued the modernist emphasis on an ethically engaged church. The 1930s thus witnessed a revival of ethical leadership from many church leaders as they tried to cope with the problems of industrialization, the economy, and an impending war.

Church activism again faded away with the drift of public events, and by the 1960s neoorthodoxy had all but run its course as an intellectual movement. As the next section reveals, the resurgence in clergy activism in the 1960s coincided with a period during which organized religion was faced with the radical implications of a demythologized religion and an increasingly secular society. Thus the conflicts brought about by the rise of new breed activism were heightened by conflicts over the meaning and purpose of religion itself.

This brief overview of the history of American Protestantism introduces two factors of prime importance to our understanding of the prophetic role of Protestant churches: the close association that has developed between Protestantism and dominant secular values and interests in this country, and the emergence of theological divisions over fundamental doctrinal issues. In the first respect, we have seen that Protestantism has tended to blend easily and comfortably with its secular environment. No anticlericalism has appeared between dominant religious and secular groups in the United States—as it has in many European countries—and both interests have benefited accordingly. This interpenetration of religious and secular values has often made it difficult to determine the extent to which Protestantism has developed independent of American values and political and economic interests.[20] With respect to social issues, however, it appears that Protestant churches have received far more than they have given in this relationship. They have been constrained by their individualistic and moralistic ethic and by their reliance on a white, middle-class membership, and they have functioned largely to support prevailing public policies and practices.[21]

Historical precedents for the recent outburst in clergy activism can be found in the social gospel movement, which began in this country at the turn of the century. Similarly, the prophetic or Kingdom of God tradition within Christianity can be traced back to the prophets of the Old Testament, to the actions of Jesus, or to the struggles of the early Christians. The activists of the 1960s have in fact identified their efforts with these earlier attempts to judge worldly affairs in terms of Christian standards.[22]

From a purely historical perspective, we might view the church activism of the past decade as a reemergence of the Kingdom of God tradition within Christianity. Yet important theological divisions have developed within Protestantism over the past half-century, and the contemporary religious situation differs in many significant respects from that of previous religious epochs. The doctrinal structure on which Christianity has traditionally rested has lost much of its validity and meaning in contemporary society, and religious modernists have attempted to confront this situation by grounding their religion in the human situation itself. Such a theological orientation brings religious leaders into closer contact with secular problems—thus increasing the likelihood that church officials will develop an active social ethic—but it also appears to undermine the traditional basis of religious authority, hence weakening the church's leadership potential in societal affairs. To understand the radical consequences of this demytholigization of contemporary religion, we turn now to a broader examination of the secular implications of religious belief systems and to the unique problems facing organized religion in its modern form.

Religious Beliefs and Social Action.   It is apparent that different religious systems have different consequences for social beliefs and actions. Max Weber, for example, distinguished between religions whose goals were "this-worldly" or "otherworldly" on the one hand and those whose actions tended to be "mystical" or "ascetic" on the other. Thus Western religions are classified as ascetic and some Western religions are more this-worldly (Judaism and Protestantism) than others (early Christianity and Catholicism). From this perspective, the Protestant Reformation is seen to have contributed to the "spirit of capitalism," as well as to a series of other secular developments.

Such distinctions continue to be useful in explaining the action-related components of contemporary religions (e.g., the different ethical implications found in Protestantism and Catholicism). Yet one increasingly hears such terms as "post-Reformation," "post-Protestant," "post-Christian," and the "death of God" being used to describe the contemporary religious situation. These phrases suggest that modern religion represents a radical departure from previous theological formulations—so radical that many theologians and sociologists see in the contemporary situation an end to Western religion as it has existed in its Judaeo-Christian form.

It is beyond our objectives to discuss the intellectual history of this development, the variety of secular factors that have contributed to it, or the specific theological attempts that have been made to create a "religion" relevant to contemporary conditions. During the 1960s, however, Protestant churches (and American religion in general) were undergoing a profound crisis of identification and reappraisal. These religious developments, we would expect, very much affected both the manner in which Protestant ministers responded to political issues in the 1960s and the nature of the conflicts that their activism caused within the church. Such developments apparently encouraged an activist commitment by many churchmen—indeed, they seem to have made some kind of ethical response an imperative—while simultaneously undermining the authority and legitimacy of the same prophetic actions. The institutional crisis within Protestantism thus led inevitably to conflict over prophetic leadership, and the resulting conflicts seem to have intensified this very crisis.

We can perhaps best grasp the radical nature of religious modernism by comparing the present religious situation with that of earlier periods. Particularly useful is the well-known discussion of Robert N. Bellah of the "evolution" of religious systems.[23] In this sweeping review of religious history, Bellah traces the evolution of religious symbol systems as they have become more differentiated, comprehensive, and rationalized. He relates these changes to those which have occurred in religious action and organization and to the role of religion in society. Such a comparative treatment of religious change serves to accentuate the radical implications in the modernist demythologization of religion.

In the earliest known religious system, that associated with primitive societies, religion pervaded the affairs of the entire community. Religious and secular roles or organizations were not separated; rather, religion was fused with other societal roles and "acted out" in the marketplace, in political functions, and in other aspects of daily life. Thus the chief function of religion in the small, homogeneous societies of primitive times was integrative. Religion bound together the members of these tribal communities and reinforced solidarity that existed along other dimensions. The religious symbol system of primitive societies was characterized by a strong ritual identification of the mythical with the real world. It served to link men with nature, and in this sense to provide meaning to the unexplainable events of daily life. Gradually, this symbolic system became more elaborate and well defined. Cults arose and distinctions appeared between men and gods; conscious systems of worship and sacrifice were developed to maintain communications between the mythical world and real world.[24] Religious roles, however, remained undifferentiated, and religious organizations continued to be merged with other social structures.

A major departure from this pattern began to occur in the first millennium B.C., when the element of transcendence was introduced into religion. Man's earthly actions were greatly devalued, and the concept arose of a superior, transcendent, otherworldly realm. Corresponding with such a belief, much of the mythology of earlier religious forms was abandoned for the idea of one God—creator and ruler of all the universe. Thus men came to think in terms of a new and important dualism between life as it is (in its corrupted form) and life as it exists in some other world (the ideal state). The obtaining of salvation in this other world became the foundation for religious action and for a radically new religious identity of the self. The individual began to see himself as somehow separate from the flow of events, with a degree of choice and responsibility for his own destiny. At the same time, the religious ideal during this period was generally one of withdrawal from rather than confrontation with the world; salvation was thought to be achieved not by individual actions alone, but through the prescribed medium of church ritual and law.

Such a conception inevitably serves to distinguish religion from other societal forms and roles. Along with the new symbolic system, then, structurally distinct religious actors and religious organizations emerged—an event of far-reaching consequences for social actions. Where religious and political forms were once merged, now they are separated into relatively independent hierarchies. Social legitimation is shared by the members of these two hierarchies, and for the first time disagreement and conflict become possible between religious and political functionaries. The idea is developed that political authorities can be judged by religious standards which they themselves do not control, and everywhere religion and religious groups inspired challenges to the existing political order. As a rule, however, such conflicts were rare. In most instances, religious and political elites were drawn from the same privileged class, and religious and political symbolisms tended to be mutually reinforcing. Religion thus served largely to provide legitimacy and support for the status quo.

The Protestant Reformation challenged many of these arrangements, although its social effects remain controversial among scholars of religion. The dualism between life in this world and life in another world was retained but acquired new significance. The world in which men lived continued to be seen as evil and debased in comparison with life in the promised hereafter. But the scope of religious reality was sharply reduced, and most of the church's role of mediation was eliminated. In this situation, salvation was to be sought not by withdrawing from the world but by directly confronting it. Men, through their faith, were now capable of acting as autonomous agents and were, in a sense, to act out God's Plan on earth.

Thus Protestantism, as Peter Berger points out, greatly limits the powerful role of mystery, miracle, and magic in religion and creates a polarization between "a radically transcendent divinity" and "a radically 'fallen' humanity."[25] By breaking the continuity that had existed between the unknown world of the divine and the observable world of man, it places an unprecedented onus on man himself. It is this tension—the need to prove oneself worthy of God's grace—that is seen as the religious basis for the worldliness of Protestantism. It is often credited with inspiring (or contributing to) a whole range of societal innovations—from the development of capitalism to the voluntaristic, self-reforming aspects of democratic society. At the same time, the individual burden of Protestantism is a heavy one. It is maintained only through a clearly defined set of doctrinal beliefs and the development of a rigid "Puritan personality."

For Protestants, the one remaining link between man and the supernatural is found in God's grace—the redemptive act whereby God forgives man for his sins and human failings. As we noted in the last section, science and historical scholarship have made it difficult for modern man to believe in the literal existence of an otherworldly realm. Science, not religion, is generally accepted as the source of knowledge about the objective world, and historical studies have demonstrated the secular origins of much of the Biblical text. In such a situation, the supernaturalism and the orthodox literalism of traditional Protestantism have lost much of their meaning and validity. The dualism between a "fallen" this world and a superior other world, which has been basic to the Judaeo-Christian tradition, is no longer tenable for many of the "faithful."

Thus in the modern situation, religion is viewed by many as symbolism rather than as divinely revealed truth. Indeed, as Bellah points out, it becomes questionable whether the term "religion" has any meaning under these new circumstances. Man is increasingly able to understand the laws of his own existence and, most importantly, to realize that such laws are discernible. What was previously recognized as religion is now seen as a symbolic attempt by humans to come to grips with the problems of their own destiny. Institutions of a purely religious nature, such as churches, seem to have no special claim for authority under such circumstances; if anything, they appear to be antiquated, especially if they continue to justify their existence in terms of an otherworldly realm.

Although not everyone would take the matter so far, the implications are obviously of major consequence. Modernist theology, as we have seen, has attempted to adjust to these conditions by developing a theology centered around man-to-man relationships. Yet this very attempt has caused a profound crisis within organized religion. What, for example, is to be the role of the religious leader in the modern religious situation? If man is not to seek his destiny in otherworldly terms, what purpose does the ministry serve? If doctrinal orthodoxy is abandoned, just what provides the basis for religious authority and for a uniquely religious perspective in human affairs? Similarly, what is to become of the institutional church under such conditions? Does the parish church serve any purpose in the modern religious situation? Is it not an outmoded form of religious organization, and might it not actually perpetuate social patterns and religious practices that might best be eliminated? Finally, what implications does such a demythologized and secular religious perspective hold for organized religion with respect to its lay constituency? Will Protestant laymen see any relevance in modernist theology? Once the certainties of traditional Protestant doctrines are removed, will they find any reason to remain "religious" and to support religious goals and institutions?

Such questions have frequently been raised with respect to modernist religion. They were discussed with particular intensity, however, and received widespread publicity in a series of best-selling treatises published in the early 1960s. Outmoded traditional Protestant beliefs came under attack in such books as Bishop J. A. T. Robinson's *Honest to God*,[26] Harvey Cox's *The Secular City*,[27] and Pierre Berton's *The Comfortable Pew*,[28] as well as in the more radical interpretations of the "death of God" theologians. The institutional forms of the church were condemned in Gibson Winters's *The Suburban Captivity of the Churches*,[29] Peter Berger's *The Noise of Solemn Assemblies*,[30] and Martin Marty's *Second Chance for American Protestants*.[31] Many of these critics also attacked the church, often in caustic terms, for its collusion with the status quo and for its failure to provide moral leadership on important social issues. The church, they charged, had not only abdicated its religious responsibility of furnishing ethical leadership on matters of moral consequence, it had formed an unholy alliance with the forces of racial bigotry, economic immorality (greed), and "jingoistic" nationalism.

All these critiques of the state of Protestantism called for a redirection in religious thought and institutional forms—fundamental changes that would make the church more "relevant" to contemporary thinking and contemporary conditions. They were widely read by religious leaders and no doubt played a role in the emergence of clergy activism during the 1960s. But what of the mass membership of Protestant churches? Does a demythologized religion provide sufficient appeal and rationale for continued religious commitment by the churches' lay constituents? If laymen reject the supernaturalism and orthodoxy of traditional Protestantism, will they remain loyal members of the church? And are they likely to accept or support the ethical implications seen by the modernist clergy in their secular-oriented religion?

Such questions are vital to modern religion, and we return to them in greater detail in a later chapter. They have been answered negatively, however, by a number of sociologists and observers of American religion. Rodney Stark and Charles Y. Glock, for example, have shown that lay loyalties and religious involvement are weak in liberal, modernist denominations. They suggest that the man-to-man theology of modern religion may not provide sufficient reason for laymen to support an institutional church, and they ask in their concluding chapter whether ethics will be the death of Christianity.[32] Similarly, in *The Gathering Storm in the Churches* Jeffrey K. Hadden documents the widening breach in Protestant churches over ethical and political issues. He demonstrates that although most clergymen support the civil rights movement and an active church involvement in racial issues, most laymen do not.[33] Glock and his colleagues move the analysis one step further. In a reanalysis of data collected in the early 1950s, they show that Episcopal laymen give much greater support to the "comforting" than to the "challenging" functions of religion.[34] Finally, recent assessments by Streiker and Strober and by Kelley, mentioned earlier, also conclude that the church's appeal to laymen lies in the comfort it provides amidst the daily traumas of life, not in its function as an agent of social change.

Thus while increasing numbers of church leaders felt compelled to speak out on controversial public issues, serious questions were being raised within religious circles over the very meaning and purpose of organized religion. Such internal developments, it would seem, could only further exacerbate the problems experienced by the activist clergy and hinder their efforts to gain lay support for their social activism. In making this point, we must be careful not to confuse the events of the 1960s with the long-term trend toward secularization; religious observers have often been misled by transitory events —some real and some more imagined—into prophesying the "decline" or "revival" of American religion. Nevertheless, these secular and religious developments did come to a head at the same period of time—undoubtedly making the institutional dilemma facing church leaders during the 1960s all the more severe.[35] On the one hand, as we have said, the crisis within Protestant religion seems to have required of clerical leaders a more active, ethically relevant commitment to public problems. On the other, the same conditions appear to weaken the public authority and legitimacy of organized religion and to make laymen more resistant (or indifferent) to the ethical admonitions of their leaders.

Religious Modernism and Clergy Activism.   This discussion of religious belief systems clearly indicates that a commitment to a critical, ethically involved church is more likely to be forthcoming from the modernist clergy. In making this statement, we must emphasize both the positive and the negative consequences of religious modernism—the ethical imperatives which we have seen to be implicit in modernist religion on the one hand, and the crisis in meaning and purpose facing contemporary modernist clergymen on the other. It is apparent that religious modernism is most compatible with the prophetic, socially active tradition within Christianity. Its perspective is highly secular, as opposed to the otherworldly emphasis on salvation found in traditional Protestantism. Modernist church leaders, moreover, have attempted to fashion a theology relevant to the conditions of men in their human experiences, and since the turn of the century it has been primarily the modernist clergy who have spoken out critically on public issues. We would therefore expect modernist ministers to be the most ethically committed in their beliefs and the most militant in their social actions.

In addition, we would expect that the modernist clergy will most often experience a loss of meaning in their religious roles and will feel the greatest need to develop new functions as religious specialists. As we have just seen, modern religion has lost much of its unique authority and functions, appearing to be an anachronism in so secular a society as the United States. Institutions, however, do not easily disappear. When organizational goals become untenable, they are often replaced by another set of goals in an effort to rationalize the organization's continued existence. Perhaps the most common means by which organized religion has responded to its precarious situation is the process of "goal displacement": taking what was once merely a means to an end and making that function the goal itself. Thus the achievement of salvation—the traditional goal of Protestantism—required the religious functionary to seek new converts to Christ. The notion of salvation may be questionable in modern society, but the pursuit of a large, supportive membership remains as a concrete and easily quantifiable goal. In such a manner, religious leaders may come to view the building up of membership rolls as an end in itself, toward which the parish minister should strive.[36] This process might explain, at least in part, the strong emphasis placed by organized religion on membership figures as an indication of "success" within the ministry.

A second means to cope with the problem of goallessness, particularly for the modernist clergy, is to seek new, essentially secular goals. An active involvement in social issues may well serve such a function for the modernist clergy. The parish church may seem to be an antiquated institution in contemporary society, religion may be highly devalued, and the clergyman may have lost some of the traditional satisfactions experienced by the man of God. But to involve oneself in such "morally right" issues as civil rights, the abolition of poverty, and peace may compensate for such doubts and such losses in traditional functions, and conflict within the parish church may even come to be viewed in positive terms. To be "socially controversial" is a sign that one is "with it"; to arouse opposition among one's parishioners is an indication of "relevance."

In this respect, we might also recall Richard Hofstadter's thesis with regard to the upheaval in status which affected the politics of the Progressive era.[37] Hofstadter argues that the loss in status suffered by the middle class to the new plutocracy contributed to the former's shift toward liberal politics and to its active role in Progressive causes. Particularly hard hit during this period were the liberal clergy. Protestant ministers not only participated in this general decline in the position of the middle class, they also lost much of their claim for moral and intellectual leadership as a result of the increasing secularization of American life. Thus Hofstadter sees one facet of the social gospel movement as an attempt by liberal clergymen to restore some of their secular influence and prestige—an effort in which they in fact achieved considerable success.[38]

An analogous situation certainly existed during the 1960s. Liberal church leaders, as we have seen, were confronted squarely with the radical implications of modernist religion to their own secular roles and functions. They seemed to have no choice but to join in the continuing secularization of American society (as in their support of the school prayer decisions). They watched public influence and recognition being bestowed on religious spokesmen who preached a bland, reassuring "civil" religion. And they themselves came under intense fire from within their own ranks, as well as from liberals with whom they had often been identified in the past.

Thus the activism of the 1960s undoubtedly had many religious roots: the theological grounding of religion in man's own experience, the crisis within modernist churches over religious roles and functions, and the mounting criticism directed at liberal churches. Given such factors, it is hardly surprising to find Protestant clergymen among the most outspoken activists of the period.

In the first part of this study, we examine the religious, ethical, and political beliefs of the parish ministers in our survey and the relation between their theological positions and their involvement in controversial public issues. It is clearly our expectation that social activism will be most common among the more modernist-oriented respondents. And we see that this is indeed the case—although by no means all members of the modernist clergy were active in the politics of the period, nor were all traditionalists politically conservative or socially inactive.

Clergy Activism and the Ministerial Profession.   The prophetic potential of Protestant churches, of course, is likely to be influenced not only by factors related to theology but also by the structural characteristics of the ministerial profession itself. Like other organizations, Protestant churches possess unique structures of communication and patterns of authority. Such organizational features, in turn, are likely to influence the views developed by parish ministers toward ethical and political questions, as well as their willingness to speak out on controversial public issues. Particularly, they place a great deal of authority in the hands of local parishioners—authority that is more likely to be exercised against than in support of the activities of the ethically committed clergy.

For these reasons, we must also consider the organizational features of the ministerial profession. In Chapter 6 we discuss in some detail the professional characteristics of the Protestant ministry and the distribution of authority and influence within Protestant churches. A short review of the path to be followed in our inquiry is useful at this point, however, to complete our description of the prophetic potential of Protestant clergymen.

The ministry is not a unique occupation. It is usually classified as one of the "professions," and we can use our knowledge of the professions in general to designate the patterns of interaction and authority we would expect to find within the ministry and to locate deviations from these expected patterns. Among the characteristics that have come to be identified with professionalism are specialized knowledge or expertise, the establishment of schools of training, relative freedom from lay evaluation or control, a service orientation toward one's clientele, a highly structured code of ethics, the establishment of a professional association, occupational control over licensing and admissions procedures, high commitment and identification with one's vocation, and a highly developed occupational ideology.[39] Such characteristics serve to differentiate the types of individual with whom professionals commonly interact in the course of their duties and who are likely to be in a position to influence their professional behavior. Within the professions as a whole, these groups are the practitioner's clientele, colleagues, and, in most instances, organizational superiors (often themselves trained professionals). Within the ministry, these groups include the clergyman's parishioners, fellow ministers, and local denominational leaders, and we look to such individuals for the major occupationally related sources of clergy activism and inactivism.

Given the institutionalization of the ministerial profession, we would expect relations between the parish minister and these three groups to be fairly stable and to be usefully studied through the concept of role. From this perspective, the members of each of these groups are likely to develop "normative expectations" concerning the proper behavior of the clergyman in his various roles. In most areas of clerical conduct, we would expect a fair amount of agreement or "consensus" in the positions taken by the members of these groups. With respect to clergy activism, or the prophetic role, however, prior research suggests that a great deal of "role conflict" exists—at least within the more liberal or modernist Protestant denominations. The lay members of these denominations are overwhelmingly white and middle class, and like their peers they tend to have conservative views on political issues. Furthermore, they seem to separate the religious and the political in their own thinking and, by and large, to oppose the notion of a critical, ethically involved church.[40]

What makes the political and ethical conservatism of Protestant laymen so very important for the development of clergy activism is the unusual role that is played by this clientele group within Protestant churches. Various unique characteristics of the Protestant ministry serve to bring the parish minister into particularly close contact with his parishioners and to render him highly susceptible to lay influence and control. First, the professional role of the minister is less limited to a specific area of competence than is the case in most other professions. The minister is not only a preacher on Sundays, a symbol of divine authority, and an educator of the young, but also an administrator, counselor, and organizer of church activities. This diffuse professional–client relationship is responsible for much ambiguity and conflict within the ministerial profession, since the minister and his parishioners often have very different ideas about the proper role behavior of the man of the cloth.

Second, unlike many other professionals, the parish clergyman does not create his own practice. Instead he is hired or appointed to a local congregation and must deal with a parish organization that has an ongoing social structure of its own. Similarly, the minister does not live in a geographical area of his own choosing but takes up residence among the members of his congregation—frequently in a house provided by the local church. He is likely to form close friendships with many of the members of his congregation, and indeed his ministerial duties (his pastoral role) include paying frequent social calls on his parishioners.

Finally, the very organizational structure of Protestant churches places a great deal of influence in the hands of local parishioners. Some denominations are more hierarchically structured than others, but laymen in most churches have much to say about the parish minister's appointment, tenure, and salary, as well as the governance of the local church. In addition, Protestant laymen can often influence church policies by withdrawing (or threatening to withdraw) their parish loyalties or financial patronage. Membership figures, as we have suggested, often serve as important signs of goal achievement within organized religion.

All these characteristics of the ministerial profession obviously contribute to the extreme vulnerability of Protestant clergymen to lay influence or control. In contrast, colleague relations within the ministry appear to be less important than in most other professions. Professional success for parish ministers is determined more by the recognition they receive from their congregational members than by praise from their colleagues; social interactions, by the same token, are more commonly conducted with the pastor's parishioners than with other ministers. Colleagues thus may provide an important source of moral encouragement and reinforcement for the ethically committed clergyman, but they can supply little concrete support for the beleaguered parish activist.

However, a major countervailing force to lay conservatism and authority within the ministry might be found in the local leadership of Protestant denominations. Prior research shows that in some denominations the official leadership holds liberal ethical and political views[41]—a product, one would expect, of both the recruitment of such leaders and the removal of such positions from direct lay control. Local church officials, moreover, are in a position to assist the activist clergy in a number of ways. They can often help the parish minister find or maintain a church position; they can provide important moral support to the parish pastor who comes under attack for his outspoken ethical conduct; and they can act as intermediaries between the local activist and irate members of the congregation. The authority available to local leaders in each of these areas seems to vary according to the denomination's polity structure. Some denominations are formally organized in a hierarchical fashion (the episcopal), some are highly decentralized (the congregational), and others represent a mixture of the two forms (the presbyterian). In theory, church officials in hierarchical denominations (Episcopal and Methodist) are in a better position to assist the socially active clergy than officials in decentralized denominations (Baptist and United Church of Christ). In practice, it is unclear how important these formal distinctions are for the exercise of authority within Protestant churches.

Our description of the organizational characteristics of the ministerial profession thus suggests that a great deal of role conflict is likely to exist within Protestant churches over the ethical actions of the parish clergy. As a general rule, we would expect clergy activism to be supported by liberal denominational leaders and opposed by conservative parishioners—although we would certainly anticipate exceptions to these patterns. However, the organization of Protestant denominations places a great deal of authority and influence in the hands of local congregations: they have much to do with the professional success and personal satisfaction obtained by parish ministers during their careers.

For reasons such as these, many dismiss the parish clergy as a major source of prophetic leadership within Protestant churches. Most sociologists feel that the church's prophetic capabilities lie primarily in its nonparish personnel—in denominational officials, theologians, seminary students, campus ministers, and the like. Such religious functionaries tend to have fewer personal interactions with Protestant laymen and to be shielded from most forms of lay reprisal.[42] In reality, relatively little is known about the ethical beliefs of Protestant laymen and about their responses to the involvement of the parish clergy in controversial social issues. It may be, for example, that many Protestant layment are equally disturbed by such problems as racism, poverty, and militarism abroad and are more tolerant and receptive of clergy activism than previous research might suggest.[43]

In any case, this discussion suggests that conflicting pressures are likely to face the parish minister who is considering speaking out on a controversial social issue. We might reasonably expect that these pressures, as well as his own ethical convictions, will influence his choice in the matter. In the second part of this study, therefore, we examine the conflicts within Protestant churches over social activism and the manner in which they influence the clergy's own ethical beliefs and behavior. Among other things, we look at the attitudes that are attributed by parish ministers to their local parishioners, close colleagues, and local denominational leaders on ethical and political questions; the actions taken by Protestant laymen in response to their minister's ethical activities; the parish clergy's professional and social relationships and their apparent impact upon clerical beliefs; and the distribution of authority within denominations of various polity structures.

NOTES AND REFERENCES

1. Lowell D. Streiker and Gerald Strober, *Religion and the New Majority* (New York: Association Press, 1972).
2. Dean Kelley, *Why Conservative Churches Are Growing* (New York: Harper & Row, 1972).
3. *Ibid.*, p. 151. For a reply to these and similar arguments by a prominent church

activist, see Richard John Neuhaus, "Going Home Again: America after Vietnam," *Worldview*, **15** (October 1972), pp. 30–36.

4.   Cf. Toyomasa Fuse, "Religion, War and the Institutional Dilemma: A Sociological Interpretation," *Journal of Peace Research*, **2** (1968), pp. 196–210; and Daniel Callahan, "The Quest for Social Relevance," *Daedalus*, **96** (Winter 1967), pp. 151–179.

5.   This review is necessarily brief, touching only on the major features of Protestant history—particularly on those most relevant to the churches' prophetic role. Also, we have chosen to omit from our discussion the country's colonial days. A recent, exhaustive survey of the history of American religion is found in Sydney E. Ahlstrom, *A Religious History of the American People* (New Haven, Conn.: Yale University Press, 1972).

6.   See, for example, Ahlstrom, *op. cit.*, pp. 379–384; and Martin E. Marty, *Righteous Empire: The Protestant Experience in America* (New York: Dial, 1970), pp. 35–45.

7.   This is the central theme, of course, of Marty's *Righteous Empire*. As Ahlstrom points out, American historians have also tended until recently to view the country's history in terms of the will of Divine Providence (*op. cit.*, pp. 2–3).

8.   See Seymour Martin Lipset, "Religion and Politics in the American Past and Present," in *Religion and Social Conflict*, Robert Lee and Martin E. Marty, eds., (New York: Oxford University Press, 1964), pp. 72–76.

9.   Accounts of these early activist movements can be found in John R. Bodo, *The Protestant Clergy and Public Issues, 1818–1848* (Princeton, N. J.: Princeton University Press, 1954); Clifford S. Griffin, *The Brothers' Keepers: Moral Stewardship in the United States, 1800–1865* (New Brunswick, N. J.: Rutgers University Press, 1960); and Charles I. Foster, *An Errand of Mercy: The Evangelical United Front, 1790–1837* (Chapel Hill: University of North Carolina Press, 1960).

10.   William G. McLoughlin, "Changing Patterns of Protestant Philanthropy, 1607–1969," in *The Religious Situation: 1969*, Donald R. Cutler, ed. (Boston: Beacon, 1969), p. 550.

11.   *Ibid.* Some historians argue that this early Protestant reform movement was social 'rather than individualistic. For this point of view, see Timothy L. Smith, *Revivalism and Social Reform in Mid-Nineteenth Century America* (New York: Abingdon, 1957).

12.   William A. Clebsch, *From Sacred to Profane America* (New York: Harper & Row, 1968), pp. 154–158.

13.   On the Protestant treatment of Indians, see Robert P. Beaver, *Church, State, and the American Indians* (St. Louis, Mo.: Concordia, 1966), and Robert F. Berkhofer, *Salvation and the Savage* (Lexington: University of Kentucky Press, 1965).

14.   For an overview of the role of Protestant churches during this period, see Ahlstrom, *op. cit.*, pp. 648–697. For more detailed analysis of the Negro and Protestantism, see Carter G. Woodson, *The History of the Negro Church* (Washington, D. C.: Associated Publishers, 1921); and David M. Reimers, *White Protestantism and the Negro* (New York: Oxford University Press, 1965).

15.   Langdon Gilkey, "Social and Intellectual Sources of Contemporary Protestant Theology," *Daedalus*, **96** (Winter 1967), p. 70.

16.   Although the term "modernism" has been defined in various ways, it appears to be the most commonly used label to describe this general movement within Protestantism, and we use it for this purpose throughout our analysis. A more detailed exposition of this theological orientation is found in the introductory comments and readings in William R. Hutchison, ed., *American Protestant Thought: The Liberal Era* (New York: Harper & Row, 1968).

17.   Major historical reviews of this period include Henry F. May, *Protestant Churches and Industrial America* (New York: Harper & Row 1948); Donald B. Meyer, *The Protestant Search for Political Realism, 1919–1941* (Berkeley: University of California Press, 1960); and Robert Moats Miller, *American Protestantism and Social Issues, 1919–1939* (Chapel Hill: University of North Carolina Press, 1958).

18.   See William G. McLoughlin, "Is There a Third Force in Christendom?" *Daedalus*, **96** (Winter 1967), pp. 43–68.

19.   Lutheranism maintained its immigrant character to a much greater extent than the other major Protestant denominations examined in this study. Partly as a result, it did not (with its large beer-drinking German membership) share the general Protestant concern with Prohibition. We see the present-day remnants of this policy when we examine clerical attitudes toward the regulation of public morality in Chapter 3.

20.   The best example of these divergent emphases can be found in the work of H. Richard Niebuhr. In his most celebrated work, *The Social Sources of Denominationalism* (New York: Holt, 1929), Niebuhr demonstrated the extent to which denominational patterns in this country were shaped by racial, ethnic, economic, and geographical divisions existing in the greater society. Yet Niebuhr remained dissatisfied with such a one-sided accounting of American religion, and in *The Kingdom of God in America* (Chicago: Willett, Clark, 1937), he attempted to show how greatly religious actions had been motivated by a prophetic tradition independent of American culture or American political and economic interests. A similar, although less pronounced, difference in emphasis can be found in Marty, *op. cit.*, and Clebsch, *op. cit.* The former reflects the adaptation of Protestant religion to its secular surroundings; the latter deals more with the independent influence of Protestantism on American values and practices.

21.   For this reason, scholars have often tried to explain the political influence of religion through the existence of some kind of "civil religion" which is a blending of religious and political values. This civil religion is influenced by Christian teachings but exists independently of any specific theological formulation. A recent, widely cited accounting of this civil religion is found in Robert N. Bellah, "Civil Religion in America," *Daedalus*, **96** (Winter 1967), pp. 1–22, reprinted in *The Religious Situation, 1970*, Donald R. Cutler, ed. (Boston: Beacon, 1970). See also Will Herberg, *Protestant–Catholic–Jew* (Garden City, N. Y.: Doubleday, 1955); and Richard John Neuhaus, "The War, the Churches, and Civil Religion," *The Annals*, **38** (January 1970), pp. 128–140.

22.   See Harvey C. Cox, "The 'New Breed' in American Churches: Sources of Social Activism in American Religion," *Daedalus*, **96** (Winter 1967), pp. 135–150. We are speaking here of the prophetic tradition within Christianity which stresses the reformation of society to bring it into conformity with God's ways. A conservative prophetic tradition also exists—one that is critical of human society but sees its restoration only in the Second Coming. The term "premillennial" is often given to this second movement; "postmillennial" refers to the first.

23.   Robert N. Bellah, "Religious Evolution," *American Sociological Review*, **29** (June 1964), pp. 358–374.

24.   Bellah distinguishes a second religious system at this stage—the "archaic"—which we have omitted.

25.   Peter L. Berger, *The Sacred Canopy* (Garden City, N. Y.: Doubleday, 1967), pp. 111–112.

26.   Philadelphia: Westminister, 1963.

27.   New York: Macmillan, 1965.

28.   Toronto: McClelland and Stewart, 1965.

29. New York: Macmillan, 1962.

30. Garden City, N. Y.: Doubleday, 1961.

31. New York: Harper & Row, 1963.

32. Rodney Stark and Charles Y. Glock, *American Piety: The Nature of Religious Commitment* (Berkeley, University of California Press, 1968).

33. Jeffrey K. Hadden, *The Gathering Storm in the Churches* (Garden City, N. Y.: Doubleday, 1969).

34. Charles Y. Glock, Benjamin B. Ringer, and Earl R. Babbie, *To Comfort and To Challenge: A Dilemma of the Contemporary Church* (Berkeley: University of California Press, 1967).

35. For a more general review of the various religious and secular trends that resulted in the activism of the 1960s, see Sydney E. Ahlstrom, "The Radical Turn in Theology and Ethics: Why It Occurred in the 1960s," *The Annals*, **387** (January 1970), pp. 1–13.

36. N. J. Demerath, III, and Phillip E. Hammond, *Religion in Social Context* (New York: Random House, 1969), pp. 176–177.

37. Richard Hofstadter, *The Age of Reform* (New York: Vintage, 1955), pp. 131–173.

38. *Ibid.*, pp. 510–512. Hofstadter's thesis, of course, has been the subject of continuing debate and reformulation among historians. For a recent critical assessment of its applicability to the clergy during the progressive period, see William R. Hutchison, "Cultural Strain and Protestant Liberalism," *American Historical Review*, **76** (April 1971), pp. 386–411.

39. References to this literature appear in Chapter 6.

40. See Stark and Glock, *op. cit.*, pp. 69–76; Hadden, *op. cit.*, pp. 131–146; and Glock et al., *op. cit.*, pp. 113–130. We discuss some of these findings in greater detail in Chapter 7. One might well suspect, however, that such lay opposition to critical clergy activism reflects the general American dislike for dissent rather than any rationalized theory of separation of church and state. Laymen seem to approve of the covert blending of religious and political forms in many areas—even, as in the case of school prayers, when such practices are disapproved by the majority of the clergy themselves. Perhaps, then, lay opposition to church activism will change as laymen themselves become more concerned about such issues as race or military actions abroad. We make this argument below in assessing future conflicts within the church over prophetic leadership.

41. Glock et al., *op. cit.*

42. See, for example, the discussions in Hadden, *op. cit.*, pp. 185–235, and Demerath and Hammond, *op cit.*, pp. 212–223. The two major studies demonstrating the structural segregation of church radicals are by the same authors: Jeffrey K. Hadden and Raymond C. Rymph, "Social Structure and Civil Rights Involvement: A Case Study of Protestant Ministers," *Social Forces*, **45** (September 1966), pp. 51–61; and Phillip E. Hammond and Robert E. Mitchell, "The Segmentation of Radicalism: The Case of the Protestant Campus Minister," *American Journal of Sociology*, **71** (September 1965), pp. 133–143.

43. Until recently the only major study on lay reactions to clergy activism involved an obviously passion-laden issue: the participation of Little Rock ministers in the desegregation crisis of 1956. See Ernest Q. Campbell and Thomas F. Pettigrew, *Christians in Racial Crisis: A Study of Little Rock's Ministry* (Washington, D. C.: Public Affairs Press, 1959). Several smaller case studies have recently appeared involving issues of the sixties: Robert Lee and Russell Galloway, *The Schizophrenic Church: Conflict over Community Organization* (Philadelphia: Westminister, 1969); Walter M. Stuhr, Jr., *The Public Style: A Study of Community Participation of Protestant Ministers* (Chicago: Center for the Scientific Study of Religion, 1972); and William C. Martin, *Christians in Conflict* (Chicago: Center for the Scientific Study of Religion, 1972).

THE STRUCTURE OF
MINISTERIAL BELIEFS

2. A logical starting point for our inquiry into clergy activism is the examination of the nature and organization of clerical beliefs. For example, we will want to know something about the positions that Protestant clergymen take on public issues, what they feel about clergy activism, and how their views on these questions are affected by their religious orientations. In more theoretical terms, we will want to know whether there exists any interrelationship or structure in the clergy's attitudes on these dimensions of belief: Do Protestant ministers think in any consistent way about religion and politics? And is this consistency great enough to allow us to predict how Protestant clergymen are likely to respond to controversial public issues?

Previous research by Benton Johnson,[1] Jeffrey K. Hadden,[2] and others has shown that a close association does exist between the religious positions of Protestant ministers and their attitudes toward certain social and political issues. Our objective in the first two chapters is to extend this analysis over a greater range of subjects—in particular, to the controversy regarding church activism and to the political issues raised so dramatically during the 1960s. For our purposes here and in a later chapter, it is useful to conceptualize these attitudinal interrelationships in terms of a "belief system" and to make use of the approach employed by Philip Converse in his suggestive study of political leaders and the mass public.[3] Following Converse, a belief system can be thought of as "a configuration of ideas and attitudes in which the elements are bound together by some form of constraint or functional interdependence."[4] Knowing a person's positions on one attitudinal dimension thus allows us to predict his positions on others as well. A person who is opposed to increased welfare expenditures, for example, might also be

50

expected to oppose federal aid to education, a more progressive income tax, or governmental regulation of corporate profits.

Two major characteristics commonly associated with such belief systems are the centrality of certain of their idea-elements and the range of subjects to which they refer. The first property indicates that some beliefs are more stable and enduring than others and that changes in these more central beliefs are likely to elicit corresponding changes in related sets of attitudes. In this sense, we can say that one belief dimension is the primary "cause" of the others, although causation is always difficult to establish in the real world. The second property refers to the narrowness or breadth of the idea-elements included within a particular system of beliefs. Belief systems may be relatively narrow in focus, pertaining to only a few areas of an individual's total beliefs, or they may be broader, containing elements that refer to many objects, as in the case of Marxism.

The usefulness of such a formulation should be readily apparent. It appears that Christianity provides the Protestant minister with a set of beliefs likely to be highly central to his definition of the clerical role and likely to extend over a wide range of related attitudes and behavior. The major function of Christian theology, on the one hand, is to give coherence and unity to the ministerial role and to show how the various elements of Christianity are in mutual harmony. The minister's religious beliefs are thus likely to provide him with the central meaning and purpose of his calling as a clergyman and to give him a teleology around which to form his personal attitudes and values. On the other hand, Christian theology explicitly attempts to show the relationship between religion and other relevant areas of secular life. In part such an extension is inherent in a belief structure that proclaims primacy over all other belief sets. To the Christian believer, temporal matters remain secondary to a faith and commitment in the "Almighty." In part such an extension of beliefs is also related to the historical development of Protestantism and to the particularly close relationship that has generally existed between religion and secular society in this country. Although some religions have stressed either an adaptation to society or a radical escape from it, most major Protestant groups in the United States have maintained an active concern with worldly affairs.

Second, we might expect such highly constrained belief systems to exist most commonly among highly educated elite groups and among organizational leaders rather than followers. Converse has suggested that such differences are likely to be observed as one goes down the information chain and belief systems become more narrowly prescribed, more concrete, and simpler. He has shown this to be the case among political leaders and the mass public and has discussed a number of interesting political phenomena that can be understood in these terms. Similar differences in attitudinal constraint appear to exist between the belief systems of Protestant leaders and followers—a pattern that is reviewed and assessed in a later chapter.

Religious Beliefs. The empirical study of religious beliefs has generated a great deal of research over the past decade, along with a complementary amount of disagreement over the measures used to tap this dimension of belief.[5] Our study objectives do not include a wholesale investigation of the variety of doctrinal positions held by contemporary ministers; rather, we wish to develop a useful, meaningful attitudinal scale that will allow us to discriminate along the traditionalist–modernist dimension of religious belief described in the previous chapter. For this reason, we have borrowed several measures from the work of Glock and Stark on laymen and from Hadden on the clergy and, in addition, have constructed three questions of our own to deal with the ethically important dimension of religious worldliness. We find that these measures are statistically meaningful, are validated by the clergy's own perceptions of their theological positions, and discriminate among Protestant ministers on a wide range of other attitudinal and behavioral dimensions.

To determine what the clergy themselves thought about their religious views, we first asked the California ministers to classify themselves according to one of four commonly delineated theological positions: fundamentalism, conservatism, neoorthodoxy, or liberalism. The term "conservatism" is most often associated with the doctrinal orthodoxy described in the previous chapter; "liberalism" stands for the modernist demytholization of orthodox Protestantism; "neoorthodoxy" is generally taken to refer to the reemphasis of the transcendent elements of Christian doctrine by such "modernist" theologians as Reinhold Niebuhr and Paul Tillich; "fundamentalism," finally, is the label attached to the most literalist and evangelistic segment of Protestantism. We have deliberately included in our study the more established or mainline Protestant denominations—those in which we would expect to find the most socially active clergy and, in line with our theoretical orientation, to be the most "professional" in their occupational attributes. Thus we should remember that our particular sample overrepresents the proportion of modernist clergymen within Protestantism as a whole and is likely to include relatively few fundamentalist ministers.

Table 2.1 indicates that most of the California ministers were able to locate themselves within one of our four broad classifications:[5] 6 percent called themselves fundamentalists, 36 percent conservatives, 18 percent neoorthodox, and 30 percent liberals. The remaining 10 percent selected the "other" category, which was also included in the question.[7] Table 2.1 also shows that adherence to these four theological positions varies widely among the nine denominations surveyed. The Methodist Church and the United Church of Christ are overwhelmingly made up of neoorthodox and liberal ministers; the Southern Baptist Convention and the Missouri Synod-Lutheran Church are composed mostly of fundamentalists and conservatives. Of the remaining five denominations, three are primarily neoorthodox or liberal and two are primarily conservative. These distributions of religious positions are similar to that found by Hadden in his national survey of six Protestant denominations.[8]

Table 2.1. Denominational Distribution of Ministers' Self-Designated Theological Positions

Denomination	Funda-mentalist	Con-serva-tive	Neo-ortho-dox	Liberal	Other	(N)
Methodist	1%	9	18	62	10	100% (350)
United Church of Christ	1%	7	18	65	9	100% (137)
Episcopal	1%	24	21	32	22	100% (204)
Presbyterian	—[a]	36	33	20	10	99%[b] (225)
Lutheran Church in America	4%	30	31	27	8	100% (80)
American Baptist	6%	61	17	10	6	100% (144)
American Lutheran Church	4%	64	17	7	9	101% (115)
Missouri Synod-Lutheran Church	9%	78	4	3	5	99% (131)
Southern Baptist	33%	61	2	—[a]	4	100% (167)
Totals	6%	36	18	30	10	100% (1559)

[a] Less than 1 percent.
[b] Percentages not totaling 100% in this and subsequent tables are a result of errors due to rounding.

Such self-classifications are important in showing that the clergy themselves recognize a certain degree of structure or regularity in their religious views; they also can be used to test the validity of other measures dealing with these dimensions of religious belief. To obtain more specific and empirically useful religious measures, we have asked our respondents their positions on several questions dealing with supernaturalism, Biblical literalism, and religious worldliness. The relation between the ministers' self-designated religious positions and their responses in the first two of these areas appears in Table 2.2,[9] where a close connection is in fact evident between these measures of clerical belief. The first two questions asked the ministers which of a series of statements came closest to expressing what they believed about God and about the Divinity of Jesus. Sixty-eight percent of the ministers replied that they had no doubts about the existence of God; 62 percent that they had no doubts about the Divinity of Jesus. Only the respondents' acceptance or rejection of this alternative is shown in Table 2.2.[10] Virtually all ministers classifying themselves as fundamentalists or conservatives report that they have no doubts about the existence of God and that they believe in the Divinity of Jesus. Slightly more than half the neoorthodox respondents take such a position, whereas 46 percent of the liberals have no doubts about the existence of God and 31 percent have no doubts about the Divinity of Jesus.

Table 2.2. Ministers' Attitudes Toward Supernaturalism and Biblical Literalism Are Consistent with Their Self-Designated Theological Positions

	Fundamentalist	Conservative	Neoorthodox	Liberal	Other	Totals
PERCENTAGE WHO AGREE						
"I know God exists and I have no doubts about it."	99% (89)	90% (559)	58% (284)	46% (466)	55% (154)	68% (1552)
"Jesus is the Divine Son of God and I have no doubts about it."	99% (90)	90% (554)	53% (283)	31% (465)	47% (154)	62% (1551)
"I believe in a literal or nearly literal interpretation of the Bible."	96% (89)	65% (545)	7% (283)	3% (465)	12% (154)	32% (1536)
REGARD AS LITERALLY TRUE						
"There is life beyond death."	99% (90)	98% (558)	78% (283)	61% (453)	74% (149)	81% (1538)
"Jesus was born of a virgin."	98% (90)	91% (556)	29% (279)	9% (459)	41% (148)	51% (1532)
"Jesus walked on water."	97% (90)	88% (554)	29% (279)	11% (457)	35% (144)	50% (1524)
"The Devil actually exists."	97% (90)	79% (553)	17% (283)	6% (464)	26% (146)	42% (1536)

Similar divisions occurred on the other questions of Christian doctrine included in Table 2.2. Fundamentalists and conservatives are much more likely to report that they believe in "a literal or nearly literal interpretation of the Bible," that they accept the historical accuracy of the Biblical account of the miracles of Jesus, that they believe in the existence of the devil, and that they believe in life after death. Most of those clergymen who regard themselves to be fundamentalists or conservatives thus maintain an unwavering belief in the traditional tenets of Protestantism. They believe that the birth of Jesus was a divine intrusion into the world and that Jesus performed miracles while on earth. They believe in life after death and in the existence of Heaven and Hell. Those ministers who regard themselves as theological liberals (and to a lesser extent the neoorthodox respondents) reject these supernatural components of Christian doctrine—the virgin birth, Jesus walking on water, and the existence of the devil. They are more divided in their attitudes toward other features of orthodox Protestant theology, however. Many believe in the existence of a personal God and in the Divinity of Jesus, and a majority believe in life after death.

In assessing such responses, of course, we should always remember that the attitudinal distributions we obtain are influenced by our wording of the question as well as by the frames of reference used by the respondents in evaluating such statements. To ask whether "the devil actually exists," for example, may elicit responses different from those to a query of whether "evil is a force in the world." Similarly, clergymen may believe in many forms of "life beyond death" or may have different conceptions of what is meant by knowing that "God exists." Thus we should keep in mind the limitations of the survey technique and the questions we may choose to measure religious beliefs. Nevertheless, the consistency in these attitudinal patterns suggests that we are dealing with meaningful differences in theological positions among Protestant ministers and that a fairly large proportion of the parish clergy do in fact hold views that we would associate with religious modernism.

Our major concern is with the ethically relevant components of the ministerial belief system. We have suggested that the salvation-oriented otherworldliness of traditional Protestantism has served as a major deterrent to the development of a more activist church. The essence of this position is captured in the following comments, the first by a Lutheran minister (Missouri Synod), the second by a Southern Baptist:

> We are concerned with social situations but we don't see our primary purpose as solving social ills. Civic groups could just as well do that. Our people become socially concerned through spiritual channels. "Christ first loved you and can now make

> you a new person through forgiveness." After believing this, they will, with opportunities presented, be socially minded.

> Most Baptist pastors believe we are duty-bound to preach the gospel alone when we go into the pulpit. We do not feel that we are called to be social reformers. Once saved, they will have the right attitude toward all people, regardless of race or color.

These ministers indicate that they are concerned in their religious duties more with life after death than with social conditions on earth. Their primary function as pastors is to bring the Word of God to the sinful, which will allow the latter to receive forgiveness and obtain salvation in the afterlife. The clergyman's role in secular affairs is thus an indirect one; Christian laymen, once they are taught the ways of God, will automatically do what is right to bring about conditions of social justice and equality.

Three additional questions were designed to deal more directly with the ethically related dimensions of religious belief. These are shown in Table 2.3, again along with the ministers' own classifications of their religious positions. Once more, we see meaningful differences between the responses of fundamentalist and conservative clergymen on the one hand and neoorthodox and liberal respondents on the other. The first set of clergymen are far more likely to disagree that "it is not as important to worry about life after death as about what one can do in this life" and to believe that the church should retain its emphasis on "individual sanctification" as opposed to "bringing human conditions into conformity with Christian teachings." The third statement deals with the crucial matter of whether the church should exercise its authority directly or indirectly to create a better society. Most of the fundamentalist and conservative ministers agree that "if enough men were brought to Christ, social ills would take care of themselves"; most of the liberal and neoorthodox clergymen disagree.

The Protestant ministers in our parish sample thus possess a consistent and structured set of beliefs on religious matters. Of the various possible ways to construct an attitudinal measure from these responses, we have chosen factor analysis because this technique can be used to identify the major components of the ministers' beliefs and can tell us whether we are confronting more than one attitudinal cluster in the several indicators of religious position. This statistical method is particularly useful in differentiating the dimensions of the respondents' attitudes toward clergy activism and toward political issues.

Applying factor analysis to the 10 measures of religious belief included in Tables 2.2 and 2.3, we find that a single dimension accounts for most of the differences found among the ministers' religious attitudes. (These data are presented in Appendix B.) This pattern indicates that the ministers' atti-

Table 2.3.   Ministers' Attitudes Toward Religious Worldliness Are Consistent with Their Self-Designated Theological Positions

	Funda-mental-ist	Con-serva-tive	Neo-ortho-dox	Liberal	Other	Totals
It is not as important to worry about life after death as about what one can do in this life."	35% (83)	47% (540)	82% (278)	92% (466)	82% (152)	70% (1519)
"It would be better if the church were to place less emphasis on individual sanctification and more on bringing human conditions into conformity with Christian teachings."	21% (80)	23% (533)	61% (274)	77% (456)	57% (143)	50% (1486)
"If enough men were brought to Christ, social ills would take care of themselves."	93% (89)	70% (549)	37% (283)	33% (460)	33% (147)	51% (1528)

tudes toward religious issues are highly structured and that they can be explained by a single dimension of belief. In measuring the ministers' religious beliefs, therefore, we use all 10 of the previously mentioned items to construct a single, continuous scale of religious commitment. In subsequent discussions, those who score high on this dimension of religious belief are referred to as "traditionalists"; those who score low as "modernists."[11] Such designations help avoid confusion when we discuss the ministers' political views in terms of their liberalism or conservatism.

As we would expect, this modernist–traditionalist scale of religious beliefs correlates highly with the ministers' own classifications of their religious positions. Among the respondents whose views fell into the most modernist fifth of the sample, for example, 80 percent regarded themselves to be liberal or neoorthodox, whereas only 4 percent were fundamentalists or conservatives. Among those in the most traditionalist fifth, 90 percent were self-designated fundamentalists or conservatives, but only 6 percent classified themselves as liberal or neoorthodox.

Table 2.4 shows the distribution of religious modernism and traditionalism among the parish ministers in the nine denominations surveyed. Modernist attitudes predominate in the Methodist Church and the United Church of Christ, followed by the Presbyterian Church, Episcopal Church, and the Lutheran Church in America. The two most traditionalist denominations are the Southern Baptist Convention and the Missouri Synod-Lutheran Church, followed by the American Lutheran Church and the American Baptist Convention.

Table 2.4. Denominational Distributions on Religious Modernism–Traditionalism Continuum

	Religious Orientation[a]					
Denomination	1	2	3	4	5	Total
Methodist	36%	34	23	6	1	100% (354)
United Church of Christ	41%	36	18	4	1	100% (137)
Episcopal	17%	27	33	16	6	99% (207)
Presbyterian	26%	22	25	20	7	100% (226)
Lutheran Church in America	15%	18	29	29	9	100% (87)
American Baptist	9%	9	16	35	31	100% (147)
American Lutheran Church	4%	12	19	34	31	100% (118)
Missouri Synod-Lutheran Church	—	1	9	29	61	100% (134)
Southern Baptist	—	2	2	28	68	100% (170)

[a] On this 5-point scale, 1 is most modernist; 5 is most traditionalist.

Attitudes Toward Clergy Activism.   A second important dimension of clerical beliefs concerns the attitudes of Protestant ministers toward clergy activism. To a very real extent, the most divisive questions being debated within church councils at the time of our survey had to do less with predominantly theological issues than with the strategy and legitimacy of social involvement. Should the Christian, for example, become involved in helping the weak and underprivileged by seeking a political solution to their grievances, or should he serve their needs in a charity capacity only? Was the Vietnam war a "moral" issue—thus one on which the clergy had a right and duty to speak out—or are moral questions to be raised only in relation to such issues as crime, pornography, sexual conduct, and drug abuse? What public activities should the clergyman engage in as a man of the cloth, and what actions should he take only as a private citizen? Can the new breed activist legitimately speak out on public issues as a representative of the church, when many of its members do not share the views he is expressing? In a more pragmatic vein, how can the socially committed clergyman maintain an activist ministry and not lose the membership and financial support of the church's most conservative parishioners?

The intensity of clerical opinions over such ethical questions was apparent in many of the ministers' comments to our survey. "While ministers may have personal opinions on political and social problems," wrote a Baptist clergyman, "I believe they should stick to religion." "This is not the minister's business," indicated another. "He has one job to do—proclaim the gospel." A third thought that the social activists had no cause to remain in the church:

> There are far too many men in the ministry who have never experienced a definite call to preach the Word of God. If they want to be a social worker or a politician, they should enter one of these fields and get out of the ministry, which they never had and do not now have any right to be serving.

Opposition to clergy activism, furthermore, was not limited to Baptists. A number of clergymen in the more liberal denominations felt that the church was, in the words of a Presbyterian minister, "betraying its unique ministry," and feared that the actions of their ethically minded colleagues would cause laymen to lose faith in the church. Some were particularly incensed because the views expressed by the new breed activists were coming to be accepted as the official positions of their denominations. A Methodist minister wrote:

> The major frustration I now experience is that the most vocal, new left, new theology, and new morality ministers make a statement which they claim represents us all and the too eager press prints it. . . . There are many ministers who are totally frustrated because weak or vacillating church officials have let this vocal minority become the voice of the church.

On the other hand, a number of respondents perceived the purpose of their ministry largely or primarily in social terms. "I feel that the hour is desperately late and that we have no other choice but to challenge," wrote one minister, "else the church will die of irrelevancy." A second hoped the church "might wake up to her mission":

> My hope is that the church might wake up to her mission. It has suffered because of very bad theology both on the part of the clergy and laity. Hopefully the world will help the church awaken. Most urban churches are still dominated by a rural mentality and a model that was designed for agrarian society rather than urban.

An Episcopal priest—in response to a question concerning factors that might impede his social involvement—wrote that he would not be discouraged, "though I may have to leave the ministry." Many activist-oriented ministers have, of course, done just that, and some of the respondents in our survey indicated that they were considering such an action. One, a Lutheran minister, reported that he was resigning from his parish position after eight years. The reasons he gave were similar to those advanced by other new breed activists who felt that the contemporary church had lost its relevance:

> . . . stagnant structure of organized church, frustration of un-committed individuals, harassment by "club" members, lack of concern for issues and people's real problems, and constant harassment and blackmail by parishioners who will not permit the clergy to be human, socially concerned, and involved in human issues.

"The acute piety of the soul-saving approach," he concluded, "has been tolerated by me as long as possible and I frankly feel that the institutional church as now constituted is so status quo oriented that its effectiveness is almost nil."

These differences are indicated in the ministers' responses to criticisms that have been levied against the church's role in public affairs. Among the most common charges are the following: (1) the church has so aligned itself with the status quo that it has abdicated whatever role it might have had in seeking social reform; (2) the church has concentrated its attention on the local parish to the exclusion of the aspects of life that are most relevant to contemporary society; and (3) by comforting individuals who do have economic or political grievances, the church has deterred them from seeking political solutions to their problems.

The respondents' positions on these three criticisms appear in Table 2.5. A majority of the California ministers agree with the first position; just under a majority with the second (a statement, incidentally, taken from an official publication of the National Council of Churches); and about a quarter with the third. In the last instance, however, the large number of "no opinion" responses suggests that many clergymen found it difficult or confusing to make such an abstract connection between the "comforting" role of religion and the political activities of lower-class laymen.

Thus both critics and supporters of the church's role in public affairs are represented among our respondents. From the tenor of their remarks—as well as from the high proportion of clergymen who were willing to take the time to fill out the long questionnaire—it appears that at the time of our survey, the debate over social activism was a salient issue to most Protestant ministers.

Table 2.5.   Some Ministers Are Critical of the Role of Protestant Churches in Public Affairs

	Agree	No Opinion	Dis-agree	Total
"Protestant churches have become too aligned with the status quo in the United States to become major agents of social reform."	52%	9	39	100% (1561)
"As long as the churches persist in re-garding the parish of the local congre-gation as their normative structure, they will not confront life at its most significant point."	43%	8	49	100% (1539)
"By comforting those who are de-prived, the church often deters such individuals from going to the political arena to solve their social grievances."	27%	21	52	100% (1540)

What proportion of the California ministers, then, support the actions of the new breed activists? To answer this question, the respondents were asked whether they approved or disapproved of clergymen engaging in 10 poten-tial forms of clergy leadership, and we use these responses as measures of the ministers' attitudes toward clergy activism. The ministers were also asked whether they themselves had ever taken any of these actions and what posi-tions they thought their local denominational officials, close colleagues, and local parishioners held on the issues. These data are reported in later chapters.

Table 2.6 shows the clergy's positions on the 10 means of ethical leader-ship.[12] Four of the items involved actions that the clergymen might take to influence the beliefs and actions of their own parishioners (church leader-ship); two involved actions they might take to influence the public generally (public leadership); and four refer to actions of a protest nature (protest leadership). By and large, the California ministers were willing to "approve" such actions on the part of their colleagues—although this does not neces-sarily mean that they themselves would engage in similar conduct. As we would anticipate, the most controversial form of social activism is the par-ticipation of clergymen in protest marches and acts of civil disobedience. Not all the respondents approved of the other methods of leadership, how-ever, and more than a third disapproved of their colleagues announcing from the pulpit a stand on a political issue or publicly supporting a political candidate. Thus although the California ministers are fairly permissive in their views toward social activism, they do not go along with all of the activities of the new breed clergy, particularly with their more publicized and expressive actions.

Table 2.6. Ministers' Attitudes Toward Clergy Activism

Acts of Clerical Leadership	Approve	No Opinion	Disapprove	Total
CHURCH LEADERSHIP				
Organize a study group within their church to discuss public affairs	87%	6	7	100% (1574)
Deliver a sermon on a controversial political or social topic	77%	4	19	100% (1557)
Organize a social action group within their church to accomplish directly some social or political goal	73%	7	20	100% (1563)
Take a stand from the pulpit on some political issue	60%	4	36	100% (1557)
OPINION LEADERSHIP				
Publicly (not from the pulpit) take a stand on some political issue	82%	3	13	100% (1569)
Publicly (not from the pulpit) support a political candidate	59%	7	34	100% (1564)
PROTEST LEADERSHIP				
Participate in civil rights protest marches	63%	5	32	100% (1567)
Participate in antiwar protest marches	54%	7	39	100% (1565)
Engage in civil rights civil disobedience (risk arrest to symbolize protest)	43%	6	52	100% (1566)
Engage in antiwar civil disobedience	38%	7	55	100% (1564)

We are dealing here, of course, only with the clergy's *approval* of these be-havioral acts; we have not asked whether the respondents believe that all ministers should engage in such conduct or that such activities are appropri-ate for them personally. As a Presbyterian minister commented in response to these questions, "Everyone has his thing, even though it may not be worthy or expedient. . . . I have my own ministry, which is personal, while others have theirs—some of which are primarily social. But the world needs us all—agnostic psychiatrists and believing social activists alike." Our measures thus provide an indication of the *support* that exists among Protestant ministers for clerical leadership in public affairs, not of the *obligation* they may or may not feel that ministers have to engage in such conduct.

In addition, the questionnaire items deal in a general way with the means by which clergymen might try to influence public affairs; only in the case of protest leadership do they mention the political content of the ministers' ac-tions. When the issue itself is highly charged with conflict or emotion, we would expect the level of disapproval to be much greater. Fewer persons, for example, would be expected to approve of the organization of a study group in the local church to discuss the morality of the war in Vietnam than one to consider the causes of starvation in Africa.

For these reasons, our measures of ministerial attitudes toward clergy ac-tivism are extremely generous estimates of their approval of the activist role. We have used factor analysis again to determine how the ministers' attitudes toward clergy activism are structured. In this instance, the clergy's positions are explained not by a single factor but by three: those dimensions of be-havior we have previously called church leadership, public leadership, and protest leadership.[13] On each of these dimensions of activism, the denomi-national pattern of responses (not shown) is identical to that found previously in examining the ministers' religious beliefs. Approval of the activist role is highest among ministers in the Methodist Church and the United Church of Christ; it is lowest among Southern Baptists and Missouri Synod-Lutherans.

Before concluding our discussion of ministerial attitudes toward clergy ac-tivism, we should clarify our definition of the term "ethicalism." As we have noted, Protestant church leaders over the years have shared an evangelistic impulse to reform American society and have often become involved in is-sues of public consequence. They have differed, of late, less over the question of activism itself than over the types of issue that warrant religious attention and the means to be employed to effect societal change. We would expect modernist ministers to be most attracted to social and political issues; the traditionalist clergy to questions dealing with individual vice and immoral-ity—acts which they see as a barrier to obtaining salvation. When we use the term "ethics" in this study, we refer to clerical concern and involvement in basically social or political matters, and we devote most of our efforts to such issues. We have, however, asked our respondents what they think about legislative efforts to regulate individual morality and how often they discuss such topics in their sermons. When this information is presented in the next two chapters, we can see more clearly how the modernist and traditionalist clergy differ in their ethical orientations.

Political Beliefs. The third set of beliefs that we analyze in detail is the clergy's attitudes toward politics—certainly a crucial consideration to our understanding of clergy activism. We are concerned both with the structure of the ministers' political beliefs and, insofar as we can determine, with how their views toward political issues compare with those of others.

The terms "liberal" and "conservative" are frequently used to describe attitudinal dimensions dealing with politics. For example, persons who favor increased governmental welfare spending, the expansion of social services, or greater regulation of corporation activities, are often said to be political liberals, whereas those who hold opposing policy views are called conservatives. Research during the past two decades, however, has shown that most Americans do not possess such highly constrained orientations toward political issues. The authors of *The American Voter* found that only 12 percent of the electorate use the labels "conservative" or "liberal" to describe either political candidates or political parties,[14] and Philip Converse determined that only 17 percent of the public possesses a correct understanding of the meaning of these terms.[15] There recently has been some dissent from the views advanced by these authors,[16] but it is apparent that most Americans do not hold consistently liberal or conservative positions—at least as these terms have been popularly understood.

Although few members of the American public are ideologically oriented, there are a number of reasons to expect that the political belief systems of Protestant clergymen will be more structured. First, most Protestant ministers are extremely well educated, and persons of high education tend to be better informed and more sophisticated politically. Among those in the present survey, 99 percent had attended college, 96 percent had attended seminary school, and 59 percent had obtained still additional higher education. Second, members of the ministerial profession generally regard it as part of their professional responsibility to be attentive to current issues. For example, 98 percent of the California clergymen agreed that "because of their positions in society, clergymen have a special obligation to stay politically informed." Finally, the existence and centrality of such highly structured religious beliefs suggest that certain political beliefs may develop in conjunction with the clergy's theological orientations. The range of idea-elements associated with the religious beliefs of Protestant ministers may extend to and include political objects as well.

To measure the clergy's political views, we asked the California ministers to state their positions on a number of specific public issues and on a number of more general statements of political belief. The questions were designed to measure the clergy's attitudes on a variety of political dimensions—civil rights, foreign policy, economic liberalism, civil liberties, and civil disobedience. Using the factor analytic techniques applied previously, we find that the political beliefs of Protestant ministers are in fact highly structured: clergymen who took liberal positions on one of the issues cited were likely to take liberal positions on the others as well; likewise, clergymen who took conservative positions on these issues were likely to do so in a consistent fashion.

Thus Protestant clergymen have highly constrained or interdependent beliefs on political as well as religious and ethical issues. Before we examine the specific configurations found in the ministers' political beliefs, however, it is interesting to review their responses to some of our questions in each of these areas of public policy.

Civil Rights. A major finding in the previously cited national survey by Jeffrey K. Hadden was that Protestant ministers are far more liberal on civil rights issues than Protestant laymen.[17] We find that the California clergymen similarly held highly liberal views on civil rights. At the time of the survey in 1968, for example, 82 percent of the parish ministers favored passage of a national fair housing law; 72 percent favored help for Negro-owned businesses and institutions; and 45 percent favored some form of bussing to deal with de facto school segregation. More than three-quarters of the California clergy, as a later chapter reveals, opposed a highly controversial constitutional amendment to repeal the state's fair housing laws, although the initiative proposal was passed by California voters by a two-to-one margin.

The clergy similarly expressed some sympathy for the black power movement as it existed in 1968, although the majority did not accept its emphasis on conflict and violence; as we see below, such questions were among the most divisive asked of the California ministers. Sixty-five percent of the respondents agreed that "the black power movement is probably necessary for white society to realize the extent of Negro frustrations and deprivations"; 71 percent, however, agreed that "black power groups such as the Student Non-Violent Coordinating Committee (SNCC) are doing the Negro cause a disservice in their emphasis upon racial conflict and violence."

Similar findings have been reported by Hadden and others, and the next chapter shows that a surprisingly high proportion of our sample had taken part in at least one civil rights protest march. Clearly there was a great deal of support for civil rights among Protestant ministers in the 1960s, although this support dropped rapidly when issues of conflict and power politics became involved.

Foreign Policy and Military Intervention.   On foreign policy issues the California ministers again had fairly liberal political views but were by no means noninterventionist or pacifistic in their orientations toward the use of military force. At the time of the survey, 58 percent of the clergymen felt that the People's Republic of China should be admitted to the United Nations, 52 percent thought that "a larger proportion of United States foreign aid should be channeled through multilateral agencies such as the United Nations," and 76 percent agreed that the United States "was spending too much money for military and defensive purposes." The California pastors also held far more dovish views than the general public on the war in Vietnam in 1968 (see Chapter 4).

Despite views such as these, however, relatively few ministers took pacifistic or noninterventionist positions on questions of United States military policy. A most interesting finding in this respect came in our attempt to determine the clergy's opinions on the "just war" argument. Crudely, the question is, Can a war be considered to be "just" and worthy of church support if its objectives are entirely or mainly defensive? To determine where the California ministers stood on this matter, we asked them whether they agreed or disagreed with the statement that "the United States should use its military forces only when it is attacked or about to be attacked." More ministers disagreed (48 percent) than agreed (43 percent) with the proposition. Because these results (first discovered during the pretest survey) were somewhat unexpected, a second series of questions was designed to measure the approval of the Protestant ministers of United States military intervention abroad. After noting that "an important issue today in the conduct of foreign policy is the extent to which the United States should use its military forces to intervene in unstable situations which communist elements might exploit," we asked which of a series of statements best represented the ministers' own views. Their responses are as follows:

13%   The United States should not intervene militarily in such situations at all.

65%   While the United States has recently been too quick to intervene militarily in such situations, it does have some responsibilities in this regard.

10%   The United States should continue at its present level of military involvement in such situations.

12%   The United States should react to such situations with greater military firmness and dispatch.

A large majority of the California ministers, in other words, are critical of recent United States interventions abroad; but in 1968 most accepted the assumptions and doctrine of interventionism associated with the cold war.[18]

Economic Liberalism. The policy dimension most often used to differentiate liberals from conservatives has to do with questions of economic liberalism— welfare, poverty, unemployment, housing, antitrust regulation, and the like. We find that the California clergy as a group have fairly liberal views in this policy area but remain divided on or opposed to major efforts to redistribute income or to regulate big business. For example, 79 percent of the respondents felt that the federal government "should do more about such social problems as poverty, unemployment, and housing," and 60 percent favored a "large-scale program, of Marshall Plan proportions, to deal with all urban problems." At the same time, less than half (43 percent) said that they would approve of a "guaranteed minimum income for all families." Few favored certain more radical economic proposals that were being voiced in 1968. Only 61 of the parish clergymen, slightly less than 4 percent of the sample, agreed that "it would be better if large corporations such as U.S. Steel were owned by the federal government."

Civil Protest and Civil Disobedience. A final attitudinal dimension often associated with political liberalism and conservatism involves the means by which the citizen should seek to secure political change and the extent to which certain actions are protected by the First Amendment. At the time of the survey in early 1968, such procedural issues were being hotly debated. On the one hand, some individuals were arguing that the American political system was so resistant to change that civil disobedience and perhaps violence were necessary to achieve certain goals. On the other hand, many were calling for repressive measures to regulate the growing dissent over the war in Vietnam and the actions of student radicals. Such questions were of particular salience to the clergy, since numerous ministers had engaged in demonstrations in support of civil rights and in opposition to the war.

These issues were clearly among the most divisive facing the clergy at the time of the survey. Sixty-three percent of the California clergymen seemed to be willing to go along with civil disobedience tactics when they agreed with the statement that "civil disobedience is permissible when an individual has carefully thought about the consequences of his actions and is willing to accept the penalties for breaking the law." Yet when the question was worded somewhat differently, the clergy showed greater reluctance to support such means of political protest. Fifty-eight percent said that they agreed that "an individual should never deliberately disobey a law he considers wrong, but should work through the proper democratic channels to have that law changed."

At the time of the survey in 1968, black power and student groups were frequently calling for even more militant means to fight racism or to stop the fighting in Vietnam. The use of such tactics clearly created problems for the California clergy, who held generally liberal views in both areas. One respondent reappraised the situation thus:

> I find the questions pertaining to possible use of violence most agonizing. I have been very much opposed but am beginning to see the necessity of revolution which will inevitably lead to violence. "Does the violence of the Detroit riot produce any more human agony than the silent suffering that goes unnoticed over decades?" is a major question. Toleration of injustice constitutes a form of violence also, it seems to me.

To determine what the clergy felt about more violent means to effect political change, we asked whether they agreed that "under certain circumstances militant procedures and even violence are legitimate means to bring about changes in the law." Twenty-nine percent replied that they did; 64 percent did not.[19]

Thus the California ministers were almost evenly divided over the issue of civil disobedience in 1968, with nearly a third willing to condone more militant procedures as a means to express dissent. Their views were much the same on various questions pertaining to civil liberties. One of the principal civil liberties issues at the time of the survey was raised by the government's response to the young men who were burning their draft cards in protest of the war in Vietnam. Half the ministers reported that they were in favor of laws "punishing individuals who burn draft cards in protest of United States policies or actions"; 34 percent opposed such legislation.

Without a comparable sample of opinions from other groups, we cannot say with certainty how liberal or conservative the views of the California clergy are in these various issue-areas. It does appear that they have fairly liberal views on civil rights, on the need to increase spending on social welfare, and on certain foreign policy issues. At the time of the survey, however, they were divided in their opinions about the black power movement, school bussing, a guaranteed minimum wage, civil disobedience, and civil liberties.

As we noted earlier, the clergy's positions on the political issues named are highly interrelated. Clergymen who take liberal positions on one issue are likely to take liberal positions on the others. Applying factor analysis to the ministers' responses to the questions, furthermore, we find that their political beliefs tend to cluster into three easily identifiable response sets commonly associated with liberalism and conservatism. One factor involves their positions on issues of economic liberalism and civil rights, a second their views toward foreign policy, and the last their attitudes toward civil disobedience and black power. These factor loadings are shown in Appendix B. The ministers' positions on the questions that load most highly on these three dimensions of political belief are used to construct our measures of political liberalism and conservatism. In each case, the ordering of denominational responses is approximately the same as that found in examining the clergy's religious and ethical views. The Methodist and United Church of Christ ministers generally take the most liberal positions, followed closely by clergymen in the Episcopal Church, the Lutheran Church in America, and the Presbyterian Church. The most conservative positions are taken by ministers in the Southern Baptist Convention and the Missouri Synod of the Lutheran Church; somewhat less conservative positions are held by clergymen in the American Lutheran Church and the American Baptist Convention.

Interrelations in Beliefs. Protestant ministers thus possess highly constrained or functionally interrelated beliefs in the areas of religion, ethics, and politics. Within each of these attitudinal dimensions, the positions taken by the California clergymen on any one idea-element are closely related to the positions they are likely to take on the others.

The consistencies found in the denominational patterns of the clergy's responses, furthermore, suggest that the ministers' attitudes on each of these issue-dimensions are themselves interrelated. Clergymen who hold "liberal" positions on one dimension of belief appear to hold liberal views on the others as well. Our data bear this out. As Table 2.7 indicates, the ministers' positions on all seven attitudinal dimensions correlate highly with one another. The ministers who maintain traditional religious beliefs also generally disapprove of clergymen engaging in social action activities and take conservative positions on questions of economic liberalism and civil rights, foreign policy, and civil protest and disobedience. The ministers who possess what we have termed modernist religious views support clergy activism and take liberal positions on each of these issue-areas.

Thus we can say that Protestant ministers have highly constrained and functionally interdependent belief systems covering a wide range of religious, ethical, and political issues. It appears from our data, as well as from our understanding of Protestantism, that the central component of the ministerial belief system is the clergy's religious commitments—the degree to which they adhere to the modernist or the traditionalist religious beliefs. A Protestant minister's stand on questions of religious authority, salvation, and other-worldliness carries direct implications for his ethical and political beliefs as well. It leads him to develop different ethical and political concerns and to define his clerical role in quite different ways. We have many occasions in

Table 2.7.   Ministers' Attitudes Toward Religion, Social Ethics, and Politics Are Highly Correlated

	Religion	Protest Leadership	Church Leadership	Public Leadership	Economic Liberalism and Civil Rights	Foreign Policy	Civil Protest and Disobedience
Religion	—	.67	.62	.38	.56	.72	.70
Protest leadership		—	.72	.49	.62	.72	.73
Church leadership			—	.55	.56	.64	.60
Public leadership				—	.32	.37	.38
Economic liberalism and civil rights					—	.61	.56
Foreign policy						—	.62
Civil protest and disobedience							—

subsequent chapters to see just how strongly the clergy's religious commitments influence a wide range of attitudes and behavior.

Although it appears that the clergy's religious beliefs are the central component in their belief systems, it does not follow that their political attitudes are without importance to their ethical behavior or have no independent influence on the manner in which they respond to public events. Politically liberal ministers often voice approval of clergy activism even when they hold more traditionalist religious views; as we see in a later chapter, the same is true of their actual involvement in public issues. Similarly, we find some variation in the responses of clergymen of different denominations to the issues covered in this study. Ministers in the United Church of Christ, for example, tend to take the most liberal positions on religious issues, whereas ministers in the United Methodist Church generally hold the most liberal views on political questions.

Thus there are some exceptions to these patterns in belief and, as we shall see, other factors helped shape the reactions of the California clergy to the political events of the 1960s. For the large majority of our respondents, however, these two belief factors reinforce each other and mutually affect the individuals' ethical views and actions.

NOTES AND REFERENCES

1.   Benton Johnson, "Theology and the Positions of Pastors on Public Issues," *American Sociological Review* **32** (June 1967), pp. 433–442.

2.   Jeffrey K. Hadden, *The Gathering Storm in the Churches* (Garden City, N.Y.: Doubleday, 1969).

3.   Philip E. Converse, "The Nature of Belief Systems in Mass Publics," in *Ideology and Discontent*, David Apter, ed. (New York: Free Press, 1964), pp. 206–262.

4.   *Ibid.*, p. 207.

5.   See, for example, Rodney Stark and Bruce D. Foster, "In Defense of Orthodoxy: Notes on the Validity of an Index," *Social Forces*, **48** (March 1970), pp. 383–393; and symposium articles in *Sociological Analysis* **31** (Fall and Winter, 1970).

6.   The question was worded as follows: "Admittedly, there are difficulties associated with describing oneself in terms of broad theological positions. However, within the following categories, which of the following best describes your theological position?" The question was taken from Hadden, *op. cit.*

7.   Those ministers who wrote in some "other" position (as they were asked to do) tended largely to be Episcopal priests who referred to themselves as "Anglicans" or liberally oriented clergymen who associated themselves with more specific theories or theologians.

8.   Hadden, *op. cit.*, pp. 81–82.

9.   The question concerning Biblical literalism was taken from Hadden, *op. cit.*; the remaining questions came from Charles Y. Glock and Rodney Stark, *Christian Beliefs and Anti-Semitism* (New York: Harper & Row, 1966).

10.   The remaining categories can be found in questions 47 and 48 in the questionnaire—reproduced in Appendix C. Most of the ministers who indicated that they had some doubts on these two questions replied that basically they believed in the existence of God or in the Divinity of Jesus—or wrote in their own statements about these matters as provided in the question. The latter responses, although not further coded, generally expressed dissent from a literal, nondoubting acceptance of God's existence and the Divinity of Jesus.

16.   Thus the ministers' positions on this scale are determined according to their relative responses to these 10 questions. Such a technique has some obvious statistical advantages, but it does obscure the actual views held by our respondents on these issues (e.g., relatively few ministers took "modernist" positions on all 10 items). We will return to these original questions, therefore, when it is useful for expository purposes.

12.   The question was worded as follows: "There are many ways by which clergymen can and do express their views on public issues. Not everyone agrees, however, that all these forms of social action are appropriate for ministers. Please indicate for each of the following whether you approve or disapprove of clergymen who take that action."

13.   See Appendix B.

14.   Angus Campbell, Philip Converse, and Warren Miller, *The American Voter* (New York: Wiley, 1960), pp. 227–234.

15.   Converse, *op. cit.*

16.   For a recent critique of Converse's position, see Robert E. Lane, "Patterns of Po-

litical Belief," in *Handbook of Political Psychology*, Jeanne N. Knutson, ed. (San Francisco: Jossey-Bass, 1973), pp. 98–105. One of the early dissenting voices from the views expressed here was that of V. O. Key, Jr., in *The Responsible Electorate* (Cambridge, Mass.: Harvard University Press, 1966).

17.   Hadden, *op. cit.*, pp. 115–181.

18.   This line of inquiry was pushed still further in another question. The statement that "the question of military intervention has come up many times in the past" was followed by a list of occasions on which "the United States had to make a decision of whether or not to send in troops" and in each instance the ministers were asked whether they thought the country "should or should not have used military force." The proportion of clergymen who favored intervention in the North-South Korean conflict in 1950 was 67 percent; in the Hungarian Revolution in 1956, 34 percent; in the Bay of Pigs invasion in 1962, 32 percent; in the Vietnam buildup in 1964–1965, 31 percent; and in the revolt in the Dominican Republic in 1965, 29 percent.

19.   Cf. J. Alan Winter, "On the Mixing of Morality and Politics: A Test of a Weberian Hypothesis," *Social Forces*, **49** (1970–1971), pp. 36–41.

RELIGIOUS BELIEFS
AND SOCIAL CONFLICT

3. A well-integrated and highly structured ministerial belief system carries with it a number of important implications both for the individual conduct of Protestant clergymen and for the organizational future of Protestant denominations. It suggests, among other things, that modernist- and traditionalist-oriented ministers will define and perform their clerical roles in different terms, will respond to public events differently, and will use the organizational power and prestige of the church for different purposes. It also brings into question whether clergymen of such diverse religious and political orientations can long coexist within the same organizational structures. In this chapter we explore other areas in which disagreements exist between modernist and traditionalist clergymen and suggest the consequences these disagreements may have for organized religion. In future chapters we examine the impact of ministerial beliefs on clergy activism and the conflicts within Protestant churches.

The extraordinary range and effect of the ministerial belief system is illustrated by the fact that the responses of the California clergy to virtually every attitudinal question included in our survey—more than 100 in all—correlate highly with one another and with their religious beliefs. In addition to the issues already considered, the ministers' religious orientations are closely related to their attitudes toward church unity, the institutional power of the church, the taxation of church property, the Supreme Court prayer decisions, Vietnam policy, crime legislation, the use of police to quell riots, the Republican and Democratic parties, the legislation of public morality, and the religious and secular charateristics of Jews.[1] Such a polarization in beliefs among Protestant ministers means that the modernist and traditionalist clergy will frequently be divided over issues pertaining to a wide range of secular and organizational problems, as well as over purely religious questions. To the extent that such issues become of greater relevance to organized religion, these ministers are likely to find it increasingly difficult to reach accommodations among themselves and to remain within the same church organizations.

Here we examine our respondents' differences in opinions on a number of important questions having to do with the institutional role of the church, party loyalties, the legislation of public morality, and church unity. We conclude with a discussion of the sources of attitudinal constraint within the ministry and the likely impact of societal unrest on organized religion.

Attitudes Toward an Action-Oriented Church.   In the last chapter we reported our respondents' attitudes toward the involvement of individual clergymen in public affairs. Perhaps as important as such individual actions, however, is the use of the organizational power and prestige of the church as an instrument of change. There are many actions that organized religious groups might undertake for such purposes. For example, Protestant churches have taken strong formal positions on important public issues, organized and assisted the poor in the use of political power, joined in local civil rights efforts, and provided sanctuary to those who have refused military induction or service. Many of these practices constitute breaks with traditional behavior by Protestant church groups, as well as a relatively new role for organized religion. They suggest a policy of conflict and confrontation with the established secular order—one in which the power of organized religion is pitted against the power of established social, political, and economic interests.

We asked the California ministers their views on a number of these measures, which have been or might be taken by Protestant denominations or local church groups to force social and political reforms. Many of the proposals were widely accepted by our respondents; others received only marginal support. As we would expect, however, they gained their greatest backing among the modernist clergy.

Most commonly, Protestant churches have attempted to influence public affairs by taking official positions on important political issues. We asked the California ministers whether they thought their national church "should take an official position on the important issues of the day" and whether it should do so "even when a substantial portion of its members are in disagreement about the issue." According to Table 3.1, most of our respondents expressed approval of these practices, although they were far from unanimous in their views and were less supportive when the issue was divisive. Three-quarters

Table 3.1. Modernist Ministers Are Most Supportive of Their National Church Taking Stands on Controversial Public Issues

	Religious Orientation[a]					
	1	2	3	4	5	Total
"Disagreement exists among many church members concerning whether the church should speak out on social and political issues. In general, do you think that your *national church* should take an official position on the important issues of the day?"						
Yes	95%	89%	79%	68%	43%	75%
Not sure	3	5	7	5	5	5
No	2	6	14	27	53	20
	100%	100%	100%	100%	101%	100%
	(309)	(320)	(312)	(296)	(304)	(1541)
"Do you think that your national church should take an official position on social and political issues even when a substantial portion of its members are in disagreement about the issue?"						
Yes	88%	81%	68%	47%	24%	62%
Not sure	6	7	7	6	6	6
No	6	12	25	47	70	32
	100%	100%	100%	100%	100%	100%
	(307)	(318)	(310)	(294)	(301)	(1530)

"Are you yourself in general agreement with most of the positions taken by your national church—or do you think that it has gone too far on most issues

Table 3.1 *Continued*

	Religious Orientation[a]					
	1	2	3	4	5	Totals
or that it has not gone far enough?"						
Think that the national church has not gone far enough	21%	19%	13%	13%	8%	15%
Generally agree with national church's positions	77	75	73	68	66	72
Think that the national church has gone too far	2	4	11	16	23	11
Not sure	—[b]	2	3	3	3	2
	100%	100%	100%	100%	100%	100%
	(309)	(314)	(311)	(295)	(299)	(1528)

[a] On this 5-point scale, 1 is most modernist; 5 is most traditionalist.
[b] Less than 1 percent.

thought that their national church should make such official statements; slightly fewer (62 percent) thought that it should do so when the issue caused conflict among many churchmen. In each case, the most modernist clergymen were the most willing to have their denominations take such actions. Almost all in the most modernist group or respondents, in fact, voiced support for such practices.

We also asked the ministers what they thought about the positions generally taken by their national churches—whether they generally agreed with the views expressed or thought that they had gone either too far or not far enough. Table 3.1 indicates that most of our respondents reported themselves to be in general agreement with their denomination's formal positions on public issues. Fifteen percent, however, believed that their church had gone too far, and 11 percent thought that it had not gone far enough. The traditionalist clergy were most likely to take the former position; the modernist respondents the latter.

Simply stating a position on political issues, of course, seldom has much influence on public policies or on the opinions held by others—and churches have been criticized by many for doing little more than issuing formal proclamations. Not only can their public statements be easily dismissed by political officials, but several studies have also shown that few laymen have any idea what their national churches have said on important social issues.[2] Even when they are aware of their church's positions, furthermore, it does not seem that Protestant laymen are in any way influenced in their own views by these policy statements.[3] Thus without taking more direct public actions, organized religion can hope to have little influence on political officials; without an attentive mass constituency, it can have little moral force over even its own members.

Many actions can be mounted by local, regional, or national church groups to influence public issues more directly and effectively. One Protestant denomination, for example, threatened to stop using a major hotel as a site for its annual meetings if it did not change its discriminatory employment practices. The hotel management eventually gave in, and the desired changes were made. A variety of such proposals, more general in scope, had been announced at the time of our survey and were known to many of our respondents. The positions taken by the California ministers on a number of such schemes are shown in Tables 3.2 to 3.4. These tables reveal substantial clergy support for some of these actions, but it drops off rapidly when the proposed measure is more direct and forceful. In each case, it is again the modernist clergymen who are most favorable to such proposals, the traditionalist clergy who are most disapproving.

Table 3.2 summarizes the responses of the California clergy to the question of whether they would approve or disapprove if their demonination were to become "directly involved in public affairs" through any of a series of fairly specific actions. The proposed activities included projects designed to oppose the war in Vietnam, to advance equal rights within the local community, and to support efforts to encourage the political organization of the poor. Most of the respondents approved of their denomination giving assistance to individuals who refuse military service as conscientious objectors: 70 percent of the ministers supported this traditional and common practice. At the time of the survey, however, many men were refusing military induction not because they objected to war in general but because they opposed the Vietnam war in particular. The most heated issue being debated within many church councils was whether the church should offer its support and assistance to "selective" objectors. We see that slightly more than half the ministers in our sample stated their approval of such an action. This figure is smaller than the 70 percent who agreed to the more abstract and "strictly religious" role of the church in aiding those who feel they cannot participate

Table 3.2. Modernist Ministers Are Most Supportive of an Action-Oriented Denomination

Would Approve if Their Denomination Were to	Religious Orientation[a]					
	1	2	3	4	5	Total
Assist those who refuse induction into the military forces because they conscientiously object to war in general	95% (306)	92% (317)	79% (313)	55% (304)	31% (317)	70% (1557)
Use its economic powers (e.g., withdrawal of patronage and trade) for forcing equal rights in your community	84% (308)	80% (315)	64% (314)	47% (304)	24% (318)	60% (1559)
Assist those who refuse induction into the military forces because they conscientiously object to the Vietnam war in particular	85% (306)	76% (317)	54% (312)	33% (305)	12% (319)	52% (1559)
Refuse to cooperate with the Government's War on Poverty unless the programs guaranteed power and participation for the poor	68% (304)	64% (315)	51% (312)	37% (297)	21% (316)	48% (1544)
Sponsor a meeting in which draft cards are turned in or burned	13% (306)	6% (316)	3% (313)	1% (307)	— (320)	5% (1562)

[a] On this 5-point scale, 1 is most modernist; 5 is most traditionalist.

in combat on moral grounds; but it is still rather substantial, considering the attitudes held by most Americans in 1968 toward the draft resisters. As our questionnaire items grew more radical, however, the California clergymen became more cautious. Only 8 percent (last item in Table 3.2), would have approved if their denomination had sponsored a meeting in which draft cards were turned in or burned—one of the major forms of antiwar protest and symbolic defiance at the time.

Table 3.3. Most Ministers Approve of an "Open Church" Policy; More Modernist Ministers Approve of Sanctions for Enforcement

| | Religious Orientation[a] | | | | | |
	1	2	3	4	5	Total
"Do you think that your denomination should attempt to induce its local churches to adopt an 'open church' policy with respect to the membership of individuals from minority racial and ethnic groups?"						
Yes	99%	98%	97%	93%	86%	95%
No	1	1	2	6	13	5
Not sure	—	—[b]	1	1	1	1
	100%	100%	100%	99%	100%	101%
	(309)	(320)	(314)	(307)	(316)	(1566)
"Do you think that your denomination should institute official sanctions (such as denying certification of pastoral assignments) against those local churches which refuse to open their membership to such individuals?"						
Yes	65%	57%	56%	38%	28%	49%
No	21	29	30	45	50	35
Not sure	13	13	11	10	8	11
Not applicable[c]	1	2	3	7	14	6
	100%	100%	100%	101%	100%	101%
	(309)	(315)	(312)	(296)	(308)	(1540)

[a] On this 5-point scale, 1 is most modernist; 5 is most traditionalist.
[b] Less than 1 percent.
[c] Gave a "No" or "Not sure" response to first question.

Table 3.4. Modernist Ministers Are Most Likely to Agree that the Church Should Help the Poor Organize Politically

"A disagreement exists among some church members as to how the church should help poor people. Some people agree with [the late] Saul Alinsky that the church should help the poor to organize themselves, while others feel that the church should help these people but should not become involved in the politics of their problems. Which position is closest to your own?"	Religious Orientation[a]					
	1	2	3	4	5	Total
Should help the poor to organize essentially as Alinsky suggests	51%	33%	25%	13%	10%	26%
Should help the poor to organize but not follow Alinsky tactics	46	58	56	43	18	44
Should help the poor as individuals but not become involved in their political problems	3	9	18	43	71	29
The church has no special duty to help the poor	—	—[b]	1	1	1	1
	100% (304)	100% (315)	100% (307)	100% (296)	100% (313)	100% (1535)

[a] On this 5-point scale, 1 is most modernist; 5 is most traditionalist.
[b] Less than 1 percent.

The same pattern of diminishing support for programs that are more concrete and come closer to involving the church directly in controversial public issues exists in other policy areas as well. Sixty percent of the clergy (Table 3.2) would approve of their denomination's using its economic power to force equal rights in their own communities. Again this constitutes rather substantial support for a potentially far-reaching and effective plan of action. However, Table 3.3 indicates that the ministers' support for change, even in the civil rights field, quickly decreases when the issue strikes closer to home. It is often said that churches are one of the most segregated institutions in American society, and Sunday church services one of the most segregated activities of the week. Almost all the respondents deplored the situation[4] and thought that their denomination "should attempt to induce its local churches to adopt an 'open church' policy with respect to the members of individuals from minority racial and ethnic groups." Less than half these ministers, however, wanted their denominations to use what powers they have to enforce this policy. Only 45 percent of the clergymen thought that their denomination should institute official sanctions against local churches that refused to open their membership to individuals of all races. Such an action, of course, would bring the church leadership in direct confrontation with many laymen.[5]

A similar pattern occurs in the clergy's attitudes toward helping the poor. Assisting the needy has been a traditional area of concern for the church, and Table 3.4 reveals that only eight ministers surveyed (0.5 percent) feel that the church has no special duty to help the poor. Traditionally, however, the church has provided direct services to the needy rather than becoming involved in the political conditions that created or contributed to the poverty state. A major issue at the time of the survey was whether the church should expand its work to include helping in efforts to organize the poor politically. This could be done through participation in the local Office of Economic Opportunity program or by becoming directly involved in the organizational process itself.

As we see in Table 3.2, 48 percent of the California ministers would have approved if their denomination refused to participate in the "war on poverty" on grounds that the poor were not guaranteed participation. By the time the survey reached the ministers in 1968, however, the relevant community action programs were all but finished in most areas, and such action was more theoretical than real. The question put to the clergy in Table 3.4 is thus a better indicator of the ministers' willingness to involve the church politically in the problems of the poor. Some of the more liberal Protestant church groups had hired the radical organizer Saul Alinsky to come into their communities to work with the poor—an action that not surprisingly disturbed many conservative churchmen. Table 3.4 indicates that although the majority of the California ministers felt that the church should help the poor organize, only 27 percent would have it follow the tactics proposed by Alinsky.[6]

Thus varying proportions of the California ministers supported the use of the church's institutional power to effect social and political reforms, but few agreed with radical proposals that would have set it more squarely against prevailing public views and practices. In all these instances, as expected, the modernist clergy were most receptive to such a role for organized religion. The differences in opinion between the modernist and traditionalist clergymen in these respects are fairly large and are consistent from one issue to the next. These data suggest once again that the polarization in views within the Protestant ministry is substantial and includes issues of fundamental importance to the clerical role itself. Our ministers differ not just in their views toward the individual conduct of clergymen, but also in the very goals and purposes they ascribe to organized religion. We have many opportunities in subsequent chapters to see the consequences of these divergent ethical orientations.

Partisan Attitudes.   Another attitudinal dimension of direct consequence to the clergy's public behavior is their partisan identification. Most Americans voice a loyalty to one of the two major political parties and support that party's candidates in national, state, and local elections. Partisan attitudes are also important in providing a major point of reference in evaluating political issues and public programs and in serving to create a sense of loyalty and attachment to the political system itself.

Given the importance of party preferences, it is not surprising to find that a number of studies have dealt with the partisan attitudes of Protestant clergymen. It has been learned that the majority of Protestant ministers are Republicans and that their partisan views are closely related to their religious positions.[7] Much the same patterns existed among the California clergy. We hope to go somewhat further than the previous studies, however, suggesting how the development of modernist or traditionalist religious commitments has led to changes in party preferences among Protestant ministers, thus demonstrating the powerful influence of the ministerial belief system on clerical attitudes. Since we do not have information about the early partisan loyalties of our respondents, we reconstruct their views by examining their socioeconomic backgrounds and the partisan attitudes of their fathers. This method of analysis involves making some major assumptions about the early attitudes of our respondents; given our knowledge about the development of partisan preferences, however, these suppositions do not appear to be unreasonable. We know from other studies that most Americans develop life-long party loyalties at a relative early age.[8] One's early preferences are shaped largely by parental attitudes and, indirectly, by the socioeconomic situation in which an individual grows up. These early influences are generally reinforced by later social and economic experiences, such that most Americans (nearly four-fifths) identify with the political party of their father.

We can use this knowledge about the manner in which partisan attitudes are formed to infer the changes that have taken place in the party loyalties of our respondents since early childhood. We will compare the partisan preferences of the California ministers with those of the fathers to determine how the clergy appear to have altered their party loyalties since they first became aware of politics. Next, we relate these apparent changes in partisan views to the ministers' religious beliefs to suggest how the development of modernist and traditionalist religious commitments have affected the respondents' partisanship.

Table 3.5 shows the relationship between the ministers' own preferences and their religious beliefs. Our findings are similar to those of other studies, although the California clergymen are somewhat more Democratic than ministers nationally.[9] Forty-seven percent of the parish clergy regard themselves to be Republicans, 34 percent Democrats, and 19 percent independents. The more modernist the respondents' religious commitments, the more likely they are to support the Democratic party; the more traditionalist, the more Republican their identification.

A most suggestive finding emerges when we relate these patterns to the ministers' early socialization experiences. Our data show, in the first place, that the majority of the California ministers grew up in middle-class,

Table 3.5.   Modernist Ministers Are Most Often Democrats; Traditionalist Ministers Are Most Often Republicans

Party Affiliation	Religious Orientation[a]					Total
	1	2	3	4	5	
Republican	23%	32%	49%	62%	67%	47%
Independent	15	22	22	20	16	19
Democrat	61	47	29	18	16	34
Other	1	—	—	—[b]	1	—[b]
	100%	101%	100%	100%	100%	100%
	(309)	(320)	(316)	(305)	(320)	(1570)

[a] On this 5-point scale, 1 is most modernist; 5 is most traditionalist.

[b] Less than 1 percent.

Republican families. In about two-thirds of the cases, the fathers held a professional or other high status job, and more fathers were Republican (51 percent) than Democratic (33 percent). No differences existed among the modernist and traditionalist clergy in either of these respects, except among the most traditionalist-oriented group of respondents: a disproportionate number of Southern Baptist clergymen grew up in Democratic, working-class families in the South. When we compare the ministers' party preferences with those of their fathers, we find indications that major shifts in partisan attitudes have apparently occurred among these Protestant ministers. Only about half the California clergymen hold the same party loyalties as their fathers: among those who had Republican fathers, 54 percent now call themselves Republicans; among those with Democratic fathers, only 45 percent are not Democrats. Of the ministers who apparently changed partisan preferences, about two-thirds support a party different from that of their father, whereas the remainder regard themselves to be independents.

As we would expect by now, these shifts are closely related to the ministers' religious commitments. The relevant information is provided in Table 3.6. Reading down each column in this table, we see that the more traditionalist the ministers' religious views, the more likely they are to be Republicans (regardless of the early partisan cues they may have received from their fathers). Reading across the columns, we see that early socialization influences still have some impact on the clergy's present party preferences (this time regardless of the attitudes they hold on religious issues).

We thus find evidence to suggest that significant changes have taken place in the clergy's partisan preferences and that these changes in party loyalties are consistent with their present religious commitments. Assuming that our respondents once held party loyalties similar to those of their fathers, modernist ministers have become more Democratic, traditionalist ministers more Republican. Since the clergy's religious views are so closely related to their political beliefs, we cannot attribute the entire change in partisan identification to religious factors. We find in fact that both the respondents' political and religious positions have an independent effect on their choice of party. For the great majority of Protestant ministers, however, these two belief variables operate together. Politically liberal, modernist clergymen have become more Democratic; politically conservative, traditionalist clergymen more Republican.

Taken together, these two trends largely counterbalance each other— at least within this sample of Protestant ministers. In this sense we can say that the high degree of Republicanism among Protestant ministers is largely a product of socioeconomic background and political upbringing. Such similarities in partisan views between our respondents and their fathers,

Table 3.6. Many Ministers Have Shifted Their Party Loyalties Consistent with Their Religious Beliefs

Ministers' Party Choice	Father's Party Identification		
	Republican	Shifted Around, Other, Don't Know	Democrat
Modernist			
1 Republican	28%	20%	18%
Independent	16	22	8
Democrat	56	57	74
	100%	99%	100%
	(154)	(50)	(96)
2 Republican	37%	26%	23%
Independent	24	21	17
Democrat	39	53	60
	100%	100%	100%
	(172)	(57)	(88)
3 Republican	55%	46%	40%
Independent	25	16	18
Democrat	20	38	41
	100%	100%	99%
	(177)	(50)	(87)
4 Republican	77%	58%	41%
Independent	14	30	26
Democrat	9	13	33
	100%	101%	100%
	(155)	(40)	(104)
5 Republican	78%	69%	56%
Independent	14	16	18
Democrat	8	15	26
	100%	100%	100%
Traditionalist	(132)	(57)	(129)

however, only serve to mask the impact of their belief systems on their partisanship. Many Protestant clergymen are changing their partisan views to make them more congruent with their present religious and political beliefs.

Attitudes Toward Public Morality. Up until now we have been concerned with social or political issues that deal with society-wide conditions or reforms rather than with the private conduct of individuals. As we pointed out in Chapter 1, however, Protestant ministers in the past have often been active in efforts to regulate individual moral conduct. Nineteenth-century Protestant church leaders were involved in legislative efforts to control prostitution, gambling, and drinking and to keep the Sabbath as a day of religious observance and rest; during the early part of this century they were among the most enthusiastic supporters of the prohibition movement.

In the past, this concern with the regulation of public morality seems to have deterred Protestant church leaders from becoming more actively involved in questions of broader social or political importance. If our argument in the previous chapter is correct, we would expect such an individualistic, moralistic ethic to remain among the more traditionalist respondents and to continue to direct their attention away from social issues. The primary concern of traditionalist clergymen, as we have said, is to bring others to Christ so that they may be forgiven for their sins, receiving then the blessing of eternal life. Thus individual transgressions are likely to be viewed as human weaknesses and barriers to the obtainment of salvation—as obstacles that must be overcome before the individual can receive God's grace and forgiveness. As a result, we would expect the more traditionalist-oriented respondents to see immorality not in terms of the conditions of society but in the behavior of the individual—not in the battlefields of Vietnam but in the actions of the sinner himself. At the same time, many modernist church leaders gave strong support to the Volstead Act. Thus concern with public morality may remain common among the modernist as well as the traditionalist clergy.

To determine where our respondents stood on such matters, we asked them what they thought about laws regulating individual conduct in four areas—the sale of liquor to adults, the use of marijuana, gambling, and the sale of "obscene" materials. In each case, we asked whether they thought that laws regulating such personal behavior should be made stronger or weaker or kept as they are. We also asked the ministers whether they had discussed such matters in their sermons (see Chapter 4).

Table 3.7 shows the positions chosen by the California clergy on the four questions concerning the regulation of public morality. The majority of our

Table 3.7. Traditionalist Ministers Are Most Favorable to the Passage of Stronger Laws to Regulate Public Morality

"Do you think that laws regulating each of the following types of social conduct should be made stronger, weaker, or kept as they are?"	Religious Orientation[a]					Total
	1	2	3	4	5	
THE SALE OF LIQUOR TO ADULTS						
Stronger	30%	47%	44%	61%	70%	51%
Kept as they are	64	48	54	37	29	46
Weaker	6	5	2	1	1	3
	100%	100%	100%	99%	100%	100%
	(304)	(317)	(313)	(303)	(319)	(1556)
THE USE OF MARIJUANA						
Stronger	19%	37%	53%	70%	84%	53%
Kept as they are	21	22	20	18	11	18
Weaker	60	41	27	12	5	29
	100%	100%	100%	100%	100%	100%
	(301)	(311)	(310)	(303)	(320)	(1545)
GAMBLING						
Stronger	45%	56%	57%	70%	76%	61%
Kept as they are	50	39	40	27	23	36
Weaker	5	4	3	3	1	3
	100%	99%	100%	100%	100%	100%
	(304)	(316)	(314)	(305)	(318)	(1557)
THE SALE OF "OBSCENE" MATERIALS						
Stronger	24%	49%	70%	83%	92%	64%
Kept as they are	59	39	22	13	6	28
Weaker	17	12	7	4	2	8
	100%	100%	99%	100%	100%	100%
	(300)	(312)	(313)	(302)	(320)	(1547)

[a] On this 5-point scale, 1 is most modernist; 5 is most traditionalist.

respondents favored stronger legislation in each area—51 percent in the case of liquor sales, 53 percent in the regulation of marijuana use, 61 percent with respect to gambling, and 64 percent in the control of allegedly obscene materials. Thus while Protestant clergymen often take liberal positions on political issues, it now appears that they have fairly conservative views on questions of public morality. The common images of men of God as pious defenders of the community's moral standards and passionate advocates of civil rights and peace thus have some substance in fact. Although not all clergymen in California fit either of these stereotypes, they do tend toward both of these extremes in their public views.

Table 3.7 also shows that the ministers' positions on the four public morality issues correspond closely with their religious views. As expected, the more traditionalist ministers are in each instance more likely to favor stronger legislation to regulate individual behavior. These differences are the greatest, furthermore, on the most contemporary and (in 1968) the most controversial of these issues—the regulation of marijuana use. Eighty-four percent of the most traditionalist group of clergymen favored stronger laws to control use of this drug; only 4 percent thought that they should be made weaker. Among the most modernist group of ministers, in contrast, 59 percent favored weaker laws, whereas 20 percent thought that they should be made stronger.

Thus we find evidence in these response patterns to support our notions concerning the contrasting ethical orientations of the traditionalist and modernist clergy. At the same time, we see that a fair number of modernist ministers also voice support for stronger legislation to regulate individual morality. For many modernist clergymen, apparently, a concern with social issues does not preclude or replace a concern with individual moral conduct.

We should also note that the relationship between the ministers' religious and moralistic views is not as strong as that found with respect to most other issues in our survey. In part, this pattern occurs because of the continuing concern of many modernist clergymen with questions of public morality. In addition, however, not all Protestant denominations share the same tradition of involvement in moralistic issues. As we noted in the first chapter, American Lutheranism was influenced more by its immigrant-based membership than the other denominations we have been examining. Partly for this reason, it did not go through the same period of moralistic reformism as the other denominations in our study and—particularly in the Missouri Synod with its large German membership—did not share the general Protestant enthusiasm for prohibition. When we look at the pattern of Lutheran responses, we find obvious traces of these historical developments. More traditionalist Lutheran clergymen do tend to favor stronger laws than their modernist colleagues in these various areas, but as a whole Lutherans' views on these issues are less conservative than those of ministers in the other six denominations surveyed. These differences are quite pronounced, moreover, with respect to the two more traditional areas of moral concern (the regulation of drinking and gambling) but are fairly small with respect to the two more recent issues (obscenity and marijuana use).

These data, then, furnish more evidence to illustrate the contrasting ethical orientations of the traditionalist and modernist clergy: the former tend to be concerned with individual sin and immorality, whereas the latter define their ethical roles in more social terms. Overlap does exist in the ethical positions of traditionalist and modernist clergymen, and we learn that Lutheran ministers are generally less concerned with the regulation of public morality than their colleagues in other denominations. These exceptions are relatively slight, however, and in the case of Lutherans only barely extend to more contemporary issues of public morality. Thus it would appear that the traditional Protestant concern with sin and salvation continues to direct the attention of church leaders away from broader social issues. We return to this question again in the next chapter when we examine the extent to which our respondents discuss these issues in their sermons.

Attitudes Toward Church Unity. A final set of questions asked the California clergy dealt with their attitudes toward church unity. The divisions in belief which we have seen to exist among Protestant ministers would obviously cast doubt on the possibility that any large-scale merger is likely to occur within Protestantism. As long as modernist and traditionalist clergymen are divided on so many issues, it seems improbable that they will find sufficient areas of consensus around which to build common organizational structures, or that they will have sufficient motivation to attempt to do so. Hadden suggested in his national survey of Protestant clergymen that although doctrinal differences remain among Protestant ministers, a consensus does exist over the church's role in the world—and this common understanding may form the basis for eventual unification.[10] His study, however, did not delve as deeply as ours into the contrasting ethical orientations of Protestant ministers and the divergent ways in which they define their clerical roles. Our data suggest that if further mergers are to occur within Protestantism, they will involve denominations with like-minded clerical memberships.

Of course, most discussions of church unity have taken place among the more liberal or modernist Protestant denominations, and we find that support for church mergers among the California clergy appears largely among the more modernist-oriented ministers. We did not, however, ask our re-

spondents whether they favored mergers with any specific church denominations—a proposal that might have elicited more favorable responses—but
whether they favored "the eventual union" of all major Protestant denominations into a single church structure, or the eventual union of all Protestant
and Catholic churches. Table 3.8 reveals that relatively few of the California
ministers favored either alternative. Only 29 percent favored the first option;
28 percent the second. The more modernist-oriented respondents were the
most receptive to these proposals, but even they were divided over the
desirability of such unifications of church organizations.

Thus little overall support exists among Protestant ministers for any
major organization changes within Christianity—even in the hypothetical
terms stated here. The responses to the first question in Table 3.8, however,
show that the California clergy are more supportive of mergers that might
occur at the local level. Sixty percent of the respondents said they would
favor the merger of their local church with one of another denomination if
such action appeared to be financially necessary. Only the most traditionalist
ministers were opposed to merger for economic reasons in any substantial
proportion; the modernist clergymen were solidly behind it.

Thus we find in these responses one possible basis on which such an organizational unification of Protestant churches might proceed: economics. Many
denominations—particularly the more modernist ones—have experienced
severe financial difficulties in recent years and, on occasion, have had to
make a decision of this type. Therefore, we might suggest that the fiscal
problems confronting liberal Protestant denominations are probably the
strongest force, albeit a negative one, toward more church mergers. As we
see below, there are good reasons to expect the financial difficulties of liberal
church groups to continue as long as the modernist clergy remain socially
active.

Polarizations Within the Protestant Ministry. The information we
have presented in Chapters 1 and 2 thus shows that Protestant ministers are
divided in their views about a wide variety of issues—about, in fact, every
substantive question raised in our survey, from the Divinity of Jesus to the
political party most capable of governing the country. Modernist and traditionalist clergy are concerned about different problems, perceive external
events in a different fashion, and favor different religious, political, and
ethical policies.

To some extent, of course, these findings are a product of the questions we
chose to ask the California clergy. Our interest in conducting such a survey
obviously directs our attention more toward areas of conflict and disagreement among Protestant clergymen than toward areas of consensus. If we had

Table 3.8. Modernist Ministers Are Most Favorable to Church Unity at the Local and National Levels

	Religious Orientation[a]					
	1	2	3	4	5	Total
"If there were more churches in your area than the neighborhood could apparently support, would you favor the merger of your church with one of another denomination?"						
Yes	93%	82%	66%	43%	18%	60%
Not sure	6	11	20	20	15	14
No	1	7	15	38	67	26
	100%	100%	101%	101%	100%	100%
	(308)	(317)	(317)	(306)	(319)	(1567)
"Do you favor the eventual union of all major Protestant denominations in a single church structure?"						
Yes	53%	42%	29%	16%	6%	29%
Not sure	30	26	27	15	5	21
No	17	31	44	69	89	50
	100%	99%	100%	100%	100%	100%
	(308)	(318)	(316)	(306)	(321)	(1569)
"Do you favor the eventual union of the Protestant and Catholic churches in a single church structure?"						
Yes	46%	40%	30%	19%	7%	28%
Not sure	34	29	31	14	6	23
No	19	31	39	67	87	49
	99%	100%	100%	100%	100%	100%
	(306)	(319)	(315)	(305)	(320)	(1565)

[a] On this 5-point scale, 1 is most modernist, 5 is most traditionalist.

asked our respondents how they felt about the need for professional standards within the ministry, for example, or about racial policies in South Africa, we might have received responses indicating greater agreement. In addition, we have discovered some subjects on which relative consensus does exist among the parish ministers. Most of the California clergy took fairly liberal positions on civil rights issues and, to a lesser degree, on programs designed to help the poor. In the next chapter we examine a heated intiative campaign that found most of the parish clergymen united in an (unsuccessful) effort to defeat a discriminatory amendment to the California State constitution. Even in the civil rights field, however, not all Protestant ministers are in agreement or maintain liberal positions. In 1968 the California ministers were almost equally divided in their views about the bussing of school children and were clearly troubled by the militancy of the emerging black power movement. Such apparent consensus on other issues similarly disappeared when we asked the clergy their views on more extreme or radical proposals. In all these cases, furthermore, the modernist clergy took the most liberal positions and the traditionalist clergy the most conservative.

Thus our survey shows that where conflict exists among Protestant ministers, we are likely to find the modernist-oriented clergy on one side of the issue and the traditionalist-oriented clergy on the other. For the most part, there is little overlap in the positions espoused by these two groups of clergymen on issues of religious, political, and ethical importance. Unlike many other groups in American society, therefore, Protestant clergymen tend to harbor divisions in belief that are largely cumulative—reinforcing and strengthening the differences that exist over religious issues rather than weakening them and diverting attention from them. At the time of our survey, modernist and traditionalist ministers had different views on most of the major religious issues that divided the clerical profession and most of the major political issues that divided the country.

Thus far we have assumed that the ministers' religious beliefs are the central component of their belief systems and, in this sense, are the primary "cause" of the polarizations noted within the ministry. Up to a point, such as assumption appears to be warranted. Christian theology provides the Protestant minister with the central purpose and meaning of his calling. He is trained in a specialized body of sacred knowledge, and it is in relation to this knowledge that he bases his own claim for professional recognition and authority. We would thus fully expect the clergy's religious perspective to have an effect on the perspectives they take on a wide variety of issues and on their definitions of their own societal roles.

In addition, of course, Christian theology is explicit in its attempt to formulate an ethic to guide the worldly actions of the relgious believer.

Traditional Protestantism maintains an otherworldly emphasis on individual salvation and continues to depreciate the importance of human affairs in this world. It perceives its primary role as bringing others to Christ and tends to be oriented in its ethics toward problems of individual sin and immorality rather than toward questions of a social or political nature. Religious modernism, in contrast, emphasizes man-to-man relationships in its ethical directives. Religion is not something "out there"; it is to be realized in the everyday actions of human beings, to provide insights into men's actions in all aspects of their daily affairs.

Such contrasting religious orientations, we maintain, lie at the core of the ministerial belief system and account for much of the polarization within the Protestant ministry. We would expect them to be the primary determinants in explaining the reactions of Protestant clergymen to events such as those of the sixties—a subject we explore in the next several chapters.

It would be misleading to push the foregoing argument too far, however. In the first place, we should remember that our information (as well as that reported in other studies) was collected quite recently. Although no sociological surveys of ministerial attitudes exist from earlier periods, it does not appear that modernist theological doctrines have always been so closely associated with political liberalism or with social activism. Thus we should maintain the historian's caution is not overgeneralizing from data collected at a single point in time; as we argue below, there are reasons to suppose that the divisions between religious modernists and traditionalists were more tightly drawn in the 1960s than they had been previously. Secondly, we should note again that a fair number of exceptions appeared to these patterns in clerical belief. Some religious traditionalists have liberal views on social issues and support an ethically oriented church, and some modernists take the opposite positions. Not all Protestant clergymen, then, seem to draw the same implications from their theological beliefs, and we look at these clerical "deviants" in some detail in a later chapter. Finally, our study amply demonstrates the effects of confounding factors on the ministerial belief system. Table 3.6, for example, illustrates the clear impact of the clergy's upbringing on their present political beliefs. Similarly, we find that younger ministers consistently take more liberal, proactivist positions despite their particular religious orientations and we pay considerable attention in later chapters to the effects of social interactions and organizational structures on clerical beliefs and behavior.

Thus polarizations within the Protestant ministry are not complete, and other factors affect the stance taken by parish clergymen on ethical and political issues. In addition, it is apparent that these divisions within the Protestant ministry are related to ideological divisions existing within the greater society. Other well-educated professional groups in American society also tend to possess highly structured belief systems and to be divided along lines similar to those within the Protestant ministry.[11] It would clearly be a mistake to isolate the ministerial belief system from broader cultural influences and values and to assess its components in theological terms alone. Rather, the ministers' belief systems should also be considered as wholes—representing common orientations toward a variety of matters, not simply adjustments to doctrinal teachings.

From the latter perspective, we might emphasize the common value orientations or images of man that run through these contrasting ministerial belief systems. One such value would certainly be the extreme individualism that developed during this country's formative years and continues to influence public perceptions and political programs today. Classical economic theory, liberalism, and Protestant theology all complement one another in emphasizing the primacy of the individual over social structures or institutions. Classical economic theory posits the existence of a society composed of autonomous, competitive, profit-seeking individuals; classical liberalism conceives of an atomized society in which individuals are free to pursue their private ends, including the acquisition and enjoyment of property; traditional Protestantism, finally, views man as a free actor who is able through personal actions to affect his own destiny (thereby adding a measure of responsibility to the emphasis on individual action). This complementary set of ideas merged during the nineteenth century to form a powerful worldview—one that was bolstered by the generally egalitarian but demanding conditions in which white Americans found themselves at the time. These conditions have, of course, changed radically over the past century, and the individualistic orientation of the earlier era has increasingly been brought into question. In this new situation, nineteenth-century individualism is often associated with conservative public perceptions and policies. A direct link exists between "rugged individualism" and the Horatio Alger myth and such present-day notions as "benign neglect," and "bootstrap theory," and the role of the United States as world policeman.

In short, underlying the various dimensions of belief is a conception of the individual as a free actor—existing in a relatively independent state from those around him and, in a normative as well as an empirical sense, holding responsibility for his own destiny.[12] We would expect those who share such a perspective to be among the stronger proponents of capitalism, limited government, a unilateral foreign policy, and a salvation-oriented religion. Correspondingly, those who tend to emphasize the interdependencies of men and the social determinism of human behavior are likely to be more sympathetic to liberal approaches to these public problems and to a religion that incorporates an understanding of social relationships among men.[13]

Although individualism is perhaps the most important value orientation influencing American political and religious beliefs, other common values or functional interdependencies can also be found between the belief systems of the modernist and traditionalist clergy. For example, a highly optimistic assessment of man's capabilities and his rationality underlies both modernist theology and political liberalism, whereas an emphasis on man's sinful and selfish nature is common to the orientations of theological and political conservatives. Similarly, we see in the conservative responses a greater degree of ideological certainty, while theological and political liberals are often obliged to make pragmatic and almost ad hoc adjustments to social reality.[14]

Thus we suggest that the polarizations in belief that appear among Protestant clergymen reflect value differences that can also be traced to broader divisions within American culture, as well as to specific theological formulations within Protestant religion. That this should be the case is not surprising, given the close interchange that has been shown to exist between Protestant religion and American society. However, it means that the ministerial belief system is likely to reflect a variety of factors—many of them external to religious considerations alone. While emphasizing the central role played by Protestant theology in these configurations of belief, we also stress the functional interdependence that exists among the various attitudinal dimensions. Theology is important because it provides an explicit theoretical framework in which to evaluate and to respond to external values and events. But Protestant theology and Protestant ethics have themselves been formulated in tension with broader societal values, interests, and problems.

Ministerial Beliefs and Social Unrest.   Thus we maintain that Protestant theology provides the central focus for the ministerial belief system, but we also expect these belief systems to be very much influenced by immediate and long-term secular forces. With these considerations in mind, we conclude our analysis of clerical beliefs by reflecting on the likely influence of the period of social unrest in the middle and late 1960s on the members of the clerical profession and on divisions within organized religion. In times of relative political calm and social tranquillity, we suggest that many of these differences between Protestant clergymen would be of slight consequence. It would make little practical difference, for example, what the parish clergy thought about the legitimacy of civil protests or about how the church might be used as an agent for social change. Such questions would be more theoretical than real—points of debate in church magazines rather than areas of contention among practicing ministers. The period prior to our survey, however, was hardly one of peace and tranquillity. It was one of the most painful and divisive times in American history. The sense of hope and destiny that marked the early 1960s had given way to great mistrust, alienation, and, for many, despair. The youthful idealism of the Kennedy years was replaced by a widespread rejection of American values and a nearly unprecedented wave of student militancy. The coalition that had existed between white liberals and blacks over racial policies broke down, and the civil rights movement gave way to new charges of racism and a growing demand for more power in the hands of black people. Most of all, the United States involvement in Vietnam continued to divide the country and made many question the morality of American values and of American political leadership. To many persons in the late 1960s, the United States appeared as a hopelessly corrupt, intractably racist, and patently immoral society.

The existence of such compelling issues among highly educated and ethically conscious religious leaders would seem likely to intensify old divisions in belief and to make salient new ones: to create conflict among Protestant clergymen over issues that in more normal times would be nonexistent or which would lie dormant. In this way, political and ethical questions became relevant to the Protestant clergy during the late 1960s as they have seldom been in American history. The heightening of social tensions brought to the forefront more issues of contention between modernist and traditionalist clergymen and made for more open and bitter disputes over differences that would not otherwise have been significant.

How strongly the modernist and traditionalist clergy disagree and the manner in which they associate their religious commitments with contemporary issues is demonstrated most strikingly by the written comments to our questionnaire of two strongly committed clergymen. The first writer is a Lutheran minister who was considering leaving the church:

> There is a great deal of ferment and change going on both in the ministry and on the American religious scene . . . . Ministers in my denomination are starting to talk about organizing—going on strike and more money. This obviously means a whole new theology and attitudes. We are flatly objecting to the early 19th-century materialism of the church and attitudes about "evangelism." We are talking about more quality and commitment by the layman and less quantity and organization. We are more and more intolerant of the layman's lousy theology and paternal God and more and more demanding of him to learn or to get out.

In contrast to the opinions expressed in this statement were those of an obviously disturbed Southern Baptist clergyman:

> I feel that the church is the place which God intended to be used as His house. I don't believe in a church being used to teach people how to riot, dodge the draft, civil rights marches, dope

dens, dance halls or numerous other things being done by it and in it.

I believe that America is the greatest land on earth and my country is right beneath my God as far as love is concerned.

Although these remarks are somewhat atypical—chosen to illustrate two extremes in viewpoint—they suggest the wide gulf between the modernist and traditionalist wings of the clerical profession. In quieter times, many of the questions we have discussed would likely be of much less importance to our respondents and would furnish less cause for dispute and acrimony. At the time of our survey, however, modernist and traditionalist clergymen were increasingly finding themselves on opposite sides of major issues, and clear signs appeared in our data and elsewhere that rancor was developing between these two groups of ministers. This is one of the ways, we suggest, that a period of intense public passion and political conflict can lead to a loosening in normal social ties and a breakdown in organizational structures. During such periods, social values frequently take on new relevance and become linked with professional values, norms, and roles. Many individuals are likely to feel a moral obligation to make their professional callings more meaningful and more relevant to the societal problems they perceive as demanding attention and solution; others are likely to see no connection between their occupational and political roles and will oppose any efforts to "politicize" their professions.

It is obvious that such a process was occurring within the Protestant ministry at the time of our survey and was taking place in other professions as well. Standard professional practices were being challenged, new roles of moral relevance were called for, and disagreements arose between those who demanded new ways of doing things and those who defended the old.

Such conflicts can create bitter divisions among Protestant ministers, threatening the harmony that characterizes many religious organizations. We deal with some of the problems clergy activism creates within Protestant churches in future chapters. For those who value moral concern and involvement, however, this intensification in moral passions and hardening of positions presents a positive side. Social unrest may make reconciliation more difficult among Protestant ministers, perhaps also placing the organizational future of some religious groups in doubt; but it draws organized religion closer to issues of secular concern and human importance. It deters parish churches from being little more than social centers—organizing women's circles and men's clubs, bowling teams, and cake bakes. It forces them to face major questions about man's condition in society and to acknowledge that churchmen may have a special duty to provide leadership on public issues. In the long run, such an acknowledgment may not only be beneficial to secular society, it may also infuse organized religion with a new relevance and a more viable organizational existence. The same might be said of other professions as well. In the next two chapters, we learn how many of the California clergy responded to these social problems and became involved in controversial public issues.

NOTES AND REFERENCES

1. The attitudes of the California clergy toward Jews are examined in Rodney Stark, Bruce D. Foster, Charles Y. Glock, and Harold E. Quinley, *Wayward Shepherds: Prejudice and the Protestant Clergy* (New York: Harper & Row, 1971).

2. Charles Y. Glock and Benjamin B. Ringer, "Church Policy and the Attitudes of Ministers and Parishioners on Social Issues," *American Sociological Review*, **21** (April 1956), pp. 148–156; Charles Y. Glock, Benjamin B. Ringer, and Earl R. Babbie, *To Comfort and to Challenge: A Dilemma of the Contemporary Church* (Berkeley: University of California Press, 1967); and W. W. Schroeder and Victor Obenhaus, *Religion in American Culture: Unity and Diversity in a Midwestern County* (New York: Free Press, 1964).

3. *Ibid.*

4. For example, 81 percent of the California clergy disagreed with the statement that "it's probably better for Negroes and whites to have their own separate churches." At least some of those who agreed with this statement, we should note, did so in condemnation of their own churches. As one Methodist minister wrote, "No Negroes should have to put up with what passes for Christianity among whites."

5. The clergy's responses to this question were influenced in part by their denomination's organizational structure. A number of ministers in the congregationally organized churches indicated that their denomination's leaders had no such authority. We examine these differences in organizational authority in Chapter 10.

6. In retrospect, it appears that this question may be somewhat biased in a liberal direction. Also, not all the respondents knew who Alinsky was or about his tactics. This percentage thus might somewhat underrepresent clerical opinion on these matters.

7. Gerhard Lenski, *The Religious Factor*, rev. ed. (Garden City, N.Y.: Doubleday, 1963), pp. 134–149; Robert Lane Brown, "Attitudes Among Local Baptist Church Leaders in Washington State," *Sociology and Social Research*, **47** (April 1963), pp. 322–330; Benton Johnson, "Theology and Party Preference Among Protestant Clergymen," *American Sociological Review*, **31** (April 1966), pp. 200–208; and Jeffrey K. Hadden, *The Gathering Storm in the Churches* (Garden City, N.Y.: Doubleday, 1969), pp. 73–76.

8. For example, Fred Greenstein, *Children and Politics* (New Haven, Conn.: Yale University Press, 1967); Robert Hess and Judith Torney, *The Development of Political Attitudes in Children* (Chicago: Aldine, 1967); M. Kent Jennings and Richard G. Niemi, "Family Structure and the Transmission of Political Values," *American Political Science Review*, **42** (1968), pp. 169–184; Angus Campbell, Philip Converse, Warren Miller, and Donald Stokes, *The American Voter* (New York: Wiley, 1960), pp. 146–149; and Angus Campbell, Gerald Gurin, and Warren Miller, *The Voter Decides* (Evanston, Ill.: Row, Peterson, 1964), p. 90.

9. Hadden, *op. cit.*, p. 82.

10. *Ibid.*, pp. 64–67.

11. At least this is true of university professors, as shown in the various reports of Everett Carll Ladd, Jr., and Seymour Martin Lipset of the Carnegie Commission on Higher Education survey conducted in 1969. Correlations among their attitudinal scales are given in *Political Science*, 4 (Spring 1971), p. 139.

12. See the discussion of this free-will conception of man in Rodney Stark and Charles Y. Glock, "Prejudice and the Churches," in *Prejudice U.S.A.*, Glock and Ellen Siegelman, eds., (New York: Praeger, 1969), pp. 80–86.

13. For a further discussion of the development of American individualism and its linkage to political perceptions, see David L. Miller, *Individualism* (Austin: University of Texas Press, 1967).

14. Such differences were readily apparent, in an unobtrusive manner, in the way in which modernists and traditionalists filled out their questionnaires. The former often inserted qualifying remarks to their answers to particular questions (as they were encouraged to do in the instructions); the latter seldom did so.

PATTERNS OF CLERGY ACTIVISM

4. We have seen in the past two chapters that a fairly large proportion of Protestant ministers approve of clergy activism and support the idea of an action-oriented church. What, we now ask, was the actual response of the Protestant clergy to the public issues that so divided Americans during the 1960s? Did many clergymen at the parish level involve themselves in the important issues of the day? Or did they remain aloof from the controversial political questions that might bring them into conflict with the members of their congregations?

Relatively little is known about how parish ministers commonly respond to public issues or how they deal with controversial political subjects in their sermons. Perhaps the best known study of clerical involvement in politics is Liston Pope's classic analysis of the 1929 strike in Gastonia, North Carolina— a strike that gained public attention because of its Communist leadership, mob violence, and murder, and the subsequent trials of the "red conspirators."[1] Pope's study examines the close association that existed between Gastonia's religious leaders and its mill owners. Church leaders publicly welcomed the textile industry to Gastonia, almost unanimously opposed the labor strike, and joined in the subsequent crusade to remove Communist "influences" from the community. The churches, in turn, were amply supported (or "rewarded") by the owners of the cotton mills. Nearly all mills provided land for the erection of new churches, many gave direct financial subsidies to a parsonage or to a minister, and mill owners themselves exerted substantial influence through positions of lay leadership. In mill villages the textile company often paid the minister directly and owned outright a number of church buildings. The use of such controls, however, was rarely necessary to obtain clergy support for the textile industry; as Pope shows, almost all the community's clergymen adopted the philosophy of the community's major economic interest.

More recently, attention has focused on the role of clergymen in issues pertaining to civil rights. Most suggestive in this respect is the study by Ernest Q. Campbell and Thomas F. Pettigrew of the actions of Protestant clergymen during the 1957 desegregation crisis in Little Rock, Arkansas.[2] The authors found that although most of their sample of ministers in main-line churches approved of school integration, only a few took vigorous public positions in support of their personal beliefs. Their initial efforts to preach racial calm and acceptance of the desegregation order were virtually abandoned when such actions met with fierce lay resistance. The community's most prestigious clergymen subsequently withdrew from the conflict and ended their activities symbolically with a Day of Prayer at which participating ministers largely ignored the racial issue and called for a reconciliation among those of all views. The few clergymen who continued to support the desegregation efforts suffered severely for their activism; most eventually lost their jobs as a direct result of their outspokenness on the issue.[3]

These studies show the extent to which organized religious groups are affected by dominant economic, racial, or political interests. When, as in Gastonia, the clergy themselves have absorbed the dominant ideology, they are likely to resist any changes in the status quo. Even when they favor reform, however, as is often the case on civil rights issues, they find themselves under strong pressures to remain inactive or to alter their views. As such conflicts become more intense and the price of activism higher, the Campbell and Pettigrew study shows that clergy activism is likely to decrease. Because Protestant ministers often privately hold liberal views or express approval of clergy activism, therefore, we cannot conclude that they invariably make their positions public. Fear of lay reprisals may inhibit their activism and cause them to remain silent during public controversies.

To determine how Protestant ministers commonly respond to political issues, we asked them many questions about their involvement in public affairs; the data are reported in this chapter and in the next. To be as concrete as possible in our examination of clergy activism, we asked our respondents to report the actions they took during three actual political controversies affecting Californians during the period just prior to our survey. We also asked them to describe the topics they discussed in their sermons during the year before the study.

Three Arenas of Conflict. Three major public controversies arose in California during the five-year period prior to our survey; these were related to an emotion-laden initiative campaign in 1964 to repeal the state's fair housing laws, a long and bitter strike by migratory farm workers over wages and working conditions in California's agricultural San Joaquin Valley, and the increasingly unpopular war being fought in Vietnam. Each issue was hotly contested among opposing segments of the population and each brought forth militant and sometimes violent tactics. In addition, many regarded the issues as involving "moral" questions, thus demanding active ethical leadership from churchmen.

Given the controversy surrounding these issues, it was decided to collect systematic information on clergy involvement in each one. To this end, we asked the California ministers a series of questions about their views on the issues and the extent of their involvement in them. In addition, they were asked about the positions taken by their congregational members, colleagues, and local denominational leaders and the reactions of their parishioners to their own described participation. The information we collected on the ministers' attitudes and behavior is presented in this chapter; the remaining data appear in later chapters when we consider the conflicts within Protestant churches over clergy activism.

Proposition 14. The first of these issues—that which caused the most bitter conflicts within Protestant churches—was the anti-fair housing initiative in 1964. The purpose of the initiative proposal was to remove from the books a recently passed fair housing law. In 1963 the California legislature had enacted the Rumford Act, prohibiting racial discrimination in the sale or rental of housing by realtors, apartment landlords, and owners of private homes that had been financed through public assistance. Shortly after the act was passed, the California Real Estate Association and the California Apartment Owners' Association joined forces to sponsor an initiative constitutional amendment that would both repeal the Rumford Act and prohibit the state from enacting similar legislation in the future. The key provision of the initiative proposal read as follows:

> Neither the State nor any subdivision or agency thereof shall deny, limit or abridge, directly or indirectly, the right of any person, who is willing or desires to sell, lease or rent any part or all of his real property, to decline to sell, lease or rent such property to such person or persons as he, in his absolute discretion, chooses.

With this wording, a positive (yes) vote was a vote cast against the fair housing law, and a negative (no) vote was in support of such legislation.[4]

An active and bitter campaign was conducted over this initiative proposal, which subsequently became Proposition 14 in the 1964 California general election.[5] An overwhelming majority of the organizations and public officials that took a public position on the issue were against the proposition. The anti-Proposition 14 forces included civil rights organizations, church groups, labor, the governor, the Democratic Central Committee, most Democratic officials and candidates, and a few prominent Republicans, most notably Thomas Kuchel, then the state's senior U.S. Senator. In favor of the amendment were the California real estate and apartment owners' associations, some neighborhood taxpayers' groups, two voluntary Republican organizations, and a few Republican officials. Although a preponderance of personal and organizational endorsements were against the initiative, however, Proposition 14 passed easily with more than 65 percent of the vote. Polls showed that as the campaign progressed, the proportion of voters favoring the proposition increased; as individuals became more aware and better informed about the meaning of the amendment, it appeared, they were more likely to approve of it.[6]

The ministers' positions on Proposition 14 are shown in Table 4.1. Clearly a large majority of the California clergymen in these nine denominations opposed the effort to repeal the state's fair housing law. In every denomination except the Southern Baptist Convention the proportion of ministers against the proposition is substantially greater than the segment approving it. As in previous chapters, the members of the American Lutheran Church,

Table 4.1. Denominational Distribution of Clergy Attitudes Toward Proposition 14 (Anti-Fair Housing Referendum)[a]

Denomination	Opposed	Favored	Not Sure	
Methodist	95%	4	1	100% (296)
United Church of Christ	91%	6	3	100% (105)
Episcopal	89%	9	2	100% (173)
Presbyterian	86%	13	1	100% (195)
Lutheran Church in America	83%	12	5	100% (66)
American Baptist	71%	23	6	100% (121)
Missouri Synod-Lutheran Church	60%	31	8	99% (96)
American Lutheran Church	54%	37	10	101% (82)
Southern Baptist	37%	55	8	100% (152)
Totals	77%	19	4	100% (1286)

[a] Question was asked only of those respondents who were in California at the time of the anti-fair housing referendum.

Missouri Synod, and American Baptist Church joined the Southern Baptists
in taking more conservative positions on this issue, whereas the Methodist
and United Church of Christ clergymen were the most liberal. Thus although California voters passed Proposition 14 by a 2-to-1 margin, Protestant
clergymen opposed its passage by better than 4 to 1.

The Delano Strike.   The second public issue we studied was the organization
of migratory farm workers in the Delano area of the San Joaquin Valley.[7]
The immediate cause of the conflict between growers and workers was a
strike called in September 1965, to demand an increase in wages and the
enforcement of standard working conditions. Farm workers at that time were
receiving $1.20 an hour, plus ten cents for each basket of grapes picked;
they demanded a raise to $1.40 an hour and twenty-five cents per basket.
The workers' negotiating position was precarious because agriculture is not
covered in either the Wagner Act or the Taft-Hartley Act. Farm laborers,
as a result, were protected neither by federal minimum wage provisions nor
by the National Labor Relations Board's procedures for union recognition.

Although worker–grower conflict was not a new phenomenon in the Valley, the farm laborers received widespread publicity and sympathy through
the skillful guidance of their chief organizer, Cesar Chavez. Chavez received
his early training and experience in organizing techniques in Saul Alinsky's
Community Service Organization, from which he resigned in 1962 to start
the National Farm Workers' Association in Delano. The NFWA, a predominantly Mexican-American group, joined with the AFL–CIO's Agricultural
Workers' Organization Committee, which was largely Filipino, to call the
1965 strike. These two groups merged in August 1965 under Chavez's leadership to form the United Farm Workers' Organizing Committee, AFL–CIO.
Thereupon, the Teamsters' Union openly challenged Chavez for the right
to represent the workers of one of the Valley's largest growers. By 1968 when
the survey was taken, Chavez and the farm workers had gained the support
of large numbers of church, labor, and political officials; had instituted a
nationwide boycott against grapes; and had been given official recognition
by two of the Valley's largest growers. At the same time, the controversy
was far from settled. The most dramatic and violent aspects of the strike had
passed, but Chavez and his allies had met with only partial success in the
implementation of their goals, and the farm labor controversy was to continue into the seventies.

Church groups and individual clergymen were among the earliest and
strongest supporters of the Delano strike. The California Migrant Ministry,
part of the Division of Homes Missions of the National Council of Churches,
had been closely connected with the farm workers' problems for many years,

and other church organizations and clergymen quickly offered their assistance to the NFWA. This assistance included public support of the NFWA's position; the collection of money, clothing, and food for the strikers; and joining in picket lines and mass rallies.

For individual clergymen who were called on to support the strike, two questions were raised. First, did he support the organization of migratory farm workers itself? Second, did he approve of clergy participation in such activities? Because these two questions raised different issues, the ministers' positions on each were obtained separately. The respondents were first asked whether they personally favored the organization of migratory farm workers in California; 76 percent replied that they did, 18 percent were not sure, and 6 percent said they were not. The first group of ministers were then asked if they favored clergy participation in the organization of farm workers. The distribution of responses to these two inquiries is given in Table 4.2. About half the ministers favored both the organization of migratory farm workers and clergy participation on behalf of such a goal; 17 percent opposed clergy

Table 4.2. Denominational Distribution of Clergy Attitudes Toward Ministerial Participation in the Organization of Migratory Farm Workers

Denomination	Favored Clergy Participation	Opposed Clergy Participation	Not Sure About Clergy Participation	Not in Favor of Organization of Farm Workers	
Methodist	66%	8	12	14	100% (347)
United Church of Christ	63%	11	13	12	99% (134)
Episcopal	54%	15	14	18	101% (205)
Presbyterian	52%	17	15	15	99% (225)
Lutheran Church in America	62%	10	14	14	100% (86)
American Baptist	39%	18	11	32	100% (145)
American Lutheran Church	37%	24	11	28	100% (117)
Missouri Synod-Lutheran Church	18%	17	9	56	100% (133)
Southern Baptist	10%	38	6	46	100% (168)
Total	47%	17%	12%	24%	100% (1560)

involvement in the issue, and the remainder were undecided. Thus support for the NFWA exceeded the opposition among these nine denominations by about a two-to-one margin. At the same time, almost a third of the respondents were undecided about their positions—indicating the apathy of many Protestant ministers, particularly those most geographically removed from the area of controversy.

Unlike the other two issues, the Delano strike was limited in its primary effects to a particular locale: the farm-producing areas of the San Joaquin Valley. This constraint provides an excellent opportunity to examine the ability of a community to control the public behavior of its clergymen. For those living in the Valley, the Delano strike quickly became an issue generating great emotion, with each side concocting myths of the other's immoral conduct and illegal activities. Since farm growers and their local allies provide a large proportion of the membership and financial support of Protestant churches in the Valley, furthermore, the clergymen from the area who supported the grape strike did so at great risk to their own parish positions. (The majority of the strikers were Catholics.) Ministers from urban or geographically remote areas, in contrast, could probably assist the strikers with little likelihood of such parishioner reprisals. Since their activities were directed at an issue in which the members of their own congregations had little direct stake or interest, they could be relatively free to support the farm workers as they desired. Such outside clerical support, according to one account, was most despised by the Delano residents who sided with the growers:

> However East Side Delano raged at the volunteers, it still reserved its purest vitriol for the clergy who came to town in support of the NFWA. What particularly infuriated Delano was the clergy's insistence that the situation involved not simply a labor dispute but a moral issue. *The outside clergy maintained that their presence in Delano was necessary because the local churchmen, by remaining neutral, had by their silence cast in with the growers.*[8]

Our survey shows that clergymen in the San Joaquin Valley were less favorable to clergy support of the striking farm workers than ministers in any other major geographical area in California. Table 4.3 reveals that support for the strikers' position was most common in the urban areas of the state, whereas opposition was most frequent in the San Joaquin Valley itself.[9] In a later chapter, we see how unpopular support of the organization of migratory farm workers was in the San Joaquin Valley and what happened to the few ministers in the Valley who ignored the wishes of their parishioners and openly backed the striking workers.

Table 4.3. Regional Distribution of Clergy Attitudes Toward Ministerial Participation in the Organization of Migratory Farm Workers

Region	Favored Clergy Participation	Opposed Clergy Participation	Not Sure About Clergy Participation	Not in Favor of Organization of Farm Workers	
San Francisco Bay area	57%	13	13	17	100% (326)
Southern California	49%	14	11	26	100% (771)
Central coast	46%	16	9	29	100% (55)
Sacramento area	45%	18	16	21	100% (100)
Mountain	44%	22	13	21	100% (63)
North coast	34%	22	12	31	99% (67)
San Joaquin Valley	30%	31	14	25	100% (178)
Total	47%	17	12	24	100% (1560)

The Vietnam War. The third issue to be studied is the clergy's positions on the Vietnam war and their activities in support of or against war policies that were current in the spring of 1968.[10] Wartime presents the church with perhaps its most acute dilemma in deciding what role to take vis à vis public affairs. On the one hand, it is during wartime that political passions are frequently at their peak and demands for conformity at their greatest. A nation's people, including its clergy, are likely to come together in a common effort against "the enemy."[11] On the other hand, the use of force to settle disputes runs contrary to some of the most central teachings of Christianity.

The Vietnam war, of course, had become unpopular among a substantial minority of the American people by 1968 and we might expect that Protestant ministers would be particularly disposed to share in this dissent. In fact, we find that our respondents were about two to three times more dovish than the general public at the time of the survey—although as a group they were split about evenly between those we would regard as "hawks" and those who were "doves."

The ministers' position on the Vietnam war are shown in Tables 4.4 and 4.5. Clergy attitudes toward the war were first elicited on five major policy proposals: (1) increasing military efforts to win the war; (2) seeking negotiations while continuing to exert military pressure on the enemy, including the bombing of North Vietnam; (3) unilaterally stopping the bombing of North Vietnam and offering to negotiate; (4) unilaterally stopping the bombing of

North Vietnam and withdrawing to the coast areas and population centers; and (5) unilaterally stopping the bombing and beginning preparations for complete withdrawal. The ministers' responses to these options are summarized in Table 4.4. The two most common choices, not surprisingly, were those closest to the current policy—seeking negotiations while continuing to bomb the North and seeking negotiations while stopping the bombing of the North. Of greater interest, however, are the other three response categories. An individual might have approved of unilateral withdrawal from Vietnam and also logically favored both withdrawal to coastal enclaves and the elimination of bombing—since all three actions constitute less militaristic policies than those in force at the time. Similarly, an individual might logically have wanted both to continue the bombing of the North and to increase military efforts, both positions arising from a desire to maintain military pressure on the enemy.

For the purposes of constructing an attitudinal scale, the respondents were assigned the most extreme policy position of those which they favored. In addition, it was decided that clergy who selected both a hawk and a dove

Table 4.4.   Ministers' Attitudes Toward Vietnam War Policies

Statement of Position	Agree	No Opinion	Disagree	Total
Increase our military efforts to win the war	29%	8	63	100% (1531)
See negotiations while continuing to exert military pressure on the enemy, including the bombing of North Vietnam	45%	6	49	100% (1523)
Unilaterally stop the bombing of North Vietnam and offer to negotiate	57%	8	35	100% (1524)
Unilaterally stop the bombing of North Vietnam and withdraw to the coastal areas and population centers	29%	19	53	101% (1500)
Unilaterally stop the bombing and begin preparations for complete withdrawal	30%	13	57	100% (1511)

position should be coded according to the hawkish response. On the basis of these two criteria, the respondents were classified according to the following ordering of policy preferences: (1) an increase in military efforts, (2) continuation of the bombing, (3) preparations for complete withdrawal, (4) withdrawal to coastal enclaves, and (5) a halt to the bombing. The results of this reclassification appear in Table 4.5. We see that the California clergymen were split almost evenly into groups holding hawkish and dovish positions at the time of our survey. The largest two groups of respondents were found at the two ends of the Vietnam scale—29 percent favoring an increase in military efforts and 26 percent advocating preparations for complete withdrawal.

Even though the ministers were in disagreement about war policy, their views were still far more dovish than those of the general public during this period. Whereas 57 percent of the ministers favored a halt to the bombing of North Vietnam in the spring of 1968, only 21 percent[12] of the public would have agreed to such a step at that time. Similarly, although the clergy were divided almost evenly between the hawk and dove positions, the public was

Table 4.5. Denominational Distribution of Clergy Hawks and Doves on Vietnam

Denomination	Increase Military Efforts	Continue the Bombing	Stop the Bombing	Withdraw to Enclaves	Complete Withdrawal	
Methodist	9%	16	22	13	40	100% (343)
United Church of Christ	13%	10	31	6	40	100% (133)
Episcopal	18%	22	22	9	29	100% (200)
Presbyterian	18%	24	16	14	28	100% (220)
Lutheran Church in America	28%	13	19	10	30	100% (83)
American Baptist	40%	25	13	7	15	100% (136)
American Lutheran Church	39%	23	20	4	14	100% (112)
Missouri Synod-Lutheran Church	50%	20	13	4	13	100% (126)
Southern Baptist	82%	15	1	—	2	100% (163)
Total	29%	19	18	8	26	100% (1516)

2.5 times as likely to be located on the hawk end of the continuum. The socioeconomic groups with which the ministers are most comparable, furthermore—professionals and the college educated—were even more hawkish in their views than the general population.

Clergy Involvement in Controversial Public Issues. Thus the positions taken by the California clergy on these three controversial public issues often varied but were generally more liberal than those held by the contemporary public and, as we shall see, by the ministers' own parishioners. On Proposition 14 a large majority of the parish ministers (77 percent) opposed the initiative proposal, which passed the electorate with nearly two-thirds of the vote. On the grape strike issue, nearly half the respondents favored clergy participation in the effort to organize migratory farm workers, although approval of such actions was lower in the San Joaquin Valley itself. On Vietnam the clergy were divided almost evenly between hawkish and dovish positions when our survey was taken, but they were nearly twice as dovish in their views as the public nationally.

As we have pointed out, little is known about how Protestant clergymen commonly respond to public controversies such as these. To obtain such information, we asked the California ministers whether they had taken any of a series of actions designed to express their views on these issues. From their responses, it is apparent that many parish clergymen do speak out on controversial public issues and do seek to involve their parishioners in community, state, and national affairs. Our respondents were particularly active in expressing their views on the civil rights issue and on the war in Vietnam— two areas in which church groups have often made public pronouncements. Most discussed these issues with the members of their congregations, from one-half to two-thirds took public positions on the matters or delivered a sermon on them, and many joined organizations either against the passage of the anti-fair housing amendment or against the war in Vietnam. In all these respects, we find that clergy activism was most common within the most modernist and politically liberal denominations in our survey: the Methodist Church, the United Church of Christ, the Episcopal Church, the Presbyterian Church, and the Lutheran Church in America. Clerical leaders in the American Baptist Convention were somewhat less active, followed by those in the American Lutheran Church. The least active respondents were found in the Missouri Synod-Lutheran Church and the Southern Baptist Convention.

Table 4.6 summarizes the actions taken by the California clergy to make their views known on Proposition 14. We have no way of knowing how direct or forceful our respondents were in their involvement in this issue (or the others examined in our survey), but we can see that a considerable proportion of them spoke out on the initiative proposal. Almost all the parish ministers in California indicated that they had discussed the matter with the members of their congregations, and many had attempted to influence the public, their parishioners, or political officials. Various degrees of activism were noted: 21 percent organized a social action unit within their churches to persuade others on the issue, 56 percent delivered a sermon on it, and 66 percent issued a public statement.

Although we do not have data with which to compare the activism of Protestant clergymen with that of other groups, these rates of ethical involvement would seem to be impressive. Certainly they are much higher than those commonly found among the general public.[13] What is more, Table 4.6 indicates that clergymen in the five liberal denominations were particularly active in expressing their views on the initiative proposal. About three-quarters of them issued a public statement on Proposition 14, slightly fewer delivered a sermon on the issue, and about half organized study groups to discuss the amendment, wrote to a public official about it, or joined an organization that campaigned on it. Among the five most liberal denominations, clergymen in the Methodist Church tended to be the most socially active, followed by ministers in the Presbyterian and Episcopal churches and ministers in the United Church of Christ and the Lutheran Church in America.

Thus a considerable proportion of the ministers in liberal Protestant denominations became involved in the conflict over passage of Proposition 14. As we would expect, most of these clergymen campaigned against the initiative proposal; we show these data shortly.

The extent of the California clergymen's active support of the organization of migratory farm workers by Cesar Chavez is reported in Table 4.7. These responses reveal that the parish ministers who participated in this issue were far less numerous than those who had been involved in the anti-fair housing campaign. Taken together, about a quarter of our respondents reported that they had made a public statement on the grape strike or delivered a sermon or a prayer on it before their congregations. Seventeen percent signed a petition, 13 percent wrote to a public official, and 11 percent organized a study group within their church to discuss the issue. Just over 5 percent of the clergy, finally, indicated that they had traveled to the Delano area itself to join in local efforts to support Chavez and his strikers.

Clergymen in the five liberal denominations most often reported that they had taken such actions to involve themselves in the issue. Leaders in the United Church of Christ had been particularly active in supporting the or-

Table 4.6. Denominational Distribution of Clergy Involvement in the Anti-Fair Housing Referendum Campaign[a]

	Meth-odist	United Church of Christ	Epis-copal	Presby-terian	Lu-theran Church in America	Ameri-can Bap-tist	Ameri-can Lu-theran Church	Missouri Synod-Lu-theran Church	South-ern Bap-tist	Total
Discussed it informally with some of the members of the congrega-tion	98% (273)	93% (99)	96% (160)	99% (184)	97% (59)	96% (110)	96% (79)	88% (94)	88% (136)	96% (1194)
Made a public statement	86% (272)	69% (97)	70% (159)	77% (183)	76% (59)	66% (109)	42% (78)	32% (94)	35% (135)	66% (1186)
Signed a petition	84% (271)	65% (98)	63% (158)	66% (183)	64% (59)	42% (108)	32% (79)	25% (93)	19% (136)	57% (1185)
Delivered a sermon or a section of a sermon on the subject	79% (272)	61% (97)	71% (160)	67% (183)	63% (59)	47% (110)	32% (79)	22% (94)	16% (136)	56% (1190)
Organized a study group within the church to discuss the subject	59% (272)	42% (97)	50% (159)	62% (182)	44% (59)	33% (109)	20% (79)	14% (94)	5% (136)	41% (1187)
Delivered a prayer before the congregation	57% (265)	51% (96)	45% (155)	59% (174)	35% (58)	33% (106)	22% (78)	7% (94)	13% (134)	40% (1160)

Wrote to a public official	53% (266)	39% (96)	37% (157)	45% (179)	43% (58)	28% (103)	14% (78)	12% (94)	8% (134)	35% (1165)
Served on a committee that campaigned for or against the proposition	48% (271)	39% (98)	45% (159)	44% (180)	37% (59)	22% (109)	5% (79)	6% (94)	6% (136)	32% (1185)
Organized a social action group within the church to persuade others on the issue	35% (269)	27% (98)	32% (159)	28% (180)	20% (59)	10% (109)	3% (79)	1% (94)	1% (136)	21% (1183)

[a] Information reported here and in subsequent tables on Proposition 14 was obtained only from respondents holding parish positions in California at the time of the anti-fair housing referendum.

ganizing efforts—and Table 4.7 shows that UCC ministers were in fact most heavily involved in the issue. Even within these liberal church groups, however, the level of clergy activism in the farm labor dispute was far lower than it had been during the Proposition 14 campaign. Apparently this issue was of relatively little importance for most Protestant ministers, particularly those more geographically removed from the strike and from areas with little direct economic interest in the matter. We examine the controversies caused by the farm labor dispute in different sections of California in a later chapter.

Turning to the last of our issues, we find that the California ministers were fairly active in expressing their views on United States policies in Vietnam, although again not equaling their participation in the anti-Proposition 14 campaign. We should keep in mind, however, that during the spring of 1968, when our survey was conducted, public opinion was still largely favorable to the war in Vietnam and antiwar activism remained highly controversial.

We see from Table 4.8 that most Protestant ministers had discussed the war with the members of their congregations and that a large proportion (85 percent) had delivered a prayer on it. Sixty-five percent reported that they had dealt with the war in Vietnam in a sermon, and 52 percent that they had made a public statement on it. Less than a third of the parish clergy, however, had organized a study group to discuss the war or had engaged in any of the other forms of activism listed in Table 4.8. Perhaps the most interesting questions in this respect are those dealing with the clergy's involvement in antiwar groups and in acts of public protest: 25 percent of the California ministers had attended a meeting to protest the war, and 16 percent had joined a peace organization. Regarding more publicized forms of clerical antiwar activism, 7 percent of the parish ministers had participated in an antiwar protest march and 2 percent had risked arrest to symbolize their opposition to the war.

Thus although not all the California clergy had spoken out on the war by the spring of 1968, our survey indicates that many had done so. Again activism was most common within the five liberal denominations, although a considerable proportion of the ministers in the conservative denominations had delivered a sermon or had made a public statement on the war. Acts of civil protest and disobedience were most common within the United Church of Christ: 16 percent of the ministers in this denomination reported that they had participated in an antiwar protest march; 10 percent in antiwar civil disobedience.

These figures thus show that a fairly substantial proportion of the California ministers became involved in one way or another in two of the public controversies investigated and that a significant minority was involved in the third. Some critics of religion might regard these levels of activism as dis-

Table 4.7. Denominational Distribution of Clergy Involvement in the Organization of Migratory Farm Workers[a]

	Methodist	United Church of Christ	Episcopal	Presbyterian	Lutheran Church in America	American Baptist	American Lutheran Church	Missouri Synod Lutheran Church	Southern Baptist	Total
Discussed it informally with some of the members of the congregation	83% (304)	81% (112)	75% (177)	88% (205)	87% (74)	60% (118)	59% (93)	48% (117)	50% (149)	73% (1354)
Made a public statement	36% (310)	44% (111)	27% (177)	33% (205)	32% (74)	25% (118)	13% (92)	3% (117)	7% (149)	26% (1353)
Delivered a prayer before the congregation	30% (308)	32% (112)	27% (176)	38% (205)	22% (74)	19% (118)	10% (93)	1% (117)	5% (148)	23% (1351)
Delivered a sermon or a section of a sermon on the subject	32% (310)	36% (112)	24% (177)	27% (206)	37% (74)	12% (118)	10% (93)	4% (117)	7% (149)	22% (1356)
Signed a petition	28% (310)	28% (111)	21% (177)	18% (205)	26% (74)	8% (118)	3% (93)	3% (117)	— (149)	17% (1354)
Wrote to a public official	21% (310)	21% (112)	14% (177)	13% (204)	16% (74)	12% (118)	3% (93)	3% (117)	— (149)	13% (1354)
Organized a study group within the church to discuss the subject	18% (308)	21% (111)	13% (177)	16% (206)	12% (74)	4% (118)	2% (93)	2% (117)	— (149)	11% (1353)
Marched or traveled to the Delano area	7% (308)	13% (111)	10% (177)	4% (206)	5% (74)	3% (117)	1% (93)	— (117)	— (149)	5% (1352)

[a] Information reported here and in subsequent tables on the organizing issue was obtained only from respondents holding parish positions in California at the time of the strike in the Delano area.

117

Table 4.8. Denominational Distribution of Clergy Involvement in the Debate Over Vietnam War Policy

	Methodist	United Church of Christ	Episcopal	Presbyterian	Lutheran Church in America	American Baptist	American Lutheran Church	Missouri Synod Lutheran Church	Southern Baptist	Total
Discussed it informally with some members of the congregation	97% (354)	96% (137)	97% (205)	99% (224)	98% (87)	98% (146)	92% (117)	95% (134)	90% (168)	96% (1572)
Delivered a prayer before the congregation	86% (353)	85% (136)	84% (202)	89% (223)	84% (87)	91% (147)	82% (117)	81% (133)	75% (168)	85% (1566)
Delivered a sermon or a section of a sermon on the subject	78% (353)	75% (137)	68% (205)	68% (223)	69% (87)	62% (146)	47% (117)	47% (133)	50% (168)	65% (1569)
Made a public statement	69% (353)	56% (137)	47% (204)	60% (222)	45% (87)	61% (145)	29% (116)	15% (133)	49% (168)	52% (1565)
Organized a study group within the church to discuss the subject	48% (353)	36% (134)	20% (203)	48% (223)	41% (86)	16% (146)	13% (117)	11% (133)	4% (169)	29% (1564)
Wrote to a public official	46% (347)	38% (137)	25% (204)	35% (221)	26% (87)	21% (144)	16% (117)	16% (134)	15% (169)	29% (1560)
Signed a petition	48% (349)	44% (136)	28% (203)	24% (222)	25% (87)	13% (144)	8% (117)	6% (134)	3% (168)	25% (1560)

Attended a protest meeting	43% (352)	43% (136)	28% (207)	25% (226)	29% (87)	10% (146)	9% (118)	9% (134)	1% (168)	25% (1574)
Joined a peace organization	27% (351)	34% (135)	21% (204)	15% (221)	13% (87)	8% (146)	3% (116)	5% (134)	— (169)	16% (1563)
Participated in an antiwar protest march	14% (353)	16% (135)	8% (206)	7% (226)	6% (86)	1% (147)	2% (118)	2% (134)	— (168)	7% (1573)
Participated in antiwar civil disobedience (risked arrest to symbolize protest)	1% (351)	10% (135)	2% (205)	2% (226)	1% (86)	1% (146)	1% (118)	1% (134)	— (168)	2% (1569)

120

appointing, especially given the church's potential role in public affairs. Compared with other groups in American society, however, the clergy are most certainly highly involved in politics. We have more to say on this matter in the next chapter, when we seek to assess clergy activism in California.

Whatever our evaluations of these patterns of activism, we find that the clergy's participation in public affairs is closely connected with their religious, ethical, and political belief systems. Ministers in the liberal or modernist Protestant denominations are most active; ministers in the conservative denominations, the least active. From the data we have presented so far in this chapter, therefore, it appears that between a third and a half of the parish clergy in the five liberal denominations in our survey are committed to an activist ministry. We learn the price these parish ministers paid for such activism in Chapter 8.

In the information we have presented concerning the clergy's activism, we have summarized together the public activities of liberal and conservative clergymen. Most criticism of the church's role in public affairs, however, has been directed not just at the failure of religious groups to speak out on important issues but also at the support they have allegedly given to dominant social, political, and economic interests in American society. For example, churches have been charged with supporting racial injustices, economic inequalities, and a nationalistic foreign policy. Of particular interest to us, therefore, is the distribution of activism among the parish ministers who took liberal and conservative positions on the three study issues. For such issues as Vietnam, on which clergy opinion is divided, Protestant ministers may be actively expressing both conservative and liberal views. Like experts testifying at a trial, those speaking out on one side of the issue may serve to counterbalance those on the other side.

It is our expectation by this time, of course, that liberal clergymen will be more outspoken in expressing their views on such social issues. This is exactly what we find—and we should adjust our description of clergy involvement in public affairs accordingly. On all three of the issues examined, the ministers who took liberal positions were the most modernist in their religious orientations and the most socially active in their ethical behavior. Table 4.9 compares the activism of ministers who opposed the passage of Proposition 14 with those who supported it. We see that the former group of clergy were far more outspoken on the issue than the latter. They were about twice as likely to make a public statement on Proposition 14; about three times as likely to sign a petition, to write to a public official, or to organize a study group within their churches; almost four times as likely to deliver a sermon on the issue; and eight times as likely to have joined a campaign committee.

Similar differences (not shown here) existed between the percentage of

Table 4.9. Liberal Ministers Were More Active During Anti-Fair Housing Referendum Campaign

	Favored Proposition 14		Opposed Proposition 14	
Signed a petition	24%	(225)	67%	(912)
Wrote a public official	16	(223)	41	(893)
Made a public statement	34	(226)	76	(911)
Served on a committee that campaigned for or against the proposition	5	(224)	40	(912)
Discussed it informally with members of their congregation	91	(227)	98	(918)
Delivered a prayer before their congregation	14	(220)	48	(891)
Delivered a sermon or a section of a sermon on the subject	16	(226)	68	(915)
Organized a study group within the church to discuss the subject	15	(225)	49	(913)
Organized a social action group within the church to persuade others on the issue	4	(223)	26	(911)

clergymen actively supporting the organization of migratory farm workers and the percentage actively opposing it. Most indicative of the political nature of the ministers' activism, however, is the pattern of their involvement in the Vietnam issue. Table 4.10 indicates an almost direct linear relationship between the California clergy's views on the war in Vietnam and their activism on the issue: the more dovish their positions, the more socially active they were with respect to the war. Again, the differences observed were considerable. Those who favored withdrawal from Vietnam, for example, were about 1.5 times as likely as those favoring a military escalation to make their views known in a public statement, about twice as likely to write to a public official or to deliver a sermon on the war, and 3.5 times as likely to organize a study group to discuss the war.

These patterns of clergy activism clearly demonstrate the overrepresentation of liberal ministers in public affairs. Not all Protestant clergymen agree on political issues, but those having liberal views are disproportionately involved in actual political controversies. Such a distribution of clergy activism

Table 4.10.   Dovish Ministers Were More Active in the Debate Over Vietnam War Policy

	Increase Military Efforts	Continue Bombing	Stop Bombing	Withdraw to Enclaves	Complete Withdrawal
Made a public statement (N = 1504)	41%	47%	50%	68%	67%
Wrote a public official (N = 1499)	20	19	27	48	45
Signed a petition (N = 1499)	4	8	31	52	55
Discussed with parishioners (N = 1511)	94	97	98	98	98
Delivered a prayer before congregation (N = 1504)	79	84	86	89	90
Delivered a sermon (N = 1507)	49	60	72	83	79
Organized a study group (N = 1505)	12	27	36	48	42
Attended a protest meeting (N = 1512)	4	11	34	48	46
Joined a peace organization (N = 1502)	1	5	16	30	39
Participated in an antiwar protest march (N = 1511)	0	1	7	12	19
Participated in antiwar civil disobedience (N = 1508)	—	0	1	4	7

obviously follows from the configurations in belief within the Protestant ministry demonstrated in the last two chapters.

Thus our survey shows that a considerable number of liberal Protestant ministers speak out on public issues involving questions of race, economic welfare, and peace. What our survey does not tell us, however, is how direct and unequivocal the parish ministers were in their ethical actions during these three public controversies. We do not know whether they approached these issues in a general and ambiguous manner—as did most of the Little Rock ministers during the desegregation crisis of 1957—or whether they were forthright and outspoken. We find some evidence to suggest that the former may be the case when we examine the California ministers' treatment of social and political topics in their sermons. We also see more clearly the contrasting ethical roles of modernist and traditionalist clergymen.

Activism at the Pulpit.   Perhaps the chief resource at the disposal of the ethically minded minister is his pulpit. The Sunday service is the central activity of Christians each week, and the sermon the accepted means by which the pastor is to instruct the faithful. Given the large number of people who attend church each Sunday, the pulpit is an obvious platform from which the parish minister can provide guidance on what he considers to be issues of ethical relevance.

We saw in the previous section that 56 percent of the California ministers delivered a sermon or a section of a sermon on Proposition 14 and that 65 percent had done so on the war in Vietnam. To determine how the California clergymen treated other social and political topics in their sermons, we inquired how often they had discussed "controversial social and political topics" from the pulpit in the year preceding the survey and how they had treated a number of specific political or moral topics. Recall again that the year preceding the survey was one of political drama and high passion for many Americans. In the period just prior to the survey, many thousands starved in Biafra; Arab–Israeli hostilities broke into open fighting in the Six-Day War; there was violence in the black ghettos in scores of American cities; and opposition to the war in Vietnam became more widespread, militant, and violent. Just before the survey was taken, the Tet offensive occurred, and midway through it President Johnson announced the cessation of bombing in North Vietnam and his decision not to run for the presidency in 1968. Shortly thereafter Dr. Martin Luther King, Jr., was shot down in Memphis and a new wave of riots swept the nation.

Few other periods in American history have been marked by issues so intense and compelling. What, then, did the California ministers have to say about these events? How did they introduce the issues into their sermons? Our data clearly show that although many ministers dealt with such topics from the pulpit, a much smaller number made them the central focus of their sermons. This distinction, we might add, was imposed on us by the respondents themselves. In a pretest mailing of an earlier draft of the questionnaire, the ministers were asked simply whether they had dealt with certain social and political topics in their sermons. Approximately a third of these respondents either refused to answer the question or qualified their responses. Most of the respondents wrote that although they sometimes touched on such topics, the matters mentioned were seldom the central theme of their sermons.

In the final questionnaire, therefore, we asked the California ministers whether they had "dealt mainly with" or had "touched on but did not deal mainly with" such issues in their sermons in the year preceding the survey. Table 4.11 indicates that almost all the California clergy reported having touched on what they considered to be "controversial social or political topics" at least once in the year preceding the survey. More than half had done so eight or more times. Yet, a much smaller percentage reported that they had dealt mainly with such subjects in their sermons. Only about a quarter indicated that they had done so five or more times in the past year; a nearly equal percentage indicated that they had never once done so.

The same pattern of behavior was encountered when the clergymen were questioned more specifically about the content of their sermons. The respondents who indicated that they had at least touched on a controversial social or political issue from the pulpit were presented with a list of topics and asked which ones they had covered in their sermons during the preceding year. The subjects ranged from racial issues and poverty to more individual problems, such as alcoholism and drug abuse. We see in Table 4.12 that a substantial proportion of the California ministers reported having at least touched on these topics in their sermons. Almost all the respondents indi-

Table 4.11. Ministers Are More Likely to Touch On than to Deal Mainly with Controversial Social or Political Topics in Their Sermons

Dealt with "Controversial Social or Political Topics" during "Past Year"	Dealt Mainly With	Touched On But Did Not Deal Mainly With
8 or more times	13%	53%
5–7 times	12	15
3–4 times	23	17
Once or twice	27	9
Never	24	4
Not applicable (not in a preaching position)	1	1
	100%	99%
	(1567)	(1570)

cated that they had discussed racial problems, world and national poverty, and crime and juvenile delinquency from the pulpit in the year preceding the survey, and most had mentioned sexual conduct, the UN and world peace, the use of drugs, and alcoholism. As previously, however, the most common way of dealing with the subjects was to introduce them into a sermon indirectly. Only on racial problems do we find even close to half the parish ministers giving directly political sermons. Relatively few of the California clergy reported that their sermons dealt mainly with any of the other topics listed in Table 4.12 in the politically tumultuous year that preceded the survey.

Table 4.12. Ministers Are More Likely to Touch On than to Deal Mainly with Specific Political and Moral Topics in Their Sermons

	Dealt Mainly with Topic	Touched On but Did Not Deal Mainly with Topic	Did Not Deal with Topic	Total
Racial problems	48%	49	3	100% (1477)
World poverty	29%	60	11	100% (1469)
National poverty	23%	62	15	100% (1466)
Crime, juvenile delinquency	21%	71	9	100% (1469)
Sexual conduct	18%	63	19	100% (1471)
The UN and world peace	18%	56	26	100% (1449)
The use of drugs	15%	69	16	100% (1473)
Alcoholism	15%	62	23	100% (1468)
Black power	8%	52	40	100% (1465)
Capital punishment	8%	40	52	100% (1465)
The conduct of public officials	5%	47	48	100% (1459)
Birth control	3%	32	65	100% (1458)
Abortion laws	2%	25	73	100% (1458)

Although the data cannot tell us the exact content of the ministers' "political" sermons, it is clear from these reports that most pastors prefer to work controversial issues into their remarks rather than to elevate them to be the prime focus of concern. To many of our respondents, this distinction is a crucial one. The following are typical of the comments written in response to these questions by both modernist and traditionalist clergymen:

... a minister should never preach a whole sermon on such topics. He should preach the Gospel and these items will come in at the proper points. (American Baptist)

I don't recall ever preaching an entire sermon on any of these important subjects, but I mention most of them often.   (Methodist)

Though I have only delivered two sermons that were strictly on social issues, most of my sermons contain in "some part" remarks on social issues.   (Methodist)

Not specifically and exclusively. Bible-centered preaching applies to many of these issues, but I don't start with these topics. (American Lutheran)

I would say Christian attitudes about these things are often brought in—not, however, to the full thrust of the measure for the day.   (Missouri Synod)

Such responses suggest that most Protestant ministers might be dealing with social and political topics in highly generalized and evasive terms, although by the nature of our survey we cannot be certain that this is the case. In any event, 62 percent of our respondents reported having taken at one time or another a stand from the pulpit on a political issue.

Once more, we find that clergymen in liberal denominations most often use the pulpit as a platform for ethical leadership. They most often speak out on social and political topics in their sermons and most often focus on such subjects. They are also the most likely to report having taken a stand on a political issue at the pulpit. Activism at the pulpit, therefore, is much greater within liberal than conservative Protestant church groups, as is social activism in its other forms. This again means that liberal views are more often expressed in the sermons given by Protestant ministers than are opinions of a conservative cast.

The types of subject included in Table 4.12 also allow us to investigate the contrasting ethical orientations of modernist and traditionalist clergymen. As we saw in the last chapter, traditionalist-oriented ministers are more likely to favor stronger state regulation of individual conduct in such areas as drugs, drinking, gambling, and "obscenity." Since these ministers are most concerned about questions of public morality because they view the related behaviors as sins, thus as barriers to the obtainment of religious salvation, we hypothesized that these ministers would be most ethically involved not in such social and political matters as racism and poverty but in efforts designed to regulate public morality: to close down gambling establishments, to keep communities dry, to restrict pornography, to punish drug users, or to fight the new sexual morality. Public actions of this type were not as widespread in the 1960s as they once were in the United States, except perhaps in the areas of drug regulation or sex education. The only such issue to receive statewide attention in California in the years just prior to our survey was an initiative proposal in 1966 to write the state's legal definition of obscenity in stricter (and probably unconstitutional) terms. The proposed initiative failed to pass despite substantial publicity, and we did not ask our respondents about it. However, some of the more conservative ministers volunteered that they had campaigned on behalf of the initiative measure.

We asked the California ministers whether they had covered a number of subjects pertaining to individual conduct and immorality in their sermons, as well as more directly political subjects. If our observations about the contrasting ethical orientations of Protestant clergymen are correct, we would expect our respondents to deal with these topics differently. We would expect the modernist clergy to spend more time discussing social and political subjects in their sermons and the traditionalist clergy to give more attention to problems of individual conduct and immorality. Table 4.13 confirms our expectations, showing that modernist clergymen are much more likely to give sermons dealing mainly with or touching on political subjects. This was true of all five topics of this type included in the survey: racial problems, world poverty, national poverty, the UN and world peace, and black power. As in the case of the ministers' activist behavior, the differences were consistent and fairly substantial.

Table 4.14 presents the relationship between the clergy's religious orientations and the percentage of ministers who gave a sermon during the year preceding the survey on the four subjects dealing more with issues of individual sin and immorality: crime and juvenile delinquency, sexual conduct, the use of drugs, and alcoholism. In contrast to Table 4.13, traditionalist-oriented clergymen appear to be somewhat more likely to include such topics in their sermons than their modernist colleagues. They are particularly more likely to speak out from the pulpit on sexual conduct and alcoholism—two of the traditional areas of concern for conservative churchmen.[14]

Thus our proposition concerning the contrasting ethical concerns of modernist and traditionalist clergymen seems to be a valid one. Again, our ignorance of the content of the parish clergy's sermons about these issues is a major limitation in our use of the survey instrument. From information gathered elsewhere in the questionnaire, however, we would surmise that the modernist and traditionalist ministers are often saying quite different things even when they are discussing the same issues. The reactions of most modernist clergymen to urban unrest, for example, is to call for measures

Table 4.13. Modernist Ministers Are More Likely to Deal with Political Topics in Their Sermons

	Religious Orientation[a]				
	1	2	3	4	5
RACIAL PROBLEMS					
Dealt mainly with	70%	59%	52%	34%	21%
Touched on	29	39	45	63	73
Did not deal with	1	1	2	4	6
	100%	99%	99%	101%	100%
	(299)	(308)	(291)	(295)	(293)
WORLD POVERTY					
Dealt mainly with	43%	34%	30%	28%	12%
Touched on	53	54	62	62	68
Did not deal with	4	12	8	10	20
	100%	100%	100%	100%	100%
	(298)	(307)	(290)	(293)	(290)
NATIONAL POVERTY					
Dealt mainly with	38%	28%	23%	17%	10%
Touched on	56	61	65	65	62
Did not deal with	5	11	12	18	28
	99%	100%	100%	100%	100%
	(297)	(305)	(290)	(292)	(291)
THE UN AND WORLD PEACE					
Dealt mainly with	34%	23%	18%	8%	4%
Touched on	56	59	61	54	51
Did not deal with	10	18	21	38	45
	100%	100%	100%	100%	100%
	(296)	(301)	(284)	(290)	(287)
BLACK POWER					
Dealt mainly with	18%	10%	5%	4%	2%
Touched on	60	59	52	46	43
Did not deal with	22	31	43	49	55
	100%	100%	100%	99%	100%
	(298)	(306)	(288)	(293)	(289)

[a] On this 5-point scale, 1 is most modernist; 5 is most traditionalist.

Table 4.14. Traditionalist Ministers Are Somewhat More Likely to Deal with Moral Topics in Their Sermons

	Religious Orientation[a]				
	1	2	3	4	5
CRIME, JUVENILE DELINQUENCY					
Dealt mainly with	19%	16%	19%	26%	23%
Touched on	67	72	71	70	74
Did not deal with	14	12	10	4	3
	100%	100%	100%	100%	100%
	(297)	(304)	(290)	(293)	(294)
SEXUAL CONDUCT					
Dealt mainly with	16%	17%	18%	17%	19%
Touched on	54	58	60	70	74
Did not deal with	30	25	22	13	7
	100%	100%	100%	100%	100%
	(297)	(307)	(288)	(295)	(293)
THE USE OF DRUGS					
Dealt mainly with	15%	16%	12%	17%	17%
Touched on	66	68	66	69	75
Did not deal with	19	16	22	14	8
	100%	100%	100%	100%	100%
	(299)	(307)	(288)	(295)	(293)
ALCOHOLISM					
Dealt mainly with	11%	13%	14%	16%	19%
Touched on	52	63	57	68	70
Did not deal with	37	24	29	16	12
	100%	100%	100%	100%	101%
	(296)	(306)	(289)	(293)	(293)

[a] On this 5-point scale, 1 is most modernist; 5 is most traditionalist.

dealing with the causes of poverty and racism—for a national fair housing law, minimum income guarantees, and help for black-owned businesses and institutions. Traditionalist ministers support some of these remedies but are more likely to favor tougher police practices in riot areas or stronger legislation to punish crime in the streets as a response to urban riots.

Not only do modernist and traditionalist clergymen frequently discuss different topics in their sermons, then, we also have reason to believe that they say different things about the same subjects. Further substantiation of this thesis is provided in Table 4.15. To obtain an idea about how the ministers themselves define their ethical objectives as preachers, we asked them how much importance they attached to four commonly stated purposes of sermons: to "illustrate the type of life a Christian should follow," to "provide spiritual uplifting and moral comfort to those who are distressed," to "apply Christian standards to judge human institutions and behavior," and to "point out the existence of human sin." We asked the ministers whether they regarded such objectives to be "very important," "fairly important," "somewhat important," or "not important at all."

Table 4.15 reveals a strong tendency for our respondents—particularly the more traditionalist ones—to regard all four goals as "very important." Our questions thus did not discriminate among the Protestant clergymen as

Table 4.15. Modernist and Traditionalist Religious Beliefs Are Related to Ministers' Views on Purpose of Sermons

Following Purposes are "Very Important" in Sermons	Religious Orientation[a]					
	1	2	3	4	5	Total
"Illustrate the type of life a Christian should follow"	64% (304)	77% (317)	78% (312)	86% (306)	93% (323)	80% (1562)
"Provide spiritual uplifting and moral comfort to those who are distressed"	49% (305)	68% (316)	75% (312)	82% (306)	92% (323)	73% (1562)
"Apply Christian standards to judge human institutions and behavior"	73% (304)	75% (316)	71% (311)	70% (305)	76% (319)	73% (1555)
"Point out the existence of human sin"	29% (303)	35% (317)	51% (311)	67% (306)	86% (323)	54% (1560)

[a] On this 5-point scale, 1 is most modernist; 5 is most traditionalist.

much as we would have liked them to. Nevertheless, the apparent differences in their responses serve to confirm the point we have been making. The traditionalist ministers were more likely than their modernist colleagues to attach importance to three of these goals; they were particularly more likely to regard pointing out the existence of human sin as an important objective in their sermons. We suspect that our respondents did not always interpret the stated goals in the same manner, but these patterns are generally consistent with our expectations.

The third objective listed in Table 4.15—applying Christian standards to judge human institutions and behavior—was designed to appeal to the modernist clergy, and the modernist ministers did in fact most often name this goal as being "very important." The traditionalist clergy were about equally likely to give the same response, but fewer rated this objective "very important," as they had for the other selections.

The ministers' own descriptions of their roles as preachers thus verify what we have said about the contrasting ethical orientations of the modernist and traditionalist clergy. The former are concerned in their ethics largely with applying Christian principles to societal conditions; the latter with helping the individual avoid sinful conduct. As we have seen throughout this chapter, these divergent religious orientations have major consequences for the pattern of clergy participation in public affairs. Modernist ministers hold relatively liberal positions on the legislation of public morality, as well as on more political issues. As a result of their religious orientations, however, the modernists are most outspoken on questions pertaining to race, poverty, and foreign policy. Traditionalist ministers, in contrast, hold generally conservative positions in these issue-areas and tend to become most involved in such moral issues as drinking, drugs, sex, and pornography. In each instance, then, the views that reach Protestant laymen (and the general public) are likely to distort the real range of opinions found within the Protestant ministry. In the case of issues of social or political consequence, the distortion will be a liberal one; in the case of issues of individual sin and immorality, the distortion will be conservative.

These patterns of activism thus help explain the existence of two common but contradictory images of the clergy: that of being highly pious protectors of the community's moral standards, and that of being highly militant advocates of civil rights and peace. We have demonstrated that the views of Protestant ministers tend to be fairly conservative on the former issues, fairly liberal on the latter. We see now that the ethical concerns of modernist and traditionalist ministers serve to accentuate further these distinctive beliefs held by members of the ministerial profession.

Ministers and Politics. Our major concern in this study lies not with issues of personal vice and immorality but with the political questions that divided Americans during the 1960s and appear to be firmly rooted in the country's institutions and ideology: race, poverty, and foreign interventions. As we have pointed out, the 1960s were a time of unusual public awareness and political activism, marked by civil rights demonstrations, urban riots, growing student activism and alienation, and mounting opposition to the country's actions in Vietnam. The decade ended with many individuals questioning the ability of the country's leaders and institutions to deal with these problems, and searching for new social and political forms of existence.

A substantial proportion of parish ministers in liberal Protestant denominations joined in these reevaluations of American society and in the efforts to solve problems posed by racism, poverty, and foreign affairs. In considerable numbers, they petitioned public officials on these issues, made public statements, and spoke out from the pulpit. Many parish clergymen also took their ethical commitments to the streets in acts of civil protest or disobedience. Although our survey suggests that Protestant clergymen may not always deal with political issues in a direct or forceful manner, it does show that they are among the most socially active groups in American society. Thus even though the parish clergy in California may not have provided the leadership on public issues that some may demand or wish of them, we find them to have been highly committed in their actions as well as their rhetoric in challenging existing inequities and injustices.

All Protestant ministers were not, of course, equally active in these political controversies; nor are all committed to an action-oriented church. In the next chapter, we take a broader look at the social activism of the California ministers and at the characteristics of the clergy activists and nonactivists. We also seek to assess the impact of the ministers' religious and political commitments on their involvement in controversial public issues.

NOTES AND REFERENCES

1.   Liston Pope, *Millhands and Preachers* (New Haven, Conn.: Yale University Press, 1942).

2.   Ernest Q. Campbell and Thomas F. Pettigrew, *Christians in Racial Crisis: A Study of Little Rock's Ministry* (Washington, D.C.: Public Affairs Press, 1959). See also Jeffrey K. Hadden and Raymond C. Rymph, "Social Structure and Civil Rights Involvement: A Case Study of Protestant Ministers," *Social Forces*, **45** (September 1966), pp. 51–61.

3.   More recently, case studies have been made of (*a*) the attempt of the Presbyterian Church to bring Saul Alinsky into Oakland, California; (*b*) community organization in

Chicago; and (*c*) a struggle with Eastman Kodak in Rochester, New York, over hiring practices. See Robert Lee and Russell Galloway, *The Schizophrenic Church: Conflict over Community Organization* (Philadelphia: Westminster, 1969); Walter M. Stuhr, Jr., *The Public Style: A Study of the Community Participation of Protestant Ministers* (Chicago: Center for the Scientific Study of Religion, 1972); and William C. Martin, *Christians in Conflict* (Chicago: Center for the Scientific Study of Religion, 1972), respectively.

4. This reverse wording caused some confusion among the electorate at first, but it appeared to have little effect on the outcome of the balloting. See Raymond E. Wolfinger and Fred I. Greenstein, "The Repeal of Fair Housing in California: An Analysis of Referendum Voting," *American Political Science Review*, **62** (September 1968), pp. 753–769.

5. For a brief account of the campaign over Proposition 14, see Thomas W. Casstevens, *Politics, Housing and Race Relations: California's Rumford Act and Proposition 14* (Berkeley: Institute of Governmental Studies, University of California, Berkeley, June 1967), pp. 53–70.

6. See *Ibid.*, p. 63; and Wolfinger and Greenstein, *op. cit.* This statement is true of white, not black voters; the latter became more opposed to the amendment as the campaign progressed.

7. For a review of the farm work strike, see John Dunne, *Delano: The Story of the California Grape Strike* (New York: Farrar, Straus, and Giroux, 1967).

8. *Ibid.*, p. 22 (emphasis added).

9. Ministers in the San Joaquin Valley tended to be slightly more conservative than ministers elsewhere on the other two issues studied as well. However, the differences in attitudes were much greater on the strike issue. The regions are composed of the following California counties: North Coast—Del Norte, Humboldt, Lake, Mendocino, Napa, Sonoma; Mountain—Alpine, Amador, Calaveras, El Dorado, Inyo, Lassen, Modoc, Nono, Nevada, Placer, Plumas, Shasta, Sierra, Siskiyou, Trinity, Toulumne, Yuba; Sacramento area—Butte, Colusa, Glenn, Sacramento, Solano, Sutter, Tehama, Yolo; San Francisco Bay area—Alameda, Contra Costa, Marin, San Francisco, San Mateo, Santa Clara; Central coast—Monterey, San Benito, San Luis Obispo, Santa Cruz; San Joaquin Valley—Fresno, Kern, Kings, Madera, Mariposa, Merced, San Joaquin, Stanislaus, Tulare; Southern California—Imperial, Los Angeles, Orange, Riverside, San Bernardino, San Diego, Santa Barbara. Ventura.

10. At the time the survey began, North Vietnam was being bombed; midway through the survey President Johnson announced a partial halt to this bombing.

11. For a bibliographical review of the involvement of clergymen in American wars, see Nelson R. Burr, *A Critical Bibliography of Religion in America, Vol. 4* (Princeton, N.J.: Princeton University Press, 1961), pp. 621–645. See also Toyomasa Fuse,"Religion, War and the Institutional Dilemma: A Sociological Interpretation," *Journal of Peace Research*, **2** (1968), pp. 196–210.

12. Unpublished findings collected by Sidney Verba and Richard Brody of Stanford University. Of course we are working with samples of different constituencies. The ministerial survey was limited to California, and the data provided by Verba and Brody are from a national sample. With the exception of the South, however, little regional variations existed in the public's positions on the war.

13. Where the data allow, we make such comparisons in the next chapter. The most recent information on the political involvement of Americans is found in Sidney Verba

and Norman H. Nie, *Participation in America: Political Democracy and Social Equality* (New York: Harper & Row, 1972).

14.   As in the last chapter, we find that Lutheran ministers are less involved than their colleagues in the drinking issue. Almost three-quarters of our Lutheran respondents reported that they had discussed alcoholism in one of their sermons during the past year. But when we control for their religious beliefs, we find that they did not discuss the issue as often as clergymen in the other six denominations surveyed. This relationship did not exist, however, for the other three issues dealing with individual moral conduct.

NEW BREED ACTIVISM IN CALIFORNIA

5. A substantial proportion of the California clergy take generally liberal positions on political issues, are committed to an action-oriented church, and involve themselves in public controversies such as the fair housing referendum and the war in Vietnam. How we wish to evaluate the extent of social activism among our respondents obviously depends on what perspective we take in interpreting these patterns of behavior. On the one hand, those familiar with the church's claim of social and moral relevance may be struck by the large number of Protestant ministers who remained inactive during such compelling public controversies as the war in Vietnam or the open housing debates; they may also be disappointed to learn that relatively few clergymen address themselves directly to social and political topics in their sermons. Such persons might choose to emphasize the lack of ethical involvement among our respondents, concluding that relatively few Protestant ministers have committed themselves to an activist ministry. On the other hand, those aware of the usual rates of political participation among the American public—or even among similarly educated elite groups in American society—are likely to be impressed by the large numbers of clergymen who are speaking out on public issues. They are likely to see Protestant clergymen as among the most politically active groups in American society, and the Protestant ministry as one of the most socially committed of occupations.

To some extent, then, the reader must decide how to interpret these patterns of activism—whether to be impressed or unimpressed by the percentage of Protestant ministers we have shown to be socially active. Since we are writing largely from the perspective of politics and political science, we must reemphasize the unusually high rates of political activism among our respondents. Those who think that organized religion has a unique moral or ethical function to play in secular society, however, may well take an opposite point of view. In a presentation of some of these data elsewhere, the latter viewpoint receives more attention.[1]

In this chapter, we look more closely at the characteristics and attitudes of the California ministers we have found to be most involved in controversial political issues—those who have sometimes been referred to as members of the "new breed." We develop a scale of social activism to use in ranking our respondents and offer a tentative definition of new breed activism in California. These ministers are distinguished from their colleagues principally by their religious and political orientations and by their membership in certain Protestant denominations, although other differences can be found between the activists and nonactivists. We also consider the reports of the California ministers themselves about the sources of their activism and nonactivism.

A Scale of New Breed Activism. Chapter 4 described the actions the California clergymen had taken to express themselves on three controversial public issues and mentioned some of the topics they had discussed in their sermons. Table 5.1 provides a more general summary of clergy activism by showing the proportion of California clergymen who reported that they had ever taken any of a series of actions to express their political views or to persuade others. As a group, Protestant ministers appear to be fairly high participants in public affairs. Most have engaged in conventional means of expressing their opinions on public issues; almost all have at one time or another taken a public position on a political issue; about two-thirds have organized a study group within their church to discuss public affairs or have taken a stand from the pulpit on a public issue; and just under half have publicly supported a political candidate or organized a social action group within their church. Perhaps the most surprising of these statistics is the number of parish ministers who have participated in a civil rights protest march: 24 percent of the clergymen in our survey. In assessing this figure, we should remember that our sample contains several highly conservative denominations; in the more liberal denominations, up to two-fifths of our respondents had engaged in such an act of public protest.[2]

Comparable information does not exist on the activism of other groups and, of course, could not be obtained on several of these dimensions. In some of these areas, however, contrasts can be made. For example, 61 percent of the California clergymen reported having personally contacted a public official, but Sidney Verba and Norman H. Nie found that only 20 percent

Table 5.1. Involvement of California Ministers in Various Acts of Ethical Leadership

Leadership Behavior	Percentage Taking Action Named
CONVENTIONAL LEADERSHIP	
Used the pulpit or church bulletins in their present church to urge parishioners to vote in a national election (N = 1561)	91%
Wrote to a public official (N = 1562)	74%
Signed or circulated a petition (N = 1570)	73%
Personally contacted a public official (N = 1550)	61%
Wrote a letter to the editor of a newspaper (N = 1562)	50%
PUBLIC LEADERSHIP	
Publicly (not from the pulpit) took a stand on some political issue (N = 1570)	84%
Publicly (not from the pulpit) supported a political candidate (N = 1569)	49%
CHURCH LEADERSHIP	
Organized a study group within the church to discuss public affairs (N = 1575)	65%
Took a stand from the pulpit on some political issue (N = 1569)	62%
Gave at least three sermons in the past year which dealt mainly with social or political topics (N = 1567)	48%
Organized a social action group within the local church in order to accomplish directly some social or political goal (N = 1568)	47%
PROTEST LEADERSHIP	
Participated in a civil rights protest march (N = 1574)	24%
Participated in an antiwar protest march (N = 1573)	7%
Engaged in civil rights civil disobedience (risked arrest to symbolize protest) (N = 1571)	5%
Engaged in antiwar civil disobedience (N = 1569)	2%

of the American public has ever contacted a local government official and 18 percent a state or national official.[3] Similarly, whereas 74 percent of our respondents said that they had written to a public official and 50 percent to the editor of a newspaper, the 1968 national survey conducted by the Michigan Survey Research Center shows that the comparable rates for the public are 20 and 2 percent, respectively. It is not surprising that the clergy are so much more active than the mass public, but the percentages for professionals in the SRC survey are not much higher—37 and 3 percent, respectively.[4]

Finally, a 1972 survey conducted by the Survey Research Center at the University of California, Berkeley, contains some useful questions on other dimensions of activism, although this information was collected four years after our own and covered only the liberal San Francisco Bay area. The Berkeley survey revealed that 39 percent of the public had talked to or written to someone in government at least once, 53 percent had signed a complaint or petition, 14 percent had taken part in a peaceful protest rally or march, and 4 percent had taken part in a protest that turned violent; the figures for professionals alone were 68, 79, 32, and 7 percent, respectively —roughly comparable to what we found for clergy throughout the state.[5]

Thus California clergymen are far more active politically than the public nationally and are least as active as professionals in the Bay Area. As political participants, then, we would rank Protestant ministers quite high, if not above most other professionals.[6] Again, those who would expect more of clergymen than of others must evaluate individually the degree of ethical commitment reflected in these figures.

In any case, we use the information provided in Table 5.1 to construct our scale of activist behavior. The major purposes of such a scale are to determine how many of our respondents we wish to count among the new breed and what characteristics distinguish these ministers from their colleagues. Our task in this respect is rather straightforward because the clergy's social activism, like their beliefs, is so highly structured. When we apply statistical techniques to these data, we are able to rank or scale these acts of ethical leadership on the part of the clergy on a Guttman scale from the most "difficult" to the "easiest."[7] As a rule, the ministers who had engaged in one of the more difficult acts in Table 5.1 (e.g., participation in an antiwar protest march) had engaged in all or almost all the more popular forms of ethical expression as well. In this way, we are able to develop a scale of social activism and to rank each of our respondents on it. The most activist-oriented ministers are those who took the most difficult actions listed in Table 5.1.

The ministers' positions on this scale of activism are arranged by denomination in Table 5.2. Eighty-two of the parish ministers, just over 5 percent of those surveyed, are classified as the most "highly active" of our respondents. These clergymen, who had risked arrest to express their support of civil rights or to oppose the war in Vietnam, can be regarded as the hard core of the new breed activists among the California clergy. Another 318 ministers, 20 percent of the respondents, reported that they had participated in a civil rights or an antiwar protest march, although they had not committed acts of civil disobedience. We also consider these ministers to be among the new breed clergy in California. Taken together, then, we estimate that about 25 percent of the parish clergymen in the nine denominations studied have committed themselves to an activist ministry. Not only had these ministers engaged in an act of civil protest to express their ethical views, but, with a few exceptions, they had also participated in most of those other acts of ethical leadership under consideration in this study.

Table 5.2.   Denominational Distribution of New Breed Activism

Denomination	Activism[a]						Total
	1	2	3	4	5	6	
Methodist	6%	34	36	10	13	1	100% (354)
United Church of Christ	15%	28	30	10	15	2	100% (137)
Episcopal	9%	27	25	14	22	3	100% (207)
Presbyterian	4%	27	33	17	17	2	100% (226)
Lutheran Church in America	2%	20	26	24	24	3	99% (87)
American Baptist	4%	10	31	27	25	3	100% (147)
American Lutheran Church	2%	6	23	24	35	11	101% (118)
Missouri Synod-Lutheran	1%	2	19	30	32	16	100% (134)
Southern Baptist	—	1	14	36	38	12	101% (170)
Total	5%	20	28	19	23	5	100% (1580)

[a] On this 6-point scale, 1 is highly active; 6 is inactive.

   This, we should note, is a fairly generous estimate of the extent of new breed activism in California. Not all these parish ministers possess the attitudes and attributes commonly associated with the activist clergy. If we include among the new breed only clergymen who hold consistently liberal views on political issues and consistently modernist positions on religious questions, we must lower our estimate of clergy activism somewhat. If we include only clergymen who possess more radical attitudes or who openly challenge the status quo, we must lower our estimate of new breed activism considerably.

The remaining respondents are grouped in Table 5.2 according to the scaling procedures just described into four additional categories. Seventy-seven ministers reported that they had never engaged in any of these 10 acts of ethical leadership and are classified as "inactive" on this measure.

Table 5.2 indicates that the denominational distribution of clergy activism follows much the same pattern found in the previous chapters in analyzing the respondents' belief systems. New breed activism is highest in the United Church of Christ and the Methodist Church, where about two-fifths of the clergy are classified as among the new breed. It is lowest in the Missouri Synod-Lutheran Church and the Southern Baptist Convention, where less than 2 percent of the ministers fall into the new breed category. Between these two extremes, the clergy's activism is distributed in about the same manner as their ethical and political beliefs. It is higher in the Episcopal Church, the Presbyterian Church, and the Lutheran Church of America; lower in the American Baptist Convention and the American Lutheran Church.

Characteristics of the New Breed Clergy.   Our major purpose in developing a scale of activism is to describe the characteristics of the new breed clergy. Among other things, we examine their personal attributes, their professional characteristics, their religious and political attitudes, and the factors they feel most influence their ethical behavior. Table 5.3 summarizes some of the more important personal characteristics of the clergy activists. (We have summed our percentages differently in this and the following tables, since we want to describe the attributes of those who are socially active, rather than the activism of those with certain attributes.) Almost a third of the new breed clergy in California come from the large and predominantly liberal United Methodist Church. As we see later, Methodist ministers are not only generally committed to an action-oriented church in their religoius and political orientations but are also encouraged in their activist behavior by their denomination's organization and leadership. The remaining new breed clergy in our sample come largely from the United Church of Christ, the Episcopal Church, and the Presbyterian Church.

Table 5.3 also reveals that although the clergy activists tend to be somewhat younger than their less ethically involved colleagues, their ranks contain ministers of all ages. The "average" new breed activist in California is in his late thirties—well beyond the usual age for members of the youth culture. A considerable proportion are in their fifties or sixties.

Some generational differences are, of course, evident in these patterns. To see them more clearly, we should sum our percentages differently—asking how many parish clergymen in different age groups had engaged in these

Table 5.3. Personal Characteristics of New Breed Activists

	Activism[a]					
	1	2	3	4	5	6
DENOMINATION						
Methodist	27%	37%	29%	11%	13%	3%
United Church of Christ	24	12	9	5	6	3
Episcopal	23	18	12	9	13	8
Presbyterian	12	19	17	13	11	5
Lutheran Church in America	2	5	5	7	6	4
American Baptist	7	5	10	13	10	6
American Lutheran	2	2	6	9	11	17
Missouri Synod-Lutheran	1	1	6	13	12	29
Southern Baptist	—	—[b]	5	20	18	26
	100%	99%	99%	100%	100%	101%
	(82)	(318)	(441)	(305)	(357)	(77)
AGE						
29 or under	17%	11%	3%	6%	6%	4%
30–34	21	20	14	12	13	9
35–39	20	21	16	16	17	13
40–44	10	10	15	14	14	13
45–49	13	12	15	12	18	14
50–59	11	19	28	27	21	28
60 or over	8	7	9	13	10	19
	100%	100%	100%	100%	99%	100%
	(82)	(316)	(440)	(303)	(356)	(77)
RACE						
White	90%	96%	97%	97%	96%	99%
Black	9	1	1	1	1	—
Other	1	3	2	1	3	1
	100%	100%	100%	99%	100%	100%
	(82)	(316)	(440)	(304)	(357)	(77)

[a] On this 6-point scale, 1 is highly active; 6 is inactive.

[b] Less than 1 percent.

various acts of ethicalism. In this instance, we find that almost half (48 percent) of our respondents who were 29 years old or younger had participated in a protest march or in an act of civil disobedience. This was true of a third of the ministers who were in their thirties and a fifth of those who were older yet. Thus the younger parish clergymen in California were clearly the most ethically involved in controversial public issues. Despite such general differences, however, the most salient fact to emerge from these age patterns is the commitment of both young and old Protestant ministers to an activist church. The youngest members of the ministerial profession are most socially active, but they are not alone in providing ethical leadership on public issues.

The last personal attribute described in Table 5.3, the ministers' race, is probably more significant for what it tells us about the Protestant ministry than about the distribution of clergy activism. Ninety-seven percent of our respondents reported that they were white; 1 percent were black. (The remaining "other" category is composed of ministers of oriental and hispanic descent.) Thus although we discover that black ministers are disproportionately active in expressing their ethical views, so few belong to these nine mainline Protestant denominations as represented in our sample that they add little to the overall proportion of new breed clergy.

In addition to these characteristics, the activist ministers are more likely to have been raised in the western part of the United States, in urban areas, and in middle-class families. These differences, however, merely reflect the recruitment patterns of the more liberal denominations surveyed. Within each denomination, there was no relationship between such background characteristics and the respondents' social activism.

Table 5.4 indicates some consistent differences in the professional characteristics of the activists and the nonactivists. Clergymen who are most involved in public affairs tend to serve larger, upper-middle-class churches located in urban areas. In part, these patterns again reflect the different organizational patterns of the nine denominations surveyed. The parish churches of the more liberal denominations are, as a group, larger, more wealthy, and more urban than those of the more conservative church groups. Within the liberal denominations, however, social activism is nevertheless more common in such churches.

Table 5.4 also points to certain exceptions to these patterns among the most activist group of clergymen. Being somewhat younger, many are just beginning their careers and are located in small rural churches or are assisting at a more urban parish. We see in future chapters that this most activist group of ministers are distinguished from their colleagues in other ways as well.

Table 5.4. Professional Characteristics of New Breed Activists

	Activism[a]					
	1	2	3	4	5	6
POSITION						
Minister	76%	80%	89%	89%	90%	91%
Assistant or associate minister	21	17	9	8	8	8
Other	4	3	2	2	2	1
	101%	100%	100%	99%	100%	100%
	(82)	(316)	(440)	(303)	(357)	(77)
CHURCH SIZE						
Less than 50	4%	3%	3%	7%	7%	12%
50–149	33	16	18	29	27	31
150–299	21	19	20	28	29	20
300–499	11	23	18	15	15	18
500–1000	18	23	28	14	13	14
More than 1000	13	17	13	8	10	5
	100%	101%	100%	101%	101%	100%
	(82)	(316)	(439)	(304)	(356)	(77)
CLASS COMPOSITION OF CHURCH						
Working class	18%	8%	15%	25%	23%	38%
Lower middle class	31	35	36	35	39	30
Upper middle class	51	57	50	40	38	32
	100%	100%	101%	100%	100%	100%
	(81)	(316)	(437)	(299)	(353)	(77)
SIZE OF COMMUNITY						
Small farming or rural community	5%	5%	5%	7%	8%	9%
Small town	6	8	10	13	15	16
Medium-sized town	5	7	10	10	12	11
Suburb	25	38	32	27	28	21
Small city	25	17	25	21	18	21
Large city	35	25	18	22	19	22
	101%	100%	100%	100%	100%	100%
	(81)	(318)	(436)	(303)	(357)	(76)

[a] On this 6-point scale, 1 is highly active; 6 is inactive.

The distribution of a final professional characteristic of clergy activists—their involvement in national, regional, and local church affairs—appears in Table 5.5. It was believed that Protestant ministers who were most active in public affairs might also be more "cosmopolitan" in their professional roles, whereas the less active, traditionalist clergy would have more "local" professional orientations (i.e., they would be more heavily involved in the life of the parish church than in broader occupational organizations and concerns). The questions in Table 5.5 are among a number touching on this local–cosmopolitan dimension. We see here that the clergy activists have higher involvement in "community service groups" and, to a lesser extent, in local councils of churches or ministerial associations. They are not, however, any more active in regional or national church affairs. As we see later, they spend the same amount of time in most of their duties within the local church as the traditionalist and less active clergy. Thus although clergy activists are most heavily involved in politics and in community organizations, they do not appear to be more cosmopolitan in their professional roles than those clergymen who are less ethically active.

The Attitudes of the New Breed Clergy. What the new breed clergy think is as important as their personal and professional characteristics. Are the ministers whom we have found to be activists relatively homogeneous in their religious, ethical, and political views? Do they take consistently liberal positions on public issues? How many of the new breed clergy possess attitudes that might be regarded as more radical—similar to those associated with the New Left during the late 1960s?

When we examine the attitudes of the most socially active clergymen, we confirm expectations stemming from our previous findings: the most active ministers are largely religious modernists, political liberals, Democrats, critics of the church's past role in public affairs, and supporters of clergy activism and of an action-oriented church. At the same time, we find relatively few ministers who we might describe as New Left activists. We find many more, in fact, who view most political issues conservatively or who are predominantly traditionalists in their religious orientations.

Table 5.6 shows the relationship between the activism of the California ministers and their positions on our measure of religious beliefs. We see the expected strong association between social activism and religious modernism —most of the clergy in our two most activist groups of respondents are located at the modernist end of our religious scale; most of the inactive clergy are at the traditionalist end. Virtually the same pattern exists if we use the ministers' own designations as our measure of religious belief. Most of the

Table 5.5. Activists and Nonactivists Are Equally Involved in Denominational Organizations; Activists are More Involved in Local Groups

"To what extent do you participate in the activities of the following organizations?"	Activism[a]						Total
	1	2	3	4	5	6	
YOUR REGIONAL CHURCH ORGANI-ZATION							
Quite a lot	43%	50%	48%	48%	43%	43%	47%
Occasionally	39	38	38	39	41	36	39
Very little	17	11	12	12	14	17	13
Never	1	1	2	1	2	4	2
	100%	100%	100%	100%	100%	100%	101%
	(82)	(315)	(435)	(303)	(355)	(75)	(1565)
YOUR NATIONAL CHURCH							
Quite a lot	10%	7%	12%	13%	10%	15%	11%
Occasionally	30	22	29	33	30	37	29
Very little	39	49	43	42	42	29	43
Never	20	22	16	12	18	19	17
	99%	100%	100%	100%	100%	100%	100%
	(79)	(311)	(429)	(296)	(351)	(75)	(1541)

activist clergy regard themselves to be religiously liberal or neoorthodox, whereas most of the less active clergymen classify themselves as religious conservatives or fundamentalists.

There are, however, enough exceptions to these patterns to warrant special attention. Table 5.6 indicates about one-tenth of the clergymen we have included among the new breed—those in our two most activist groups of respondents—hold relatively traditionalist positions on our scale of religious beliefs, and others in this group fall in the middle category on our measure. Similarly, 12 percent of these clergymen call themselves religious conservatives. Thus at least some of the Protestant ministers in California who are highly active in public affairs maintain orthodox views on religious matters.

This condition can be illustrated most clearly by returning to some of the

Table 5.5. *Continued*

"To what extent do you participate in the activities of the following organizations?"	Activism[a]						
	1	2	3	4	5	6	Total
A LOCAL COUNCIL OF CHURCHES OR MINISTERIAL ASSOCIATION							
Quite a lot	45%	49%	49%	37%	35%	16%	42%
Occasionally	27	36	32	36	34	40	34
Very little	20	11	16	20	20	28	18
Never	8	4	3	6	11	16	6
	100%	100%	100%	99%	100%	99%	100%
	(82)	(315)	(437)	(303)	(357)	(75)	(1569)
COMMUNITY SERVICE GROUPS							
Quite a lot	56%	41%	39%	25%	21%	9%	32%
Occasionally	38	41	44	40	38	37	41
Very little	5	15	15	32	36	33	23
Never	1	3	2	3	5	20	4
	100%	100%	100%	100%	100%	100%	100%
	(82)	(316)	(437)	(303)	(355)	(75)	(1568)

[a] On this 6-point scale, 1 is highly active, 6 is inactive.

specific questions we asked the clergy about their religious positions. So doing, we find that a fairly large minority of the activist ministers hold to at least some tenets of Protestant orthodoxy. Among the most activist group of ministers (i.e., those who had engaged in acts of civil disobedience), 30 percent express no doubts about Jesus being the Divine Son of God, 19 percent believe that Jesus walked on water, 15 percent accept the virgin birth as historical fact, and 10 percent believe in the existence of the devil. The comparable figures among the next most active group of clergymen are 40, 19, 20, and 12 percent, respectively. Of more direct relevance, perhaps, are our questions about religious worldliness. Again, some of the socially active clergy gave responses associated with religious otherworldliness. Among the

Table 5.6.   New Breed Activists Have Modernist Religious Beliefs

	Activism[a]					
	1	2	3	4	5	6
Modernist						
1	44%	42%	21%	7%	8%	—
2	38	27	26	12	14	3
3	10	20	23	22	20	9
4	8	9	18	28	25	25
5	—	2	12	31	33	64
Traditionalist						
	100%	100%	100%	100%	100%	101%
	(82)	(318)	(441)	(305)	(357)	(77)

[a] On this 6-point scale, 1 is highly active, 6 is inactive.

most activist group of ministers, 23 percent agree that "if enough men were brought to Christ, social ills would take care of themselves." Fifteen percent of these respondents *disagree* that "it would be better if the church were to place less emphasis on individual sanctification and more on bringing human conditions into conformity with Christian teachings." Finally, 7 percent disagree with the statement that "it is not as important to worry about life after death as about what one can do in this life." The comparable results from the next most active group of ministers are 30, 20, and 10 percent, respectively.

When we examine the political views of the activist clergy, we find much the same pattern exhibited for their religious commitments. Most of those clergymen we have included among the new breed take consistently liberal positions on our measures of political belief. They score high on all three of our political measures—those dealing with economic liberalism and civil rights, foreign policy, and civil protest and disobedience. At the same time, there are some exceptions to these patterns, and about 10 percent of the activists might be considered to be primarily conservative in their political orientation.

Thus although most of those we have included among the new breed activists in California have modernist positions on religious issues and liberal views on political questions, some do not. We investigate the impact of these two belief factors on clergy activism among this group of conservative activists in the next section.

New breed activism is sometimes associated with rather radical politics—with a rejection of the economic and political status quo and with the use of confrontation tactics as a device to effect political change. Indeed, the great number of ministers who risked arrest to show support for civil rights or opposition to the war in Vietnam suggests that many Protestant clergymen are committed to fairly extreme political tactics. Closer examination of the positions of the California activists, however, indicates that relatively few hold attitudes similar to those associated with the New Left during the late 1960s. Table 5.7 presents the ministers' views on several previously reported questions dealing with programs and tactics of the left. According to this table, the most socially active ministers give the most support to such positions, but relatively few subscribe to radical views. Even among clergymen who had committed civil disobedience, we find little evidence of acceptance of confrontation politics, a noninterventionist foreign policy, or government ownership of big business. Somewhat surprisingly, only slightly more than half (54 percent) of these civil protesters agreed that "militant procedures and even violence" can under certain circumstances be legitimate means to bring about changes in the law. Apparently many felt compelled to reject the statement because of the inclusion of the word "violence." Other responses in Table 5.7 reveal that 76 percent of these ministers favored Alinsky-like tactics to organize the poor, 40 percent felt that the United States should never use its military forces to intervene in situations "which communist elements might exploit," 33 percent said that they would approve if their denominations were to sponsor a meeting in which draft cards were turned in or burned, and 17 percent favored government ownership of large corporations.

Such responses indicate that these ministers are much to the "left" of the American public in general, but they can hardly be used to classify even this most activist group of Protestant clergymen among the Radical Left of the era. The percentage of clergymen holding such radical orientations is considerably lower, furthermore, among the next most activist group.

Thus there seems to be only a small group of clergymen whom we might label as Radical Left activists—ministers who are religiously modernist, socially active, who took "left" positions on at least four of these five questions. We find that 21 parish clergymen fit such a description, and all are members of one of the five liberal denominations surveyed. Another 38 gave radical responses to three of the pertinent questions; all but one were members of liberal church groups. At best, we can consider about 4 percent of the parish clergy in California to be Radical Left activists—ministers who were socially active, religious modernists, holding fairly radical views on political issues.

Table 5.7. Few New Breed Activists Have Radical Views on Political Issues

	Activism[a]						
	1	2	3	4	5	6	Total
Feel the church should help the poor to organize essentially as Alinsky suggests	76% (82)	44% (312)	26% (429)	16% (297)	13% (341)	8% (74)	27% (1535)
Agree that "under certain circumstances militant procedures and even violence are legitimate means to bring about changes in the law"	54% (82)	44% (312)	31% (434)	24% (302)	18% (353)	8% (76)	29% (1559)
Agree that the United States should not intervene militarily in "unstable situations which communist elements might exploit"	40% (82)	22% (315)	13% (431)	6% (296)	8% (346)	4% (75)	13% (1544)
Would approve if their denomination were to sponsor a meeting in which draft cards were were turned in or burned	33% (81)	10% (314)	2% (438)	1% (300)	1% (353)	— (76)	5% (1526)
Agree that "it would be better if large corporations such as U.S. Steel were owned by the federal government"	17% (81)	5% (317)	3% (441)	3% (303)	2% (355)	3% (77)	4% (1574)

[a] On this 6-point scale, 1 is highly active; 6 is inactive.

150

Religion, Politics, and Clergy Activism.   It appears that although the California activists have many characteristics in common, they are by no means identical in their personal and professional attributes or even in their religious and political attitudes. The ministers whom we have identified as being among the new breed tend to be members of the more liberal Protestant denominations in California; they are usually somewhat younger than their colleagues; and they often serve large, middle-class congregations. They are also predominantly political liberals and religious modernists.

Enough exceptions do exist to the last pattern to warrant a closer look at the impact of the ministers' religious and political beliefs on their ethical behavior. We have maintained throughout our analysis that the central component of the clergy's belief systems is their religious commitment, and that religious modernism serves to encourage an ethically active ministry. It has sometimes been charged, however, that the church activists are acting more from political than religious convictions in their public involvements —that they have used their positions as religious leaders as an excuse to speak out on political issues on which they have particularly strong opinions. There is no doubt that the ministers' political beliefs figure prominently in their social activism. Both our respondents' religious and political beliefs correlate highly with their activism, and both have a statistically independent effect on their involvement in public issues. Moreover, the clergy themselves, as we will see shortly, say that their political beliefs are an important factor in encouraging their social activism.

There is no method by which we can judge how much each dimension of belief contributes to clergy activism, since most of our activists are both political liberals and religious modernists. However, we can arbitrarily separate our sample to show the relation of these two factors to the ministers' ethical actions and to indicate the number of Protestant clergymen who hold generally congruent or incongruent attitudes along these two belief dimensions. For this purpose, we have divided our respondents in half according to their positions on our scales of religious belief and economic liberalism and civil rights; we consider those in the first half of our sample to be religious modernists and political liberals, respectively, and those in the second half to be religious traditionalists and political conservatives. The results of these classifications, along with the positions of these respondents on our activism scale, are given in Table 5.8. The table tells us, in a more general way, that both these belief factors are independently related to the clergy's social activism. We also see that religious modernism is slightly more related to the ministers' activism than political liberalism (cf. the positions of the conservative modernists with those of the liberal traditionalists). Again this pattern occurred throughout our analysis, showing that the ministers'

Table 5.8.   Both Religious Modernism and Political Liberalism Are Associated with Clergy Activism

	Activism[a]						Total
	1	2	3	4	5	6	
Liberal modernist	12%	38	32	7	10	—[b]	99% (559)
Conservative modernist	3%	18	34	20	22	3	100% (227)
Liberal traditionalist	3%	18	26	20	28	5	100% (216)
Conservative traditionalist	—[b]	4%	22	30	33	10	99% (578)

[a] On this 6-point scale, 1 is highly active; 6 is inactive.
[b] Less than 1 percent.

religious orientations have a somewhat greater impact on their participation in public affairs than their political views.

We can use the designations in Table 5.8 to obtain a rough estimate of how many of the new breed activists hold consistently liberal attitudes toward religious and political issues and how many do not. Summing our totals differently, we find that the members of the two most activist groups of ministers fall into the following attitudinal categories: liberal modernists, 70 percent; conservative modernists, 12 percent; liberal traditionalists, 11 percent; and conservative traditionalists, 7 percent.

Thus most, but not all, of those we have designated as new breed activists are religious modernists and political liberals. In total, 18 percent of the ministers in these nine Protestant denominations held liberal views on both dimensions of belief and reported that they had participated in an act of civil protest.

Denominational Affiliation and Clergy Activism.   Religious and political convictions are not the only factors influencing the manner in which Protestant ministers respond to public issues. Indeed, ministers in certain Protestant denominations are more likely than others to take liberal positions on controversial political questions and to speak out on public issues, regardless of where they stand on our measures of religious and political belief. Such a pattern appeared during all three of the public controversies examined in Chapter 4, as well as in relation to the activist scale we have developed in this chapter. It suggests that conditions in some denominations encourage clergy activism, whereas in the others the opposite may be the case. As we would expect from our previous findings, such encouragement appears to occur most frequently in the more liberal or modernist denominations in our survey. Since we discuss denomination-related influences in the next several chapters, we need not mention this effect further here.

Source of Activism: The Views of the Clergy.   The data we have presented thus far suggest that the religious and political beliefs of Protestant ministers are the primary determinants of their social activism; however, they show that other factors also influence the individuals' ethical behavior. Before turning to these additional influences, we must learn what the California clergy themselves have to say about the sources of their activism and inactivism. We asked our respondents to assess the effects of eight possible factors on their "participation in social action activities."[8] The factors included not only religious and political beliefs but also the clergy's goals as parish ministers, their personalities, the community in which they live, and the attitudes of their local denominational leaders, colleagues, and parishioners.

From the ministers' responses to these questions (Table 5.9), we see that the factors reported to be most encouraging are religious and political beliefs. Sixty-eight percent of the California ministers listed their theological views and 65 percent their political views as generally encouraging to their participation in public affairs; 21 and 28 percent, respectively, saw them as generally discouraging. A similar distribution of responses existed in the ministers' evaluations of their goals as parish pastors. Thus about two-thirds of the clergy see a positive connection between their own beliefs and their social activism.

Three of the factors listed in Table 5.9 deal with the attitudes held by the groups having the most control over the ministerial profession—the clergy's local denominational leaders, colleagues, and parishioners. The first two groups are reported to have a generally positive effect on the ministers' social activism; the last, a predominantly negative one. We examine the impact of these three occupationally related groups on our respondents' activism in the next five chapters.

Of the two remaining factors in Table 5.9—the individual clergymen's personalities and the communities in which their churches are located—only the latter receive attention in our analysis. Clearly, a large percentage of the parish ministers regard their local communities as exerting a predominantly negative effect on their social activism. In part, the ministers' responses to this item reflect the layman's hostility to clergy activism that can be observed in most communities. In addition, however, it is evident that geographical limitations pose certain restraints on the ministers' involvement in public

Table 5.9. Influence Attributed to Various Factors Relating to Ministers' Participation in Social Action Activities

Factor	Generally Encourage	Neither	Generally Discourage	Total
Own theological views	68%	11	21	100% (1558)
Own political beliefs and attitudes	65%	17	18	100% (1547)
Own goals as a parish minister	59%	16	25	100% (1554)
Attitudes of local denominational officials	53%	38	9	100% (1560)
Attitudes of colleagues among the clergy	51%	35	14	100% (1546)
Own personality	49%	21	30	100% (1548)
Community in which church is located	20%	32	48	100% (1555)
Attitudes of local parishioners	18%	38	44	100% (1552)

affairs—particularly in the more rural areas of the state. A number of respondents indicated that they would like to have been involved in civil rights or antiwar activities but that little opportunity existed for such involvement in their own communities. One would not normally expect, for example, to find organized protest movements outside the larger urban areas of the state or the vicinity of a college or university. We also know that clergymen in the immediate area of the California grape strike were under especially strong pressures not to lend public support to the workers' position. When they ignored community sentiment and did speak out, they suffered severely for their disregard of community sentiment, as we see in a later chapter.

Six of the participation factors thus reportedly encourage clergy involvement in public affairs; two have a primarily negative impact. The most encouraging factors, according to the California ministers, are their personal beliefs and goals; the most discouraging, the views of their parishioners.

The pattern of clerical responses to these questions, furthermore, serves to corroborate our previous statements about the impact of religious and political beliefs on social activism. Table 5.10 shows that virtually all the ministers in our two new breed groups felt these belief factors to have a generally encouraging effect on their participation in social action activities. The less socially active clergymen are less likely to give such a response, although there is a general tendency among the parish clergy to see the impact of these two factors in positive terms.

Finally, the relative influence ascribed by Protestant ministers to the

Table 5.10. Modernist Ministers Are Most Likely to Feel that Their Theological and Political Beliefs Encourage Their Social Activism

	Activism[a]					
	1	2	3	4	5	6
THEOLOGICAL VIEWS						
Generally encourage	96%	95%	80%	53%	48%	13%
Neither	1	2	7	16	18	25
Generally discourage	2	3	12	32	34	61
	99%	100%	99%	101%	100%	100%
	(82)	(315)	(433)	(304)	(349)	(75)
POLITICAL BELIEFS AND ATTITUDES						
Generally encourage	96%	92%	79%	50%	43%	9%
Neither	2	4	8	21	32	51
Generally discourage	1	4	13	29	25	40
	99%	100%	100%	100%	100%	100%
	(82)	(314)	(432)	(299)	(343)	(77)

[a] On this 6-point scale, 1 is highly active; 6 is inactive.

participation factors becomes even more apparent when we ask them to state which is the "most encouraging" and which is the "most discouraging" to their activist behavior. Most clearly, Protestant ministers attach a great deal of importance to their theological beliefs in both respects. During the pretesting of the questionnaire, we found that the dominant tendency of the respondents was to name their theological views as the primary determinant of their activism and, to a lesser extent, of their inactivism as well. Such a response plainly demonstrates the central role given by Protestant ministers themselves to their theological convictions.

Although this pretest finding was in itself significant, we also wanted to know what relative influence the clergy would ascribe to the other factors listed in Table 5.9. Therefore, we decided to eliminate the religious variable as a response category in the final questionnaire and to ask the respondents to choose among the remaining seven factors. Even when this was done, many clergymen persisted in writing in that their theological views were most important, or indicated this response by selecting the "none of these" category or by naming as most important their own goals as parish ministers.

Table 5.11. Ministers See Their Own Beliefs and Goals as the Most Encouraging to Their Social Activism; the Attitudes of Their Local Parishioners as the Least Encouraging

	Most Encouraging	Most Discouraging
Own goals as a parish minister	30%	19%
Own political beliefs and attitudes	28	9
Attitudes of local denominational officials	7	3
Own personality	6	11
Community in which church is located	5	12
Attitudes of colleagues among the clergy	3	2
Attitudes of local parishioners	3	30
None of these	17	14
	99%	100%
	(1535)	(1560)

Nevertheless, a suggestive pattern emerges from the ministers' remaining selections (see Table 5.11). It is the respondents' personal beliefs that are most often named as the most encouraging influence on their social activism; the attitudes of their parishioners are most often identified as the most discouraging. Many ministers report that their denominational leaders and colleagues lend support to their participation in public affairs, but few feel that these two groups are the most important factor in their activist involvement. In contrast, the ministers' parishioners are frequently named as the most discouraging among the factors listed.

These patterns suggest that although many Protestant ministers wish to pursue an activist role in ethical matters, the system of rewards and sanctions within the ministerial profession discourages such behavior. The remainder of our analysis bears out this contention in many cases. The next five chapters represent a broadening of our inquiry into clergy activism to include factors related to the ministerial profession itself. In Chapter 6 we present the theoretical foundations for such an investigation and look more closely at the conflicts within Protestant churches over clergy involvement in public issues. In subsequent chapters we examine the belief systems of Protestant laymen, the reactions of the ministers' congregational members to their social activism, and the impact of the lay–clergy relationship on the manner in which Protestant clergymen respond to public events. We also investigate more fully the role of denominational leadership in encouraging or discouraging clergy activism.

NOTES AND REFERENCES

1. Rodney Stark, Bruce D. Foster, Charles Y. Glock, and Harold E. Quinley, *Wayward Shepherds: Prejudice and the Protestant Clergy* (New York: Harper & Row, 1970), pp. 86–95.

2. We also asked the clergy how often they discussed public affairs with the members of their congregations. Fifty-five percent replied that they do so "frequently," 44 percent said "occasionally," and 1 percent indicated that they never did so.

3. Sidney Verba and Norman H. Nie, *Participation in America: Political Democracy and Social Equality* (New York: Harper & Row, 1972), p. 31.

4. These data are made available through the Inter-University Consortium for Political Research. The data were originally collected by the Survey Research Center Political Behavior Program, Institute for Social Research, the University of Michigan.

5. These data come from the Bay Area Survey No. 2, conducted in 1972 by the Survey Research Center, University of California, Berkeley. They were made available to the author by J. Merrill Shanks, Director of the Survey Research Center.

6. The California clergy and college professors in the Boston area also were about equally involved in the Vietnam issue. See David J. Armor, Joseph B. Ciacquainta, R. Gordon McIntosh, and Diana E. H. Russell, "Professors' Attitudes Toward the War in Vietnam," *Public Opinion Quarterly,* **31** (1967), pp. 159–175. Although comparable studies have not been conducted on the political behavior of other professional groups, it is apparent that occupational norms and practices are related to different political styles within the professions. Doctors, for example, tend to be relatively uninvolved in politics, whereas career considerations often require lawyers to be politically involved. For an explanation of these phenomena in the United States, see William A. Glaser, "Doctors and Politics," *American Journal of Sociology,* **66** (November 1960), pp. 230–245; and Heinz Eulau and John Sprague, *Lawyers in Politics* (Indianapolis, Ind.: Bobbs-Merrill, 1964). For a more general review of some of the hypothetical linkages between professionals and politics, see Seymour Martin Lipset and Mildred A. Schwartz, "The Politics of Professionals," in *Professionalization,* Howard M. Vollmer and Donald L. Mills, eds. (Englewood Cliffs, N.J.: Prentice-Hall, 1966), pp. 299–310; and Heinz Eulau, "Skill Revolution and Consultative Commonwealth," *American Political Science Review,* **67** (March 1973) pp. 169–191.

7. The respondents, in other words, were coded according to the most difficult of the 10 stated forms of social activism in which they had engaged. The categories used were as follows: (1) engaged in either civil rights or antiwar civil disobedience; (2) participated in either civil rights or antiwar protest march; (3) organized a social action group within the local church; (4) publicly supported a political candidate; (5) publicly took a stand on a political issue, organized a study group within the local church, took a stand from the pulpit on a public issue, or gave at least one sermon in the past year dealing mainly with a controversial social or political issue; and (6) engaged in none of these 10 forms of activist behavior.

The coefficient of reproducibility of this scale is .89; the coefficient of scalability, .58. Factor analysis of these behavioral items shows that the clergy's behavior clusters into the same groupings we found with respect to their ethical beliefs—those related to church, public, and protest leadership. We have combined these behavioral acts here, however, since we are interested in developing a composite measure of our respondents' activism.

8. The question was worded as follows: "There are many reasons why some clergymen participate in social action activities while others do not. Indicate for each of the factors listed below whether you feel it generally encourages or discourages your participation in such activities. Please answer in terms of your present situation."

CONFLICT OVER THE ACTIVIST ROLE

6. We have noted many times that clergy involvement in public affairs is a controversial issue. Not everyone within the church or outside it agrees that clergymen should play an active role in social and political issues. In previous chapters we have considered the divisions among Protestant ministers over the question of social activism—whether they agree that the church has been derelict in its moral judgments of secular society, whether the church has any direct role to perform in public affairs, and whether it is permissible for parish ministers to engage in certain forms of activist behavior. These questions, however, are controversial not only among Protestant ministers but also among others involved in the affairs of the church—most specifically, the members of the ministers' congregations and the denominational officials who are responsible for implementing church policy and for ensuring that the church thrives as an institution. These churchmen are also likely to have pronounced views on questions of social activism, and by virtue of their positions within Protestant denominations, they may seek to influence the conduct of clergymen in public affairs.

We turn now to an examination of the impact of such individuals on the clergy's own attitudes and behavior. Our analysis utilizes the insights provided by occupational sociology and role theory. The Protestant ministry is characterized by a unique set of sociological attributes that tend to create a great deal of homogeneity among its members, also serving to shape their attitudes and behavior on a wide range of issues. Many of these characteristics are derived from the ministry's status as a profession and the position it occupies within American society. We begin our analysis, therefore, by reviewing the attributes commonly associated with professionalism and the manner in which these factors operate with the ministerial profession. It will become

160

apparent that the Protestant ministry deviates in a number of important respects from the patterns of influence and authority that exist in most other
professions.

In our efforts to link certain structural features of the ministerial profession with clergy activism, we rely heavily on the role concept. Role theory
predicts that in an institutionalized setting such as the ministry, mutual
norms and expectations will develop between the role incumbent and those
"significant others" (role partners) with whom he commonly interacts and
who are in a position to reward or punish his behavior.[1] During the course
of his career, a minister may come into contact with and take cues from a
number of such individuals or groups. He may receive his primary inspiration
from a teacher, a prominent member of his profession, or from the example
of one of his relatives. More systematic and enduring, however, are the minister's relations with the groups that control and influence significant aspects
of his vocation. For the professions in general, such groups include the practitioner's clientele, colleagues, and organizational superiors. Therefore, our
analysis focuses on the attitudes held by the ministers' parishioners, fellow
clergymen, and local denominational leaders, and the sanctions at the disposal of these groups to influence the individual's behavior.[2]

Our source of information about these groups—the respondents' own perceptions of their positions on ethical and political issues—may introduce an
element of bias into our data, and we consider its effects more fully below.
By and large, however, it is the ministers' perceptions of what they believe
others think about social activism—rather than the precise positions of these
groups—that are most likely to affect clerical behavior. Furthermore, it
appears from independent studies to be cited that our respondents are highly
accurate in their reporting of the views of their parishioners and denominational officials.

The Ministry as a Profession. The Protestant minister is a professional
and, like the members of other professions, finds himself in a situation that
is sociologically unique. In the United States the professions have traditionally been accorded high status and, with some exceptions, a great deal
of individual autonomy. Partly because of the privileges accorded professionals, many occupations have sought recognition as a "profession," and
much of the writing on professions has been concerned with whether a particular occupation has obtained such a status. In their classic treatise in 1933,
however, Carr-Saunders and Wilson suggested that a profession be treated
as a complex of characteristics and that an occupation be judged as such
according to the degree to which it possesses "professional" characteristics.[3]

This approach has recently been adopted by most sociologists studying the professions, who have sought to define the characteristics of professional status and the stages through which a particular occupation becomes professionalized.[4] Their conclusions can be summarized in terms of the following ideal-type constructions.[5]

Specialized Knowledge and Expertise.   The possession of a specialized body of knowledge and expertise is often held to be the primary mark of distinction between the professional and nonprofessional.[5] The practical application of such knowledge to the vital problems of men forms the basis of an occupation's claim for professional recognition and its members' claim for status and authority. The skill of the professional, however, is not technical but intellectual; it is based on a systematic body of theory organized into a series of operational propositions.[6] This body of knowledge may be scientific (as in the case of the medical profession), nonscientific (as in the ministry), or a combination of the two (as with the law).[7] In any case, the professional's vocation is to subject the problems of his clients to theoretical analysis; his "skill" lies not only in the application of these conclusions but in the theorizing itself.

It follows from this need for theorizing and theory construction that as an occupation gains in professional stature, it will develop specialized schools to transmit the requisite knowledge and skills. This development implies a number of important characteristics, all easily recognized within the ministry. First, the establishment of specialized schools is likely to create major differences between those who have received the training offered there and those who have not; this characteristic is included in the church–sect distinction often drawn by those studying religion. Second, the aspiring student must now make his vocational decision relatively early in life, and he must be financially and psychologically prepared to endure a long period of apprenticeship. The professions, as a result, are likely to recruit their members from the more wealthy segments of society, and especially from those whose parents held similar positions. This characteristic is reflected in our data: 17 percent of the parish clergy in our sample reported that their fathers had been clergymen, and an additional 22 percent indicated that another close relative had held a ministerial position. Third, because of the long period of intensive training, those who survive are likely to be highly socialized into the norms and ways of their calling. Finally, the development of a separate theory-oriented branch of the profession often institutionalizes individual differences in professional norms and goals, personal values, and political attitudes. In the ministry, such a differentiation occurs not only between those who teach and those who practice, but also between those who work in the parish church and those in more insulated positions, such as the cam-

pus ministry. The latter position, it has been held, provides an institutionalized outlet through which clergymen with radical predispositions can safely
function.[8]

Professional Autonomy.   If the professions are characterized by a high degree
of knowledge and expertise, only those who have been trained in this body
of theory will be capable of making judgments concerning the adequacy of
professional service. The professional thus holds extraordinary power over
those who seek his services; only he can determine the exact nature of the
client's difficulty and only he can offer the proper prescriptions to deal with
the problems.[9] In a buyer–seller relationship, in contrast, the customer de-
termines his own needs and shops around until he is satisfied with the bar-
gain he receives.[10] Although the nonministerial professional client may be
physically free to seek out the services of another professional, he is seldom
able to appraise the value of the services he is given.

From the professional's point of view, such surrendering of authority is
frequently essential to the successful solution of the client's ailments. Unless
a certain degree of trust and cooperation exists in the clientele relationship,
the professional may not be able to ascertain the cause of the client's difficulties. This authority is not without limits in most professions, however,
but is confined to what Parsons has termed "specificity of function."[11] The
professional can prescribe to his client only with respect to the areas in which
he has obtained the requisite training. The absence of such rigid boundaries
between the minister and his parishioners, we see below, constitutes one of
the most important differences between the ministry and other professions.

Service Orientation.   A further protection for the client exists in the acceptance of the norm of service. The client is often extremely vulnerable both
because of his lack of knowledge and because of the urgency of his problem.
For this reason the professions have been characterized as occupations in
which the principle of *caveat emptor* cannot be allowed to prevail.[12] The basic
norm of this service orientation is that all clients are to be given the best
service possible regardless of financial or personal considerations. Professional decisions are thus to be based on "universalistic" rather than "par-
ticularistic" criteria—on the objective features of the *case* rather than on
who the client is or *what* he can offer.[13] The major corollaries of the service
orientation are: the professional must provide his services at request; he
must not be influenced by personal factors such as sex, religion, age, race,
family, position, or friendship; he must aid others regardless of the financial
resources of the recipients; and he must not allow personal discomfort or
disadvantage to interfere with the treatment of a client.[14]

Protestant churches have been severely criticized for not being open to all comers. Protestant churches are in fact highly segregated both racially and in terms of class composition. The ministers in the California survey, as we have seen, generally deplore the segregated state of their profession but are often unwilling to approve concrete steps to end discrimination at the parish level. Thus we might question the extent to which this service orientation is operative within the ministry; others have questioned it for the professions in general.[15]

Professional Self-Control.   Because these norms are ideals that cannot ever be satisfied in full, all professions have established institutionalized procedures to enforce them. Since the professional's skills are of such vital importance to the welfare of the community, and since the client himself is so dependent on the professional for his services, it is apparent that the regulation of these services cannot be left to the individual practitioner. The imposition of regulations, however, can be carried out by the state, by the profession, or by a combination of the two. The professions in this country have been allowed an extraordinary degree of self-control. Among the major mechanisms for such self-regulation are internalized codes of ethics, control over entrance into the profession, professional associations, and licensing procedures.

The ministerial profession—aided by the traditional American concern with the separation of church and state—has had almost unparalleled autonomy from direct state influence or control. At the same time, however, authority within Protestant churches rests more in the hands of the clientele than it does in virtually any other profession. We have more to say about this matter below.

Professional Ideology.   The final major characteristic of the professions is their ideology. The members of all occupations—by virtue of their sharing common social roles—will develop a distinctive way of viewing the world and interacting with it. This common set of attitudes and behavior has been variously referred to as an occupation's ethics, milieu, culture, and ideology. It is formed by the personal characteristics, occupational demands, and life experiences that its members have in common, and it can be expected to influence an individual's behavior both on the job and outside it.

From the previous discussion, it is apparent that the professions will possess highly structured ideologies: their members have experienced long periods of training and socialization, they have developed elaborate codes of ethics and means of enforcement, and their social prestige is relatively high. Thus professionals are likely to develop a distinctive set of ideological traits—some they will share with middle-class society, some will be characteristic of all professionals, and some will be unique to a single profession. Among those which professionals as a group generally share are a high career orientation and the belief that the profession operates for the welfare of the society. These beliefs, in turn, serve to strengthen the professional's ideological beliefs and commitment to his career.

Role Relations Within the Ministry. Various important characteristics are associated with professional status in American society, and it is not difficult to see how these factors operate within the Protestant ministry and how they might influence the attitudes and behavior of parish clergymen. Protestant ministers, for example, are highly trained and socialized in seminary schools in the proper knowledge and skills of their chosen vocation. They hold relatively high status positions in American society and are strongly committed to their profession. They possess a set of systematized and rationalized sacred beliefs that serves to guide their occupational conduct and to orient their relations with others. They have, finally, a peculiar relation of authority and responsibility with those to whom they provide their services.

All these factors are likely to create a great deal of attitudinal consistency within the Protestant ministry and to serve to stabilize the clergy's relations with their occupationally related role partners—their parishioners, colleagues, and denominational superiors. The members of these groups are thus uniquely placed to influence the clergy's attitudes and behavior. This effect is likely to occur through two related social processes. On the one hand, the clergyman's parishioners, colleagues, and denominational superiors will frequently serve as major "reference groups" in shaping his own beliefs and actions. They will provide cues on a variety of matters and most particularly in those areas which are most closely associated with their respective role relationships with the parish minister. As the clergyman comes to identify and interact with the members of these groups, therefore, we can expect him to develop similar beliefs and opinions—partly in an effort to avoid dissonance with these role-related groups and partly because of the development of common interests and common perceptions. (Such a process, of course, may take place among the clergy's occupational referents as well, causing their attitudes to become more consonant with those of the clergyman.) As a result, systematic differences in attitudes are likely to exist among clergymen in various occupational settings: for example, in liberal rather than conservative denominations, in urban rather than rural settings, and in nonparish rather than parish positions. In each case, persons of identical clerical status work within occupational milieus that are likely to transmit quite different sets of attitudes toward such issues as politics, social ethics, and the minister's proper relations with his congregational members. As the clergyman accommodates himself to the occupational milieu within which he works—and as he develops friendship ties with the members of these three role groups—he will tend to become more like those around him in his own beliefs, values, and behavior. The operation of such a process in the parish church is described in Chapter 9.

On the other hand, even when the minister maintains his disagreement with these groups or avoids identification with them, he is not completely immune to their influence. The members of each occupational group possess certain sanctions that may be exerted against the clergyman if he engages in disapproved conduct. The minister's parishioners may take their member-ship and financial loyalties elsewhere, his colleagues may prevent him from receiving certain professional benefits or recognition, and his denominational officials may assign him to an undesirable post. The parish clergyman thus must also take care not to antagonize unnecessarily anyone in a position to either reward or punish his behavior. If one of his role partners, for example, believes that the minister should not engage in certain types of public action, he must determine the possibilities of that individual's applying such sanc-tions and decide whether the risk is worth the potential price.

Our efforts to determine the effects of the ministerial career on social ac-tivism thus focus on the perceived attitudes and sanctions of these three occu-pationally related reference groups and the clergy's associations with them. We assume that these groups are the major occupational referents within the ministerial profession, that they have control over major aspects of the ministerial career, and that their positions enable them to reward or to punish the parish clergy for activism, thus to influence the latter's public behavior.

Clientele, colleague, and organizational pressures are presumed to exist within all professions, but it is obvious that their relative effects on profes-sional behavior will vary according to the circumstances of a given profes-sional and the ability of the reference groups to reward or punish his behavior. In some professions or in some situations we would expect certain role group influences to be more important than the others. For example, we might expect clientele influences to be especially important when professionals are forced to compete for a scarce market, colleague influence when referral practices are common, and organizational influence when the professional is directly responsible to an administrative agency or bureaucracy. Such patterns appear to exist among solo lawyers, medical specialists, and "house" attorneys, respectively.

Although Protestant ministers share many characteristics with the mem-bers of other professions, their relations with these three role groups are in some ways unique. For a variety of reasons, the clergy's clients (parishioners) are in a position to exercise extraordinary influence over their ministers' attitudes and behavior and, we would hypothesize, are a major career-related obstacle to the development of an activist Protestant ministry. Most importantly, the minister's relations with his lay followers are far more diffuse and multifaceted than those between most other professionals and their clients. In most professions the practitioner's specialized expertise creates both a need and desire to maintain distance between himself and his clientele. The professional role of the parish pastor, however, is not limited to a specific area of competence, such as preaching; it often includes many aspects of his parishioners' personal and public lives. "His calling as a godly man," as James Gustafson puts it, "is to *interpret* the life of the people, individual persons, and their organized relationships with one another, in the dimension of the relation of life to God."[16] The parish minister thus plays numerous roles in his relations with his congregational members. He is a symbol of the divine and an administrator of the local church, a counselor of the old and an educator of the young, a preacher on Sunday mornings and an organizer of church activities during the remainder of the week.[17] At least in some cases, our data show, he is often an active participant in public affairs and a cajoler of his parishioners to follow his example.

Being diffuse, the clerical role gives the Protestant minister a unique opportunity to attempt to influence his clientele on issues of public consequence—probably he is better placed to do this than most other professionals—but it also carries the seeds of ambiguity and conflict. The diffuseness of the ministerial role means that the boundaries between professional competence and private exhortation cannot always be well delineated. The laymen may demand of the minister services for which he may not feel or be qualified, as, for example, in providing counsel on sexual or marital matters or on death. Similarly, the minister may include in his definition of his professional role areas of expertise that are not recognized by the layman. Active leadership on social and political issues is likely to fall into this category.

Thus the role relationship between Protestant ministers and their parishioners differs markedly from that between most other professionals and their respective clienteles. The diffuse clergy–lay relationship bears the potential for both greater contact and greater conflict. Three additional peculiarities of the ministerial profession serve to draw the Protestant minister close to his congregational members and to make him especially vulnerable to clientele influence. The parish minister comes to what can be regarded as a "ready-made practice." He responds to a call from the laity of a particular church or is appointed to his position by his denominational superiors (generally the process involves a combination of these two procedures). He does not create his own practice, as does the solo lawyer or the solo doctor; he comes to a congregation having preexisting norms, values, and social structure. The result is that most clergymen experience a "breaking-in" process.[18]

They must alter some of their goals and expectations to conform to those of the new clients. To do otherwise would be to risk alienating substantial portions of the laity and would make the clergyman's duties all the more difficult.

Complementing this give-and-take process between the parish clergyman and his parishioners, the minister takes up residence among the members of his congregation. His relationship with his clients thus is not a purely professional one. Indeed, a part of the minister's professional duties engages him to become involved in the private lives of his constituents, and the minister's relationship with his parishioners is intimate, continuous, and personal. He sees his clients not just in his office or on Sundays but often makes visits to their homes. Frequently he forms close friendships with the members of his congregation, and his social life tends to involve primarily local church members. In most other professions, as we have pointed out, strong norms exist to deter the professional from becoming too closely enmeshed in the personal lives of his clients. He lives among and interacts primarily with other professionals and generally makes special efforts to avoid befriending those he serves in a professional capacity.

The members of the parish church, finally, possess a vast array of formal and informal sanctions by which they can seek to control the behavior of their pastor.[19] Laymen influence or control the clergyman's initial parish appointment, the success of his church programs, and his continuing employment. As individuals, they can bring private pressure to bear on him in personal conversations or through the local church. They can also withdraw financial support from the local parish or resign in sufficient numbers to necessitate a change in clerical behavior or denominational policies. Since ministerial success is still often measured in terms of membership and financial statistics, these actions are an effective form of protest.

Thus the minister–parishioner relationship is expected to dominate the clergy's associations with his other role partners, and a major portion of our subsequent analysis deals with the impact of this relationship on clergy activism. Our previous discussion indicates that an individual's colleagues are likely to occupy such a dominant position in most other professions—particularly when the professional's specialized knowledge is so theoretical and abstract that it can be shared only with highly trained specialists, or when the profession itself is strongly self-regulating. Neither of these situations exists to any great extent within the Protestant ministry. Protestant theology does not give the clergyman a position of preeminence over the untrained layman, as it does in the Catholic Church.[20] Protestantism, rather, is composed of a "brotherhood of all believers"; the Protestant minister is better trained in theology than his lay followers, but this does not give him the sole privilege of declaring religious truths. All men have such a right. Similarly, authority within Protestant churches is shared between the laity and the clergy. Even in the highest denominational councils—the equivalent of professional associations or governing bodies—laymen are given a major voice and a vote.

The ministers' colleagues are expected to play a far less influential role in the Protestant ministry than in most other professions. Nevertheless, the expressions of approval that the clergy receive from fellow ministers can be an important source of encouragement and influence, particularly when the parish pastor finds himself in conflict with his parishioners.

The third occupational-related group, the ministers' local denominational leaders, appear in many denominations to be a major force in offsetting the authority of Protestant parishioners. The ability of church officials to perform this function, however, may vary substantially from denomination to denomination. Three forms of church government exist within Protestantism: the episcopalian, the presbyterian, and the congregational. (Moberg compares these organizational forms with political monarchies, aristocracies, and democracies, respectively.[21]) In the first governmental structure, authority is exercised in hierarchical fashion, passing from the bishop down to the local congregations and supposedly freeing the parish pastor from local parish pressures. The Episcopal and Methodist churches possess such policy structures. In denominations organized along congregational principles, in contrast, the members of the local church are relatively autonomous from any higher organizational control. They select their own minister, who is subject to their supervision and can be replaced on the vote of the congregation. Denominations in our sample with congregational governmental structures are the American Baptist and Southern Baptist Conventions and the United Church of Christ.

In the final organizational form, the presbyterian, authority is held jointly in local synods or presbyteries by church officials and elders representing local churches. In fact, Moberg argues, such an arrangement is dominated by the clergymen who control these groups and comprise a "hierarchy of ecclesiastical oligarchs."[22] Furthermore, since the parish clergyman must be approved by the elders of the local church, he is subject to pressures both from above and below.[23] The Presbyterian Church, among the denominations surveyed, possesses such a policy structure, as do the three Lutheran groups.

Despite these formal differences in organizational structure, it appears that Protestant denominations are becoming more and more similar in their authority patterns. In Chapter 10 we explore the manner in which authority is exercised in the local church and the manner in which local denominational officials supervise the activities of parish ministers. We would expect clergy activism to be most encouraged in those denominations which are most hierarchical and in which control over the sanctions of the ministerial pro-

Table 6.1. Ministers Report that Close Colleagues and Local Denomina-

	Parishioners				
	Ap-prove	Even-ly Di-vided	Dis-ap-prove	No Opin-ion	(N)
Organize a study group within the church	59%	24	11	6	100% (1570)
Publicly take a stand on a political issue	30%	37	27	6	100% (1568)
Organize social action group within the church	30%	34	30	6	100% (1569)
Deliver a sermon on a controversial politi-cal or social topic	26%	38	32	3	99% (1569)
Take a stand from the pulpit on a political issue	18%	29	50	3	100% (1567)
Publicly support a political candidate	17%	24	53	6	100% (1569)
Participate in a civil rights protest march	8%	21	68	3	100% (1572)
Participate in an antiwar protest march	4%	16	76	3	99% (1573)
Be arrested to symbolize civil rights protest	2%	7	88	3	100% (1573)
Be arrested to symbolize antiwar protest	1%	6	90	3	100% (1572)

fession rests in the hands of the clergy's organizational superiors.

We devote the remainder of this chapter to describing the attitudes held by the members of these three occupationally related groups toward clergy activism and toward specific political issues, and the apparent effects of their attitudes on the ethical activities of our respondents. We use the ministers' own reports as our source of data in this undertaking.

Conflict over the Activist Role. Disagreements between Protestant ministers and their occupationally related role partners may arise over both ethical and political issues—over whether clergymen should become in-volved in political controversies and over the positions they take in their ac-

tional Leaders Are More Favorable than Parishioners to Clergy Activism

Colleagues					Local Denominational Leaders				
Ap-prove	Even-ly Di-vided	Dis-ap-prove	No Opin-ion	(N)	Ap-prove	Even-ly Di-vided	Dis-ap-prove	No Opin-ion	(N)
78%	10	4	8	100% (1556)	81%	6	4	8	99% (1550)
66%	19	8	8	101% (1571)	68%	13	8	11	100% (1562)
65%	17	10	8	100% (1555)	70%	12	9	9	100% (1554)
64%	18	10	8	100% (1570)	67%	13	10	10	100% (1555)
57%	21	16	7	101% (1568)	56%	17	18	9	100% (1553)
47%	26	18	9	100% (1569)	41%	22	25	13	101% (1559)
41%	27	26	6	100% (1570)	47%	20	24	9	100% (1559)
34%	27	33	6	100% (1571)	39%	22	29	10	100% (1560)
23%	27	43	7	100% (1570)	22%	26	41	11	100% (1560)
21%	27	45	7	100% (1570)	20%	25	44	11	100% (1550)

tivist behavior. To identify the type of conflict that exists within the ministry over ethical behavior, therefore, we asked the California ministers to report the positions taken by their local denominational officials, close colleagues, and parishioners on both issues. We asked whether the majority of the members of these groups approve of the 10 forms of clergy activism we have discussed previously and whether the majority took liberal or conservative positions on the three public controversies we considered in earlier chapters.

Table 6.1 shows the attitudes reportedly held by the ministers' local denominational leaders, colleagues, and parishioners toward clergy activism. There seem to be large differences among the members of these groups regarding the ideal conduct of a clergyman's ethical role. Most of the ministers thought that their local denominational leaders and close colleagues would be generally receptive to their activism, but most perceived their parishioners to be generally opposed to clerical leadership in social and political affairs. Furthermore, the positions reportedly held by the clergy's colleagues and the local denominational officials are similar in distribution to the views of the respondents themselves. Approval of clergy activism was said to be the highest for such actions as organizing local study groups and publicly taking a stand on political issues; it was lowest on the four forms of protest leadership. Only on the two civil disobedience measures did more ministers report that their local denominational leaders and close colleagues held disapproving than supportive views.

Thus these first two groups of ministerial role partners can be expected generally to support the positions and activities of the liberal activists among the parish clergy. Very few of the parish respondents, however, felt that the members of their own congregations would respond approvingly to attempts they might make to provide ethical leadership on public issues, either within the church or outside it. The only action to which a substantial proportion of the respondents felt that the majority of their own parishioners would agree was the organization of a study group within the local church to discuss public affairs—a behavioral act, as we have pointed out, that can cover a wide range of relatively innocuous as well as potentially explosive subjects. (In fact, we find that Protestant ministers were far less likely to organize local church groups to study such questions as the anti-fair housing initiative, the California grape strike, and the Vietnam war than to engage in more approved conduct, such as expressing their views on these matters publicly or including them in their sermons.) On none of the other behavioral items did as many as one-third of the clergy indicate that they could count on the approval of the lay members of their own churches. On three of these issues, the ministers were divided almost equally in their perceptions of their parishioners' attitudes. The number reporting that their parishioners would approve was nearly the same as the number stating that disapproval would result if the ministers took a public stand on a political issue, organized a social action group within the local church, or delivered a sermon on a controversial political or social topic. Half or more of the ministers felt that the members of their congregations held negative attitudes on the six remaining issues listed in Table 6.1. Engaging in protest marches or civil disobedience as a means of political expression appeared to be especially noxious to the respondents' local laymen. Only 17 percent of the clergy felt that their parishioners would approve of their participation in a civil rights protest march (as opposed to 24 percent who had actually engaged in such conduct), but only 2 percent indicated that their parishioners would approve of their being arrested to express their views on civil rights. The corresponding percentages on antiwar activities were 4 and 1 percent, respectively.

Wide differences thus exist in the attitudes the California ministers attribute to their occupationally related role partners with respect to social activism. A large proportion of the respondents report that their colleagues and denominational leaders would approve of most forms of clergy activism but that most of the members of their congregations would disapprove. Other studies have found that similar conflicts exist between Protestant laymen and church leaders on related issues. We review some of their findings in a subsequent chapter.

When we examine these responses according to each minister's denominational affiliation, we see more clearly the nature of the conflict over the activist role. The reported positions of the respondents' local denominational leaders and colleagues vary widely among the nine denominations surveyed but follow the same patterns found previously in analyzing the clergy's own belief systems. Approval of social activism was highest within the Methodist Church, the United Church of Christ, the Episcopal Church, the Presbyterian Church, and the Lutheran Church in America; it was lowest in the Southern Baptist Convention and the Missouri Synod-Lutheran Church. The views of these two occupational reference groups toward clergy activism thus serve largely to reinforce the ethical positions held by the clergy themselves. The reported positions of the respondents' parishioners, in contrast, only slightly resemble these distributions of denominational response. By and large, only small differences exist among the nine denominations in the ministers' predictions of parishioners' reactions to the former's social activism. Parishioner opposition to clerical involvement in public affairs, apparently, is only slightly greater in the conservative denominations than in the liberal church groups.

Before studying these differences in attitudes and their effects more closely, let us review conflicts reported by the clergy to exist among these groups over political issues.

Conflict over Political Issues.   We followed much the same procedure outlined earlier to determine the attitudes held by the clergy's local denominational leaders, close colleagues, and parishioners during each of the three public controversies explored in Chapter 4. On the first issue, Proposition 14, the clergy were asked whether the majority of the members of these groups favored or opposed passage of the initiative proposal. Similarly, they were asked whether the majority of the members of these groups favored or opposed clerical participation in the organization of migratory farm workers. Because of the greater complexity of the third issue, United States policy in Vietnam, we could not ask the ministers to state precisely the policy favored by their occupational associates. Instead we asked them whether the position of the majority of their close colleagues and parishioners was "more hawkish" or "more dovish" than their own. We also asked them whether their local denominational leaders had ever made a formal statement either in favor of greater efforts to negotiate a settlement of the war or in support of current government policies. Again, we must specify the time of our survey—the spring of 1968.

The clergy's responses to the first two sets of questions (Table 6.2) reveal that essentially the same division in views found earlier existed among the clergy's role partners during both the campaign to repeal California's fair housing laws and the efforts undertaken to organize migratory farm workers. In each case, the California ministers reported that their local denominational leaders and close colleagues had predominantly liberal views and their parishioners predominantly conservative ones. These differences were particularly sharp during the campaign over Proposition 14. It will be recalled that although most of the parish ministers (77 percent) opposed the initiative proposal, it passed the electorate with almost two-thirds of the vote. Table 6.2 indicates that a large proportion of the ministers' denominational leaders and colleagues also opposed the amendment, but more ministers reported that the majority of their parishioners favored its passage than opposed it (40 vs. 14 percent).

Table 6.2.   Ministers Report that Their Close Colleagues and Local Denominational Leaders Held More Liberal Positions than Their Parishioners on Proposition 14 and the Organization of Migratory Farm Workers

	Majority Opposed Passage	Evenly Divided	Majority Favored Passage	Not Sure	Total
PROPOSITION 14					
Local denominational leaders	72%	5	9	14	100% (1181)
Close colleagues	70%	11	11	8	100% (1183)
Parishioners	14%	34	40	12	100% (1187)
CLERGY PARTICIPATION IN ORGANIZATION OF MIGRA- TORY FARM WORKERS					
Local denominational leaders	48%	11	8	33	100% (1358)
Close colleagues	39%	22	11	28	100% (1361)
Parishioners	6%	23	30	41	100% (1362)

On Vietnam we find a similar pattern, although the questions we used were somewhat different (see Table 6.3). If the ministers' local denominational leaders had made any formal statement on the war at the time of the survey, it was likely to be a liberal one. Half the respondents reported that their local officials had formally called for greater efforts to negotiate an end to the war; only 4 percent said that they supported policies then in existence. As we might expect, the clergymen's closest colleagues reportedly held about the same views on the war as the respondents; but their parishioners, like the public generally, were more supportive of the current governmental policies. Forty-eight percent of the ministers believed that the majority of their parishioners held views on the war more hawkish than their own; only 4 percent said that their congregations were more dovish.

According to our respondents, then, their occupationally related role partners—those with whom they interact most often professionally and who can influence their careers—were divided in the positions they took on all three issues. On each, the clergy's local denominational leaders and close colleagues generally took what was recognized as liberal positions, whereas the majority of their parishioners held conservative views.

Conflict thus exists among these groups over political issues, as it does over ethical questions. Furthermore, we find once more that although the denominational distribution of these responses follows much the same pattern among the clergy, their colleagues, and their local leaders, it varies little among the laity; parishioners in modernist denominations are reported to be only slightly more liberal than parishioners in traditionalist ones.

The occupational milieu that appears to have existed on most controversial public issues during the 1960s is represented in Table 6.4. On the one hand, the liberal ministers—in this case, the large number of clergymen who opposed Proposition 14—were joined in their positions by most of their denominational leaders and colleagues, but were generally opposed by the majority of the members of their congregations. They were somewhat more likely than the conservative ministers (those who favored the initiative) to feel that their parishioners supported the liberal position, but most faced hostile or divided congregations, nevertheless. On the other hand, the conservative ministers found themselves in much closer agreement with their almost uniformly conservative parishioners, but received less reinforcement from their denominational leaders and colleagues. Almost as many members of these groups opposed Proposition 14 as favored it. An identical pattern does not necessarily exist on all public issues, and in this instance an unusually large proportion of Protestant clergymen held liberal views. However, very similar patterns of support and opposition occurred during the grape strike controversy and the debate over Vietnam war policy.

Table 6.3. Ministers Report that Their Local Denominational Leaders and Close Colleagues Held More Dovish Positions than Their Parishioners on the Vietnam War

"Churchmen throughout the country have increasingly become concerned about the situation in Vietnam. Have the local denominational officials in your immediate jurisdiction made a formal statement on the Vietnam War?"

Yes, in favor of greater efforts to negotiate	50%
Yes, in support of present policies	4
No, they did not take a position	40
Not sure	6
	100%
	(1553)

"Do you think that the majority of your close colleagues among the clergy would take a more hawkish or a dovish position on the war than your own?"

More hawkish	11%
About the same position	50
More dovish	24
Not sure	15
	100%
	(1565)

"Do you think that the majority of your congregation would take a more hawkish or dovish position on the war than your own?"

More hawkish	48%
About the same position	34
More dovish	4
Not sure	14
	100%
	(1567)

Our survey thus shows that many clergymen experienced conflict situations during the political controversies of the sixties. Liberal clergymen found support for their views among most of their colleagues and denominational officials but were generally opposed by their parishioners. Conservative clergymen seemed to be in agreement with most of their congregational members but received less support from their colleagues and denominational officials. Such conflicts, of course, were the sharpest in the more lib-

Table 6.4. Ministers Who Opposed Proposition 14 Were Reportedly in Closest Agreement with Their Local Denominational Leaders and Colleagues; Ministers Who Favored It Were Closest to Their Parishioners

	Opposed to Proposition 14	In Favor of Proposition 14
LOCAL DENOMINATIONAL OFFICIALS		
Favored	5%	27%
Opposed	84	30
About evenly divided	4	9
Not sure	7	34
	100%	100%
	(916)	(222)
CLOSE COLLEAGUES AMONG THE CLERGY		
Favored	4%	38%
Opposed	83	23
About evenly divided	8	22
Not sure	5	17
	100%	100%
	(916)	(224)
MEMBERS OF CONGREGATION		
Favored	37%	54%
Opposed	16	5
About evenly divided	38	21
Not sure	10	19
	101%	99%
	(918)	(224)

eral or modernist-oriented denominations; a relative (conservative) consensus existed over the issues we have been examining within the Southern Baptist Convention and, to a lesser extent, within the Missouri Synod-Lutheran Church.

Role Conflict and Clergy Activism.   As we pointed out in the last chapter, clergymen in some denominations take more liberal positions on controversial public issues and are more activist in their behavior even when we control for differences in their religious and political beliefs. We understand now some of the causes of these patterns in denominational activism. Church leaders give far more support to clergy activism and hold far more liberal political views in the more modernist denominations in our survey than in the conservative ones. Similarly, would-be activists in liberal denominations receive greater reinforcement of their positions and actions from their colleagues than those in conservative church groups. There is some evidence, finally, to suggest that Protestant laymen may be somewhat more receptive to clergy activism in the liberal denominations.

With survey data such as ours, it is difficult to establish causality in a conclusive sense between the attitudes or actions of these reference groups and the clergy's own beliefs and behavior. We cannot isolate the importance of any single factor or influence, as we could if we were to focus on a single minister or a single situation. We cannot, for example, show just what actions a local denominational leader took or what promises he made to cause a parish minister to decide to speak out on an issue. In addition, these responses were obtained by asking the clergy about the views of their role partners—not by interviewing the actors themselves. Although we have reason to believe that the ministers' reports are fairly accurate, we should be cautious in how we use such information. On the one hand, it is common for an individual to misperceive or to distort the attitudes of others in an unconscious effort to reduce dissonance. Therefore, we might expect some respondents to understate the amount of disagreement existing between themselves and those with whom they commonly interact. On the other hand, many ministers may well regard parishioner conflict as a sign of relevancy and social concern. Particularly among the modernist clergy, being in trouble with "the people" may be seen as a necessary part of the prophetic role. In this case, we might expect ethically oriented ministers to overstate the degree of resistance they encountered with their congregational members over social activism—a possibility we should keep in mind when we analyze lay reactions to the new breed clergy in Chapters 8 and 9.

Finally, in comparing the attitudes of our respondents with those of their role partners, we must remember that influence can and is likely to be reciprocal. It is obviously circular to argue that all clergymen are influenced by the attitudes of their close colleagues; some role incumbent must be influenced as well as being an influencer. Similarly, church leaders may be reacting to the sentiments of their clerical members in approving clergy activism, whereas local parishioners may be responding to the admonitions of their parish pastor. In particular, we suspect that the latter is frequently the case. It is likely that activist clergymen have been able to convert some of the members of their congregations to their positions. Also, it may be that the greater proportion of liberal constituents reported by the activist clergy may exist largely because conservative churchmen have left the parish churches of such ministers.

For these reasons, we must be cautious in drawing inferences from the information presented in this chapter. Nevertheless, it seems clear that the attitudes of the ministers' local denominational leaders, close colleagues, and parishioners have a marked impact on their own political views and activist behavior. For example, clergymen reporting that the members of these three groups took liberal positions on Proposition 14 and on the grape strike were themselves most likely to take liberal positions on the same issues and to speak out on them. Similarly, ministers reporting that their role partners approved of these 10 forms of social activism were in turn more likely to engage in such conduct. Finally, we have the ministers' own word on the matter. As we saw in the last chapter, slightly more than half these California clergymen said that the attitudes of their local denominational leaders and colleagues served to encourage their participation in social action activities. Such reports, we find, were most likely to come from ministers whose role partners held liberal attitudes and who were themselves most active in public affairs.

It is not necessary to repeat all these calculations here—we study the influence of these groups in greater detail in future chapters. The impact of the three role groups on the ministers' political positions, however, is illustrated in Table 6.5. In Table 6.4, it will be recalled, we took the ministers' own positions on Proposition 14 as our basis for reference and examined the occupational milieu of clergymen who favored or opposed the initiative proposal. Our objective was to determine the degree of conflict or consensus existing between the parish ministers and their role partners over this issue. By summing our percentages the other way, we answer a somewhat different question: What positions did our respondents take on the anti-fair housing referendum when their occupationally related role partners held different views? Additionally, we can control for the ministers' religious commitments, since we wish to separate the influence of their belief systems from that of their role partners. When we carry out these operations (see Table 6.5), a consistent pattern of correspondence emerges between the views of our respondents on Proposition 14 and those reportedly taken by the local denominational leaders, close colleagues, and parishioners. In each instance, the ministers were more likely to support the initiative proposal when the members of these groups also did so.

Such patterns suggest that these groups influence the positions commonly taken by Protestant ministers on controversial public issues. Very similar patterns occur, furthermore, in relation to the type of actions taken by the clergy to express themselves on Proposition 14 and in relation to their attitudes and actions toward the organization of migratory farm workers. Thus

Table 6.5. Ministers Were Likely to Take Positions on Proposition 14 Similar to Those of Their Role Partners

| | Percentage Opposed to Proposition 14 | | | | | |
| | Religious Orientation[a] | | | | | |
	1	2	3	4	5	Total
PARISHIONERS' ATTITUDES						
Majority in favor of	97%	89%	88%	56%	24%	72%
Proposition 14	(99)	(100)	(93)	(86)	(93)	(471)
Evenly divided, not	96%	95%	86%	70%	49%	78%
sure	(112)	(103)	(107)	(108)	(124)	(554)
Majority opposed to	94%	94%	91%	94%	88%	91%
Proposition 14	(31)	(32)	(32)	(33)	(32)	(160)
COLLEAGUES' ATTITUDES						
Majority in favor of	63%	60%	50%	34%	10%	30%
Proposition 14	(8)	(15)	(14)	(35)	(59)	(131)
Evenly divided, not	94%	94%	58%	48%	40%	52%
sure	(16)	(17)	(24)	(64)	(107)	(230)
Majority opposed to	97%	95%	94%	87%	76%	92%
Proposition 14	(218)	(203)	(193)	(127)	(79)	(822)
LOCAL DENOMINATIONAL LEADERS' ATTITUDES						
Majority in favor of	71%	72%	61%	36%	11%	40%
Proposition 14	(7)	(18)	(18)	(31)	(35)	(109)
Evenly divided, not	91%	81%	71%	49%	34%	48%
sure	(11)	(16)	(21)	(59)	(118)	(225)
Majority opposed to	97%	95%	92%	84%	71%	91%
Proposition 14	(223)	(202)	(193)	(136)	(91)	(845)

[a] On this 5-point scale, 1 is most modernist; 5 is most traditionalist.

on both issues we find evidence that the clergy's role partners affect the ministers' own attitudes and behavior.

We also note a positive relationship between the clergy's social activism and the attitudes reportedly held by these groups toward clergy activism (as shown in Table 6.1). Using partial correlations to control for the ministers' religious positions, we find that a statistically significant relationship remains between the positions reportedly held by these groups on each of

our previously studied forms of activism and the ministers' own tendencies
to engage in such conduct.

All these patterns suggest that the attitudes of the individuals with whom
Protestant clergymen commonly interact in their careers and who control
most of the rewards and sanctions of their profession—their local denominational leaders, colleagues, and parishioners—do have a major influence on
their own response to public issues. The more liberal the attitudes of these
groups, and the more supportive they are of clergy activism, the more the
Protestant ministers take liberal positions on controversial political issues
themselves and the more they appear to be socially active. In practical
terms, this means that ministers who are most oriented toward clergy activism will generally be supported by their local denominational leaders and
close colleagues and opposed by the members of their congregations.

We can verify these inferences by returning to the parish ministers' perceptions of these matters. This information is provided according to the
respondents' positions on our scale of social activism in Table 6.6. As expected, the most active clergy tend to feel that the attitudes of their local
denominational officials and close colleagues encourage their involvement in
public affairs and the attitudes of their parishioners generally discourage it.
The less active ministers are more likely to report that all these groups are
irrelevant to their participation in public affairs.

Two additional patterns of interest are reflected in the ministers' responses
in Table 6.6. First, consistent with the data presented in the previous two
sections, we see that some of the most active clergymen feel that the attitudes
of their parishioners do in fact facilitate their ethical involvement. This suggests that some of the ethically oriented clergy—including those who had
committed acts of civil disobedience—have (a) been able to gain lay support
for their actions, or (b) served congregations with a large proportion of liberal members. A future chapter reveals that this is indeed the case. Second,
we also find that the most active group of ministers are somewhat less likely
than their more conventionally active colleagues to regard the attitudes of
their denominational leaders and colleagues as lending encouragement to
their activist activities. Some of the new breed activists, we would suggest,
have gone beyond the bounds of accepted behavior even within the most
liberal Protestant denominations in our survey, thus finding themselves at
variance with their generally liberal church leaders and colleagues. Data to
support this conclusion appear later in our analysis.[11]

The Ministerial Profession and Clergy Activism.   In this chapter we
have laid out the theoretical framework within which we examine the effects
of certain features of the ministerial profession on clergy activism. We use

Table 6.6. Activists and Nonactivists Report that Attitudes of Their Role Partners Have Different Effects on Their Social Activism

	Activism[a]						
	1	2	3	4	5	6	Total
ATTITUDES OF LOCAL DENOMINATIONAL OFFICIALS							
Generally encourage	63%	74%	65%	38%	39%	10%	51%
Neither	24	22	27	52	53	65	35
Generally discourage	12	4	8	10	8	25	14
	99%	100%	100%	100%	100%	100%	100%
	(82)	(315)	(434)	(304)	(348)	(77)	(1546)
ATTITUDES OF CLOSE COLLEAGUES AMONG THE CLERGY							
Generally encourage	56%	75%	63%	36%	34%	6%	65%
Neither	21	19	24	47	49	64	17
Generally discourage	23	6	13	17	17	30	18
	100%	100%	100%	100%	100%	100%	100%
	(80)	(313)	(427)	(301)	(348)	(77)	(1547)
ATTITUDES OF LOCAL PARISHIONERS							
Generally encourage	34%	24%	24%	10%	12%	1%	18%
Neither	22	33	29	45	48	57	38
Generally discourage	44	44	47	45	40	42	44
	100%	101%	100%	100%	100%	100%	100%
	(80)	(312)	(430)	(304)	(349)	(77)	(1552)

[a] On this 6-point scale, 1 is highly active, 6 is inactive.

role theory for this purpose, since it provides focus to our inquiry and allows us to compare certain features of the ministerial profession with those of other professions. Role theory also directs our attention toward the individuals with whom Protestant clergymen commonly interact in their professional duties. It leads us to study the attitudes and norms characterizing the members of these role groups, the occupational rewards and sanctions at their disposal, and the ministers' relations with them. We have pointed out that the most important role groups within the professions are the practitioners' clientele, colleagues, and organizational superiors—and we have focused on the ministers' parishioners, fellow clergymen, and local denominational officials. We have shown that various characteristics of the ministerial profession give laymen an unusually large degree of potential influence and authority within Protestant churches and make them a special object of concern.

The data in this chapter demonstrate most clearly the nature of the conflict that exists among these occupationally related role partners over clergy activism and the effects of these groups on the ministers' response to political issues. We see that the major obstacle to clergy activism in this respect is the ministers' parishioners—who generally hold conservative positions on political issues and who oppose most forms of clergy activism. In the next three chapters we look more closely at the attitudes of Protestant laymen, their reactions to clergy involvement in controversial issues, and the manner and effects of their relations with their parish ministers. In Chapter 10 we examine the attitudes and authority of the ministers' local denominational leaders, as well as their ability to offset such lay conservatism and to encourage clerical participation in public affairs.

NOTES AND REFERENCES

1. For a general discussion of role theory, see Robert K. Merton, *Social Theory and Social Structure*, rev. ed. (Glencoe, Ill.: The Free Press, 1957); Neal Gross, Ward S. Mason, and Alexander W. McEacheron, *Explorations in Role Analysis* (New York: Wiley, 1958); and Bruce J. Biddle and Edwin J. Thomas, eds., *Role Theory: Concepts and Research* (Wiley, 1966).

2. Campbell and Pettigrew used a similar cross-pressure model to study Little Rock ministers during the desegregation Crisis of 1956. They saw the ministers as responding to three pressures: (1) their own personal convictions, (2) the positions of their denominational leaders and colleagues, and (3) the views of their congregational members. See Ernest Q. Campbell and Thomas F. Pettigrew, *Christians in Racial Crisis: A Study of Little Rock's Ministry* (Washington, D.C.: Public Affairs Press, 1959).

3. A. M. Carr-Saunders and P. O. Wilson, *The Professions* (Oxford: Clarendon, 1933).

4. See in particular Howard M. Vollmer and Donald L. Mills, "Some Comments on

'The Professionalization of Everyone?' " *American Journal of Sociology*, **57** (January 1965), pp. 480–481, and *Professionalization* (Englewood Cliffs, N.J.: Prentice-Hall, 1966). Also, Ernest Greenwood, "Attributes of a Profession," *Social Work*, **2** (July 1957), pp. 45–55; and William J. Goode, "Encroachment, Charlatanism, and the Emerging Profession: Psychology, Sociology, and Medicine," *American Sociological Review*, **25** (December 1960), pp. 902–914. For a similar application of these ideal-type constructions to the ministry, see Paul M. Harrison, "Religious Leadership in America," in *The Religious Situation, 1969*, Donald R. Cutler, ed. (Boston: Beacon, 1969), pp. 957–979.

5.   See, for example, A. M. Carr-Saunders, *Professions: Their Organization and Place in Society* (London: Humphrey Milford, 1928), p. 5; and Morris L. Cogan, "Toward a Definition of Profession," *Harvard Educational Review*, **23** (Winter 1953), pp. 48–49.

6.   See Greenwood, *op. cit.*, and Cogan, *op. cit.*

7.   Harold L. Wilensky, "The Professionalization of Everyone?" *American Journal of Sociology*, **70** (September 1964), pp. 138–140.

8.   Phillip E. Hammond and Robert E. Mitchell, "Segmentation of Radicalism—The Case of Protestant Campus Ministers," *American Journal of Sociology*, **71** (September 1965) pp. 133–143.

9.   See Greenwood, *op. cit.*; Everett Hughes, *Men and Their Work* (Glencoe, Ill.: Free Press, 1958); and T. H. Marshall, "The Recent History of Professionalism in Relation to Social Structure and Social Policy," *Canadian Journal of Economics and Political Science*, **5** (August 1939), pp. 315–340.

10.   This proposition is increasingly open to doubt in contemporary capitalist society, with its need to create an expanding market for consumption and its increasingly powerful advertising techniques to do so. For a general discussion, see John Kenneth Galbraith, *The New Industrial State* (Boston: Houghton Mifflin, 1967); and Paul A. Baran and Paul Sweezy, *Monopoly Capital* (New York: Modern Reader Paperbacks, 1966), pp. 112–141.

11.   Talcott Parsons, "The Professions and Social Structure," *Essays in Sociological Theory* (New York: Free Press, 1954), pp. 34–49.

12.   See most particularly Hughes, *op. cit.*, p. 141, and Marshall, *op. cit.*

13.   Parsons, *op. cit.*, p. 41.

14.   Theodore Caplow, *The Sociology of Work* (Minneapolis: University of Minnesota Press, 1954), p. 114.

15.   C. Wright Mills, *White Collar* (New York: Oxford University Press, 1956), Chapter 6.

16.   James M. Gustafson, "Analysis of the Problem of the Role of the Minister," *Journal of Religion*, **32** (July 1954), p. 187.

17.   See Charles Y. Glock and Rodney Stark, *Religion and Society in Tension* (Skokie, Ill.: Rand McNally, 1965), pp. 124–129; S. W. Blizzard, "The Minister's Dilemma," *Christian Century*, **73** (1956), pp. 508–509; and Kaspar D. Naegele, "Clergymen, Teachers, and Psychiatrists: A Study in Roles and Socialization," *Canadian Journal of Economics and Political Science*, **22** (Feburary 1956), pp. 46–62.

18.   See David O. Moberg, *The Church as a Social Institution* (Englewood Cliffs, N.J.: Prentice-Hall, 1962), p. 502.

19.   Paul M. Harrison, "Church and the Laity Among Protestants," *Annals of the American Academy of Political and Social Science*, **332** (1960), pp. 37–49.

20.   See Robert E. Mitchell, "The Decline of the Protestant Clergy's Influence and Prestige: Some Historical and Inter-Faith Comparisons," Survey Research Center, University of California, Berkeley (mimeographed), January 1966.

21.   Moberg, *op. cit.*, p. 94.

22.   *Ibid.*

THE STRUCTURE OF LAY BELIEFS

7.
It is clear from the information we have just presented that the conservatism of Protestant laymen constitutes a major obstacle to parish clergymen who wish to pursue an active role in public affairs. Most local parishioners are reported to oppose both the tactics and the politics of the ethically oriented clergy. Chapter 8 identifies the problems created by such lay attitudes for California clergymen who speak out on controversial social and political issues.

Before turning to these data, however, it is useful to look more closely at the structure of beliefs among Protestant laymen and the consequences of these configurations in belief for the activist clergy. In particular, we wish to know whether lay conservatism and lay opposition to clergy activism are rooted in the religious commitments of Protestant laymen—as they are among the traditionalist clergy—or whether lay attitudes on such issues are affected largely by nonreligious factors. On the one hand, it may be that Protestant laymen who oppose liberal church activism do so because they maintain traditionalist attitudes toward religious issues. In this case, the ethically committed clergy's problem is too many traditionalists among the laity; as more laymen come to reject traditional orthodoxies, however, we would expect them also to embrace the ethicalism of the modernist clergy. On the other hand, it may be that Protestant laymen hold conservative political views and oppose clergy activism irrespective of their positions on religious issues. In this case, the modernist clergy could not expect to increase their support among the laity simply by a growth in the number of non-orthodox laymen; these churchmen would not draw from their new theological orientations the same implications assumed by the modernist clergy.

In approaching this important question, it is useful to return to some of the theoretical considerations raised in Chapter 2 concerning belief systems and to the work of Philip Converse concerning the attitudes of political elites and the mass public. We followed Converse in defining a belief system as a set of attitudes or idea-elements bound together by a high degree of constraint or functional interdependence. Two distinguishing characteristics of belief systems are the centrality of certain idea-elements and the range of subjects to which they refer. We have seen most clearly that religious beliefs play a central role in a ministerial belief system that extends over a wide range of ideas and has major attitudinal and behavioral consequences for Protestant clergymen. Converse was concerned with the political belief systems of political leaders and their mass constituents. He hypothesized that as one moves down the information scale from elites to masses, two important changes are likely to occur in the belief systems: first, the degree of constraint among the idea-elements in the belief system is likely to decline and the range of elements to become increasingly narrow; second, objects central to the belief system are likely to shift from the "remote, generic, and abstract to the increasingly simple, concrete, or 'close to home.' "[1] Converse found that although such terms as "liberalism" and "conservatism" are widely used in the press and are generally descriptive of the political beliefs of public leaders, they have less meaning for the public at large. Most Americans do not possess highly constrained political belief systems, nor are they able to define these terms accurately.

Following this reasoning, we might expect that the religious issues we have seen to be crucial in understanding clerical attitudes and behavior will have little meaning for most churchmen. If this is the case, we must conclude that the combination of lay conservatism and opposition to ethicalism is caused largely by factors external to religious commitments. Such a disassociation of beliefs carries serious consequences for liberal denominations and for the ethically committed clergy—and we deal with them briefly in this chapter before returning to the problems encountered by the California activists with their own parishioners. For the purposes of this investigation, we rely chiefly on two sources: a survey of lay attitudes in the San Francisco Bay area carried out by Charles Y. Glock and Rodney Stark a few years before our own study[2] and the national presidential survey conducted by the Survey Research Center at the University of Michigan in 1968.[3]

The Nature of Lay Beliefs. Numerous studies have been conducted on the religious commitments of Protestant laymen and the impact of religious values on lay attitudes toward social ethics and politics. Despite such efforts, the precise influence of the laity's religious commitments on either their ethical or political attitudes is still not known. Part of this confusion arises from the many dimensions involved in being a religious person. For example, religious commitment has been associated with holding to certain doctrinal positions, belonging to a national denomination, attending services each Sunday, involving oneself in the associational life of the church, developing friends within the local parish, engaging in religious rituals and practices, and having a knowledge and understanding of religious teachings. All these dimensions of religious commitment have been investigated in an attempt to determine their impact on the political beliefs of churchmen.[4]

Our concern here is with the influence of lay theological views on the parishioners' ethical and political beliefs, since we wish to know whether Protestant laymen and their church leaders draw the same inferences from their religious convictions. The evidence we have shows that a fairly substantial minority of Protestant laymen take nonorthodox positions on theological issues but apparently do not join the modernist clergy in supporting either an action-oriented church or liberal political programs. With a few exceptions, status-related differences rather than religious factors appear to account for the range in attitudes found among Protestant laymen of different denominations.

Religious Beliefs.   Six of the religious belief questions used in our survey were adopted directly from the study by Glock and Stark and thus can be used to compare the attitudes of Protestant laymen and ministers on questions of religious orthodoxy. These questions dealt with the existence of God, the Divinity of Jesus, life after death, the virgin birth, Jesus' walking on water, and the existence of the devil. When we compare the positions taken by laymen in Glock and Stark's sample with those of our own respondents, we find many similarities in the religious positions of these religious leaders and followers. Not only do Protestant laymen often join in the rejection of traditional orthodoxies, they do so in roughly the same fashion as the California ministers. Nonorthodox views are most common in the United Church of Christ and the Methodist Church, followed by the Episcoal Church, the Lutheran Church in America, and the Presbyterian Church. Orthodox views are most common in the Southern Baptist Convention, followed by the Missouri Synod-Lutheran Church, the American Lutheran Church, and the American Baptist Convention.[5]

Thus the rejection of traditional Protestant orthodoxies (as measured, at least, by these questions) is not uncommon among Protestant laymen and exists most frequently in the denominations served by modernist clergymen. What is more, the laity in our sample possess a highly structured set of attitudes on these six measures of religious orthodoxy. On 12 of the 15 possible pairings between these belief items, in fact, the correlations among the Protestant laymen are higher than the comparable correlations among the clergy. For this reason, it is not improper to speak of "orthodox" and "nonorthodox" laymen, and we followed the same techniques used with our ministers to construct a single unidimensional scale of lay attitudes toward religious orthodoxy.

The Glock–Stark survey was conducted in 1963—prior to the outburst in social unrest in the country and the mounting opposition to the war in Vietnam. Also, their sample of laymen was restricted to the San Francisco Bay area and included only actual members of local churches. We can supplement their findings, however, with the data gathered in the 1968 presidential survey conducted by the Survey Research Center of the University of Michigan. The respondents to this national poll were asked which of four statements about the Bible best represented their personal views. These four statements and the responses given by laymen in the Protestant denominations under consideration appear in Table 7.1. The majority of Protestant laymen in these mainline denominations clearly regard the Bible as containing the unerring Word of God, and most of the remaining number consider the Bible to be "inspired by God," even if written by men and susceptible to human error. Unfortunately, the SRC survey did not ask the respondents to give their exact denominational affiliations; thus we must be content to group together the Lutherans, Baptists, and Presbyterians (where a separate southern-based denomination exists). Table 7.1 indicates that the denominational distribution of lay responses is similar to that in the Glock–Stark data and in our own survey of Protestant ministers, but some major differences exist. Nationally, we find that Episcopal laymen hold the most nonorthodox religious views, followed by the laity in the United Church of Christ, the Presbyterian Church, the various Lutheran denominations, and the Methodist Church; the most orthodox views are maintained by the members of the various Baptist denominations.

Social Ethics. Relatively little information exists on the ethical positions of Protestant laymen. Previous accounts have generally assumed that Protestant laymen are antagonistic to church activism and that such lay conservatism is a major reason for the failure of many Protestant clergymen to speak out on controversial political issues. Only recently have greater efforts been undertaken to examine the attitudes of laymen toward social ethics and the factors that help shape their views on such matters. These studies show that although Protestant laymen often approve of church activism in the abstract, they give much less support to more specific actions that might be taken by the church or by religious leaders to influence public affairs.

Table 7.1. Lay Attitudes Toward Biblical Literalism

"Here are four statements about the Bible, and I'd like you to tell me which is closest to your own view."	Epis-copal	Congre-gational, United Church of Christ	Pres-byte-rian	Lu-theran	Metho-dist	Bap-tist	Total
"The Bible is God's Word and all that it says is true."	16%	39%	44%	51%	51%	69%	54%
"The Bible was written by men and inspired by God but it contains some human errors."	59	56	49	45	44	29	41
"The Bible is a good book because it was written by wise men, but God had nothing to do with it."	22	6	7	3	3	2	4
"The Bible was written by men who lived so long ago that it is worth very little today."	3	0	0	1	1	0	1
	100% (32)	101% (18)	100% (80)	100% (100)	99% (177)	100% (384)	100% (610)

Source. 1968 American National Election Study conducted by the Survey Research Center, University of Michigan.

The national survey conducted by Jeffrey K. Hadden in 1967 provides the best example of the reluctance of Protestant laymen to support clergy activism. Hadden found that 89 percent of the laymen in his sample agreed that "the best mark of a person's religiousness is the degree of his concern for others," and 84 percent agreed that "clergymen have a responsibility to speak out as the moral conscience of this nation." Yet when Hadden asked his respondents what they thought about various ways that clergymen might exert such moral leadership, the degree of approval dropped sharply. Seventy-seven percent of the Protestant laymen, for example, thought that "clergymen who participated in demonstrations and picketing do more harm than good for the cause they support," and an identical proportion agreed that "I would be upset if my minister were to participate in a picket line or demonstration."[7]

Somewhat greater support for church activism was reported in the recent survey by Thomas C. Campbell and Yoshio Fukuyama of lay attitudes in the United Church of Christ. Sixty-nine percent of the laity in this liberal denomination agreed that "ministers have a right to preach on controversial subjects from the pulpit," whereas 53 percent thought that "churches should support the Negro's struggle to achieve civil rights." At the same time, only 38 percent agreed that "demominations have a right to issue policy statements on social and economic issues."[8] (By way of contrast, 78 percent of the California ministers in the same denomination said that their national church "should" take an official position on social and political issues.)

As previously, we have some reservations about the importance that should be attached to such expressed attitudes. It is one thing for a congregational member to say that his minister can speak out from the pulpit on a controversial subject; it is often quite another for him to listen to his pastor condemn the war in Vietnam or support local school bussing. The layman, in other words, may agree in principle that the church should exercise its moral influence in public affairs, but he may be less tolerant when his minister expresses an opinion different from his own or becomes involved in an unpopular local issue.

Nevertheless, the various surveys tend to corroborate what our respondents told us about the ethical beliefs of their own parishioners. Some support exists for church involvement in social issues, but the type of activity practiced by the new breed activists is widely disapproved by Protestant laymen.

Our major concern here is with the sources of such lay attitudes toward ethical issues—whether a nonorthodox or modernist orientation among Protestant laymen leads to a greater emphasis on social ethics, as it does among the clergy. The answer seems to be that it does not. There is little or no relationship between these two dimensions of belief, which we found to be so strongly related among Protestant ministers. The Glock–Stark data perhaps best illustrate the irrelevance of ethical attitudes to the religious commitments of the Protestant laity. In their own report, the authors formed an "ethicalism" scale from the degree of importance attached by their respondents to "doing good for others" and "loving thy neighbor" as a means of achieving religious salvation.[9] They found that the Protestant laymen who scored highest on this scale tended to be members of the liberal denominations and to be somewhat less orthodox in their religious views.[10] These differences were slight, however—far lower than those found among the clergy on questions related to religious worldliness, religious salvation, or activist approval. Correlating these two individual questions with our own scale of religious orthodoxy, we find only a .10 correlation in the first instance and an insignificant .01 in the second.

Possessing such orientations toward religious salvation is not, of course, equivalent to supporting church activism. Three additional statements in the Glock-Stark survey deal more directly (although abstractly) with this dimension:

> Aside from preaching, there is little that churches can really do about social and economic problems.
>
> Churches should stick to religion, and not concern themselves with social, economic, and political questions.
>
> It is proper for churches to state their positions on practical political questions to the local, state, or national government.

The majority of the Bay Area laymen in the nine Protestant denominations we have been examining took proactivist positions on each of these general statements relating to church activism: 84 percent disagreed with the first, 67 percent diasgreed with the second, and 57 percent agreed with the third. These responses again show that many Protestant laymen support the general principle of church involvement in public affairs. When we examine the distribution of the responses, however, we find very little difference in the positions taken by orthodox and nonorthodox laymen. In Table 7.2 we have broken down the laity's responses to the second question according to religious orthodoxy, socioeconomic status (as measured by income), and frequency of church attendance. All three factors, it appears, have some relation to the support these respondents give to church activism—approval is greater among those who have higher incomes, who attend church most frequently, and who hold nonorthodox religious beliefs. The relationship between the laity's religious and ethical beliefs, however, is quite weak and certainly does not approach that found to exist among the California clergy. Almost identical patterns emerged, furthermore, in the laymen's responses to the other two questions included in the Glock–Stark survey.

The findings thus show that the attitudes of these Protestant laymen toward church activism are only slightly related to their religious orthodoxy. We should of course avoid generalizing to all Protestant laymen from this single study, since it is limited by the questions asked, the geographical constraints of the sample, and the time period in which it was conducted. We might well find some such relationships in other sections of the country or when more detailed questions are asked the laity about their ethical views. Furthermore, Protestant laymen may form a more religiously integrated set of attitudes toward church activism as clergy involvement in public affairs becomes more

Table 7.2. Lay Approval of Church Activism Is Slightly Related to Socioeconomic Status (SES), Church Attendance, and Religious Orthodoxy

	Disagree that Churches Should Stick to Religion and Not Concern Themselves with Social, Economic, and Political Questions			
	High Orthodoxy		Low Orthodoxy	
	Low SES	High SES	Low SES	High SES
High attendance[a]	67% (401)	73% (270)	71% (172)	76% (241)
Low attendance	55% (118)	61% (114)	61% (224)	67% (300)

Source. Survey of lay attitudes in the San Francisco Bay area conducted by Charles Y. Glock and Rodney Stark in 1963.

[a] Includes those who report that they attend church every week or nearly every week.

common and as they are forced to respond to such situations personally. In a recent study of Presbyterian churches in Colorado, Barbara W. Hargrove noted enough differences in lay beliefs to classify congregations into "sacred," "mainstream," and "secular" types. Only a few congregations fit into the secular or change-oriented category, however, and the members of these churches hold the most disparate set of religious-related attitudes.[11] In a study of four Indiana congregations, James D. Davidson likewise discovered a relationship between religious orthodoxy on the one hand and the comforting and challenging functions of religion on the other. None of the questions used in this study dealt explicitly with church activism, however, and the generality of the behavioral items used to measure the prophetic dimension makes that linkage highly suspect.[12] A more suggestive line of inquiry involves studying the beliefs of laymen for whom religion is particularly important. In a study of Indianapolis churchgoers, David R. Gibbs et al., found that a relationship exists between orthodoxy and social ethics among laymen whose religious membership is of very high salience—although the same relationship was not found on social and political issues.[13]

Thus some semblance of the attitudinal patterns we have found among the clergy exists among Protestant laymen as well, and may be further clarified in future studies. Such linkages are quite weak, however, and appear to occur only under special conditions. As we will see shortly, rather than joining the modernist clergy in their ethical commitments, nonorthodox laymen appear to be losing interest in religion and drifting away from the institutional church.

Political Beliefs.   As we argued previously, the differences in political beliefs between the new breed clergy and their parishioners are probably most responsible for the conflicts over social activism that have arisen in parish churches. Protestant laymen, we suspect, are more likely to tolerate clergy involvement in political causes with which they agree than in issues about which they hold different opinions.

Much greater attention has been given to the political attitudes of Protestant laymen and the manner in which they are shaped by the laity's religious commitments. In his national survey of lay attitudes, Hadden shows that Protestant clergymen are far more supportive of civil rights than are Protestant laymen—a pattern we also found to exist between the California clergy and their parishioners. It also appears from our own survey that ministers are more liberal on foreign policy issues and perhaps on questions of economic liberalism as well. We find, then, that most Protestant laymen oppose not only the new breed's social ethics but also their politics.

Again our major interest lies in the links that might exist between the religious orthodoxy of Protestant laymen and their political beliefs—we want to know whether the patterns found among Protestant ministers are repeated among their lay constituents. Our two sources of data indicate that some associations in belief exist between the laity's religious and political views, but these associations are relatively weak and occur only in relation to certain issue-areas. Findings from other studies generally corroborate these patterns in lay belief.

Both the Glock–Stark data and the Michigan SRC survey results point to a consistent and relatively strong relationship between the religious beliefs of Protestant laymen and their views toward Communist-related issues. Such patterns emerge most clearly from the Bay Area study, which reveals that orthodox laymen take anticommunist positions in a variety of policy areas. They are more likely than nonorthodox laymen to agree that "the races would probably get along fine in this country if Communists and other radicals didn't stir up trouble," that "communism is as much a threat inside the United States as outside it," that "the House un-American Activities Committee ought to be encouraged in the work it is doing," and that "a high school teacher who pleads the Fifth Amendment while being questioned by a congressional committee ought to be fired at once." Somewhat weaker

but similar relationships are found in the positions taken by Bay Area laymen toward the admission of the People's Republic of China to the United
Nations and toward the invasion of Cuba.

The same associations between religious orthodoxy and anticommunism
appear in the 1968 SRC survey data (see first part of Table 7.3). Laymen
who believe that the Bible is God's Word (the literalists) are more likely to
oppose trading with Communist countries and the admission of Communist
China to the United Nations. We should also note that the laity's attitudes
toward these issues are strongly related to socioeconomic position, as are
their attitudes toward most other political issues included in these two
surveys.

The SRC data suggest the specter of communism alone is responsible for
these associations between religious orthodoxy and foreign policy attitudes.
We do not find any such associations in belief on the other two foreign policy
questions included in the SRC survey—the provision of foreign aid (shown
in Table 7.3) and Vietnam war policy (not shown here). Furthermore, as
we shall see, no such consistent and strong relationship occurs on any of the
other issues covered in these two surveys.

Turning to a second issue-area, we find some evidence of an association
between the laity's religious beliefs and their attitudes toward civil rights:
that nonorthodox laymen are more supportive than orthodox laymen of civil
rights measures. These associations vary from issue to issue, however, and
emerge much more clearly in the SRC data than in the Glock-Stark survey;
in addition, they are influenced at least in part by the tendency of Southerners
to hold orthodox religious beliefs. Table 7.3 shows the relationship between
the laity's attitudes toward the Bible and several political questions included
in the Michigan survey. We see that nonliteralist laymen are consistently
more supportive of civil rights on the more general questions (favoring desegregation and housing integration), but the differences are smaller and
less consistent on the more specific policy questions (school integration and
public accommodations). The same patterns exist on two questions not
shown here—the speed with which civil rights leaders have pushed their
views and the extent to which the government should help blacks obtain
equal employment. Thus on at least some racial issues we find associations
in religious and political beliefs similar to those among the clergy. Other
studies have likewise demonstrated that orthodox laymen tend to be more
intolerant or prejudiced than nonorthodox laymen.[14] At the same time, these
relationships are not nearly as strong as those found among the Protestant
clergy, and they emerge only weakly in the Glock–Stark data.[15] When we
eliminate the South from this national sample, furthermore, we find that this
relationship remains only with respect to the three more general statements
about civil rights.

Table 7.3. Lay Attitudes Toward Politics Are Associated with Their Religious Beliefs Only on Certain Issues

Attitude Toward the Bible	Yearly Income				
	Under $4000	$4000–7999	$8000–14,999	$15,000 and over	Total

FOREIGN POLICY ISSUES[a]

Farmers and businessmen should be able to do business with Communist countries as long as the goods are not used for military purposes.

	Under $4000	$4000–7999	$8000–14,999	$15,000 and over	Total
Literalists	26%	25%	31%	33%	28%
	(50)	(88)	(67)	(21)	(228)
Nonliteralists	45%	44%	50%	68%	51%
	(29)	(55)	(98)	(41)	(227)

Communist China should be admitted to the United Nations[b]

	Under $4000	$4000–7999	$8000–14,999	$15,000 and over	Total
Literalists	13%	20%	34%	50%	27%
	(31)	(65)	(56)	(18)	(170)
Nonliteralists	27%	51%	41%	68%	48%
	(22)	(51)	(93)	(40)	(208)

We should give aid to other countries if they need help

	Under $4000	$4000–7999	$8000–14,999	$15,000 and over	Total
Literalists	34%	40%	41%	61%	40%
	(62)	(103)	(81)	(23)	(273)
Nonliteralists	30%	44%	49%	63%	48%
	(37)	(72)	(108)	(49)	(271)

CIVIL RIGHTS ISSUES[a]

Blacks have a right to live wherever they can afford to

	Under $4000	$4000–7999	$8000–14,999	$15,000 and over	Total
Literalists	54%	56%	66%	74%	59%
	(78)	(104)	(80)	(23)	(290)
Nonliteralists	72%	80%	78%	94%	81%
	(32)	(69)	(109)	(47)	(262)

Table 7.3 *Continued*

Attitude Toward the Bible	Yearly Income				
	Under $4000	$4000–7999	$8000–14,999	$15,000 and over	Total

The government should guarantee the right of blacks to go to any hotel or restaurant they can afford

Literalists	34%	46%	51%	67%	46%
	(67)	(103)	(77)	(24)	(276)
Nonliteralists	50%	51%	55%	68%	56%
	(38)	(72)	(114)	(44)	(272)

The government should see to it that white and black children are allowed to go to the same schools

Literalists	25%	31%	36%	42%	31%
	(71)	(104)	(76)	(24)	(281)
Nonliteralists	36%	41%	25%	40%	33%
	(36)	(71)	(110)	(48)	(268)

Favoring desegregation

Literalists	20%	19%	26%	36%	22%
	(82)	(111)	(84)	(25)	(309)
Nonliteralists	29%	37%	31%	56%	37%
	(42)	(79)	(115)	(45)	(287)

ECONOMIC ISSUES[a]

Approving of the government helping people get doctors and medical care at low costs

Literalists	76%	49%	49%	32%	55%
	(75)	(101)	(73)	(22)	(276)
Nonliteralists	49%	60%	43%	54%	50%
	(35)	(70)	(100)	(41)	(252)

Table 7.3. *Continued*

Attitude Toward the Bible	Yearly Income				
	Under $4000	$4000–7999	$8000–14,999	$15,000 and over	Total
	The government should help towns and cities provide education for grade and high school children				
Literalists	24%	17%	28%	9%	21%
	(63)	(93)	(65)	(23)	(247)
Nonliteralists	34%	25%	17%	34%	25%
	(38)	(69)	(105)	(44)	(260)
	The government should see to it that every person has a job and a good standard of living				
Literalists	41%	22%	23%	31%	27%
	(73)	(101)	(80)	(24)	(283)
Nonliteralists	24%	19%	19%	26%	21%
	(37)	(74)	(110)	(47)	(272)

Source.   1968 American National Election Study conducted by the Survey Research Center, University of Michigan.

[a] On all these questions the respondents were first asked whether they were interested or concerned enough to hold an opinion on one side of the issue or the other. These percentages include only those who were interested and who had an opinion on the issue.

[b] Only those who knew that the People's Republic of China was a Communist country and not a member of the United Nations were asked this question.

Thus on racial issues we must conclude that the association between the laity's religious and political views is tenous. On the last of these policy areas, economic liberalism, we find no such relationship in beliefs—except perhaps among high-income, nonorthodox laymen. Table 7.3 gives the breakdowns on several questions taken from the SRC survey, revealing somewhat irregular patterns from issue to issue. Among the respondents of the highest income level, however, there is a tendency for the nonliteralists to take more liberal positions on economic issues. The importance of this relationship, if it is found to exist on other issues, would be obvious: the new breed clergy are predominantly drawn from high-status, nonorthodox congregations. If there is a reservoir of support for economic liberalism among such parishioners, these ministers should find it easier to speak out on behalf of liberal issues. We should not forget, however, that these differences are only relative and that the majority of these high-status, nonorthodox laymen continue to hold conservative views on such political issues; moreover, this pattern did not exist on the two economics questions included in the Glock–Stark survey. Thus the finding, although suggestive, does not indicate that modernist clergymen are likely to have congregations that support liberal political programs.[16]

The data collected in these two surveys furnish mixed evidence concerning the associations between the Protestant laity's religious and political beliefs. Religious orthodoxy appears to accompany conservative views on some racial issues and—among upper socio-economic status groups— liberal views on economic questions. Such patterns are similar to those recently reported by Seymour Martin Lipset and Earl Raab using a slightly different classificatory scheme.[17] Only with respect to Communist-related issues, however, does a strong and consistent relationship appear between religious orthodoxy and the positions taken by Protestant laymen on political issues. Orthodox laymen at all income levels are clearly the most opposed to rapprochement with Communist nations abroad and are the most worried about the spread of communism at home. Our general conclusion from this analysis is thus consistent with that of Robert Wuthnow, who recently reviewed 58 different findings concerning the relationship between religious orthodoxy and political beliefs: "orthodoxy, in spite of being charged with legitimating the status quo, seems to be of little consequence for political and social views, at least outside of the South and among adults."[18]

Thus the attitudes of Protestant laymen toward political issues are not nearly as closely related to their religious beliefs as they are among Protestant clergymen. As with Converse's findings with respect to political actors, the degree of attitudinal constraint among religious leaders is far greater than that observed among religious followers.

In assessing these findings, we should keep in mind Converse's remarks concerning the differences in attitudinal constraint likely to exist between any group of elites and nonelites. As we move down the information scale from leaders to followers, the subjects' belief systems are likely to become increasingly narrow in scope and less abstract and sophisticated in content. Such attitudinal patterns reflect a variety of differences likely to characterize leaders and followers, including training, level of attention, and personal involvement in the issues under consideration. Viewed from this perspective, we would always expect a gap to exist between the religious, ethical, and political attitudes of religious leaders and the mass membership of organized religion.

On the other hand, however, it is clear from these findings and from our earlier considerations that the gap between Protestant leaders and followers is exceedingly large. For most Americans it appears that religion has indeed become a private affair: that religious values have become compartmentalized from the important issues facing society, thus having little or no effect on the everyday actions of the church-going public. For clergymen who wish to develop an action-oriented church, this privatization of beliefs constitutes a serious problem. Many laymen in liberal denominations have joined their ministers in rejecting the orthodox view of Biblical truths and religious salvation, but they have not shared their ethical commitment to provide church leadership on the major social and political issues of the day. They have abandoned many of the traditional conceptions of the church's function and purpose, in other words, but they have not accepted the modernist version of the church's role in society.

Thus the religious convictions of Protestant laymen do not carry with them the same ethical and political implications that we have observed among the clergy. Perhaps Protestant laymen are simply "behind" their ministers in the development of new religious orientations, and nonorthodox laymen will eventually come to believe as the modernist clergy do on political and ethical matters. From all appearances, however, Protestant religion seems to be losing its influence in American society rather than becoming more salient or authoritative. If the trends toward modernism and secularization described in the first chapter are accurate, we might expect such compartmentalization of religion to increase rather than to diminish.

At the same time, all laymen do not hold conservative views on political and ethical questions, nor do they always actively oppose the clergy activists. As we have seen, some churchgoers voice support for liberal political programs and for an ethically involved church, and some ministers—particularly the most socially active—report that the views of their parishioners have a generally encouraging effect on their own activist behavior. As the next chapter reveals, many congregation members openly supported the efforts of their pastors to involve the church critically in political issues.

Furthermore, lay beliefs are by no means uniform, either within or between Protestant denominations. Of particular importance is the tendency of some churches to take on a "conservative" or a "liberal" character. The existence of such ideologically oriented churches are well known both to local laymen and to church leaders. Laymen often join (or transfer to) churches that correspond with their own beliefs, and parish appointments are generally made with the idea of matching like-minded ministers and congregations. The result is that ministers in some churches are given much greater latitude to pursue an active ethical role than ministers in others. From our survey, it is apparent that the socially active clergy tended to serve such "liberal" congregations; the obvious problem for ethically inclined ministers is that there are relatively few such parishes.

Some differences in lay attitudes toward public issues also exist between denominations—caused less by religious differences than by the socio-economic characteristics of the lay members of these denominations. As Table 7.3 indicates, upper socioeconomic status laymen have more liberal views on foreign policy and civil rights issues and more conservative positions on economic questions. Since modernist, new breed activists tend to be drawn predominantly from high-status denominations, we would expect to find greater lay receptivity for clerical involvement in issues of the former type than of the latter. If so, the level of conflict within Protestant churches may depend in part on the kinds of issue arising in the future. Conflicts may be greater if these issues are economic (e.g., welfare reform, job guarantees, or the closing of tax loopholes) than if they involve civil rights or foreign policy questions. We return to such considerations in the closing chapter.

Lay Beliefs and Religious Involvement.   The absence of support for a more ethically engaged church among laymen who have turned away from orthodox Protestantism obviously has some disturbing implications for liberal denominations and for the modernist clergy. We must first ask what will tie the nonorthodox layman to the institutional church once he no longer accepts its traditional goals and functions. Traditional Protestantism is explicit in its supernaturalism and in its focus on redemption and religious salvation. It specifies man's relationship to God and enumerates the consequences of holding to the faith or of abandoning it. To accept God and Jesus Christ is to be saved and to receive the blessing of eternal life; to reject them is to be eternally damned. Such a doctrine obviously provides a firm rationale for the church's existence and, for the believer, a strong motivation not to stray from the faith.

Although modernist clergymen have largely replaced supernaturalism and otherworldliness with an ethical concern with man's relations in secular society, we have seen that most laymen have not. What, then, will motivate these laymen to remain active members of the church? Stark and Glock, who address themselves to this question at the end of their important study, show that the more ethically oriented laymen are the most likely to stay home on Sundays and the least likely to contribute financially to their churches.[20] This relationship held within all the denominations surveyed, even when class controls were introduced, thus suggesting that ethicalism has not provided a theological substitute for those laymen who no longer accept the orthodoxies of traditional Protestantism.

Not surprisingly, then, the liberal Protestant churches are in the poorest organizational health. As Stark and Glock discovered, the members of liberal denominations are far less committed to organized religion on a variety of dimensions—from the importance they attach to religion in their personal lives to their involvement in the affairs of the local parish. They summarize their findings as follows:

> ... the majority of members of liberal bodies are dormant Christians. They have adopted the theology of the new reformation, but at the same time they have stopped attending church, stopped participating in church activities, stopped contributing funds, stopped praying, and are uninformed about religion. Furthermore, only a minority of members of the liberal bodies feel that their religious perspective provides them with the answers to the meaning and purpose of life, while the overwhelming majority of conservatives feel theirs does supply the answers. Finally, the liberal congregations resemble theater audiences, their members are mainly strangers to one another, while conservative congregations resemble primary groups, united by widespread bonds of personal friendship.[21]

Not all observers give such a bleak assessment of the current circumstances of the liberal Protestant denominations. However, it is clear that non-orthodox laymen are less loyal or committed to the institutional life of the church than the orthodox laity and that many liberal churches are suffering severe losses in membership and finances. Dean Kelley, in the book discussed in the first chapter, presents an impressive array of official membership statistics to document the poor organizational health of the liberal denominations.[22] In addition, we can turn again to the SRC survey for corroboration of these patterns of church attendance on a national scale. According to the data of Table 7.4, Protestant laymen who believe that the Bible is God's Word and contains nothing but truth report that they attend church most regularly. More than half the laymen who feel that the Bible was "written by men and inspired by God," however, report that they attend church "seldom" or "never."

Many modernist ministers may experience a similar loss in religious meaning and professional conviction as a result of their acceptance of a demythologized theology. As we have suggested at various points in this analysis, their involvement in ethical activities may represent an effort to find new meaning and relevance in their religious roles: social activism may serve as a substitute for their loss in traditional functions and goals; being "in trouble" with their parishioners may serve as a sign that their ministry is "relevant" and "prophetic." Our concluding chapter presents some evidence

Table 7.4. Laymen Who Have Literalist Views Toward the Bible Attend Church Most Frequently

"Would you say you go to church regularly, often, seldom, or never?"	Attitude Toward the Bible		
	God's Word	Written by Men; Inspired by God	Written by Men; of Little Worth Today
Regularly	42%	32%	11%
Often	20	15	—
Seldom	33	46	59
Never	5	7	30
	100%	100%	100%
	(325)	(246)	(27)

Source. 1968 American National Election Study conducted by the Survey Research Center, University of Michigan.

to support this position. Modernist clergymen are in fact the least satisfied with their chosen profession and are the most likely to think about leaving the church.

Our concern at this point, however, lies with the religious commitments of nonorthodox laymen. Two very serious questions arising from the contrasting belief systems of Protestant ministers and laymen ask whether the laymen who have turned away from orthodox Protestantism are likely to accept the new ethicalism of the modernist clergy and whether this ethicalism is sufficient in itself to give meaning and purpose to the laity's religious involvement. The present evidence suggests that it is not. As the next chapter reveals, substantial conflict exists in California between the modernist, ethically active clergy and their parishioners over social activism. A substantial number of Protestant laymen have left the church or are withdrawing their loyalty in other ways as a direct result of new breed activism. Unless the new ethicalism becomes more relevant to Protestant laymen—or unless church leaders are able to develop new alternatives to traditional Protestant orthodoxy—the future of liberal Protestant denominations as organizations appears to be uncertain. We have more to say on this matter after reviewing our findings in subsequent chapters.

Lay Beliefs and New Breed Activism. A more immediate problem brought out by the above-mentioned patterns in lay belief has to do with how the ethically committed clergy will be able to gain lay acceptance of their actions and how they will be able to attract others to their views on public issues. Since laymen and the clergy do not make the same connections between their religious beliefs and their ethical and political positions, it follows that modernist ministers will find it difficult to appeal for lay support on religious grounds alone. Unless the laymen who have rejected religious orthodoxies begin to see a relationship between their new theology and ethical and political issues, it seems unlikely that arguments about religious doctrine will be sufficient in themselves to win lay support for clergy activism.

It is possible, of course, that Protestant laymen will come to see more connections between their own religious values on the one hand and societal problems on the other. We find that clergy activists were supported in their ethical endeavors by a small but significant minority of laymen during the sixties, and we suspect that the events of this period did result in some church-goers seeing a more positive relationship between certain of their religious beliefs and such public issues as racism, poverty, and militarism. If the politicization of the church continues for a long period of time, we might expect more laymen to be forced to consider the relevance of their religious commitments to social issues. Any major transformation in lay attitudes seems to us to be quite unlikely, however. American society appears to be becoming more secular, not less, and nonorthodox laymen are currently turning away from the church rather than finding new meaning in it. Furthermore, it seems improbable that liberal denominations can operate for long under the intensely political conditions of the sixties; they are likely to become bankrupt before they can "convert" significant numbers of their members to a more activist social ethic.

What kinds of strategy are available to ministers who wish to involve the church in controversial social and political issues? On what other grounds can they seek support for their ethical activities? We can think of at least four. They can attempt to influence the ethical and political attitudes of their members directly through official pronouncements on public issues, study materials, or the activities of individual ministers. They can try to reach an "understanding" with conservative laymen by paying close attention to their other ministerial roles and by appealing for lay support on personal grounds. They can move to attract new members to their congregations— churchmen who are more politically liberal and more sympathetic to the activism of the modernist clergy. Finally, they can simply ignore the con-servatism of their parishioners and seek allies outside the church among those who are like-minded politically—with no attention to the consequences such actions might have for their parish churches, for organized religion, or for themselves.

The first strategy is unlikely to meet with success as long as religion remains peripheral to the lives of most Americans. If the average Protestant layman forms his ethical and political views independently of his religious commitments, there is little reason to expect that church leaders will be able to obtain his support on other grounds. The dilemma faced by religious leaders in making such direct political appeals is obvious.[23] On the one hand, if they are specific in their political references and in calling for church action on public problems, they risk losing their moral authority and their distinctive role in society. Churchmen who oppose such policies or actions may feel that the church has failed to preserve the separation of church and state, coming to view it as simply another political pressure group. On the other hand, if church leaders state their political and ethical messages in general terms, they will have little impact on the personal beliefs of churchmen or on the problems facing American society. Abstract principles can be easily ignored, and moral expressions without a specific plan of action can have little effect on social conditions.

Thus the use of direct political or ethical appeals to the Protestant laity would appear to be a poor substitute for gaining religious adherents to ethicalism. Most churchmen do not feel that their religious leaders have any special political wisdom or authority, and surely such lay conservatism and resistance to church activism will be difficult to overcome without laying a religious foundation for proposed changes. If this cannot be done, religious leaders must compete with the other influential forces that shape the political thinking of Americans—a task for which they are not especially well qualified, skilled, or legitimized.

The second strategy involves devoting a great deal of personal attention to the members of the local church and trying to develop a relation of mutual trust and understanding with them. Hopefully, laymen will respond by allowing the parish minister more latitude in his ethical actions and by joining him in his activities. Such a course of action would produce the same problems we have just described. In addition, it is fraught with danger and compromise for the ethically committed clergy, since it implies that the parish minister should temper his own activities, to "stay in touch" with his parishioners. Since we asked the California clergymen a number of questions about their professional and social relations with their parishioners, we can comment further on this matter in a later chapter.

A third strategy for the activist clergy is to recruit from outside their churches new parish members who are more sympathetic to an ethical role for organized religion and who are drawn to the church by a minister's ethical leadership. During the sixties many modernist church leaders advocated such a procedure. They felt (urged on by sociological critiques) that the church could regenerate itself by becoming more socially relevant and could thereby attract new types of individuals to the church. We must ask in this respect, however, just which groups are likely to be attracted to organized religion for such reasons. The obvious answer is, the individuals in American society who share the modernist clergy's concern with the course of public events and their views on social and political issues: those individuals, in other words, who look with favor on the civil rights and black power movements, who support the efforts of the poor to organize, and who oppose such military adventures as the war in Vietnam. A curious sight at many of the political rallies of the past decade has been the intermingling of lavishly robed or white-collared clerics and bearded, bedraggled members of the youth culture. These two groups, along with some academicians and intellectuals, have been at the forefront of the political protest movements of the past 10 years.

One possible alternative for the ethically minded clergy, then, might be to seek new support and new religious "converts" from the members of the groups with which they are aligned politically—from among college students, hippies, young academicians, and intellectuals. Some clerical leaders have spoken optimistically about such an audience for their new theology, and class enrollments in religious studies have continued to rise dramatically since the late sixties. Yet everything we know about the sources of religious commitment and institutional loyalty to organized religion tells us that the members of these groups are among the least likely to be recruited to Protestantism or to become involved in the institutional life of the church. As one minister wrote when asked if he had gained any new members as a result of his ethical activities, "Liberals and intellectuals who support this kind of activity rarely make commitments to the church."

Thus ethically committed clergy who ignore the usual middle-class base of Protestantism may well find themselves with political rather than religious allies. Such individuals may find a compatible environment for their activism in college chaplaincies—and new breed activists have in fact been disproportionately drawn to such positions. But the institutional base, the wealth, and the rationale for the church exist on the parish level, not on university campuses or in special denominationally supported ministries. As we discuss in the next chapter, clergy activism seemed to attract some new members to liberal churches during the sixties, but the losses in these respects far outdistanced the gains.

NOTES AND REFERENCES

1. Philip E. Converse, "The Nature of Belief Systems in Mass Publics," in *Ideology and Discontent*, David Apter, ed. (New York: Free Press, 1964), pp. 208–209.

2. A description of this study is contained in Charles Y. Glock and Rodney Stark, *Christian Beliefs and Anti-Semitism* (New York: Harper & Row, 1966), pp. 215–248. The

analysis of lay beliefs to which we refer frequently in this chapter is contained in Stark and Glock, *American Piety: The Nature of Religious Commitment* (Berkeley: University of California Press, 1968).

3. These data, like those in Chapter 5, were originally collected by the Survey Research Center, University of Michigan, and made available through the Inter-University Consortium for Political Research. Neither the Survey Research Center nor the Consortium bear any responsibility for the analyses or interpretations presented here.

4. See Robert Wuthnow, "Religious Commitment and Conservatism: In Quest of an Elusive Relationship," in *Religion in Sociological Perspective: Essays in the Empirical Study of Religion*, Charles Y. Glock, ed. (Belmont, Calif.: Wadsworth, 1973).

5. Lay responses to most of these questions are presented in Stark and Glock, *op. cit.*, pp. 33–37.

6. These percentages refer to whites only. We have eliminated nonwhites from the analysis that follows because their church affiliations and political loyalties differ so markedly from those of whites.

7. Jeffrey K. Hadden, *The Gathering Storm in the Churches* (Garden City, N.Y.: Doubleday, 1969), pp. 146–154.

8. Thomas C. Campbell and Yoshio Fukuyama, *The Fragmented Layman: An Empirical Study of Lay Attitudes* (Philadelphia: Pilgrim Press, 1970), p. 239. For a similar pattern among lay Episcopalians, see Charles Y. Glock, Benjamin B. Ringer, and Earl R. Babbie, *To Comfort and To Challenge: A Dilemma of the Contemporary Church* (Berkeley: University of California Press, 1967). The data for the Episcopal study were collected in 1952.

9. Stark and Glock, *op. cit.*, pp. 58–64.

10. Among Catholic laymen this relationship was reversed. *Ibid.*, pp. 214–215.

11. Barbara W. Hargrove, "Local Congregations and Social Change," *Sociological Analysis*, **30** (Spring 1969), pp. 13–22.

12. James D. Davidson, "Religious Belief as an Independent Variable," *Journal for the Scientific Study of Religion*, **11** (March 1972), pp. 65–75. Individuals of high socioeconomic status are likely to be active participants in politics and to hold nonorthodox religious beliefs. Since the SES variable was not controlled, we have no way of knowing the independent relationship that may exist between these religious measures and the respondents' political behavior.

13. David R. Gibbs, Samuel A. Mueller, and James R. Wood, "Doctrinal Orthodoxy, Salience, and the Consequential Dimension," *Journal for the Scientific Study of Religion*, **12** (March 1973), pp. 33–52. For similar results with a student sample, see Howard M. Bahr, Lois Franz Bartel, and Bruce A. Chadwick, "Orthodoxy, Activism, and the Salience of Religion," *Journal for the Scientific Study of Religion*, **10** (Summer 1971), pp. 69–75. In both instances, the relationship was found only among subjects for whom religion was of extremely high salience. In the Glock-Stark study a large proportion of laymen in our nine denominations (44 percent) said that their church membership was "extremely important" to them, and no major differences in belief structure were found between this group and the remaining respondents. Our use of the church membership variable in Table 7.2 is an attempt, therefore, to introduce this dimension of saliency.

14. Glock and Stark, *op. cit.*; Milton Rokeach, "Faith, Hope and Bigotry," *Psychology Today*, **3** (April 1970), p. 33ff; and Seymour Martin Lipset and Earl Raab, *The Politics of Unreason* (New York: Harper & Row, 1970), pp. 468–472.

15. The Glock–Stark questions did not refer so specifically to civil rights policies or

principles but dealt in general terms with attitudes toward blacks or toward the separation of blacks and whites in different institutions. About half these questions reveal a slight tendency by the more orthodox group of laymen to hold conservative or anti-civil rights views. These differences are rather small, however, and could not be considered to be significant, taken by themselves.

16.   We find some evidence in these data—particularly in the SRC survey—to support the proposition that religion serves as the "opiate" of the masses. On all four economic liberalism questions in the SRC survey, as well as both those included in the Glock–Stark study, low-income laymen who attend church most frequently also appear to hold the most conservative political opinions; this pattern occurred most consistently and strongly, furthermore, among the more orthodox lay respondents. These differences were fairly small, however, and they emerged most clearly in the SRC survey—where our religious measure has been more crudely formulated. Also, we are dealing here with a relatively small sample size.

17.   Lipset and Raab, *op. cit.*, pp. 468–472.

18.   Wuthnow, *op. cit.*

19.   These differences emerge most clearly in the SRC survey, where there is a greater economic range in the members of various Protestant denominations. In Glock and Stark's study of laymen in the San Francisco Bay area, we find that the socioeconomic differences in the membership of these nine denominations is relatively slight.

20.   Stark and Glock, *op. cit.*, pp. 204–224.

21.   *Ibid.*, p. 221.

22.   Dean Kelley, *Why Conservative Churches Are Growing* (New York: Harper & Row, 1972).

23.   See Daniel Callahan, "The Quest for Social Relevance," *Daedalus*, **96** (Winter 1967), p. 203.

LAY REACTIONS TO CLERGY ACTIVISM

8. Although the conservatism of Protestant laymen is generally recognized as a major obstacle to the development of an action-oriented church, little is known about how the laity commonly respond to clergy activism. Does the opposition of lay members to social ethics, for example, often go beyond mere verbal admonishments? Do Protestant laymen frequently use their formal control over the governance of the local church to censor ethically active ministers? How often, finally, do parishioners leave a church or withdraw their financial contributions in reaction to the pastor's ethical activities?

Certainly the most comprehensive and suggestive examination of lay reactions to clergy activism is the previously mentioned study by Campbell and Pettigrew of the involvement of Protestant ministers in the desegregation crisis in Little Rock, Arkansas, in 1957.[1] The authors found that clergymen who preached racial tolerance in Little Rock elicited extremely hostile reactions from the members of their congregations. They were told by their parishioners that the church had no business becoming involved in the issue, their parish churches lost members, and they saw church attendance swell in the churches served by prosegregationist clergymen. Such reactions proved to be highly effective. When the pressures became too great—and absenteeism from Sunday services too high—the city's most influential Protestant ministers withdrew from the controversy, ending their protest with a symbolic day of prayer. The few clergymen who remained steadfast in their support of racial integration suffered severely for their commitment. They faced mass defections in membership, and most were eventually driven from their parish positions as a direct result of their stand on the issue. Despite the sympathy of church leaders for integration, denominational officials in

Little Rock were unable or unwilling to come to the assistance of the committed clergymen and in fact urged them to restrain their actions and to conform to the wishes of their parishioners.

The Campbell–Pettigrew study thus shows that in Little Rock, at least, Protestant laymen reacted strongly against parish ministers who showed signs of exerting leadership on a controversial local issue. They were able to silence most integration-minded clergymen and later took vengeance on the few recalcitrants who disregarded their warnings. California, of course, is less conservative than Arkansas, and few public issues have been as explosive as the Little Rock crisis of 1957. We might not expect laymen anywhere to be as hostile to clergy activism as southern whites during the early civil rights days. Campbell and Pettigrew also dealt with a relatively small number of ministers—they studied the clergy who most actively took the desegregation side during the controversy.

To ascertain how Protestant laymen react on other issues and in other circumstances, we asked the California clergymen a number of questions about the response of their parishioners to their involvement in each of the three public controversies examined in previous chapters. The ministers' responses to these questions allow us to study the actions of Protestant laymen in a wide variety of circumstances—on three diverse issues of public policy, among clergymen who take opposing liberal and conservative positions on political issues, and among those who are most active in expressing their ethical views. We also asked the California ministers about both the opposition and the support they received from their parishioners during these three public controversies. In the former instance we asked each respondent whether the members of his congregation had shown their opposition to his activism in any of five ways: by privately expressing their opposition to him, by publicly expressing their opposition before the local church board, by reducing their contributions to the church, by trying to have him removed from his position, or by withdrawing their membership from the church. To determine what, if any, support the ministers received from their parishioners during these three controversies, we also asked corresponding questions about the manner in which lay members had expressed approval of the ministers' public activities. A large number of our respondents reported that their ethical activities had elicited actions of support and of opposition from the members of their congregations.

Proposition 14. We have already mentioned Proposition 14, the bitterly fought initiative proposal in the 1964 California general election, designed to repeal the state's fair housing laws and to amend the state constitution to prohibit the passage of such legislation in the future. Most of the Protestant clergy in California took one side of the issue, and most of the Protestant laity the other. Seventy-seven percent of our respondents reported that they had opposed the initiative proposal, but it was passed by the electorate with more than 65 percent of the vote. It likely received even greater support from the ministers' predominantly white, middle-class parishioners—and the clergy in fact reported that most of the members of their congregations had favored passage.

Not surprisingly, clerical efforts to organize opposition to Proposition 14 created conflicts within a large number of parish churches in California. Many Protestant ministers who actively campaigned against the initiative proposal were opposed both privately and publicly by members of their congregations and met with rather extreme punitive actions. Somewhat more surprisingly, however, many of them were supported by their parishioners and felt that they had gained new members and financial contributions as a result of their activism.

Table 8.1 summarizes the situation. The negative responses of the ministers' parishioners indicate that clergymen who were actively opposed to the proposed constitutional amendment frequently faced hostile congregations: 83 percent reported that they met with private opposition to their actions, 47 percent lost contributions, 32 percent had their positions publicly attacked before their church boards, and 11 percent faced efforts to have them removed from their parish positions. Such reactions from our respondents' parishioners must certainly be regarded as severe. More than any other data we have presented, they illustrate the conflict between modernist, ethically committed Protestant clergymen and their predominantly conservative parishioners. Not only do most Protestant laymen hold conservative positions on public issues and stand opposed to ethicalism, but many also feel so strongly about these matters that they attempt to censor the actions of their ministers. We learn how common such lay response is as we proceed with our analysis in this chapter.

Table 8.1 also illustrates the extent to which lay–clergy conflict over social activism largely involves the liberal clergy. We see that clergymen who took conservative positions in supporting Proposition 14 faced some opposition to their involvement in the issue, but not nearly as much as their liberal colleagues. These ministers, of course, not only took conservative positions on Proposition 14 but were also relatively inactive during the anti-fair housing campaign.

Table 8.1 also indicates that many parish ministers were actively supported by some of their parishioners on the issue, and those who were opposed to Proposition 14 most frequently received such support. Eighty-six percent of the clergymen who campaigned against the initiative proposal reported that

Table 8.1. Ministers Who Actively Opposed Proposition 14 Most Often Reported Lay Opposition and Lay Support for Their Actions

	Opposed to Proposition 14	In Favor of Proposition 14	All Clergy
ACTION TAKEN BY PARISHIONERS IN OPPOSITION TO CLERGY'S ACTIVISM			
Privately expressed their opposition	83% (877)	39% (175)	76% (1078)
Reduced their contributions to the church	47% (844)	9% (172)	40% (1041)
Publicly expressed their opposition before the church board	32% (871)	5% (174)	27% (1070)
Tried to have the minister removed from the church	11% (862)	2% (175)	9% (1062)
ACTION TAKEN BY PARISHIONERS IN SUPPORT OF CLERGY'S ACTIVISM			
Privately expressed their approval	86% (876)	63% (176)	82% (1077)
Joined the minister in some public expression of his views	50% (872)	16% (174)	43% (1071)
Publicly expressed their approval before the church board	33% (870)	7% (174)	28% (1069)
Increased their contributions to the church	12% (806)	2% (170)	10% (1001)
EFFECT OF CLERGY'S ACTIVISM ON CHURCH MEMBERSHIP			
Both gained and lost members	22%	8%	19%
Gained members	2	3	2
Lost members	29	4	25
Neither gained nor lost members	47	85	54
	100% (876)	100% (177)	100% (1079)

some of their parishioners privately expressed their approval of their actions, 50 percent said that they were joined in some public statement of opposition to Proposition 14, 32 percent indicated that they were backed by lay members of their church when the issue came up at a church board meeting, and 12 percent felt that they had gained church contributions as a result of their activism. A fairly large proportion of liberal activists were able thus to find some support for their ethical actions among the members of their congregations to counterbalance the opposition also present. By and large, the ministers who experienced lay opposition of the type just described were most likely to report such expressions of lay support. Two-thirds of the clergymen who said that their activism had met with opposition before their church boards, for example, noted that some laymen had also spoken out in support of them.

Such support can be important for the ethically committed clergy, and we expand on this point later. Our data show, however, that on balance the losses suffered by the clergy activists far outnumber the gains in such crucial areas as church finances and membership. Four times as many parish ministers reported having lost contributions as a result of their activism than having gained. Our inquiries do not tell us the exact amounts of these financial losses; but in any event, they appear to be far greater than the gains.

Probably the most important question in this area involves the impact of clergy activism on church membership. These data show much the same pattern we have just described. Some of the liberal clergy did feel that they had gained members because of their active opposition to Proposition 14, but many more felt that they had lost them. Thus 2 percent said that they had gained members, 29 percent said that they had lost some, and 22 percent that they experienced both losses and gains. Less than half the ministers who spoke out against the initiative proposal, in other words, reported that membership loyalties remained unaffected by their involvement in the issue. Again this is a firm indication of the controversy surrounding the anti-fair housing issue and the degree to which some laymen will go to express their opposition to clergy activism. In contrast to these figures, only 15 percent of the ministers who took conservative positions in supporting Proposition 14 reported that their activities had led to individuals leaving or joining the church, and almost as many reported membership gains as losses.

Even these gross figures show that Protestant laymen often react in punitive ways to the social activism of their parish ministers. Nevertheless, Table 8.1 includes all respondents who expressed their views on the issue in any way. Some of these ministers had done nothing but discuss the issue with the members of their congregations; others had done little more. Even more indicative of the characteristic lay response to clergy activism, therefore, is how the California laymen reacted to the more socially active respondents.

The information we have collected does not tell us quantitatively how active the clergy were during the initiative campaign or just what the ministers said in their public admonitions. But we do know whether they had engaged in various acts of ethical leadership, and we find a consistent pattern to their activism. Using the same techniques described in Chapter 5, we can arrange our respondents along a continuum from those who had participated in the most "extreme" or "difficult" of these acts to those who had participated in the least extreme or "easiest." By and large, ministers who engaged in one of the more difficult acts reported that they had engaged in all the easier ones as well, and the statistical requirements for Guttman scaling are satisfied.[2]

According to Table 8.2, the parishioners were far more reactive to the activities of the more socially active respondents. Again this included both the amount of support and the amount of opposition faced by the clergy— although the losses appear to far outnumber the gains. In this case, the most activist clergy are those who had organized a social action group within their churches to campaign against the amendment (as well as serving on a Committee against Proposition 14 and engaging in many other acts of ethical leadership). They numbered 240, or more than one-fifth of the ministers surveyed who were serving in parish positions in 1964. We see that 90 percent of these ministers were privately opposed by members of their congregations, 67 percent lost contributions, 50 percent faced opposition before their church boards, and 20 percent underwent efforts to have them fired. Such opposition is certainly substantial. We did not ask our respondents how many of these efforts to have them fired actually succeeded, but a number did note that they had lost their jobs over the issue.

Table 8.2 also reveals that a large proportion of these ministers received lay backing for their actions. For example, more reported that they had been publicly supported by members of their congregation before the local church board than opposed. In addition, 27 percent felt that they had gained contributions as a result of activism on the issue. Again, however, the situation is best summarized by the impact of the activities of these ministers on their church membership. We see that more than three-quarters of the most active ministers believed that their parishioners had left or joined the church as a result of their involvement in the issue. Some thought that their activism had gained members, but more reported losses: 4 percent indicated that they had gained members, 37 percent said that they lost some, and another 37 percent reported both losses and gains.

Our survey thus shows that the anti-fair housing campaign brought many California ministers into conflict with the members of their congregations, but it also elicited some support. We discover that this pattern is repeated with the other two issues we have been examining.

Table 8.2. Ministers Who Were Most Active in Their Opposition to Proposition 14 Most Often Reported Lay Opposition and Lay Support for Their Actions

	Activism[a]					
	1	2	3	4	5	6
ACTION TAKEN BY PARISHIONERS IN OPPOSITION TO CLERGY'S ACTIVISM						
Privately expressed their opposition	90% (239)	89% (185)	87% (145)	81% (182)	70% (57)	45% (49)
Reduced their contributions to the church	67% (232)	58% (173)	47% (140)	31% (176)	23% (56)	6% (48)
Publicly expressed their opposition before the church board	50% (238)	36% (184)	28% (143)	21% (180)	11% (57)	2% (49)
Tried to have the minister removed from the church	20% (232)	14% (182)	6% (145)	7% (179)	2% (56)	— (49)
ACTION TAKEN BY PARISHIONERS IN SUPPORT OF CLERGY'S ACTIVISM						
Privately expressed their approval	97% (239)	91% (185)	90% (145)	79% (182)	72% (57)	52% (48)
Joined the minister in some public expression of his views	84% (239)	63% (186)	41% (142)	26% (181)	11% (56)	6% (48)
Publicly expressed their opposition before the church board	58% (238)	35% (184)	32% (143)	16% (181)	13% (56)	— (48)
Increased their contributions to the church	27% (220)	13% (165)	5% (131)	7% (169)	— (53)	— (48)

216

Table 8.2. *Continued*

	Activism[a]					
	1	2	3	4	5	6
EFFECT OF CLERGY'S ACTIVISM ON CHURCH MEMBERSHIP						
Both gained and lost members	37%	23%	18%	15%	5%	2%
Gained members	4	2	1	1	—	—
Lost members	37	40	30	22	18	2
Neither gained nor lost members	22	35	52	62	77	96
	100% (240)	100% (184)	100% (145)	100% (181)	100% (57)	100% (48)

[a] On this 6-point scale, 1 is highly active; 6 is inactive.

The California Grape Strike. The California grape strike centered around the efforts of Cesar Chavez to organize migratory farm workers in the Delano area of the San Joaquin Valley. At the time of our survey, the most open and bitter hostilities between the workers and growers had temporarily passed, and accommodations had been reached in some areas. The issue was hardly settled, however, either for the grape pickers or for other agricultural workers in the state, and the effort to organize the Valley's farm workers has continued into the 1970s.

We saw in Chapter 4 that although many California clergymen became involved in the farm labor controversy, fewer did so in this case than in the other two conflicts under study. More than a quarter, for example, reported that they had not even discussed the issue with any of their parishioners. For this reason, we would not expect lay reactions to be as great during this issue as during the others—and indeed they were not. We also saw in Chapter 4 that parish clergymen in the immediate area of the grape strike, the San Joaquin Valley, gave considerably less support to Chavez and his striking farm workers than ministers elsewhere in the state. Fifty-six percent of the clergymen in the San Joaquin Valley either opposed the organization of farm workers or opposed clerical involvement in the issue; only 30 percent said that they favored the assistance given by members of the clerical profession to the organizational effort. Given this pattern of attitudes, we pay particular attention in this section to the occupational climate in the San

Joaquin Valley during the grape strike and the reactions of Protestant lay-men to the ministers in the Valley who actively supported the workers' position.

Table 8.3 breaks down the parishioners' reported responses to clergy involvement in the issue, either in support of or against the striking workers. A much smaller number of ministers who spoke out on the grape strike experienced either positive or negative lay reactions than was the case during the anti-fair housing campaign. As in the previous conflict, however, both types of lay reaction were most common among clergymen who took liberal positions (i.e., favoring clerical support of the striking grape pickers). Fifteen percent of these ministers reported having lost financial contributions because of their involvement, 14 percent were opposed before their church boards, and 14 percent indicated a loss of members due to the conflict. Again, a smaller number of these clergymen also reported financial and membership gains because of their social activism. Thus within the state as a whole, the grape strike was not nearly as controversial as Proposition 14, but ministers who actively supported the striking workers suffered for their choice.

Once again we examined the reactions of our respondents' parishioners according to the ministers' degree of activism. In this case, 64 ministers reported having taken the most extreme act—namely, marching or traveling to the Delano area to express their views. We need not repeat all our calculations here, but again we found that this most active group of clergymen faced considerable opposition to their public activities. Seventy-five percent met with private opposition, 33 percent lost contributions, 30 percent were opposed before their church boards, and 11 percent faced efforts to have them fired. Thus clergymen who were most outspoken in their support of Chavez often encountered substantial lay opposition to their actions—although not nearly as much as those who were most active during the anti-fair housing campaign.

Finally, many of the most active ministers also enjoyed some lay support. Ninety-two percent reported private expressions of approval, 56 percent were joined by some of their parishioners in a public statement of support for the farm workers, 37 percent were supported before their church boards, and 16 percent felt that they gained financial contributions as a direct result of their activism. Again, however, the net impact of the clergy's activism on local church membership was to cause losses. Sixteen percent of these clergymen reported having lost congregational members over the issue, 5 percent had gained some, and 17 percent had experienced both losses and gains.

Thus we find that lay reactions to ministerial support of the striking grape workers were generally less frequent than were reactions to clergy opposition to Proposition 14, but the same pattern was followed in both cases. The most active of the clergy liberals most frequently received from the laity expres-

Table 8.3. Ministers Who Actively Supported the Organization of Migratory Farm Workers Most Often Reported Lay Opposition and Lay Support for Their Actions

	In Favor of Clergy Participation	Not in Favor of Clergy Participation	All Clergy
ACTION TAKEN BY PARISHIONERS IN OP- POSITION TO CLERGY'S ACTIVISM			
Privately expressed their opposition	55% (479)	43% (350)	50% (829)
Reduced their contributions to the church	15% (463)	7% (344)	12% (807)
Publicly expressed their opposition before the church board	14% (478)	9% (350)	12% (828)
Tried to have the minister removed from the church	4% (476)	1% (348)	2% (824)
ACTION TAKEN BY PARISHIONERS IN SUP- PORT OF CLERGY'S ACTIVISM			
Privately expressed their approval	67% (476)	50% (348)	60% (824)
Joined the minister in some public expression of his views	24% (474)	10% (345)	18% (819)
Publicly expressed their approval be- fore the church board	17% (473)	9% (347)	13% (820)
Increased their contributions to the church	5% (451)	2% (339)	4% (790)
EFFECT OF CLERGY'S ACTIVISM ON CHURCH MEMBERSHIP			
Both gained and lost members	7%	3%	5%
Gained members	1	1	1
Lost members	7	5	6
Neither gained nor lost members	85	91	87
	100% (473)	100% (349)	99% (822)

sions of both approval and opposition to their ethical activities. Unlike our other two issues, however, the California grape strike had a definite geographical focus: the Delano area of California's San Joaquin Valley. We suggested earlier that clergy support of Chavez and his striking workers would be most controversial in churches in the San Joaquin Valley, and we showed that ministers from this area were the most likely to oppose the organization of migratory farm workers or clergy participation in support of the workers' position. We can use the clergy's responses to the questions examined here and in previous chapters to determine just how controversial the grape strike issue was for ministers in the Valley, as well as the problems it caused for local clergymen who supported the workers' position.

Table 8.4, which shows the occupational climate in the San Joaquin Valley and elsewhere in California during the farm labor dispute, indicates how very different the situation was for ministers in the immediate vicinity of the strike. Clergymen in the Valley were far more likely than clergymen elsewhere to report that their local denominational leaders, close colleagues, and congregational members were opposed to clergy involvement in the organization of migratory farm workers. In most of California the issue was clearly one of low salience. Many of these ministers were "not sure" of the positions of their occupational role partners, and existing clerical attitudes were predominantly in favor of ministerial support of the farm workers. Even the clergy's parishioners were much less negative toward the position of the striking workers than they had been to their ministers' opposition to Proposition 14. In the San Joaquin Valley, in contrast, the climate was more hostile. More of the ministers from this area reported that the majority of their local leaders favored (33 percent) than opposed (23 percent) clerical support of the workers; but the opposite was true of their colleagues, and the prevailing sentiment among the parishioners was definitely negative.

Given this climate of opinion, it is not surprising to find that more San Joaquin Valley Protestant ministers opposed clerical involvement in the farm workers' cause then in any other area of the state. What, we might ask, happened to the few ministers in the Valley who actively supported Chavez and the striking grape workers? Table 8.5 provides the answer. Forty-one ministers from this area reported that they favored clergy involvement in the issue and that they had at least discussed the matter with their parishioners.[3] Half these clergymen reported losses in contributions as a result of their participation, more than one-third lost members, and 18 percent faced attempts to have them removed from their parish positions. Far fewer clergymen elsewhere in the state reported such reactions to their support of the migratory farm workers. Some of the ministers in the San Joaquin Valley received the backing of their parishioners on the issue, but not more than those in areas where the conflict was of less immediate importance.

Table 8.4. Ministers in the San Joaquin Valley Reported Opinion To Be Least Favorable to Clergy Participation in the Organization of Migratory Farm Workers

"Did the majority of the members of the following groups favor or oppose the participation of clergymen in the organization of migratory farm workers?"	Favored	About Evenly Divided	Op- posed	Not Sure	Total
LOCAL DENOMINATIONAL OFFICIALS IN YOUR IMMEDIATE JURISDICTION					
Ministers in San Joaquin Valley	33%	20	23	24	100% (154)
Ministers elsewhere in state	50%	10	26	34	100% (1204)
YOUR CLOSE COLLEAGUES AMONG THE CLERGY					
Ministers in San Joaquin Valley	25%	27	34	14	100% (154)
Ministers elsewhere in state	41%	21	8	30	100% (1207)
MEMBERS IN YOUR CONGREGATION					
Ministers in San Joaquin Valley	3%	19	64	15	101% (155)
Ministers elsewhere in state	6%	23	26	45	100% (1207)
YOUR LOCAL COUNCIL OF CHURCHES OR MINISTERIAL ASSOCIATION					
Ministers in San Joaquin Valley	25%	26	25	25	101% (151)
Ministers elsewhere in state	38%	14	7	41	100% (1192)

The California grape strike thus illustrates the difficulties encountered by parish ministers when a local issue becomes highly controversial or, as in this case, involves the economic self-interest of many of their parishioners. Clearly, they come under intense pressures to conform to the dominant views of the community and of their laymen. As we have seen, many clergymen in the San Joaquin Valley apparently bowed to these pressures and gave less support to the striking workers than clergymen elsewhere in the state.

Table 8.5. Ministers in the San Joaquin Valley Who Actively Supported the Organization of Migratory Farm Workers Most Often Reported Lay Opposition to Their Actions

	Clergy in San Joaquin Valley	Clergy Elsewhere in California
ACTION TAKEN BY PARISHIONERS IN OPPOSITION TO CLERGY'S ACTIVISM		
Privately expressed their opposition	81% (41)	53% (438)
Reduced their contributions to the church	49% (41)	12% (422)
Publicly expressed their opposition before the church board	39% (41)	12% (437)
Tried to have the minister removed from the church	18% (40)	2% (436)
ACTION TAKEN BY PARISHIONERS IN SUPPORT OF CLERGY'S ACTIVISM		
Privately expressed their approval	67% (39)	67% (437)
Joined the minister in some public expression of his views	18% (39)	25% (435)
Publicly expressed their approval before the church board	23% (39)	16% (434)
Increased their contributions to the church	3% (38)	6% (413)
EFFECT OF CLERGY'S ACTIVISM ON CHURCH MEMBERSHIP		
Both gained and lost members	3%	8%
Gained members	3	1
Lost members	36	4
Neither gained nor lost members	59	87
	101% (39)	100% (434)

Ministers who disregard the wishes of their parishioners are likely to pay a high price for their activism, too, and the small number of clergymen in the San Joaquin Valley who actively supported the strike frequently caused themselves to lose members and financial contributions, often facing efforts to have them removed from their parish positions, as well.

The farm labor dispute was a relatively minor and noncontroversial issue for clergymen elsewhere in the state, but it was hardly so for ministers in the agricultural areas directly affected by the strike. Clergymen from this region underwent pressures not unlike those experienced by some Little Rock ministers during the desegregation crisis of 1957, and the fate of those who were active resembled that of the southern integrationists. "This issue continues to convulse the Valley churches," wrote one minister on our questionnaire. "Parishioners are still leaving the church, three years later, if a new minister such as me indicates his support, in the past or the present, for unionization of farm workers."

The Vietnam War.   The third issue we have been considering in detail involves the debate over Vietnam war policy. In Chapter 4 we classified our respondents' views toward the war into five categories. The most hawkish group included those who in 1968 advocated an increase in military efforts "in order to win the war"; the most dovish were those who believed that the United States should "unilaterally stop the bombing and begin preparations for complete withdrawal." Ministers between these two extremes were arranged according to whether they favored a continuation of the bombing of North Vietnam, a stop to the bombing, or a withdrawal to the coastal areas and population centers of South Vietnam. On this basis, we found that although public opinion was still largely favorable to the war at the time of our survey, the California clergy were split almost evenly into hawkish and dovish groups.

The reactions of Protestant laymen to the activism of these five groups of clergymen illustrates even more distinctly than the previous two issues the political nature of their responses. Indeed, the more dovish the ministers' views on the war, the more likely their parishioners were both to oppose and to support their actions (see Table 8.6). On the one extreme, the most hawkish group reportedly met with few lay reactions of either type. Far more of these clergymen, furthermore, reported that their parishioners privately supported (68 percent) than opposed (28 percent) their advocacy of an escalation of military efforts in Vietnam. Yet the most dovish group of parish ministers frequently experienced both opposition and support from the laity regarding their antiwar activism. Twenty-four percent of the ministers who advocated partial or complete withdrawal from Vietnam, for

Table 8.6. Ministers Who Actively Opposed the War in Vietnam Most Often Reported Lay Opposition and Lay Support for Their Actions

	Increase Military Efforts	Continue Bombing	Stop Bombing	Withdraw to Enclaves	Complete Withdrawal	All Ministers
ACTION TAKEN BY PARISHIONERS IN OPPOSITION OF CLERGY'S ACTIVISM						
Privately expressed their opposition	28% (381)	41% (258)	59% (250)	77% (122)	69% (377)	51% (1430)
Reduced their contributions to the church	2% (378)	4% (251)	14% (232)	27% (113)	24% (350)	12% (1365)
Publicly expressed their opposition before the church board	3% (381)	7% (256)	6% (248)	12% (121)	20% (374)	9% (1422)
Tried to have the minister removed from the church	— (380)	1% (259)	3% (247)	4% (118)	8% (369)	3% (1414)
ACTION TAKEN BY PARISHIONERS IN SUPPORT OF CLERGY'S ACTIVISM						
Privately expressed their approval	68% (378)	70% (259)	77% (248)	89% (122)	85% (376)	76% (1425)
Joined the minister in some public expression of his views	11% (373)	12% (257)	21% (247)	33% (122)	34% (374)	21% (1415)
Publicly expressed their approval before the church board	7% (378)	12% (256)	10% (248)	17% (121)	19% (374)	13% (1419)
Increased their contributions to the church	3% (367)	1% (250)	4% (236)	4% (110)	9% (346)	4% (1351)
Both gained and lost members	2%	3%	9%	17%	14%	8%
Gained members	4	1	2	2	3	3
Lost members	1	3	11	17	14	8
Neither gained nor lost members	93	93	79	64	69	81
	100% (374)	100% (258)	101% (248)	100% (121)	100% (372)	100% (1417)

example, indicated that they lost financial contributions because of their active opposition to the war; 20 percent were publicly opposed before their church boards, and 8 percent found their jobs to be in jeopardy. A much higher percentage of these clergy also were backed in their antiwar views by the members of their congregations. Thirty-four percent said that they had been joined by some of their parishioners in a public statement against the war, 19 percent had received public support before their church boards, and 9 percent felt that they had gained contributions as a result of their antiwar activities.

Again an important indication of the impact of the issue on organized religion is found in the effects of the clergy's war-related activism on church membership. Table 8.6 reveals that only a small proportion (7 percent) of the two most hawkish groups of clergymen indicated that the composition of their churches had been affected in any way by their support of the war. More of the parish ministers who called for a military victory, in fact, felt that they gained members than lost them as a result of their hawkish views. A third of the clergymen who openly advocated total or partial withdrawal, in contrast, reported that the membership of their churches had been affected. As we would expect, their losses exceeded their gains. Taken together, 15 percent of the two most dovish groups indicated that they had lost members because of their antiwar activities, 3 percent had gained some, and 15 percent had experienced both losses and gains.

Ministers who disagreed with United States policies in Vietnam, of course, often engaged in fairly militant acts of dissent, including antiwar protest marches and civil disobedience. We saw in Chapter 4 that 7 percent of our respondents had taken the former action at the time of our survey; 2 percent, the latter. Of particular interest to us is the fate of the antiwar clergymen. To what extent did such ministers lose money and members as a result of their antiwar activities? And how much lay support could they muster for their actions?

Parish clergymen who engaged in the two acts named—particularly those who committed antiwar civil disobedience—met with considerable opposition from the members of their congregations; as on the other issues, however, many were also able to attract some lay support. The relevant information is provided in Table 8.7.

Thirty of the ministers who advocated complete or partial withdrawal of American troops from Vietnam reported having engaged in acts of civil disobedience to symbolize their opposition to the war; another 65 indicated that they had participated in an antiwar protest march. Of these two groups of clergymen (listed in Table 8.7 as the two most active categories of respondents), a considerable number faced stiff opposition from the members

Table 8.7. Ministers Who Were Most Active in Their Opposition to the Vietnam War Most Often Reported Lay Opposition and Lay Support for Their Actions[a]

	Activism[b]					
	1	2	3	4	5	6
ACTION TAKEN BY PARISH-IONERS IN OPPOSITION TO CLERGY'S ACTIVISM						
Privately expressed their opposition	90% (30)	88% (65)	78% (109)	69% (148)	65% (80)	46% (67)
Reduced their contributions to the church	57% (28)	44% (61)	30% (99)	20% (135)	16% (75)	3% (65)
Publicly expressed their opposition before the church board	40% (30)	29% (65)	25% (108)	16% (146)	8% (80)	— (64)
Tried to have the minister removed from the church	21% (28)	20% (65)	9% (105)	3% (145)	3% (78)	2% (68)
ACTION TAKEN BY PARISH-IONERS IN SUPPORT OF CLERGY'S ACTIVISM						
Privately expressed their approval	100% (30)	97% (65)	93% (109)	86% (147)	83% (80)	66% (67)
Joined the minister in some public expression of his views	57% (30)	55% (65)	42% (108)	33% (147)	24% (79)	4% (67)
Publicly expressed their opposition before the church board	37% (30)	31% (65)	20% (108)	21% (146)	11% (79)	1% (67)
Increased their contributions to the church	57% (30)	55% (65)	42% (108)	33% (147)	24% (79)	4% (67)

Table 8.7. *Continued*

	Activism[b]					
	1	2	3	4	5	6
EFFECT OF CLERGY'S ACTIV-ISM ON CHURCH MEMBERSHIP						
Both gained and lost members	30%	15%	17%	17%	10%	3%
Gained members	10	5	1	3	3	1
Lost members	33	29	16	11	11	4
Neither gained nor lost members	27	51	66	68	76	91
	100%	100%	100%	99%	100%	99%
	(30)	(65)	(107)	(145)	(79)	(67)

[a] Includes only ministers who favored a partial or complete withdrawal from Vietnam.
[b] On this 6-point scale, 1 is highly active; 6 is inactive.

of their congregations. Among those who had engaged in civil disobedience, 57 percent lost financial contributions, 40 percent were opposed before their church boards, and attempts were made to remove 21 percent of them from their positions. Many of these ministers also were supported by some of their parishioners, but the price of their activism was high. Again perhaps the best indication of the response of Protestant laymen to antiwar activism is in the impact of the clergy's actions on church membership. Seventy-three percent of the clergymen who had engaged in antiwar civil disobedience reported that such activities has affected the loyalties of Protestant laymen to their local churches. Thirty-three percent reported having lost members over their involvement in the issue, whereas 10 percent said that they had gained members, and 30 percent noted that they had experienced both gains and losses in membership.

Liberal Losses in the 1960s. With almost tedious regularity this chapter demonstrates that socially active clergymen in California encountered frequent and severe resistance to their ethical actions from the members of their congregations. Many lost financial contributions and members, and some lost their jobs because of their involvement in these three public disputes. Moreover, punitive actions were most frequently taken against ministers who were most active in expounding the liberal position on these three issues.

Negative reactions from Protestant laymen to clergy activism present obvious difficulties both for the new breed clergy and for liberal Protestant denominations. Such hostile lay actions place strong pressures on the activist clergy to curtail their activities or to stay out of controversial public issues altogether. As we have pointed out, parish ministers are highly dependent on those they serve in a professional capacity for their occupational success and personal satisfactions. Not only does the organization of Protestant churches place much authority in the hands of laymen, it also brings the parish clergyman into a peculiarly close association with his parishioners. Knowing that Protestant laymen possess so much formal and informal influence, the parish clergyman will think carefully about the effects of his ethical activities on his parishioners and on his own chances for professional advancement.

We have no way of telling from our survey the number of California ministers who deliberately avoided taking controversial positions on public issues for fear of lay reprisals or in what ways they restricted their public activities to placate the members of their congregations. It is obvious, however, that many have done just that. We saw in Chapter 6 that the modernist clergy generally feel that their parishioners have a negative effect on their social activism and are in fact less ethically active when they perceive the majority of their congregational members to hold conservative views on a particular issue. We asked the California ministers directly whether they would like to increase their social activism: "If it were possible, would you like to be more or less involved in social action activities than you presently are?" At the time of our survey in 1968, a substantial proportion of the California ministers (46 percent), replied that they wanted to become "more" involved; only 3 percent said that they would like to be "less" so. Consistent with our comments about the conflict between the modernist, ethically oriented clergy and their parishioners, we find that the more modernist respondents most frequently indicate a desire to increase their level of involvement in social action activities.

Finally, we have the direct testimony of a number of our respondents to the effectiveness of lay opposition to clergy activism. "Sometimes you lose your job for telling the truth," said an Episcopal priest. "I helped organize a peace movement in Salinas," said another clergyman, "but then had to withdraw because of congregational pressure." Others indicated that they were "afraid to do much joining" (of peace groups) or that after facing stiff lay opposition to their ethical actions, they had decided to be more careful in the future. A Methodist minister who reported that he had lost both members and financial contributions because of his opposition to the anti-fair housing referendum was most explicit. "After getting burned by laymen over Proposition 14," he wrote, he had decided "to keep my mouth shut and my ear open" in response to the issues raised by the organization of migratory farm workers. Similarly, he had avoided involvement in the Vietnam issue "because I want to stay on and serve this church."

Few of our respondents were so blunt in their assessments of the situation, and we cannot say with certainty from our data how many parish ministers are restricting their ethical activities for fear of lay reprisals. We can only use our survey to show in a general way how the clergy perceive the situation and how they respond to it. It would be taxing the limits of the research instrument—as well as our respondents' patience—to ask each clergyman to describe the situation within his own parish church. Furthermore, it is likely that many clergymen are not fully conscious of the ways in which they may have tempered their activism to avoid conflict with their parishioners. In the next chapter we examine one common social process by which parish clergymen often unconsciously assume the conservative views of the members of their congregations.

For these reasons, we cannot describe precisely the effects of lay conservatism and opposition to ethicalism on clergy activism in California. However, it is apparent that these forces were very powerful. Given the control exercised by Protestant laymen over a minister's occupational success—if not over his peace of mind and contentment in his job—it is difficult to see how clergy activism can grow in the face of such severe lay reaction.

Lay opposition to clergy activism can have potentially far-reaching consequences for liberal denominations as well as for the new breed clergy themselves. Protestant churches are voluntary associations and cannot long survive in their present organizational forms without the loyalty and support of their lay members. If large numbers of parishioners leave the church or withdraw financial support, the organizational stability of Protestant denominations will be threatened, and new pressures toward nonactivism will be felt.

When we inspect the financial and membership losses resulting from the activism of the California ministers, we are not surprised to find that they are highly concentrated in the denominations most often served by the new breed clergy: the Methodist Church, the United Church of Christ, the Episcopal Church, the Presbyterian Church, and, to a lesser extent, the Lutheran Church in America. Table 8.8 lists the percentages of ministers in the various denominations who reported losing or gaining contributions because of their involvement in the three public controversies we have been examining. Again we have no way of telling from our survey what these losses amounted to in terms of dollars and cents. But it is apparent from the table that liberal Protestant denominations have lost considerable financial support because of the social activism of their parish ministers. More than half the clergy in these five liberal denominations reported losing contributions because of their active opposition to the anti-fair housing referendum in California in 1964. Almost one out of five had lost financial support because of activism on the war issue (even though a third of the ministers in these denominations supported the war policies in effect at the time of our survey). Even on the relatively low-keyed conflict over the organization of migratory farm workers, 13 percent of the clergy in liberal denominations felt that their activism had cost them financial contributions.

Certainly such financial setbacks must be regarded with apprehension by liberal church leaders and by the ethically committed clergy. They provide obvious threats to the church's ability to grow and to expand its programs in the directions desired by liberal churchmen. If allowed to continue long into the future, they jeopardize the ability of liberal denominations to sustain even their present programs and organizational commitments. Table 8.8 does indicate the belief of some of the socially active ministers in California that their ethicalism had attracted new financial contributions to their churches. This must certainly be regarded as a hopeful sign for the church activists—and we return to it in a moment. As we have shown all along,

Table 8.8. Ministers in Liberal Denominations Most Often Reported Losing and Gaining Contributions as a Result of Their Social Activism

Denomination	Proposition 14		Grape Strike		Vietnam War	
	Lost Contributions	Gained Contributions	Lost Contributions	Gained Contributions	Lost Contributions	Gained Contributions
Methodist	52%	10%	14%	4%	19%	5%
	(254)	(243)	(274)	(272)	(312)	(314)
United Church of Christ	48%	15%	15%	5%	21%	9%
	(91)	(86)	(102)	(100)	(117)	(112)
Episcopal	69%	25%	10%	3%	18%	9%
	(149)	(144)	(154)	(154)	(186)	(182)
Presbyterian	59%	15%	13%	4%	16%	3%
	(169)	(158)	(174)	(165)	(195)	(194)
Lutheran Church in America	27%	4%	6%	—	12%	1%
	(56)	(53)	(68)	(66)	(75)	(77)
American Baptist	16%	4%	—	2%	4%	2%
	(93)	(91)	(105)	(105)	(132)	(131)
American Lutheran Church	5%	—	1%	—	2%	1%
	(67)	(67)	(83)	(83)	(105)	(102)
Missouri Synod-Lutheran Church	1%	1%	1%	1%	3%	2%
	(81)	(80)	(114)	(114)	(111)	(107)
Southern Baptist	1%	—	—	—	—	1%
	(118)	(116)	(132)	(130)	(156)	(156)
Totals	38%	10%	8%	3%	12%	4%
	(1078)	(1038)	(1206)	(1189)	(1389)	(1375)

however, far fewer parish ministers reported having gained financial support because of their activism than reported having lost it.

Of greater threat to the organizational future of liberal Protestant denominations, perhaps, are the numerous Protestant laymen who are leaving the church, apparently because of clergy activism. Once again, we do not know exactly how many parishioners in California took this course of action during any of these three public controversies, but a considerable number appear to have done so during two of them (see Table 8.9). We see that 71 percent of the parish ministers in one liberal denomination—the Episcopal Church—reported having lost members because of their active involvement in the anti-fair housing referendum.[4] Sixty-three percent of the Presbyterian respondents mentioned such losses, and more than half the clergy in the Methodist Church and the United Church of Christ also lost members because of their conduct on the issue. Some parish clergymen in conservative denominations also reported losses, but the percentages are relatively small.

The proportion of clergymen who had lost members because of their leadership on the Vietnam war—far lower at the time of our survey than it had been on the earlier issue—was still considerable within the liberal denominations. More than one out of every five parish clergymen in the five liberal denominations reported losing members over the Vietnam conflict. Perhaps this issue better illustrates the often contrasting effects of clergy activism on liberal and conservative churches. Most of the clergy in the five liberal denominations held more dovish views on the war than their parishioners, and a fairly large proportion lost members for expressing these opinions. Most of the clergy in the four conservative denominations, however, held hawkish views on the war—more similar to those held by the members of their congregations. We see that relatively few parish ministers in these denominations lost members for expressing such views, and in fact as many reported gaining members as a result of their Vietnam-related activities as reported losing them.

Thus our survey shows that the activism of the sixties poses a severe threat to the organizational growth and stability of the denominations served by socially active ministers. In such circumstances, we might expect great pressures on the ethically committed clergy to be less outspoken in expressing their views, and on church officials to give less encouragement to the activists within their denominations.

Polarizations on the Lay Level.   In concluding this review of the laity's response to social activism, we might consider the effects of the activism of the sixties on the attitudes of Protestant laymen and on relationships on the

Table 8.9.   Ministers in Liberal Denominations Most Often Report

	Proposition 14			
	Both Gained and Lost Members	Gained Members	Lost Members	Neither Gained nor Lost Members
Methodist	19%	1	38	42
United Church of Christ	24%	2	31	43
Episcopal	41%	3	30	26
Presbyterian	29%	1	33	37
Luthern Church in America	11%	2	26	61
American Baptist	5%	4	11	79
American Lutheran Church	4%	—	4	91
Missouri Synod-Lutheran Church	4%	1	4	91
Southern Baptist	2%	1	2	96
Total	18%	2	24	56

parish level. We must necessarily be speculative in the inferences drawn from these findings, but would suggest that the sixties heightened political sensitivities among large numbers of laymen, as they did among the clergy, leading to new polarizations within and between Protestant denominations.

The behavior of parish activists, in the first place, undoubtedly led many Protestant laymen to reexamine their religious commitments and to determine their relevance to social and political issues. The information reported here indicates that most laymen concluded that their religious values had nothing to do with politics and that they either opposed the activist clergy or remained apathetic to ethical issues. A significant minority of Protestant churchgoers, however, reached a different conclusion. They rallied to the support of the activist clergy and joined them in their ethical admonitions and public activities. Thus we would suggest that the events of the 1960s had not dissimilar impacts on the Protestant laity and on the clergy: they brought new issues into the church and made relevant questions that in less political periods would have lain dormant. In this fashion, many local congregations became politicized, and new divisions developed among the laity resembling those existing among the clergy.

We would expect the polarizations among laymen to be much less intense than those among the clergy, although the former may have long-term conse-

Losing and Gaining Members as a Result of Their Social Activism

	Vietnam War				
	Both Gained and Lost Members	Gained Members	Lost Members	Neither Gained nor Lost Members	
100% (269)	14%	2	11	73	100% (334)
100% (93)	14%	4	11	71	100% (125)
100% (153)	9%	4	11	76	100% (191)
100% (178)	8%	3	12	76	99% (207)
100% (57)	9%	1	11	79	100% (79)
99% (97)	2%	3	2	93	100% (134)
99% (69)	—	—	2%	98	100% (103)
100% (80)	2%	1	2	95	100% (109)
101% (122)	—	4%	1	95	100% (159)
100% (1118)	8%	3	8	82	101% (1441)

quences for Protestant religion, as well. As we have seen, many laymen disagreed with their ministers' ethical activities so strongly that they left the churches served by such clergy. Those who felt this way had three options: they could shop around for another parish within the same denomination (or within another liberal denomination) which was more compatible with their views, they could switch their loyalty to a church in a more conservative denomination, or they could drop out of organized religion altogether. Similar choices faced laymen who favored an active church involvement in public affairs and felt that their local minister was not sufficiently concerned with ethical questions. One effect of the activism of the sixties, then, was to create new alignments within Protestant churches, with laymen switching from liberal to conservative churches—and, to a lesser extent, from conservative to liberal ones—to find a minister and a congregation more compatible with their own views. We do not know which option was most often taken by dissident laymen, but our observations suggest that most transfers involved parishes within the same denomination. In this respect, the activism of the sixties had the effects of creating more like-minded congregations at the local level and producing more sharply defined divisions among parish churches in the liberal denominations. At the same time, the trend in membership since the sixties indicates that many former members of liberal churches have joined more conservative denominations or have dropped out of organized religion altogether.

Thus it would seem that the events of the 1960s made ethical and political issues more relevant to many churchgoers and created more serious polarizations within and between Protestant denominations. It should be apparent from the information presented that unless significant numbers of laymen change their attitudes toward ethical and political issues, liberal churches and denominations are bound to come out on the short end of this process of realignment. Conservatives far outnumber liberals among the lay membership of Protestant churches, and to the extent that politicization of the churches continues, ethically oriented ministers are likely to experience increasing losses of members and funds. This dilemma of the new breed activists during the sixties is likely to remain for liberal denominations in the future.

NOTES AND REFERENCES

1.   Ernest Q. Campbell and Thomas F. Pettigrew, *Christians in Racial Crisis: A Study of Little Rock's Ministry* (Washington, D.C.: Public Affairs Press, 1959).

2.   The coefficients of reproducibility for these three scales are .88 for Proposition 14, .94 for the strike issue, and .92 on Vietnam. The scale items are as follows. Proposition 14: (1) organizing a social action group, (2) serving on a committee that campaigned for or against the proposal, (3) organizing a study group, (4) delivering a sermon or a prayer, (5) making a public statement, and (6) discussing the issue with parishioners. Delano grape strike: (1) marching or traveling to the Delano area, (2) organizing a study group, (3) delivering a sermon or prayer, (4) making a public statement, and (5) discussing the issue with parishioners. Vietnam war: (1) engaging in antiwar civil disobedience, (2) participating in antiwar protest march, (3) joining a peace organization, (4) attending a protest meeting or organizing a study group, (5) making a public statement, and (6) delivering a sermon or a prayer or discussing the issue with parishioners. The "inactive" category on each scale includes respondents who had not engaged in any of these actions.

3.   We do not know from our data exactly what these 41 ministers in the San Joaquin Valley said on the issue. However, they engaged in the various acts of involvement examined in Chapter 4 to a slightly higher degree than clergymen elsewhere in the state. The same is true for the Valley ministers who were unsympathetic to Chavez's organizing efforts.

4.   It is interesting to speculate why such losses are greatest within the Episcopal Church, since our survey shows that parish clergymen were not as active in this denomination as in some others. Part of the answer may lie in the higher socioeconomic status of lay Episcopalians, hence their greater conservatism. More probably, these patterns result from the large number of nonparish Episcopal priests who were active during this period. At the time of our survey, the Episcopal Church had many clergymen serving in special urban ministries, and it was these church officials who seemed most often to receive publicity for their acts of symbolic protest—particularly for their antiwar civil disobedience. In this respect, our survey probably does not give a fair accounting of the degree of commitment to an ethically involved church among Episcopal priests.

LAY RELATIONS AND CLERGY ACTIVISM

9. In the last three chapters we have shown that most Protestant laymen are strongly opposed to clergy activism, reacting negatively to the involvement of parish clergymen in controversial public issues. Although some laymen have joined the modernist clergy in their rejection of traditional Protestant orthodoxies, relatively few have joined them in support of an action-oriented church. Protestant laymen apparently do not draw the same ethical and political implications from their religious convictions as their clerical leaders. Furthermore, some of the socially active clergy report gaining members and lay support for their activism, but many more say that their involvement in public issues met with fierce resistance from the members of their congregations. Parishioners have left the church, ceased to make financial contributions, and sought to censor their church leaders in protest of the ethical actions described earlier.

Under such circumstances, we might expect the manner in which the liberal, ethically committed clergy carry out their professional and social relations with their parishioners to be of considerable importance. If ethically oriented ministers are unable to gain more lay converts to their brand of ethicalism, it would appear necessary for them to pay particularly close attention to their parishioners on a more personal level. If the modernist clergy cannot change their parishioners' minds about the need for a more action-oriented church, perhaps they can gain the personal trust and confidence of their congregations and persuade the members to go along with certain ethical actions.

This is a position often voiced by the modernist clergy and by church leaders who are sympathetic to clergy activism. Stated in the extreme, the conflicts experienced by the new breed clergy with their parishioners are perceived essentially as problems of communications and human relations. Mutual trust and confidence must be established between the minister and his congregational members, it is argued, before the clergyman can hope to gain lay sympathy for his ethical goals. Once such a relationship is created, the minister will generally find himself free to engage in the ethical activities he wishes to pursue. As we stated in Chapter 7, however, it is also possible that parish ministers who hold such views may become overly concerned about maintaining smooth lay relations. In taking pains not to antagonize their parishioners, they may voluntarily restrict their own ethical actions. Such a position was stated baldly by a liberal Methodist respondent:

> While many of us believe in being on the "cutting edge" of things, there is the obligation of a clergyman (if he is to minister) to maintain "communication" with his parishioners. A value judgment must therefore be made concerning social and political and economic activities as to what these will do to help or hinder the communication.

To be in proper "communication" with his parishioners, this clergyman suggests, a minister often must avoid certain types of social, political, and economic involvement. Such decisions call for a "value judgment" from the individual.

In the first two sections of this chapter, we examine various aspects of our respondents' professional relations with their parishioners. We compare the amount of time and attention given by modernist and traditionalist ministers to their parishioners in their professional roles, and we determine whether actions of this type bear any relation to the clergy's activist behavior or to the conflicts they encounter with their parishioners over public issues.

As we have noted elsewhere, Protestant ministers interact with their congregational members not only in a professional capacity but also socially. The organization of the ministry places the parish pastor in extremely close contact with the members of his local church. He lives among them, calls on them socially, and appears to have far more contact with lay members of the church than with his fellow professionals. In such circumstances, it would not be surprising for large numbers of Protestant ministers to form close friendships with the members of their congregations and for such friendships to have a strong influence on clergy response to public issues. We would expect those who are closest to their parishioners to take more conservative or "safe" positions on political issues and to be less radical in their public behavior.

In the balance of this chapter, we discuss the ministers' social relations and the impact of their choice of friends on their social activism. We see that the manner in which clergymen interact socially with their parishioners appears to have a considerable influence on their response to public issues.

Professional Relations within the Parish Church.   The role of the Protestant minister is most certainly highly diverse or multifaceted.[1] He is a preacher, a counselor, an educator, and an administrator; frequently he assumes active leadership in public affairs as well. The variety of roles the parish minister is called on to play inevitably places severe demands on his time and often produces a situation in which contradictory actions or attitudes are expected of him. Recent research has shown that the ministerial work week is long and disproportionately loaded with administrative duties. The contemporary clergyman devotes the bulk of his efforts not to preaching or counseling but to being an administrator—attending meetings, supervising the church's clerical work, and taking care of church finances. One study found that the parish minister spends about 40 percent of his work week attending to administrative duties, whereas 25 percent is devoted to his pastoral work (counseling and making visitations), and 20 percent to his role as preacher and priest. The remaining 15 percent was spent on organizational work and educational activities.[2]

Neither Protestant ministers nor their parishioners appear to be happy with this situation. The same study indicated that parish ministers attach the most importance to their roles as preacher, pastor, and priest; the least to their activities as administrators. According to a survey of lay attitudes, Protestant laymen also feel that their ministers are spending too much time on administrative matters and should devote more effort to their preaching and pastoral duties.[3] It is sometimes charged, furthermore, that in their quest for social activism the new breed clergy are neglecting their traditional roles as men of God and are not paying sufficient attention to their parishioners' personal needs. Conservative churchmen in particular are likely to argue that the preoccupation of such clergymen with social ethics prevents them from taking proper care of the "spiritual needs" of their lay followers.

To learn how much attention the California ministers in our sample give to several of their professional roles, we asked how much time they devote each week to five activities unrelated to their preaching and priestly duties: attending to administrative matters, counseling their parishioners on personal problems, counseling their parishioners on religious matters, educating the youth of the church, and participating in public affairs. To study their pastoral duties, we also asked how many "social visits" they have with their parishioners each week.

The ministers' responses to the first inquiry appear in Table 9.1. The California ministers, like churchmen elsewhere, devote the greatest single amount of effort to administrative matters. Sixty-seven percent of the parish pastors reported that 7 or more hours each week were consumed by such activities. Counseling one's parishioners on personal problems was the next heaviest task, followed by religious counseling and educating the youth of the church. As a group, the clergy reported that they spent less time participating in public affairs than on any other ministerial roles mentioned.

Table 9.1. Ministers Reportedly Spend the Most Time Each Week on Administrative Matters

| Activities | Hours per Week | | | | | |
	7 or more	5–6	3–4	1–2	Less than 1	Total
Attending to administrative matters	67%	16	10	5	2	100% (1544)
Counseling parishioners on personal problems	34%	24	25	14	3	100% (1548)
Counseling parishioners on religious matters	17%	18	30	28	7	100% (1541)
Educating the youth of the church	13%	17	27	31	13	100% (1530)
Participating in public affairs	10%	13	22	31	24	000% (1534)

Our findings thus substantiate previous reports of the disproportionate amount of time the parish minister devotes to administrative matters. We also see that despite the controversy over clergy activism among many churchmen, parish ministers do not spend a very large proportion of their work week participating in public affairs. The average minister, these data suggest, gives between 2 and 3 hours each week to such activities. In contrast, he spends about 9 or 10 hours a week counseling his parishioners on personal problems or on religious matters.

What differences, then, exist between the divisions of the ministerial work week made by the modernist and traditionalist clergy? Do modernist ministers devote any less attention to their parishioners than their traditionalist colleagues? These questions are answered in Table 9.2. We see that modernist and traditionalist clergymen reportedly spend an equal amount of time each week counseling parishioners on personal problems, attending to adminis-

Table 9.2.   Ministers Divide Their Time in a Way Generally Unrelated to Their Religious Beliefs

Hours per Week Spent on Activities	Religious Orientation[a]				
	1	2	3	4	5
ATTENDING TO ADMINISTRATIVE MATTERS					
7 or more	68%	70%	68%	67%	63%
5–6	16	16	15	14	17
3–4	10	8	11	10	11
1–2	4	4	5	7	7
Less than 1	2	2	2	2	2
	100%	100%	100%	100%	100%
	(306)	(312)	(304)	(304)	(318)
COUNSELING PARISHIONERS ON PERSONAL PROBLEMS					
7 or more	31%	34%	37%	37%	31%
5–6	29	25	20	22	23
3–4	23	23	28	23	30
1–2	14	15	13	14	13
Less than 1	3	3	2	3	4
	100%	100%	100%	99%	101%
	(307)	(310)	(310)	(303)	(318)
COUNSELING PARISHIONERS ON RELIGIOUS MATTERS					
7 or more	9%	12%	18%	24%	24%
5–6	17	16	15	19	24
3–4	26	31	32	29	30
1–2	34	31	29	24	19
Less than 1	14	9	7	4	3
	100%	99%	101%	100%	100%
	(304)	(310)	(307)	(307)	(318)

Table 9.2. *Continued*

Hours per Week Spent on Activities	Religious Orientation[a]				
	1	2	3	4	5
EDUCATING THE YOUTH OF THE CHURCH					
7 or more	16%	13%	13%	8%	13%
5–6	12	14	14	22	23
3–4	24	28	28	31	23
1–2	30	33	34	27	29
Less than 1	18	13	11	11	12
	100%	101%	100%	99%	100%
	(306)	(308)	(302)	(301)	(313)
PARTICIPATING IN PUBLIC AFFAIRS					
7 or more	17%	15%	8%	8%	3%
5–6	20	19	11	12	5
3–4	27	23	26	19	14
1–2	24	31	35	34	32
Less than 1	12	12	20	28	46
	100%	100%	100%	101%	100%
	(305)	(306)	(306)	(301)	(316)

[a] On this 5-point scale, 1 is most modernist; 5 is most traditionalist.

trative matters, and educating the youth of the church. Traditionalist ministers spend more time counseling parishioners on religious matters, and modernist ministers spend more time participating in public affairs.

These patterns are about what we would have expected on the basis of the clergy's religious orientations alone, and do not suggest that any significant differences exist in the way that the modernist and traditionalist clergy relate to their parishioners. We know that traditionalist ministers define their clerical role largely in terms of bringing others to Christianity so that they may receive forgiveness and obtain salvation in the afterlife; and our data here reveal that the most traditionalist ministers devote more time to counseling their parishioners on what are considered by our respondents to be "religious matters." Modernist ministers, who define their role more in ethical terms, appear to participate more regularly in public affairs. No differences exist, however, between the modernist and traditionalist clergy in the amount of time they give to their other three roles—and, most significantly, in the amount of time they spend counseling parishioners on personal problems.

As throughout this chapter, we are dealing with general differences in behavior between modernist and traditionalist clergymen. We cannot conclude from these findings that no modernist ministers are ignoring the personal needs of their parishioners in their quest for ethical involvement in social issues. We can say, however, that insofar as these questions provide accurate indicators of how parish clergymen spend their time, they show that modernist clergy are not much different from the traditionalist clergy in the performance of their professional relations with parishioners.

The similarity between the two groups of ministers in this respect is shown even more clearly in our inquiry into the ministers' pastoral roles (see Table 9.3). "On the average," the respondents were asked, "how often do you usually have social visits with your parishioners in their homes or in your own home?" Again, there are fairly broad differences in the visitation practices of the California ministers, but there are no differences in this respect between the modernist and traditionalist respondents. The clergy's religious views have no relation to their visitation policies.

Table 9.3.   The Number of Social Calls Ministers Make on Their Parishioners Each Week Is Unrelated to Their Religious Beliefs

Average Number of Social Visits Each Week	Religious Orientation[a]					
	1	2	3	4	5	Total
5 or more times	32%	23%	27%	25%	29%	27%
3–4 times	15	23	17	18	13	17
1–2 times	25	21	24	28	25	24
Less than once	29	33	32	30	33	21
	101%	100%	100%	101%	100%	99%
	(304)	(315)	(312)	(301)	(319)	(1551)

[a] On this 5-point scale, 1 is most modernist; 5 is most traditionalist.

Modernist ministers thus do not appear to be ignoring their other clerical roles or to be dealing with their parishioners on a less personal basis than traditionalist clergymen. They report that they devote an equal amount of time to personal counseling, youth education, and administrative matters within their churches and have social visits with their parishioners equally often each week. An identical pattern is found among our respondents if we divide them according to the degree of their activism rather than, as we have done here, by religious orientation.

Parishioner Relations, Lay Conflict, and Clergy Activism.   In considering the lay relations of Protestant ministers, it is important to know whether they in any way influence the response of their parishioners to their activist behavior. As we have pointed out, it is sometimes argued that socially active clergymen could eliminate or substantially reduce lay hostility to their ethical actions if only they would pay closer personal attention to their parishioners. From this perspective the problems their social activism raises with the members of their congregations are largely ones of communications and human relations rather than the result of deep-seated antagonism by Protestant laymen to an action-oriented church.

Before examining data relevant to this question, we should make clear how widespread conflict is between Protestant ministers and Protestant laymen— especially between the modernist clergy and their parishioners. A recent study sponsored by the National Council of Churches found that by far the most common sources of occupational stress among Protestant ministers resulted from their relations with their congregational members.[4] More than half the respondents in this survey of 5000 Protestant ministers reported that they had at some point experienced major difficulties over lay-related problems. The author of the study found that such responses were common among ministers of all ages and concluded that these conflicts "will probably remain the dominant sources of stress in all stages of the minister's career."[5]

The report just cited did not indicate whether the modernist clergy are any more likely to experience such conflicts with their parishioners than their traditionalist colleagues. Our survey, however, shows most definitely that they are—not only in relation to their ethical behavior but also with respect to other facets of the ministerial role. We asked the California ministers whether they had ever had "serious differences of opinion" with members of their congregations in each of four areas: their theological views, the church budget, church organization, and their own participation in social activities. Only a few ministers report having had "many" such differences, but about half indicated that they had experienced at least "some" differences over each issue (see Table 9.4). Most significantly, the proportion of clergymen reporting such problems was greater among the modernist clergy in all four areas. These differences were particularly large with respect to the theological views of the modernist respondents and their participation in social action activities. For example, 76 percent of the most modernist group of clergymen indicated that some or a great deal of conflict had existed be-

Table 9.4. Modernist Ministers Most Often Experience Serious Differences of Opinions with Their Parishioners over Church Matters

"Have you ever had any serious differences of opinion with some of the members of your congregation over the following matters?"	Religious Orientation[a]					Total
	1	2	3	4	5	
THEOLOGICAL VIEWS						
Many	10%	2%	4%	2%	—[b]	4%
Some	66	62	43	38	27	47
None	24	36	53	60	73	49
	100%	100%	100%	100%	100%	100%
	(308)	(320)	(316)	(306)	(321)	(1571)
CHURCH BUDGET						
Many	6%	2%	5%	3%	2%	3%
Some	55	51	45	49	39	48
None	39	47	50	48	59	49
	100%	100%	100%	100%	100%	100%
	(308)	(319)	(314)	(305)	(321)	(1567)
CHURCH ORGANIZATION						
Many	7%	3%	3%	2%	2%	3%
Some	53	54	52	50	35	49
None	39	43	45	48	63	48
	99%	100%	100%	100%	100%	100%
	(307)	(319)	(316)	(307)	(321)	(1570)
PARTICIPATION IN SOCIAL ACTION ACTIVITIES						
Many	12%	6%	3%	2%	—	5%
Some	59	55	38	27	8%	37
None	29	39	59	71	92	58
	100%	100%	100%	100%	100%	100%
	(307)	(319)	(315)	(304)	(319)	(1564)

[a] On this 5-point scale, 1 is most modernist; 5 is most traditionalist.
[b] Less than 1 percent.

244

tween themselves and their parishioners over their theological beliefs, in comparison with 27 percent of the most traditionalist group. The contrast between these two groups of ministers was even greater with respect to conflict over their social activism—71 and 8 percent, respectively.

To some extent, these differences may reflect a greater tendency by the modernist clergy to see lay conflict as a "normal" part of their clerical duties or, as we have said, to regard it in more positive terms as an indication that one's ministry is in fact "prophetic." Modernist clergymen thus may be more likely than traditionalist ministers to perceive or to report the existence of "differences of opinion" with their parishioners. Even when we take these possibilities into consideration, however, we would regard these patterns to be still another indication of the breach between modernist, ethically active clergymen and the bulk of the Protestant laity.

If, in these circumstances, we were to find that modernist clergymen can reduce this conflict by paying close attention to their professional relations with their parishioners, we would have uncovered a pattern of considerable importance. We could show at least one way in which modernist ministers can maintain their personal commitments to an action-oriented ministry without driving Protestant laymen away from the church or into open rebellion against their activities. Unfortunately for clergymen who wish to pursue an activist role, we find no support for this proposition in our survey. Table 9.5 presents the levels of lay conflict experienced by those ministers who reportedly spend the greatest amount of time in providing personal and religious counsel to their parishioners and who make the most social calls on their church members each week. Clearly, these clergymen were no better able to avoid disagreements with the members of their congregations over their theological views or over their social activism than those who were less attentive to their parishioners. The same patterns hold, moreover, with respect to the reported reactions of Protestant laymen to our respondents' involvement in major public controversies. Ministers who were most attentive to their parishioners were no less likely to report hostile lay reactions to their leadership in the three political conflicts we have been examining than ministers who were equally active but less involved with their congregational members.

This is a rather disquieting conclusion for the ethically committed clergy, and we should specify exactly what our data tell us about this relationship. They do not say that an individual clergymen cannot reduce the level of lay opposition to his ethical activities by spending more time with his parishioners or by improving his services to them; undoubtedly, some clergymen have followed that strategy with success. The data do show, however, that within the Protestant ministry as a whole there is no relationship between

Table 9.5. Ministers Who Give the Most Attention to Their Pastoral Duties Are No Less Likely to Experience Differences of Opinion with Their Parishioners

	Religious Orientation[a]				
	1	2	3	4	5
SOME (OR A GREAT DEAL OF) DIFFERENCES OF OPINION WITH PARISHIONERS OVER MINISTERS' THEOLOGICAL VIEWS					
Ministers who had devoted 7 or more hours a week to counseling parishioners on personal problems	78% (94)	76% (105)	51% (113)	43% (111)	32% (97)
Ministers who had devoted 5 or more hours a week to counseling parishioners on religious matters	73% (79)	69% (87)	45% (101)	43% (130)	31% (148)
Ministers who had had an average of 5 or more social visits with their parishioners each week	75% (95)	72% (74)	49% (84)	42% (74)	28% (91)
All ministers	76% (308)	64% (320)	47% (316)	40% (306)	27% (321)
SOME (OR A GREAT DEAL OF) DIFFERENCES OF OPINION WITH PARISHIONERS OVER MINISTERS' PARTICIPATION IN SOCIAL ACTION ACTIVITIES					
Ministers who had devoted 7 or more hours a week to counseling parishioners on personal problems	79% (94)	73% (105)	42% (113)	38% (110)	13% (97)
Ministers who had devoted 5 or more hours a week to counseling parishioners on religious matters	71% (79)	66% (87)	44% (101)	36% (129)	8% (147)
Ministers who had had an average of 5 or more social visits with their parishioners each week	68% (95)	62% (74)	51% (84)	24% (74)	13% (90)
All ministers	71% (307)	61% (319)	41% (315)	29% (304)	8% (319)

[a] On this 5-point scale, 1 is most modernist; 5 is most traditionalist.

these indicators of professional service and lay–clergy conflict. Modernist ministers apparently have been unable to reduce lay opposition to their ethical activities or to their theological views through greater efforts of the type described.

Apparently, the manner in which the parish clergymen in California perform their professional roles vis à vis their parishioners bears no relation to their religious and ethical attitudes or behavior. We suggested in the introduction to this chapter that some Protestant clergymen may be so concerned about maintaining harmonious relations with their congregational members that they tend to restrict their ethical actions or stay out of controversial issues altogether. This behavior may occur in individual cases, but we find no relation in our survey between the amount of attention our respondents give to their various professional roles and the extent of their involvement in public issues. Those who devote the most effort to their pastoral roles—counseling parishioners and calling on them socially—are as socially active (controlling for religious differences) as those who reportedly devote the least effort. The manner in which our respondents conducted their professional roles is thus unrelated to their religious beliefs, to the conflicts they experience with their parishioners, or to their own activist behavior.

Of course, all the questions we asked the California ministers concerning these professional roles are quantitative rather than qualitative: they deal with the amount of attention the respondents give their parishioners in these several respects; they do not elicit data about the specific ways these roles are performed. If we had more detailed information about what Protestant ministers actually say or do in each of these professional roles, we might find such relationships to be more important to the clergy's ethicalism. From the questions we asked, however, they do not appear to be related to the central concerns of this study. Traditionalist ministers devote no more time or attention to their pastoral roles than the modernist clergy; modernist ministers who give the most attention to their parishioners are no better able to avoid conflicts with them over their social activism and are no less ethically active themselves.

Thus although we do not have a full picture of the clergy's professional relations with their parishioners, our information suggests that such associations have little relevance to the divisions existing within the church over religious or ethical issues. The conflicts between Protestant laymen and their parish ministers are rooted far more in their belief systems than in the manner in which Protestant clergymen carry out their pastoral roles. Yet whereas the foregoing statement applies to the ministers' professional associations with their parishioners, it is not true of their social relations with them. We turn now to an examination of these patterns.

Social Relations and Clergy Activism.   In previous discussions we have made much of the fact that Protestant ministers live among their parishioners and interact with them on such a continual and intimate basis. We suggested that as a result many parish ministers may develop close social ties with the members of their congregations and that such friendships may influence the ministers' desire or ability to engage in controversial ethical actions. Unlike our previous propositions, we find a great deal of support in our survey for such a thesis. We discover important differences in the manner in which Protestant clergymen interact socially with the members of their congregations, and these differences appear to be related both to the ministers' belief systems and to their social activism.

To learn about the ministers' social relations, we asked the California clergymen how often they "visit informally" with other clergymen and whether most of their close friends are found among their parishioners or their colleagues. The clergy's responses to both questions indicate the central role of lay members in the network of social relations among parish pastors. From Table 9.6, which shows the frequency with which the California ministers reportedly interact on an informal social basis with other clergymen, we see that they spend comparatively little time socializing with their professional colleagues. On the average, our respondents report visiting informally with colleagues in their own denomination only about twice a month and with colleagues in other denominations about once a month. By way of contrast, Table 9.3 indicated that the same ministers have "social visits" with their parishioners on an average of two to three times *each week*. These two questions are not entirely comparable, of course, since clerical duties involve making such pastoral calls. Whatever the motive behind such social interactions, however, they demonstrate the closer contact that parish clergymen have with their parishioners; the consequences of these patterns of social interaction are revealed shortly.

Table 9.6 also shows that colleague interaction is nearly the same among modernist and traditionalist ministers. No differences exist between these two groups of ministers in the extent of their social visits to clergymen within their own denomination; the former are only slightly more likely to interact socially with clergymen from other denominations. These patterns thus complement our findings in Chapter 5 concerning the local–cosmopolitan orientation of our respondents and those in the last section concerning the performance of their professional roles. In all these instances of professional conduct, little or no difference appears between the modernist, socially active clergy on the one hand and their traditionalist, largely inactive colleagues on the other. The two sets of ministers are equally involved in denominational organizations, devote an equal amount of attention to their pastoral roles, and interact with their colleagues in a roughly similar fashion.

Table 9.6. Extent of Ministers' Informal Visiting with Clergymen in Own Denominations Is Unrelated to Their Religious Beliefs; Modernist Ministers Visit More Often with Clergymen in Other Denominations

Frequency of Informal Visits with Other Clergymen	Religious Orientation[a]					
	1	2	3	4	5	Total
CLERGY OF OWN DENOMINATION						
6 or more times a month	16%	16%	19%	13%	14%	16%
3–5 times a month	24	21	22	23	25	23
1–2 times a month	38	41	41	44	41	41
Less than once a month	22	22	18	20	21	20
	100%	100%	100%	100%	101%	100%
	(309)	(320)	(317)	(309)	(321)	(1576)
CLERGY OF OTHER DENOMINATIONS						
6 or more times a month	8%	12%	9%	4%	5%	8%
3–5 times a month	22	18	19	13	10	16
1–2 times a month	42	42	39	36	32	38
Less than once a month	28	29	33	47	52	38
	100%	101%	100%	100%	99%	100%
	(308)	(318)	(316)	(306)	(318)	(1566)

[a] On this 5-point scale, 1 is most modernist; 5 is most traditionalist.

Of greater importance than the frequency with which Protestant ministers interact with their colleagues and parishioners, however, is the extent to which they look to these two groups for their closest friendships. We might expect that parish clergymen who form the closest friendships with the members of their congregations will tend to take on attitudes more similar to those of Protestant laymen.

Table 9.7 shows the sources of closest social relations of traditionalist and modernist ministers.[6] Forty-two percent of the California ministers said that their closest friends were among their parishioners, and 37 percent named their colleagues as the source of their closest friendships. The remaining 21 percent selected the "other" category—most saying that their closest friends were divided about equally between these two groups. Thus many parish ministers have a close social and professional relationship with the members of their congregations. Unlike the situation in most other professions, Prot-

Table 9.7. Traditionalist Ministers Most Often Report That Their Closest Friends Are Among Their Parishioners

Source of Closest Social Relations	Religious Orientation[a]					
	1	2	3	4	5	Total
Colleagues among the clergy	41%	39%	35%	35%	37%	37%
Parishioners	35	35	42	48	48	42
Mixed, others	24	26	23	17	15	21
	100%	100%	100%	100%	100%	100%
	(305)	(317)	(314)	(307)	(318)	(1561)

[a] On this 5-point scale, 1 is most modernist; 5 is most traditionalist.

estant ministers at the parish level look more to their clients than to their fellow professionals for their most important friendships.

Table 9.7 also reveals that the more traditionalist clergymen are somewhat more likely to maintain close social relationships with the members of their congregations than the modernist clergy. Forty-eight percent of each of the two most traditionalist groups reported that their closest friends are individuals in their parishes, as compared with 35 percent of the two most modernist groups. We cannot say with certainty what causes these differences; it is likely, however, that they result from the greater similarities in attitudes between traditionalist ministers and Protestant laymen. Those who see things in much the same way are more likely to become close friends than those who do not.

The most important feature of these patterns of friendship is their clear influence on the clergy's ethical beliefs and on the manner in which they respond to public issues. Protestant clergymen who are closest friends with the members of their congregations are more conservative on political issues and are less socially active than those who look more to their colleagues for their major social relationships. These patterns existed on all three of the public controversies we have been examining, and they remain when we control for differences in the ministers' religious orientations.

We can demonstrate this effect most clearly by following the procedures adopted in Chapter 6 for the analysis of the influence of role group attitudes. Table 9.8 shows the relationship between the clergy's choice of friends and their positions on the three public issues studied previously; as in Chapter 6, we are controlling for the differences in the ministers' religious views to separate this influence from the effects of the respondents' friendship groups. We see that on all three controversial issues the ministers who are closest friends with their parishioners take more conservative positions than other ministers with similar religious orientations. On Proposition 14—where the clergy's position was almost uniformly liberal—this relationship occurred among both modernist and traditionalist clergymen. On the remaining two issues, the California grape strike and the war in Vietnam, it occurred among all but the most traditionalist group of clergy. For these ministers it apparently made little difference which group served as a major source of social contact, since both were reported to have predominantly conservative opinions on these issues.

The consistent and fairly large differences evident in Table 9.8 show one major way in which Protestant laymen influence clergy activism. Our respondents may not always be aware of it, but the development of close friendships with their parishioners clearly results in their taking more conservative or "safe" positions on important public issues. Such influence seems to be exerted whenever conflicting positions are taken by the ministers' generally liberal colleagues and denominational leaders on the one hand and their generally conservative parishioners on the other. It is apparently operative for issues as diverse as civil rights, war, and the organization of the poor.

We should also point out that most parish ministers develop at least some close friendships among the members of their congregations. Even clergymen who name their colleagues as the source of their most important social relations are likely to interact socially with their parishioners on a fairly regular basis, thus being exposed to these conservative influences. Table 9.8 gives only the differences in attitudes among Protestant ministers according to the source of their closest friendships; it cannot be used to determine the overall impact of the development of lay–clergy social ties on ministerial activism. We can only suggest that this overall impact of social relations between Protestant ministers and laymen appears to be considerable.

In helping to shape the positions that parish ministers take on public issues, Protestant laymen are clearly reducing the number of clergymen who speak out on such issues as peace, racial relations, and programs for the poor. Clergymen who take conservative positions on these issues, as we have seen, are less active than those who hold liberal views. There is also evidence to suggest that a minister's choice of friends directly influences his activist behavior, although this effect is much more limited. By and large, our survey shows that the clergy's social relations are linked to their social activism in a more indirect fashion by influencing the positions they take on public issues, rather than their actions once their views have been formed.

Table 9.8. Ministers Whose Closest Friendships Are Among Their Parishioners Most Often Take Conservative Positions on Controversial Political Issues

Major Friendship Group	Religious Orientation[a]					Total
	1	2	3	4	5	
OPPOSING PROPOSITION 14[b]						
Parishioners	95%	88%	80%	66%	42%	70%
	(43)	(51)	(64)	(70)	(82)	(310)
Colleagues	100%	96%	90%	81%	52%	81%
	(46)	(44)	(38)	(47)	(63)	(238)
Mixed, others	90%	88%	97%	63%	27%	76%
	(29)	(32)	(33)	(27)	(22)	(143)
FAVORING CLERGY PARTICIPATION IN ORGANIZATION OF MIGRATORY FARM WORKERS[b]						
Parishioners	76%	54%	41%	24%	15%	38%
	(66)	(68)	(88)	(101)	(99)	(422)
Colleagues	81%	73%	55%	33%	6%	48%
	(59)	(71)	(56)	(70)	(85)	(355)
Mixed, others	80%	65%	49%	43%	9%	52%
	(39)	(48)	(43)	(30)	(32)	(192)
DOVISH ON VIETNAM WAR						
Parishioners	61%	49%	38%	16%	9%	32%
	(108)	(112)	(133)	(146)	(151)	(650)
Colleagues	68%	55%	44%	25%	6%	40%
	(124)	(123)	(109)	(108)	(118)	(582)
Mixed, others	59%	45%	39%	13%	14%	37%
	(73)	(82)	(72)	(53)	(49)	(329)

[a] On this 5-point scale, 1 is most modernist; 5 is most traditionalist.
[b] Totals do not include ministers who were in different churches or were not in the ministry when these controversies existed.

Social Activism and the Ministerial Career. The organization and government of Protestant churches thrust the parish ministers into extremely close contact with a predominantly conservative laity. The clergymen are dependent on the members of their congregations for much of the psychological satisfactions they derive from their professions, as well as for the more formal aspects of their career success. We have learned that many parish ministers form close friendships with their parishioners and that such friendships apparently cause them to take more cautious, conservative positions on controversial political issues. The importance of these findings cannot be overemphasized, since the relationships cited serve to undermine the ethical directives perceived by many clergymen in their religious commitments and to make them less outspoken on public issues. Such a conservatizing influence, furthermore, appears to be far more extensive than we can demonstrate in a survey of this kind. We have documented only the differences that exist in this respect between parish clergymen who are closer to their liberal-oriented colleagues and those who are closer to their congregational members. We have not shown the overall consequences of such close lay–clergy social relations for an action-oriented church; undoubtedly, they are substantial.

Given the nature of our study, we cannot trace exactly how such social relationships develop and come to influence the clergy's ethical attitudes and behavior. However, it does appear from our findings—as well as those from other studies[7]—that career patterns within the Protestant ministry lead the clergy into taking progressively more conservative positions on controversial public issues. We can describe this process (in idealized terms, of course) roughly as follows. Protestant clergymen fresh from seminary school are the most idealistic and purposive in defining their ministerial goals and are likely to be the least cautious in speaking out on public issues. At this point, they experience relatively few cross-pressures over their clerical goals and are less settled into their parish positions. Like others of the same age, they have smaller families and generally have less perceived need to worry about income or job security. As they settle into their first jobs, however, they often find that their parishioners have very different ideas about the proper roles and duties of the cleric. They are "shown the ropes" and told that they must conform to certain behavioral norms if they hope to succeed in their new position.[8]

Such a breaking-in period—when the individual finds that reality does not always correspond to his idealized picture—occurs in most professions. Among ministers, however, the process is particularly severe, since the practitioner finds that the norms to which he must conform are defined not by similarly trained colleagues but by his new clientele. Furthermore, he faces

his clients not in individual, dyadic relationships but as a social unit: as an
ongoing social structure with values, role preconceptions, and structured
authority relationships that predate his arrival at the scene. Certain aspects
of his theological teachings—the source of his authority—even serve to
legitimize the directives he receives from his laymen. Finally, to a greater or
lesser extent, his clients control his ability to enact his church programs, his
job security, and the impression he will make on his denominational
superiors.

For all these reasons, then, the pressures on the young cleric to conform
to the wishes of his parishioners are great. He has much to gain by playing
along; much to lose if he does not. His adaptation may be partly conscious—
as it was for the California clergymen who told us that they avoided certain
actions to keep their jobs. Equally often, however, it will be an unconscious
act, particularly as the new minister comes to make friends with the members of his congregation and to "see" things their way.

Our findings indicate that such conflict and role adjustment are the most
severe for modernist-oriented clergymen. These disagreements are a product not only of the general liberalism of the modernist clergy and the general
conservatism of Protestant laymen, but also of the patterns of recruitment
within the ministry. Modernist ministers tend to serve in denominations
with a high proportion of upper-income members, and, within these denominations, in churches located in more affluent, suburban areas. Differences in political beliefs, moreover, are clearly more likely to become subjects of contention in congregations served by modernist, ethically active
clergymen; they will be of little relevance in parish churches in which traditional ethical norms are followed.

Finally, we should keep in mind our broad description of religious goals
within the modernist situation. Orthodox Protestantism is specific in its doctrinal teachings and provides the minister with a concrete and easily defin-
able goal: the saving of souls. Modernist religion is far more ambiguous in
its theological message and in the objectives it posits for organized religion.
It devalues religious authority and undermines the distinctive role that religion is to play in secular society. As we saw in Chapter 7, laymen who have
turned away from traditional Protestant orthodoxies are less attached to organized religion than more orthodox church members and appear to derive
fewer satisfactions from their religious affiliation. Evidence exists to suggest
that modernist clergymen likewise suffer from a lack of significant theological
reality and purposive goal orientation. They tend to view the ministry more
as a "profession" than as a "calling" and to be more dissatisfied with their
chosen occupation than the traditionalist clergy.[9] In this situation, as we
have suggested, prophetic leadership may serve partly as a substitute for this
loss in traditional religious authority and function. Being in disagreement

with one's parishioners—being "on the cutting edge," in the words of several of our respondents—may become a sign of one's social relevance and prophetic actions. For many modernist ministers, then, open conflict with local congregational members may come to be expected—indeed may be viewed as a virtue, rather than as something to be avoided at all costs.

Thus role conflict, ambiguity, and adjustment seem to be more common among modernist, ethically oriented clergymen than among the more orthodox members of the clerical profession. It is among these ministers that we would expect conservative lay pressures to be most strongly felt and to lead to the greatest amount of conflict and compromise.

We should be careful, of course, not to overstate our description of these career-related pressures toward conformity. It is obvious from our previous findings that all Protestant clergymen do not succumb to these influences. Given these strong pressures toward conservatism and inactivism, in fact, we might exclaim at the large numbers of Protestant ministers who *are* active in public affairs. Clearly parish clergymen do not act from career considerations alone in forming their ethical views and in deciding what to say on public issues. Our point here is not that these influences are overriding, but that the structural features of the ministerial profession are such as to create greater political conservatism and to constrain clergy activism. It is in this sense that we are arguing that the career cycle within the Protestant ministry is associated with conservatism and inactivism.

As noted earlier, our study does not provide the type of information needed to test conclusively these propositions about the ministerial career. To do so, we would have to trace the attitudes and actions of Protestant clergymen over time. In social science terms, we would have to construct a longitudinal study—one that examines the attitudes and behavior of Protestant ministers at some initial point in time (t_1) and compares the findings with their attitudes and behavior at some later date (t_2). We would then attempt to explain any changes we found (or did not find) between t_1 and t_2 by looking for the existence (or absence) of these career-related factors. We do not, of course, have such data. Rather, our information about the clergy's goals, behavior, and patterns of interaction was collected at a single point in time. Thus the only way we can test any of these propositions is to draw inferences from cross-sectional data. We can assume that the differences we find between parish clergymen at different stages in their ministerial careers are a result of career-related influences; by linking these differences with certain explanatory factors, we can suggest how the changes may have occurred. Such a technique is obviously risky and necessarily inconclusive. For example, when we find that the older modernist ministers are less socially active than their younger, equally modernist colleagues, we cannot automatically conclude that the older ministers have changed their behavioral patterns or beliefs over time.

It may well be that ethical issues were less salient to clergymen entering the ministerial profession 15 or 30 years ago, and that modernist-oriented ministers did not at that time develop a commitment to an action-oriented church. Other equally logical reasons can be proposed to explain these differences between our older and younger respondents.

Therefore, we can only draw suggestive inferences from our survey to explain the generational differences among our respondents. Our data do, however, strongly suggest that such career-related changes are occurring in the clergy's attitudes and behavior. We find, for example, that the longer a minister has been in his parish position, the more likely he is to name his congregational members as the source of his most important social relations. As we have seen, ministers who have their closest friendships with their parishioners tend to be more politically conservative and socially inactive. In addition, a smaller proportion of the older respondents expressed approval of our 10 measures of clerical leadership in public affairs. This relationship persists even when we control from the ministers' religious commitments— and it is particularly strong on the questions dealing with protest marches and civil disobedience. The older ministers, finally, are less socially active and are somewhat less likely to report that their religious and political views serve to encourage their participation in social action activities. Again these patterns remain when we control for religious beliefs.

All these findings suggest that there is validity to our description of the ministerial career cycle. Thus the data we have presented in this chapter— together with those in the previous three chapters—show very distinctly the opposition of most Protestant laymen to clergy activism and how much their opposition influences ministers who wish to speak out on public issues. Most importantly, we have seen that lay–clergy conflict over church activism does not occur idiosyncratically but is firmly rooted in the contrasting belief systems of Protestant ministers and laymen and in certain organizational features of Protestant churches and of the ministerial profession. For these reasons, such conflicts are likely to continue in the future, and lay conservatism will probably remain as a major force inhibiting the development of an action-oriented church.

As we saw in Chapter 6, Protestant churches contain some counterbalancing forces to such lay influences. Particularly, Protestant church leaders take generally liberal positions on political and ethical questions and have some authority at their disposal with which to encourage church activists. We turn now to these data to complete our analysis of the impact of occupationally related factors on clergy activism.

NOTES AND REFERENCES

1.   See the discussion in Charles Y. Glock and Rodney Stark, *Religion and Society in Tension* (Skokie, Ill.: Rand McNally, 1965), pp. 124–129.

2.   Samual W. Blizzard, "The Minister's Dilemma," *Christian Century*, **73** (1956), pp. 508–509. More recent studies have found similar patterns.

3.   Glock and Stark, *op. cit.*, pp. 144–150.

4.   Edgar W. Mills, "Occupational Stress in the Ministry: A Progress Report," mimeographed, Ministry Studies Board, National Council of Churches, Washington, D.C., February 11, 1971.

5.   *Ibid.*, p. 4.

6.   The exact wording of the question was: "In which social group are most of your *close* friends located?"

7.   For example, Hadden found considerable age-related differences in clerical attitudes in his nationwide survey. Jeffrey K. Hadden, *The Gathering Storm in the Churches* (Garden City, N.Y.: Doubleday, 1969), pp. 56–60, 126–132, 283–285, 288–289.

8.   See Lee Braude, "Professional Autonomy and the Role of the Layman," *Social Forces* (May 1961), pp. 297–301 for a discussion of some of these influences on the young rabbi.

9.   Data to support these assertions are presented in Chapter 11.

10.   From this perspective, parish clergymen will be most protected from such informal lay influences when they frequently change parish positions. Among the liberal denominations surveyed, the United Methodist Church most often employs this practice as a deliberate policy. The hierarchical polity structure of this denomination, as the next chapter indicates, is important in several respects in encouraging more active social commitment among its parish pastors.

DENOMINATIONAL LEADERSHIP
AND CLERGY ACTIVISM

10. In the preceding three chapters we focused largely on the role of lay-related factors in influencing the nature and extent of clergy activism. As expected, we find Protestant laymen to hold generally conservative views on ethical and political issues and to act as a brake on the development of a more action-oriented church. Local congregations, however, do not have a monopoly over important organizational inducements and constraints within the ministerial profession. It is recalled from Chapter 6 that local denominational leaders share authority with local congregations in several important respects and thus may be in a position, if they so choose, to counterbalance such lay conservatism and lay resistance to social activism. In this chapter we complete our investigation of the impact of occupational factors on clergy activism by examining the role of local denominational leaders in encouraging or discouraging the ethical actions of the California clergy.

We first consider the attitudes of local denominational leaders toward ethical and political issues. Prior research on this question suggests that Protestant church officials generally maintain liberal views on ethical and political issues. A survey of the attitudes of Episcopal bishops, priests, and laymen carried out in 1952 shows that liberalism increases as one goes up the hierarchy in this high-status denomination. Episcopal bishops hold the most liberal views on ethical and political issues, followed by ministers at the parish level and, last, by Episcopal laymen.[1] A survey of the delegates to the 1966 Triennial Assembly of the National Council of Churches produced somewhat similar results. Nonparish church leaders at the convention were the most likely to take nonorthodox positions on religious issues and to favor a withdrawal policy in Vietnam. Parish clergymen were the next most liberal in their religious and political positions, followed by the lay delegates in attendance.[2]

We saw in Chapter 6 that the California ministers likewise report their local leaders to hold generally liberal views on political issues and to support most forms of clergy activism. Such a pattern is obviously important, and we begin this chapter by looking more closely at the denominational distributions of these responses.

Because Protestant church leaders personally approve of clergy activism, it does not follow that they will play a major role in encouraging the development of a more action-oriented church. Authority is highly decentralized within Protestant denominations, and as we know from Chapter 8, many congregational members are not reluctant to use or to threaten to use the sanctions at their disposal to put a stop to a minister's ethical actions. However, local Protestant leadership may be in a position to counterbalance, at least in part, such lay resistance to clergy activism. In particular, local denominational officials may play an important role in helping the parish clergyman obtain and maintain employment; thus they may be in a position to provide a measure of occupational security to ministers who do speak out on controversial public issues.

Our second concern in this chapter is the distribution of authority within the nine denominations surveyed. We asked the California ministers a series of questions about the manner in which their parishioners and their local denominational leaders supervise their activities, and we use the responses to gauge the relative influence of these two groups within Protestant churches. We are especially interested in whether each denomination's formal polity structure—espiscopal, presbyterian, or congregational—has any apparent effect on the role of laymen and local officials in church governance.

Even if local denominational officials possess such authority, of course, they will not necessarily exercise it to the benefit of the socially active clergy. They may be reluctant to take sides in local lay–clergy disputes, or they may be hesitant to support the more outspoken new breed clergymen. Our final set of questions thus deals with the actual assistance our respondents feel they would receive from their local denominational leaders in case of conflict with their parishioners; we also try to ascertain how they feel their chances of receiving choice parish appointments are affected by their being socially active.

The information presented in this chapter is important in showing that the parish activist does not stand alone before a hostile laity. At the same time, it also indicates that most new breed activists believe their careers will suffer as a result of strong stands taken on controversial social issues. Together with the data presented in Chapter 9, this material illustrates the strong structural restraints that act on the ethically oriented clergy at the parish level.

The Ethical and Political Attitudes of Local Church Leaders.
Local church leaders in California take generally liberal positions on ethical and political issues—they approve of most of the 10 forms of activism on which we are focusing and generally hold liberal views on the three public issues explored in our analysis. As we noted in Chapter 6, however, this is not true within all nine denominations we surveyed. Local officials in some churches are more liberal than those in others, and conservative views dominate in at least two of these denominations. We begin our examination of church leadership, therefore, by looking more closely at the denominational patterns of these clerical reports. We find that these patterns are much the same on both ethical and political issues and are similar, although not identical, to those found among the parish ministers themselves.

Table 10.1 shows the percentages of local church leaders in California who approve of the various forms of clergy activism.[3] (Recall that the data were collected by asking our respondents whether they felt that the majority of their local denominational officials would approve or disapprove of each action.) For reasons of space, the responses in Table 10.1 are abbreviated to include only the proportion of ministers in each denomination who reported that their local leaders looked on these actions favorably. A fairly consistent pattern appears—for each question, local church leaders in the United Church of Christ and in the Methodist Church most often approve of clergy activism, followed in order by officials in the Presbyterian Church, the Lutheran Church in America, and the Episcopal Church. As we have seen, the distribution of clerical responses followed much the same order—the major differences being the relatively greater liberalism of Episcopal priests and the relatively greater conservatism of local Presbyterian ministers.

Among the four conservative denominations, the ordering is identical to that found previously among the clergy. Local church leaders are reported to be the most supportive of clergy activism within the American Baptist Convention, followed in order by church leaders in the American Lutheran Church, the Missouri Synod-Lutheran Church, and the Southern Baptist Convention. The relative differences in views among church leaders in these four denominations vary somewhat from issue to issue, but greater support for ethicalism appears among American Baptist leaders. Church officials in this denomination, in fact, seem to be more similar in their ethical views to officials in the five liberal denominations than to those in the other three conservative church groups. As we see below, this pattern holds on our other questions as well.

Turning to some of the specific items in Table 10.1, we see that at the time of our survey a large majority of the church leaders in the liberal denominations reportedly approved of the six following ethical actions: organizing a study group within the local church to discuss public affairs, organizing a social action group to accomplish directly a social or political goal, delivering a sermon on a controversial political or social topic, publicly taking a stand on a political issue, taking a stand on a political issue from the pulpit, and participating in a civil rights protest march. Only on the question dealing with antiwar civil disobedience do we find more ministers reporting that their local denominational leaders would disapprove than approve. Even in this instance, furthermore, the differences are small: 33 percent of the clergy in the liberal denominations feel that the majority of their local officials would disapprove of such conduct, whereas 29 percent believe that they would approve.

Thus church officials in liberal denominations were seen as holding fairly permissive views on ethical issues during the 1960s, and the forms of social activism most controversial among the clergy were also most controversial among their leaders. Identical differences exist in the manner in which local church officials in the four conservative denominations were reported to respond to clergy activism. Some support existed for the more common forms of social activism, but it dropped off sharply in response to acts of civil protest.

These questions regarding social ethics are, of course, somewhat abstract and ambiguous, since they refer to the response of church leaders to hypothetical acts of clergy activism. Not so with our questions concerning the positions of church leaders on the three issues examined in previous chapters: the anti-fair housing referendum, the California grape strike, and the debate over Vietnam war policy. The ministers' reports of their denominational leaders' views on these issues are summarized in Table 10.2. Again the table is abbreviated to include only the percentage of local officials who reportedly took liberal positions on these public controversies.

The distribution of denominational responses to these questions resembles the distribution of Table 10.1, although some variations occur from issue to issue. We see most clearly in this table the great opposition to Proposition 14 within liberal church groups. Only 6 percent of the respondents in the five liberal denominations felt that the majority of their local leaders favored the initiative proposal. (Again we should recall that the measure was supported by most Protestant laymen and passed with 65 percent of the vote.) Even within the more conservative denominations, church leaders generally broke with their parishioners and lined up against the proposed discriminatory amendment. Only within the highly conservative Southern Baptist Convention did more parish ministers report that their local leaders favored

Table 10.1. Ministers in Liberal Denominations Most Often Report that Their Local Denominational Leaders Approve of Clergy Activism

Majority of Ministers' Local Denominational Leaders Would Approve of Their Taking the Following Actions	Methodist	United Church of Christ	Episcopal	Presbyterian	Lutheran Church in America	American Baptist	American Lutheran Church	Missouri Synod-Lutheran Church	Southern Baptist	Total	
PROTEST LEADERSHIP											
Participate in a civil rights march	70%	76%	57%	69%	54%	38%	15%	10%	1%	48%	(1559)
Participate in an antiwar protest march	63	71	39	54	45	24	7	1	—[a]	39	(1560)
Be arrested to symbolize civil rights protest	30	45	27	31	22	15	4	2	1	22	(1560)
Be arrested to symbolize antiwar protest	30	47	21	27	20	13	2	1	1	20	(1558)
CHURCH LEADERSHIP											
Organize a study group within the local church to discuss public affairs	95	91	85	95	99	84	78	57	30	81	(1556)
Organize a social action group within the local church to accomplish directly some social or political goal	87	87	74	88	92	72	52	32	21	70	(1554)
Deliver a sermon on a controversial political or social topic	87	84	73	90	79	65	35	25	24	67	(1555)
Take a stand from the pulpit on a political issue	80	72	62	72	67	51	23	12	23	57	(1553)

PUBLIC LEADERSHIP

Publicly (not from the pulpit) take a stand on a political issue	87	85	69	83	85	63	39	33	31	67	(1562)
Publicly (not from the pulpit) support a political candidate	55	56	29	50	48	40	20	25	25	41	(1559)

[a] Less than 1 percent.

Table 10.2. Ministers in Liberal Denominations Most Often Report that Their Local Denominational Leaders Take Liberal Positions on Political Issues

	Methodist	United Church of Christ	Episcopal	Presbyterian	Lutheran Church in America	American Baptist	American Lutheran Church	Missouri Synod-Lutheran Church	Southern Baptist	Total
Majority opposed Proposition 14	90% (272)	89% (98)	88% (160)	91% (184)	95% (57)	66% (110)	44% (77)	34% (92)	12% (131)	72% (1181)
Majority favored clerical support of striking farm workers	64% (310)	85% (112)	54% (180)	63% (207)	69% (75)	40% (120)	20% (94)	4% (115)	3% (145)	48% (1358)
Officials had made formal statement favoring greater efforts to negotiate Vietnam war	87% (352)	63% (136)	61% (203)	57% (224)	54% (85)	33% (143)	17% (117)	8% (128)	10% (165)	50% (1553)

(21 percent) than opposed (12 percent) the initiative proposition. At the same time, it is clear that clergymen and church officials in these four conservative Protestant denominations were less involved in the issue than their liberal colleagues. About two-fifths of the clergymen in these four denominations reported that they were "not sure" of the positions of their local leaders on Proposition 14, but no more than 3 percent of the respondents in any of the liberal denominations indicated this to be the case.

The church leaders' opinions were less uniformly liberal on the other two political issues under consideration, but roughly the same denominational patterns in attitudes emerge. The California grape strike, as we pointed out earlier, was a less controversial issue than the others, and more than a third of the parish clergymen did not know where their leaders stood on the matter. Again this was particularly true within the more conservative church groups. Only in the Missouri Synod and Southern Baptist Convention, however, did more clergymen report that their local leaders opposed clerical support of the striking workers than favored it. The strongest support for the workers' position was found in the United Church of Christ—a denomination that was closely involved, both publicly and financially, with the Migrant Ministry.

A similar distribution of opinions apparently existed on the Vietnam issue at the time of our survey. As we indicated earlier, by the spring of 1968 more than half the local denominational officials in California had reportedly taken a formal position on the war. Almost all these statements called for greater efforts to negotiate an end to the war; only 4 percent of the respondents indicated that their local leaders had publicly supported the policies then in effect. Again, these dovish views were more prevalent in the liberal denominations. Eighty-seven percent of the Methodist ministers, for example, reported that their local denominational leaders had publicly opposed the war, as compared with less than 10 percent of the Missouri Synod and Southern Baptist clergymen.

The attitudes of local denominational leaders in California toward both ethical and political issues thus tend to parallel the distribution in attitudes found among the parish ministers themselves. Such a pattern in attitudes comes as no surprise, of course, since denominational leaders are themselves ordained ministers and in many denominations still retain parish positions. Thus we would not expect their attitudes to differ too markedly from those found among the parish clergy. As we proceed in this chapter, however, we see just how important such supportive positions can be for socially active ministers.

In trying to learn the views of the local denominational leaders, we are chiefly interested in their impact on the ethical behavior of parish clergymen:

whether local leaders are in any way acting to encourage or to discourage social activism within their respective denominations. We saw in Chapter 6 that a majority of the California ministers feel that the attitudes of their local officials serve to encourage their activist behavior. Fifty-three percent report that the attitudes of these officials "generally encourage" their participation in social action activities, and only 9 percent indicate that they have a discouraging effect. The ministers' responses to this question are listed by denomination in Table 10.3; clearly their evaluations are consistent with their reports concerning their denominational leaders' ethical and political views. The majority of the parish ministers in the five liberal denominations indicate that the attitudes of their local leaders serve to encourage their social activism; the majority of the ministers in the four conservative denominations indicate that they do not—most respondents reporting that they neither encourage nor discourage their response to public issues. More specifically, these responses correspond almost exactly to those in Tables 10.1 and 10.2. Three-quarters of the clergymen in the Methodist Church and the United Church of Christ report that the attitudes of their local leaders generally serve to encourage their social activism. Somewhat fewer Presbyterian ministers make such a claim (70 percent), followed by clergymen in the Lutheran Church in America (65 percent) and the Episcopal Church (63 percent).Only a few ministers in these five liberal church groups—an average of 5 percent—feel that the attitudes of their local church officials have a generally discouraging effect on their activist behavior. Within the four conservative denominations, we again find that church leaders within the American

Table 10.3. Ministers in Liberal Denominations Most Often Report that Attitudes of Their Local Denominational Leaders Serve to Encourage Their Participation in Social Action Activities

Denomination	Generally Encourage	Neither	Generally Discourage		
Methodist	75%	22	3	100%	(353)
United Church of Christ	75%	18	7	100%	(135)
Episcopal	63%	26	11	100%	(206)
Presbyterian	70%	25	5	100%	(223)
Lutheran Church in America	65%	29	6	100%	(86)
American Baptist	41%	50	9	100%	(143)
American Lutheran Church	25%	56	19	100%	(117)
Missouri Synod-Lutheran Church	9%	65	26	100%	(131)
Southern Baptist	10%	83	7	100%	(166)
Totals	53%	38	9	100%	(1560)

Baptist Convention are felt to be substantially more activist oriented than local leaders in the other three church groups. As we see below, there is evidence to suggest that the church hierarchy within this denomination may be more liberal in California than most of its parish ministers.

Thus we find consistent patterns in the ethical and political attitudes attributed to the local leaders in these nine denominations in California and in their reputed impact on the ministers' activist behavior. To understand how church leaders can encourage clergy activism within their respective denominations, we asked the California ministers a number of questions concerning the exercise of authority within their churches. We turn now to these data.

Authority Patterns Within Protestant Churches. We inquired into the exercise of authority within Protestant churches to determine the relative control exerted by generally conservative laymen on the one hand and generally liberal church leaders on the other over important aspects of the ministerial career. To the extent that authority rests in the hands of local parishioners, we might expect parish ministers to be deterred from speaking out on public issues. To the extent that it resides with local church leaders, we might expect more of the modernist clergy to assume active roles in public affairs.

Theoretically, at least, such authority patterns are affected by the formal organizational structures within each of the nine denominations surveyed: the episcopal, the presbyterian, and the congregational forms of government. In theory, authority resides in the denominational hierarchy in the first of these policy structures, is shared by the clergy and specially selected lay representatives in the second, and is exercised primarily by the members of the local congregation in the third. In practice, however, it is frequently held that all Protestant churches are now governed in much the same way. Glock and Stark, for example, point out that most local churches are moving toward a congregational authority structure as they strive for autonomy from their national denominations. The minister remains the central figure in local church government, but ultimate authority over the affairs of the parish church rests in an elected council of laymen. These church councils, furthermore, tend to be dominated by the wealthier and better educated members of the local congregation, and are thus likely to reinforce the conservatism of Protestant laymen generally.[4]

Such lay authority over the affairs of the local church would seem to be a major obstacle to the development of an action-oriented church. With respect to employment practices within Protestant churches, however, the

Table 10.4. Ministers Report that Their Parishioners Closely Supervise Many of Their Church Activities; Little Relation Exists to Denominational Polity Structure

Degree of Lay Supervision	Episcopal Polity		Presbyterian Polity				Congregational Polity			Total
	Episcopal	Methodist	American Lutheran Church	Lutheran Church in America	Missouri Synod-Lutheran Church	Presbyterian	American Baptist	Southern Baptist	United Church of Christ	
THE CHURCH BUDGET										
Closely	47%	50%	63%	56%	72%	65%	46%	50%	61%	54%
Moderately	46	42	33	35	24	28	37	36	26	35
Little	13	8	4	8	4	7	15	10	11	9
Not at all	4	1	—	1	—	—	2	4	2	2
	100% (204)	101% (353)	100% (116)	100% (87)	100% (134)	100% (224)	100% (142)	100% (170)	100% (137)	100% (1567)
THE MINISTER'S SALARY										
Closely	29%	52%	63%	48%	63%	52%	45%	58%	44%	50%
Moderately	32	34	31	31	27	35	37	29	31	32
Little	18	10	4	16	8	11	15	7	17	12
Not at all	21	4	2	5	2	2	3	6	8	6
	100% (199)	100% (351)	100% (116)	100% (87)	100% (134)	100% (221)	100% (145)	100% (169)	100% (135)	100% (1557)

Closely	7%	14%	21%	21%	25%	30%	12%	31%	17%	19%
Moderately	46	63	61	48	60	54	56	49	60	56
Little	39	21	18	28	14	16	27	16	22	22
Not at all	8	2	—	3	1	—[a]	5	4	1	3
	100%	100%	100%	100%	100%	100%	100%	100%	100%	100%
	(204)	(353)	(117)	(87)	(134)	(224)	(144)	(170)	(137)	(1570)

THE MINISTER'S PARTICIPATION IN SOCIAL ACTION ACTIVITIES

Closely	2%	3%	6%	2%	6%	7%	3%	4%	6%	4%
Moderately	16	24	25	21	19	30	15	14	32	22
Little	37	42	38	47	39	37	42	32	38	39
Not at all	45	31	30	30	36	27	40	49	24	35
	100%	100%	99%	100%	100%	101%	100%	99%	100%	100%
	(204)	(350)	(115)	(87)	(133)	(224)	(144)	(168)	(135)	(1560)

[a] Less than 1 percent.

trend appears to be toward more denominational than lay control. Given the increasing size of churches and church denominations, it is difficult for local churchmen to screen all applicants and to choose, independent of denominational assistance, their own ministers. Local church officials thus may be coming to play a relatively important role in most denominations in helping the parish clergy obtain employment.

To determine how the California clergymen view the situation, we asked them a number of questions about the manner in which their parishioners and their local church officials supervise their clerical activities. We will be particularly interested, in this respect, in the distribution of authority within the five more liberal, activist-oriented denominations. Two of these denominations have episcopal organizational structures (the Methodist and the Episcopal), two are presbyterian (the Presbyterian and the Lutheran Church in America), and one is congregational (the United Church of Christ). We want to know whether the more hierarchically organized denominations do in fact place greater authority in the hands of local church officials and whether such authority patterns work to the benefit of the socially active clergy.

Table 10.4 shows the degree to which the California ministers feel their local parishioners supervise their actions in each of four areas: the church budget, the individual's salary, the church's programs, and the individual's participation in social action activities. The responses are arranged according to the formal authority structure in each denomination, thus facilitating our assessment of the impact of these hypothetical organizational forms. The totals in Table 10.4 indicate that local congregational members exercise the closest authority over fiscal matters. Fifty-four percent of the ministers report that their parishioners "closely" supervise the church budget; 50 percent say that they "closely" supervise ministerial salaries. Few parish clergymen report that lay authority in either of these areas is "little" or nonexistent. Such lay control over church finances—particularly with respect to the minister's own salary—would seem to give Protestant laymen a very important means of influencing clerical behavior. As a Lutheran minister commented on his questionnaire, "A pastor . . . has no outside union, board, etc., to assist in establishing a fair salary; it is left to the whims of his congregation. If he is well-liked—good salary, if not, well. . . ."[5]

Lay supervision of clerical conduct is reportedly less severe in the other two areas covered in our survey. Nineteen percent of the California ministers indicate that their parishioners closely supervise their churches' programs, whereas 56 percent say that lay authority in this area is moderate. Most important for our purposes, even less formal lay control is exercised over the clergy's ethical actions. Only 4 percent of our respondents report that their parishioners closely supervise their participation in social action activities, and 22 percent say that such supervision is moderate. Thus parish ministers clearly do not feel that their congregational members regulate their ethical behavior as closely as they do their conduct in the other cited areas of church policy. In part, this pattern undoubtedly reflects the smaller amount of time and attention given by Protestant clergymen to ethical matters, as opposed to other clerical functions. Even within the liberal denominations, however, most California ministers report that lay supervision in this area is slight or nonexistent. Apparently, relatively few parish congregations attempt to oversee their ministers' ethical conduct directly and formally. Rather, their influence in this respect comes through their informal contacts with the parish pastor and through their control over other aspects of the minister's career and programs.

We also observe from these responses that formal polity structures apparently have little effect on the manner in which congregational members oversee clerical conduct in these four areas. By and large, according to the data of Table 10.4, ministers in all our nine denominations report that their parishioners supervise their activities in the same manner. The only major exception to this pattern is found within the Episcopal Church, where a hierarchical polity structure seems to allow the local minister greater autonomy from lay supervision. The same situation does not exist within the hierarchical Methodist Church, however, nor do clergymen in denominations organized according to presbyterian principles experience more freedom from lay control than ministers in congregational polities.

Thus the pattern of ministerial responses to these questions serves to confirm the observations that local parishioners have a great deal of control over many aspects of local church policies and that their authority in this respect varies little from denomination to denomination. Only within the Episcopal Church do these formal organizational forms have any apparent effect on authority patterns, and even in this case congregational members still retain a substantial degree of influence.

What role, then, do local denominational leaders play with respect to the ministerial career? What authority can they exert to counteract lay conservatism and lay opposition to social activism? Thus far it appears that their major influence lies in the area of clerical employment—in the manner in which parish clergymen are hired and fired. For this reason, we asked a parallel question about how closely the California ministers perceive their local denominational leaders to supervise the appointment and removal of parish ministers within their own denominations. These data are reported in Table 10.5. The responses suggest that Protestant denominational officials as a group have fairly substantial influence over hiring and firing practices at the parish level. In total, 39 percent of the California ministers indicate that their local leaders "closely" supervise the appointment of parish ministers within their denominations, and 27 percent say that their authority in this respect is moderate. Similarly, 32 percent report that their local leaders closely supervise the removal of parish ministers from their positions, with 16 percent indicating that such supervision is carried out moderately.

Thus local denominational leaders have major sanctions with which to reward parish ministers with whom they are pleased and to punish those whom they regard with disfavor. They often play a significant role in helping the parish clergy obtain parish appointments and in supervising their dismissal. Moreover, differences in organizational structure are quite important with respect to denominational authority in this area (see Table 10.5). Local officials in the hierarchically governed Methodist Church have by far the most control over the employment of parish ministers. Following them in influence are the leaders of the Episcopal Church and the four denominations governed by combined lay–clerical bodies—the three Lutheran denominations and the Presbyterian Church. Church officials in the denominations organized according to the congregational principle play a much more minor role in the hiring and firing of parish clergymen, particularly within the highly conservative Southern Baptist Convention. To take the two extremes in our survey, 87 percent of the ministers in the Methodist Church report that their local leaders closely supervise the appointment of clergymen to parish positions; 78 percent say that they closely supervise their removal as well. Within the highly decentralized Southern Baptist Convention, only 1 percent of the respondents make either of these claims.

We are primarily interested in these authority patterns as a means of clarifying the situation in the denominations most often served by modernist and ethically oriented clergymen. Here the role of denominational leadership does indeed vary accordingly to polity structure. Local church leaders closely control the appointment and removal of parish ministers in the Methodist Church and are in an optimal position, if they so choose, to encourage the development of church activism. Church leaders in the Episcopal Church, the Lutheran Church in America, and the Presbyterian Church have less influence over the appointment of parish clergymen in their denominations and less still over their removal. Yet they retain a fair amount of authority in both respects. Denominational leaders in the congregationally organized United Church of Christ have the least amount of protection from their conservative parishioners. Again, however, such authority is relative to that which exists in other modernist denominations; even in this decentralized denomination, more than half the parish clergymen report that their local denominational officials play at least a moderate role in the appointment process.

Table 10.5. Most Ministers Report that Their Local Denominational Leaders Closely or Moderately Supervise the Appointment Process; Strong Relation Exists to Denominational Polity Structure

Degree of Lay Supervision	Episcopal Polity		Presbyterian Polity				Congregational Polity			Total
	Episcopal	Methodist	American Lutheran Church	Lutheran Church in America	Missouri Synod-Lutheran Church	Presbyterian	American Baptist	Southern Baptist	United Church of Christ	
THE APPOINTMENT OF PARISH MINISTERS										
Closely	41%	87%	39%	55%	23%	31%	9%	1%	8%	39%
Moderately	38	6	42	33	28	38	45	2	44	27
Little	18	5	12	8	29	23	26	12	28	17
Not at all	4	2	7	3	20	9	20	85	20	17
	101%	100%	100%	99%	100%	101%	100%	100%	100%	100%
	(205)	(353)	(118)	(87)	(134)	(226)	(146)	(163)	(137)	(1569)
THE REMOVAL OF PARISH MINISTERS										
Closely	32%	78%	32%	29%	25%	23%	2%	1%	4%	32%
Moderately	19	13	25	26	16	26	10	1	11	16
Little	36	7	35	33	37	36	38	4	39	26
Not at all	13	2	8	12	22	15	50	94	47	26
	100%	100%	100%	100%	100%	100%	100%	100%	100%	100%
	(204)	(350)	(117)	(87)	(134)	(226)	(144)	(163)	(137)	(1562)

Church Leadership and Clergy Activism. We have thus the responses of the parish ministers to two major questions related to the role of local denominational officials in influencing clergy activism: the attitudes taken by local leaders on political and ethical issues, and the authority they wield within their respective denominations. Church leaders in the modernist denominations have generally liberal views on ethical and political issues and to a greater or lesser extent, play important roles in helping the parish clergy find and maintain employment. Our major goal in asking these questions is to determine whether liberal-minded church officials have sufficient authority at their disposal to lend positive encouragement to activist-oriented clergymen. Thus we asked the California clergymen two additional questions about the likely consequences of their involvement in controversial social issues. First, how much assistance would they expect to receive from their local denominational leaders if they were to come in conflict with their parishioners over various issues, including their social activism? Second, what effect would speaking out on controversial social issues have on a minister's chances of receiving a choice parish position within his own denomination? The data from these questions show that denominational leaders have an important influence on the development of an action-oriented church—particularly in the most liberal and hierarchical denominations surveyed.

The ministers' responses to the first question are presented in Table 10.6. We asked the members of our sample if they would expect to receive "a great deal," "some," "little," or "no" assistance if they were to come into conflict with their parishioners over each of three issues: their theological views, their participation in social action activities, and the content of their sermons. The responses indicate that most Protestant ministers would expect at least some assistance in each of the circumstances named. Forty percent say that they would expect to receive "a great deal" of assistance from their denominational leaders in conflicts over their theological views, and 35 percent expect to receive at least "some." A slightly lower proportion of parish ministers expect such assistance in response to lay-related conflicts in the other two areas: 30 and 38 percent, respectively, in regard to the clergy's activist behavior, and 28 and 36 percent, respectively, in regard to the content of their sermons. Thus most parish ministers feel that if they were to experience difficulties with the members of their congregations, their local denominational leaders would come to their aid.

Again important differences are found in the denominational distribution of responses. As in the previous section, we have arranged the denominations according to their formal governmental structure rather than the liberalness of their members. Here we see even more sharply the effects of organizational structure on the role of Protestant church leaders. Clergymen in denominations organized along episcopal or presbyterian lines expect to receive much greater assistance from their church leaders in each of these situations than clergymen in denominations organized along congregational principles. Methodist ministers in particular feel that they would be given substantial support if they were to come into open conflict with the members of their congregations over any of these issues. Clergymen in the three Lutheran denominations also expect to receive a great deal of assistance in such circumstances from their local leaders, especially with respect to disagreements over theological issues. Official denominational support was least expected within the two Baptist denominations and, to a lesser extent, within the United Church of Christ.[7]

From the responses to these questions, we want to learn how much assistance the ethically oriented clergy expect to receive from their local denominational leaders when conflicts develop over the ministers' social activism. Table 10.6 reveals that a large majority of the ministers in all five liberal denominations would expect to receive at least some aid from these church officials. Such aid is apparently most common within the highly liberal and hierarchical Methodist Church; it is least common within the equally liberal but more decentralized United Church of Christ. In both instances, however, relatively few parish ministers feel that local church officials would do nothing if the individual's ethical activities created conflicts with his congregational members.

We did not probe the California ministers further on the specific forms such denominational assistance might take. From what we have said previously, however, it appears that the influence of these local officials over the appointment process is a major source of encouragement for the ethically active clergy. Informal consultations, bargaining sessions, statements of support, and comparable forms of moral backing can be important to a beleaguered parish activist. They can provide valuable encouragement and, on occasion, strategic support to ministers who find themselves under fire from parishioners for their ethical activities. In the long run, however, they cannot supply the type of job security and assurance of professional success that parish clergymen, like persons in other occupations, can be expected to seek. Without some formal, career-related incentive to maintain an active commitment to ethical leadership, therefore, we believe that far fewer parish ministers would become involved in controversial public issues, risking the types of lay reaction described in earlier chapters. Without the expectation that their denominational leaders will help them maintain their positions or find new ones elsewhere, Protestant clergymen would be far more reluctant to risk antagonizing their employers within the parish church.

Local denominational leaders, of course, do not have exclusive control over employment procedures even within the most hierarchical of Protestant denominations. Laymen can, if they are so moved, use their control over

Table 10.6. Most Ministers Expect at Least Some Assistance from Their Local Denominational Leaders When Conflicts Arise with Their Parishioners; Strong Relation Exists to Denominational Polity Structure

Assistance Expected when in Conflict with Parishioners over Various Issues	Episcopal Polity		Presbyterian Polity				Congregational Polity			Total
	Episcopal	Methodist	American Lutheran Church	Lutheran Church in America	Missouri Synod-Lutheran Church	Presbyterian	American Baptist	Southern Baptist	United Church of Christ	
YOUR THEOLOGICAL VIEWS										
A great deal	47%	53%	64%	68%	67%	30%	10%	9%	15%	40%
Some	34	35	29	25	26	44	41	22	47	35
Little	13	9	6	6	5	21	34	14	21	14
None	6	3	1	1	2	5	15	55	16	11
	100%	100%	100%	100%	100%	100%	100%	100%	99%	100%
	(203)	(352)	(118)	(87)	(132)	(223)	(145)	(161)	(137)	(1558)
THE CONTENT OF YOUR SERMONS										
A great deal	33%	45%	39%	40%	37%	22%	5%	6%	9%	28%
Some	39	36	41	39	42	36	39	13	42	36
Little	19	14	14	17	17	31	34	11	27	20
None	9	5	6	3	4	11	22	70	22	16
	100%	100%	100%	99%	100%	100%	100%	100%	100%	100%
	(203)	(351)	(118)	(87)	(131)	(225)	(145)	(161)	(137)	(1558)

YOUR PARTICIPATION IN
SOCIAL ACTION ACTIVITIES

A great deal	41%	53%	15%	45%	16%	32%	8%	2%	23%	30%
Some	39	38	49	44	32	48	45	8	48	38
Little	16	8	28	8	37	18	30	14	17	18
None	4	1	8	3	15	3	17	76	12	14
	100%	100%	100%	100%	100%	101%	100%	100%	100%	100%
	(202)	(353)	(117)	(87)	(132)	(225)	(145)	(161)	(137)	(1559)

279

ministerial salary as a means to influence their pastor's conduct or to punish him for certain actions. Within the more decentralized denominations, they form "search" committees to select clergymen who satisfy the qualifications required by the local congregation and can, often without notice, fire their minister at will.[8]

Thus although denominational leaders are able to provide some support for clergy activists through their influence over the appointment process, they are seldom in a position to guarantee that the professional career of a would-be activist will not suffer as a result of his ethical activities. Protestant laymen, even within the most hierarchical denominations, have extensive control over the ministers' careers. In addition, many denominational leaders themselves are sensitive to losses in membership and finances and are likely to view with alarm the parish clergyman whose actions cause a major drop in either. As a Lutheran (ALC) minister wrote, "In my opinion, my denomination wants to preserve the establishment and maintain the status quo. Money and members count with them."

Despite the sympathy of many denominational leaders for clergy activism and despite their ability to offer some protections to the ministerial activist, it remains unclear how much assistance church leaders are able to offer. Do clergy activists jeopardize their chances of career success by engaging in controversial public issues, or can they enhance their careers through the active support of generally liberal and sympathetic church leaders? Are denominational leaders, in short, able to offer clergy activists enough support to offset the opposition of members of their congregations to social actvism? It was with this potential cross-pressure in mind that we asked the California ministers the following question:

> In some denominations a minister who raises controversial social issues with his parishioners will have difficulty obtaining choice ministerial positions in the future, while in others a controversial minister will often receive the choice positions. Which of the following statements most closely describes the situation in your denomination?

The options given the clergy and their responses (see Table 10.7) furnish a wealth of suggestive information and validate many of our previous remarks. The totals reveal that more than half the respondents feel that involvement in controversial social issues will damage a minister's chances of receiving choice positions in their own denomination. Thirty-seven percent of the parish clergymen said that controversial ministers in their denominations "are often able to obtain suitable positions even though many do suffer because of their activism," and 21 percent selected the more strongly

Table 10.7. Most Ministers Expect that Controversial Clergymen Will Not Receive Choice Ministerial Positions; Slight Relation Exists to Denominational Polity Structure

Situation in Respondent's Denomination	Episcopal Polity		Presbyterian Polity				Congregational Polity			Total
	Episcopal	Methodist	American Lutheran Church	Lutheran Church in America	Missouri Synod-Lutheran Church	Presbyterian	American Baptist	Southern Baptist	United Church of Christ	
"The way to obtain a choice ministerial position in my denomination is to remain noncontroversial on social and political issues."	26%	7%	25%	18%	27%	25%	28%	27%	19%	21%
"Controversial ministers in my denomination are often able to obtain suitable positions even 'though many do suffer because of their activism."	49	42	27	29	23	49	29	13	51	37
"A minister's social activism has little relation to the type of ministerial position he receives in my denomination."	16	35	46	49	50	17	26	55	19	32
"Ministers who are socially active in my denomination are more likely to receive choice ministerial positions than those who do not speak out on social issues."	9	16	2	4	1	9	17	5	11	10
	100% (198)	100% (350)	100% (112)	100% (85)	100% (123)	100% (221)	100% (143)	100% (148)	100% (129)	100% (1509)

worded response: "The way to obtain a choice ministerial position in my denomination is to remain noncontroversial on social and political issues." Of the remaining respondents, 32 percent did not think that such an action would have any effect on a minister's parish appointment, and 10 percent felt that activist ministers actually received the best positions. Thus there is no consensus among the California clergy regarding the effects of social activism on their careers, but most feel that ethical leadership would damage their chances of obtaining choice parish positions. Despite the sympathy and encouragement which they feel their denominational leaders give to clergy activism, most parish ministers believe that their careers would suffer if they were to raise controversial issues with the members of their congregations.

As in our previous discussions in this chapter, the denominational distributions of these responses are also revealing. They show that among the five liberal church groups social activism creates the fewest career-related problems for parish ministers within the United Methodist Church—a pattern consistent with earlier findings. We suggest that local Methodist officials have much to do with the high degree of activism among Methodist ministers at the parish level in California. They possess liberal views on most ethical and political issues and also exercise a relatively large amount of authority over church affairs. Local clergymen are guaranteed employment by conference officials, and parish appointments are made by the bishop, not the local congregation (although some type of consultation may take place). Furthermore, Methodist ministers are rotated in their positions quite often and thus escape at least some of the informal social pressures that build up over time.

We see in Table 10.7 that polity structure is generally unrelated to the manner in which parish clergymen in the remaining liberal denominations evaluate the impact of their social activism. Ministers in the Lutheran Church in America are somewhat less likely to feel that they would suffer as a result of speaking out on controversial public issues, but the responses are much the same in the remaining three church groups. Whether this lack of further differentiation is a result of organizational factors or differences in denominational leaders' viewpoints (i.e., the greater liberalism of United Church of Christ officials and the greater conservatism of Episcopal leaders), we cannot say. At any rate, we find that a large majority of ministers in all but the Methodist Church and Lutheran Church in America feel that social activists experience difficulties obtaining choice parish positions. Only about a quarter of these ministers believe that speaking out on controversial social issues would either help their careers or not affect them.

We can also see more clearly from these breakdowns the somewhat peculiar situation within the American Baptist Convention. We know from other tables that clergymen within this denomination are more socially active than those in other church groups we have labeled "conservative" and that their denominational leaders are fairly liberal on political issues and sympathetic to social activism. We see here that social activism is a more divisive issue within the American Baptist Convention than in the other conservative denominations. Thus conditions within this generally conservative denomination may be encouraging the further spread of clergy activism. In any event, it seems that Baptist church leaders have more in common with church liberals than church conservatives.

The Costs of New Breed Activism. The information presented in this chapter completes our examination of the conflicts within Protestant churches over new breed activism and the effects of these conflicts on the ethical activities of parish clergymen. The local leadership in most Protestant denominations appears as a positive force in the development of a critical, action-oriented church, but the support it is able to give the new breed clergy is limited. On the one hand, California ministers feel that their local denominational officials approve of most forms of clergy activism, reporting that these attitudes generally serve to encourage their own participation in social action activities. They also indicate that their local leaders play a major role in the appointment process within most Protestant denominations and are generally expected to provide at least some assistance to parish clergymen who come into conflict with their parishioners over ethical issues. Thus we find that a liberal leadership exists in the more modernist Protestant denominations and apparently does lend important encouragement to the ethically oriented clergy.

On the other hand, the data presented in this chapter show that this support is not without limits and does not entirely offset the conservatism of Protestant laymen. Not all church leaders, even in the liberal denominations, give unqualified approval to clergy activism. They are divided in their views toward clergy participation in acts of civil protest and at the time of our survey were reported to disapprove of ministers who engaged in antiwar civil disobedience. In addition, although church officials influence employment procedures within most Protestant denominations, they share authority over the ministers' careers with local parishioners. The local congregational members exercise fairly tight control over fiscal policies in the parish church, including the minister's own salary, and they have extensive influence over the church's programs. Their authority in these areas is great even within the more hierarchically organized denominations. In all Protestant denominations, then, local parishioners have authority over significant aspects of the careers of parish clergymen and can make them pay dearly for their involvement in controversial public issues. In Chapter 8 we gave evidence of parishioners' willingness to use such authority to censor ministers who were most outspoken in their ethical behavior.

Our survey thus clearly demonstrates the cross-pressures under which socially active ministers operated in the late 1960s. A fairly large proportion of Protestant ministers in California wanted to provide leadership on public issues and were supported in their efforts by the majority of their colleagues and denominational leaders; at the same time, they met frequent and often hostile opposition from the members of their own congregations. We have given many examples of the direct and indirect effects of such conflicting role pressures on the responses of parish ministers to public issues. Clergymen who interact primarily with liberal role partners are more liberal and outspoken in their political conduct than we might otherwise expect them to be; clergymen who interact primarily with conservative role partners are more conservative and inactive. Many Protestant ministers consciously stay out of controversial public issues to avoid conflict the members of their congregations.

The information presented in this chapter is important in showing the pervasive authority of laymen within Protestant churches and the consequences of this authority for the socially active clergy. Despite a very liberal hierarchy in most Protestant denominations, most parish ministers believe that their careers would suffer if they became overly involved in controversial public issues. Table 10.8 summarizes the situation as the socially active clergy perceived it at the time of our survey. More than two-thirds of the new breed activists in our study—clergymen who had participated in acts of civil protest—felt that controversial ministers had more difficulty receiving choice parish positions within their own denominations. The hard-core activists who had engaged in acts of civil disobedience, furthermore, were the most pessimistic about the chances of socially active ministers obtaining choice appointments. Forty percent of this group agreed with the following strongly worded statement: "The way to obtain a choice ministerial position in may denomination is to remain noncontroversial on social and political issues."

Thus liberal church leaders provide support and encouragement for the new breed clergy, but they are apparently unable to counteract completely the conservatism of Protestant laymen and the hostile reactions of local parishioners to liberal clergy activism. This is not only because the leaders do not possess sufficient authority over church affairs; in the late 1960s they themselves were not entirely sympathetic to some of the actions of the new breed activists. As a result, parish ministers who were most committed to an action-oriented church often spoke out on public issues at great risk to their personal careers. They lost members, contributions, and often their jobs be-

Table 10.8. Socially Active Ministers Most Often Say that Controversial Clergymen Will Not Receive Choice Ministerial Positions

Situation in Respondent's Own Denomination	Activism[a]						Total
	1	2	3	4	5	6	
"The way to obtain a choice ministerial position in my denomination is to remain noncontroversial on social and political issues."	40%	19%	19%	20%	18%	30%	21%
"Controversial ministers in my denomination are often able to obtain suitable positions even though many do suffer because of their activism."	28	52	42	31	31	14	37
"A minister's social activism has little relation to the type of ministerial position he receives in my denomination."	21	19	30	38	41	56	32
"Ministers who are socially active in my denomination are more likely to receive choice ministerial positions than those wo do not speak out on social issues."	11	10	9	11	10	—	10
	100%	100%	100%	100%	100%	100%	100%
	(81)	(312)	(423)	(288)	(335)	(70)	(1509)

[a] On this 6-point scale, 1 is highly active; 6 is inactive.

cause of their ethical activities, and at the time of our survey they apparently had difficulty obtaining the most desirable parish appointments.

The rise in social activism among Protestant ministers in the 1960s was costly for the new breed clergy and for liberal denominations. We suspect that similar conflicts occurred in other professions during this period and that other practitioners suffered similar fates for their outspoken public conduct. The unique organization of the ministerial profession, however, gives extraordinary influence and authority to the parish clergy's conservative clients rather than to their more liberal colleagues or to their organizational superiors. Therefore, the problems the ministers encountered in speaking out on public issues differed substantially from those of most other professionals, and the risk to their personal careers would seem to be much greater. Viewed purely in sociological terms, one might marvel over the large number of clergymen who risked the wrath of their parishioners and involved themselves in controversial public issues during the period of our study. It is doubtful that we would find in other professions such a large proportion of individuals who deliberately placed their careers in jeopardy to provide leadership on such issues as racism and the Vietnam war.

The church, of course, purports to be different from other institutions in American society. It claims to be a voice of prophecy as well as one of comfort. Organized religion has often been criticized for its support of the status quo and for its failure to provide leadership on important social and political issues. In the middle and late 1960s, we find that a significant number of Protestant clergymen had in fact renewed the prophetic tradition within Christianity.

NOTES AND REFERENCES

1.   Charles Y. Glock, Benjamin B. Ringer, and Earl R. Babbie, *To Comfort and To Challenge: A Dilemma of the Contemporary Church* (Berkeley: University of California Press, 1967).

2.   The survey was conducted by Dr. Glen W. Trimble and reported as "A Study Report on the Miami Assembly: Some Characteristics and Opinions of 521 Church Leaders," *Information Service*, 17, No. 9 (May 6, 1967). These data were interpreted in the form reported here by Jeffrey K. Hadden, *The Gathering Storm in the Churches* (Garden City, N.Y.: Doubleday, 1969), pp. 224–233.

3.   The denominations we have surveyed are not all organized in the same manner, and the titles and duties of such local church officials vary from denomination to denomination. We tried to gain as much comparability as possible in our questions by asking the California ministers to discuss the local denominational officials in their "immediate jurisdiction." Some ambiguity undoubtedly remains, however, and may account for some of the differences we find in the ministers' responses here and elsewhere.

4.   Charles Y. Glock and Rodney Stark, *Religion and Society in Tension* (Skokie, Ill.: Rand McNally, 1965), pp. 129–134.

5.   The socially active clergy in California apparently do not feel discriminated against in their salaries. We asked our respondents the following question: "Compared with other parish ministers in your own denomination, how would you describe your salary and benefits?" The choices they were given were: "much above average," "somewhat above average," "about average," "somewhat below average," and "much below average." There was no difference in the way that socially active and inactive clergymen answered this question. Interestingly, there was a strong tendency for the parish ministers in our sample to see their salaries in favorable terms. The percentages giving these responses were 9, 28, 39, 17, and 7 percent, respectively.

6.   To compare the authority of local church leaders with that of local parishioners, we also asked the California ministers how closely their denominational officials supervised

the programs of the local church. Three percent said they did so "closely," 31 percent "moderately," 41 percent "little," and 25 percent "not at all." These responses also were related to policy differences among the nine denominations surveyed.

7.   Some of the comments written by our respondents on their questionnaires illustrate the importance of these polity differences. Methodist ministers were clearly the most complimentary in their remarks toward their denominational leaders. One Methodist minister, for example, wrote that "it has meant a lot to have the support of a strong bishop who gives clear leadership in areas of social concern." Another noted that, "Our Methodist leadership has been very forward-looking and helpful. It has made me feel backed up in whatever I have felt was my job to do." These comments may be contrasted with those of an American Baptist clergyman: "Denominational leaders are secure and can say anything, even foolish things, but the minister who follows their pronouncements may find himself with violent opposition and will have to paddle his own canoe and may sink, because his leaders do not protect him in any way. Since the church is autonomous, we Baptists have absolutely no security."

8.   Practices vary in this respect, but the policy in at least some decentralized denominations is to give the parish clergymen 60-day notice of dismissal. Baptist ministers probably have less security in this respect than United Church of Christ clergymen.

THE PROTESTANT RESPONSE
TO THE POLITICS OF THE 1960s

11.

Protestant churches have pursued many different courses of action in responding to public events. Our study captures this process at a particular point in time—the middle and late 1960s, when political passions ran high in this country and many individuals attempted to redirect the nation's foreign and domestic policies. It shows that Protestant churches were polarized by the events of the period, and that many religious leaders were actively involved in the issues of the day.

In putting together our findings, it is useful to return to some of the considerations raised in the introductory chapter about the role of organized religion in public affairs. Protestant religious groups have developed in close harmony and interpenetration with the dominant secular values and interests of American society. Throughout most of the nineteenth century, Protestant church leaders openly identified the nation's destiny with Divine Providence. They saw their new nation as the veritable promised land and its settlers as the new chosen people. Their preachments provided a strong justifying ideology for early Americans, and Protestant churches grew in strength and influence with the expanding nation. Largely ignored in the process were the fates of those not of colonial stock—the country's native inhabitants and its enslaved black population—and the emerging problems caused by industrialization. The ethical concerns of nineteenth-century Protestant leaders were primarily individualistic and moralistic. They gave their attention to such issues as drinking and prostitution and used their positions to support rather than to criticize the existing social and political order.

Protestant hegemony and alliance with the status quo began to break down by the end of the nineteenth century. The massive influx of immigrants brought new customs, languages, social problems, and a loyalty to the

Catholic Church. Internally, Protestant church leaders were divided by the challenge to religious orthodoxy due to scientific theories of evolution and historical criticisms of the Bible. Largely because of these events, Protestantism split into opposing modernist and traditionalist camps—a schism that exists in its essential features today. For the most part, both groups have stayed out of controversial political issues in the past, but a small number of modernist church leaders aligned themselves with liberal political programs during the Populist and Progressive eras and later during the New Deal period.

We have pointed out that this very close relationship between Protestantism and American society has carried with it both strengths and weaknesses for the church's ethical role in public affairs. On the one hand, such a close relationship has kept the church in constant touch with societal values and problems and has contributed much to its organizational strength and influence. Churchmen have not tried to escape from the trials of the temporal world, nor have they so isolated themselves from social issues or intellectual currents that they have become irrelevant to secular concerns.[1] This interpenetration of values and institutions has also contributed to the social legitimacy of organized religion and to its membership growth, wealth, and unique status in American society.

On the other hand, the same features have served to deter the church from playing a critical role in public affairs. Protestants have joined in the general celebration of the American way of life—indeed, they have often led it— and by and large have shown little awareness of or sympathy toward social injustices or inequities. The Protestant worldview has primarily been that of its white, middle-class membership; the overwhelming majority of Protestant churchmen have continued to align themselves with the dominant social, economic, and racial interests of American society. The few modernist church leaders who have resisted such support of the status quo have generally been excluded from the mainstream or ignored by other churchmen. They have seldom been able to make a living as parish pastors.

Thus the dilemma for the ethically committed clergy in the 1960s was posed by the need to overcome the complacency and conservatism that commonly grips Protestant churches and to utilize the church's potential to provide critical leadership on public issues: how could they engage Protestant churchmen in social issues and induce them to see in their religious beliefs a moral commitment to build a better society?

What light does our study shed on this dilemma? How did Protestant clergymen respond to the public issues that were so explosive during the period of our study? Certainly we must acknowledge that the church of the middle and late 1960s was not the conservative, status-quo-oriented organization that existed historically and was criticized so sharply a few years earlier by Berger, Berton, Cox, and others. A substantial number of Protestant ministers at the parish level were speaking out on controversial public issues—often against the wishes of their congregations and to the detriment of their personal careers. A large majority of the parish clergymen in California campaigned actively against a discriminatory initiative proposal in 1964, about a third were active in the antiwar movement at the time of our survey, and from 10 to 15 percent openly supported the efforts of Cesar Chavez to organize migratory farm workers in the San Joaquin Valley.

Thus many Protestant clergymen at the parish level were actively involved in issues of civil rights, poverty, and peace at the time of our survey—although such ethicalism clearly did not encompass all the ministers in California. Thus we can choose to stress the strong commitment to an action-oriented church reflected by these data, or we can remain disappointed by the large numbers of Protestant clergymen who had little to say on such compelling issues as civil rights or the war in Vietnam. Let us reemphasize, however, that these rates of social activism are most impressive when compared with those of other groups in American society. Furthermore, although no comparable surveys were taken during earlier periods of clergy activism, it appears likely that more parish ministers spoke out critically on these important public issues in the middle and late 1960s than during any earlier period of church activism.

The Religious Belief System and Clergy Activism. However we choose to assess the significance of these rates of new breed activism, it is evident from our study that they are strongly influenced by the ministers' theological orientations. Clergymen who adhere to traditional Protestant orthodoxies and an otherworldly conception of Christianity are generally politically conservative and socially inactive; those who possess what we have termed "modernist" religious views are the most liberal in their political positions and the most outspoken in their activist behavior.

Table 11.1 provides a general summary of the linkages revealed in our study between the ministers' religious orientations and their social activism. In each of the policy areas examined in our survey, the more modernist-oriented respondents most often spoke out critically or attempted to involve their parishioners in the issue. Modernist ministers most actively opposed the anti-fair housing referendum in California in 1964, went the furthest in supporting the organizing efforts of Cesar Chavez, and most actively pressed for military withdrawal from Vietnam. They were also the most likely to engage in the more publicized forms of dissent often associated with new breed activism—protest marches and acts of civil disobedience. Table 11.1

indicates that except for the anti-fair housing referendum campaign, it was almost entirely the modernist clergy in California who were critically involved in public affairs in the late 1960s.

Such a strong association between the ministers' theological perspectives and their social activism is certainly not unexpected. Modernist church leaders in the past have attempted to provide leadership on important public issues, while traditionalist churchmen have generally aligned themselves with more conservative political policies. The strength of these behavioral patterns and associations in belief, however, should make clear that the primary obstacle to the development of a more action-oriented church is not the conservatism of Protestant laymen but the persistence of religious traditionalism among so many members of the clergy. As we have seen, supernaturalist, otherworldly, and moralist beliefs are common even within these nine established, mainline denominations. They are more pronounced yet in the rapidly growing Protestant sects, in the South, and probably in areas of the country more conservative than California. Thus traditionalist religious views remain dominant among a large majority of Protestant ministers in the United States. Traditionalism is strongly associated with political conservatism and a highly individualistic and moralistic ethical orientation. It is therefore unlikely that many such ministers will be won over to the new ethicalism. To embrace a liberal, action-oriented church would be to upset a worldview that is highly integrated, philosophically, cognitively, and psychologically. It would mean subscribing to a system of beliefs that runs contrary to one's orientation toward life.

This is not to say, we hasten to add, that all orthodox ministers stand inexorably opposed to clergy activism or are totally acquiescent when it comes to politics. Certainly there is some support for clergy activism within conservative denominations, and for at least one issue- the anti-fair housing referendum in California—a significant minority of traditionalist clergymen became actively involved. Perhaps, then, under certain conditions, more traditionalist ministers will speak out on controversial public issues.

By and large, however, our survey shows that clergy activism is associated with a modernist orientation toward Protestant theology. We have offered several explanations for this association between Christian beliefs and clerical involvement in social issues. Primary among these is the worldliness of religious modernism: its efforts to accommodate religion with secular knowledge and to look for the "religious" in the experience of men rather than in the relationship between man and the supernatural. Such an orientation would seem to bring modernist ministers into close contact with societal conditions and problems, in effect making them dependent on secular events for an understanding of their own religious roles and functions. The history of religious modernism, in fact, is largely a history of church involvement in

Table 11.1. Modernist Ministers Most Often Spoke Out Critically on Important Political Issues

	Religious Orientation[a]				
	1	2	3	4	5
ACTIVE OPPOSITION TO CALIFORNIA ANTI-FAIR HOUSING REFERENDUM IN 1964[b]					
Issued a public statement	85% (241)	77% (235)	69% (227)	46% (230)	19% (247)
Discussed in a sermon	83% (242)	71% (234)	60% (230)	38% (229)	13% (249)
Considered in a study group	59% (242)	55% (234)	44% (228)	27% (228)	6% (249)
Joined an anti-Proposition 14 campaign committee	54% (239)	48% (235)	33% (227)	18% (229)	4% (249)
Organized a social action unit in the local church	33% (239)	30% (234)	23% (228)	9% (227)	2% (249)
ACTIVE SUPPORT OF EFFORT TO ORGANIZE MIGRATORY FARM WORKERS[c]					
Issued a public statement	41% (267)	24% (269)	17% (260)	9% (265)	4% (283)
Discussed in a sermon	38% (268)	21% (269)	15% (262)	6% (265)	2% (283)
Considered in a study group	17% (268)	13% (268)	9% (260)	2% (265)	1% (283)
Marched or traveled to the Delano area	12% (266)	8% (267)	3% (262)	2% (265)	1% (283)

Table 11.1. *Continued*

	Religious Orientation[a]				
	1	2	3	4	5
ACTIVE OPPOSITION TO THE WAR IN VIETNAM[d]					
Discussed in a sermon	54% (309)	36% (320)	27% (314)	11% (305)	5% (321)
Issued a public statement	47% (307)	31% (320)	23% (313)	7% (304)	4% (321)
Considered in a study group	35% (306)	21% (320)	12% (313)	3% (304)	1% (321)
Joined a peace organization	31% (306)	21% (319)	6% (311)	2% (304)	1% (323)
INVOLVEMENT IN ACTS OF CIVIL PROTEST					
Participation in a civil rights protest march	53% (308)	34% (321)	22% (317)	11% (308)	3% (320)
Participation in an antiwar protest march	22% (307)	11% (320)	4% (317)	1% (308)	— (321)
Engaged in an act of civil rights civil disobedience	11% (307)	8% (320)	3% (317)	2% (307)	— (320)
Engaged in an act of antiwar civil disobedience	5% (304)	4% (320)	—[e] (316)	1% (308)	— (321)

[a] On this 5-point scale, 1 is most modernist; 5 is most traditionalist.

[b] Includes only respondents who held parish positions in California at the time of the anti-fair housing referendum; percentages include only those who opposed the anti-fair housing referendum.

[c] Includes only respondents who held positions in California at the time of the strike in the Delano area; percentages include only those who supported the organizing effort.

[d] Percentages include only ministers who advocated partial or total U.S. withdrawal from Vietnam.

[e] Less than 1 percent.

the most outstanding secular problems in American society—science and evolution, political reformism, disillusionment and realism, conformity and alienation, and, most recently, social protest and change.[2]

The social activism of the 1960s can be viewed as an inevitable product of a theological perspective that looks for religion in the human condition itself rather than in a transcendent, otherworldly realm. As long as public problems remain as urgent and salient as they were in the 1960s, we can expect to find many modernist clergymen speaking out on public issues. Certainly at the time of our survey there was evidence of a large reservoir of support for an action-oriented church among the modernist clergy. As we noted in Chapter 8, almost half our respondents indicated a desire to increase their involvement in social action activities. We see in Table 11.2 that such sentiments were most often expressed by the more modernist-oriented ministers.

Thus in the late 1960s there appeared to be a potential for still greater public involvement on the part of parish ministers. Whether such an increase in activist commitment materializes, we suspect, will depend largely on the nature of future political conflicts and public issues. Civil rights and the war in Vietnam were public problems presenting a particularly strong moral imperative to the modernist clergy. For church leaders to have remained silent on such compelling issues as racism and the war most certainly would have undermined the churches' claim for moral relevance and leadership. It would have exposed them to the strong charges of hypocrisy and collusion with the status quo that were made by critics in the early 1960s. Yet the

Table 11.2. Modernist Ministers Most Often Wanted to Become More Involved in Social Action Activities

"If it were possible, would you like to be more or less involved in social action activities than you presently are?"	Religious Orientation[a]					
	1	2	3	4	5	Total
More	65%	61%	48%	35%	22%	46%
Continue present degree of involvement	34	37	50	62	74	51
Less	2	2	2	3	4	3
	101%	100%	100%	100%	100%	100%
	(304)	(319)	(314)	(308)	(315)	(1560)

[a] On this 5-point scale, 1 is most modernist; 5 is most traditionalist.

forms of political controversy will surely change, as they already have since the peak of the protest movements in the late 1960s. Public concern over racism and militarism has cooled considerably since the time of our study, and the liberal churches, like many other institutions, have tended to focus more on their own organizational problems. Whether modernist church leaders continue to speak out on public issues once they become somewhat removed from the public eye will provide an indication of the depth of their commitment to a critical, action-oriented church.

As we have noted at many points in our analysis, there are other ways to view this association between religious modernism and clergy activism. The demythologization of Christian theology not only orients churchmen toward secular issues, it also brings into question the very meaning and purpose of religion in contemporary society. It contradicts the historical Christian concern with salvation—a religious goal that has given Protestantism much of its missionary zeal and fervor. It accelerates the process of secularization by recognizing that science, not religion, is the source of objective knowledge about the observable world. Finally, it exposes the church as an "antiquated" institution and the clergy as practitioners of an obsolete craft.

The widespread involvement of modernist church leaders in the political upheavals of the 1960s can also be interpreted as an effort to develop new religious roles and to regain some of their lost prestige and authority in American society. A personal commitment to the "morally right" issues represented by the civil rights and antiwar movements can be seen as providing a greater degree of focus and certainty to the relativistic worldview of modernist theology. An active involvement in such political causes may be said to offer modernist clergymen new clerical roles and new means to receive satisfaction from their chosen profession. The assumption of prominent positions of leadership in the political movements of the period, finally, appears as a means for modernist church leaders to renew their influence and prestige in a highly secular society in which liberal religion itself has come under attack for moral irrelevance.

Certainly there is some truth to such propositions. The activist role was fervently embraced by some, and a tone of self-congratulation was not uncommon in liberal pronouncements or in activist literature. Liberal churchmen, moreover, assumed major leadership roles in the political movements of the period and succeeded in reestablishing the churches' image as a force for social change. This image was probably viewed negatively by most Americans, but it did serve to reunite modernist church leaders with the liberal intellectual community. Church involvement in controversial public issues may have been unpopular with most of the Protestant laity, but it was almost mandatory if Protestant religion was to stay in communication with its own liberal intellectual tradition and with liberals outside the church.

Thus the roots of the modernist response to the public issues of the 1960s, like the roots of other activist groups of the period, were undoubtedly many. We can only speculate about the relative importance of the various factors that linked religious modernism with social activism. In explaining this linkage in sociological terms, however, we should not lose sight of the nature of the political problems besetting the country during the 1960s. The political controversies of the period were undeniably real—and they brought forth an active public commitment by many Americans. Protestant ministers, like others, felt a moral obligation to deal with these societal problems, and in so doing behaved as attentive citizens as well as religious actors.

The Conflict in Protestant Churches over Clergy Activism. A large part of our study has been concerned with the conflicts caused by clerical commitment to ethical leadership within Protestant churches during the 1960s. In particular, we have paid a great deal of attention to the attitudes of California laymen toward ethical issues and to their responses to clergy activism. We have seen that the lay members of Protestant churches in California are no less antagonistic to church activism than they have been said to be. Most have conservative views on political questions and strongly disapprove of clergymen who speak out on controversial public issues. More importantly, laymen possess substantial authority within all Protestant denominations—even the most hierarchical ones—and they do not hesitate to use the sanctions at their disposal to punish parish ministers who disregard their directives on ethical matters. Almost all the highly active ministers in our survey reported that at least some of their parishioners had expressed opposition to their ethical activities, and many had the issues taken up before their church boards. Even more threatening to the careers of the new breed clergy was the frequency with which Protestant laymen tried to have ministers dismissed because of social activism. One out of every ten parish clergymen in our sample (about one out of six in the liberal denominations) reported that efforts had been undertaken in their churches to have them fired as a direct result of their involvement in public issues.

Many Protestant laymen are also resigning their memberships or reducing their financial contributions to their parishes in protest against their ministers' ethical conduct. Most of the clergymen we include among the new breed suffered membership and financial losses during at least one of the three public controversies examined here, and liberal Protestant denominations have been especially hard-hit in both respects. In many ways, such a withdrawal of patronage is the most effective and unanswerable sanction available to church members who oppose new breed activism. Churches are voluntary associations; in a sense, they compete with one another and with secular organizations for the loyalty and support of large numbers of the public. Any action that detracts from their ability to recruit and hold members is an obvious cause for concern among religious leaders. Protestant churches could be forced to go out of existence—or at least to reduce radically their activities and services—if laymen continue to resign in large numbers.

Protestant clergymen are highly dependent on a generally conservative and antiactivist laity. They rely on their parishioners not only to pay the churches' bills, but also for the very rationale of their existence. In California, Protestant laymen vigorously fought clergymen who wanted to develop an action-oriented ministry; we can reasonably expect that similar lay reactions took place elsewhere.

We have shown at various points in our analysis that the opposition of Protestant laymen to church activism has a definite inhibiting effect on the development of clergy activism. Both directly and indirectly, the actions of local congregational members influence parish clergymen to take more cautious, conservative positions on public issues. At the same time, parish activists are not without allies in the church. Ethically oriented ministers reported receiving support from at least some of their parishioners, from most of their close colleagues, and from the majority of their local denominational leaders. The last group in particular can be an important counterbalance to lay conservatism and censorship, since local denominational officials play a major role in church governance—particularly with respect to hiring practices—often assisting clergymen who get in trouble with their parishioners over ethical issues.

Many ethically oriented clergymen during the sixties, then, experienced conflicting role pressures and discovered sources of both support and discouragement. In liberal denominations, such ministers generally were supported by their colleagues and denominational leaders, being opposed by their local parishioners. On balance, however, the new breed activists usually paid a price for their activism. Most lost members and contributions because of their social actions, some lost their jobs, and a large majority felt that their activism hurt their chances of career advancement.

Such role conflict often led parish clergymen to restrict their activist conduct or to stay out of controversial public issues altogether. They also have the option of withdrawing from the conflictual situation in which they find themselves. They may attempt to move to another position within the church, or they may become disillusioned with their roles as clergymen and resign from the ministry. Many ministers were leaving the church at the time of our survey, and it was widely believed that the new breed were most often taking this step.

With this possibility in mind, we asked the California clergymen two questions about their careers: whether they would like to move to another

Table 11.3.   Modernist Ministers Most Often Wanted to Move to Another Position

	Religious Orientation[a]					
Would Like to Move	1 (297)	2 (312)	3 (309)	4 (293)	5 (308)	Total (1519)
To another position	45%	36%	30%	28%	24%	33%
To another congregation	22	20	19	15	14	18
To a teaching position	8	6	6	5	4	6
To a denominational position	4	2	2	1	3	2
To something else	13	10	7	7	4	8

[a] On this 5-point scale, 1 is most modernist; 5 is most traditionalist.

position, and whether—if they had it to do again—they would once more go into the ministry. Their responses are not quite what we had expected, but they are most revealing. We see in Table 11.3 that a fairly sizable proportion of the parish ministers in California—33 percent—are unhappy with their parish situations and would like to move to another position. Most of these respondents indicated that they would like to move to another congregation; but 6 percent said that they would like to begin teaching, and 8 percent wanted to go into "something else." What is more, Table 11.3 indicates that it is primarily the more modernist clergymen who feel this way. Forty-five percent of the most modernist group of respondents indicated that they would like to move to another position, as compared with 24 percent of the most traditionalist group. The modernist clergy were also the most likely to say that they would like to move to another congregation, to a teaching position, or to "something else."

Given our previous findings, the explanation for such attitudes on the part of modernist clergymen is not difficult to discern. It is they who most often experience serious differences of opinion with the members of their congregations over a wide variety of church matters—from their participation in public affairs to the organization of the local church. Not surprisingly, the same beleaguered clergymen most often want to move to another position. Among the ministers who reported experiencing "a great deal" of differences of opinion with their parishioners over their social activism, for example, 57 percent indicated that they would like to change positions. Among those who reportedly experienced "some" such conflict the figure was 39 percent, whereas among those who had experienced "none" it was 26 percent. Similar differences exist among ministers who encountered conflicts in other areas of their ministerial duties.

Such responses again demonstrate the deep-seated problems that religious modernism has created for the ministerial profession. It not only leads to divergent religious and ethical orientations between the modernist clergy and the bulk of the Protestant laity, it is also responsible for conditions of conflict and personal discomfort for large numbers of modernist ministers serving in parish positions. At the same time, we should also take note of the general level of dissatisfaction running throughout the Protestant ministry. Even among the traditionalist clergy—as well as among ministers who report no serious differences of opinion with their congregational members—a quarter or more of our respondents wish to change their positions.

How upset were the California ministers with the state of affairs within the ministerial profession? We know that many Protestant clergymen were leaving the ministry in the late 1960s as a result of problems such as those examined in this study. Since we have included in our survey only respondents who were serving in parish positions, we cannot tell from our data how many California ministers had in fact resigned from the church. To determine how satisfied they were with their careers, however, we asked the California clergy how certain they were that they would enter the ministry if they could make that choice again. Once more, a fair proportion of parish ministers are seen to be unhappy with their chosen profession, and the modernist clergy are most disillusioned with the ministry. According to Table 11.4, 6 percent of the California ministers feel that they "probably" or "definitely" would not enter the ministry if given another chance, and 11 percent were not sure what they would do. These figures, like those quoted earlier, seem

Table 11.4. Modernist Ministers Most Often Said that Given Another Chance, They Would Not Go into the Ministry Again

"Looking back on things—if you had it to do over—how certain are you that you would enter the ministry?"	Religious Orientation[a]					
	1	2	3	4	5	Total
Definitely would	28%	43%	61%	71%	80%	57%
Probably would	38	36	27	22	13	27
Not sure	19	16	9	5	4	11
Probably would not	14	3	2	2	3	5
Definitely would not	1	2	1	1	—	1
Total	100%	100%	100%	100%	100%	101%
	(309)	(319)	(313)	(304)	(321)	(1566)

[a] On this 5-point scale, 1 is most modernist; 5 is most traditionalist.

to be quite high for a profession requiring such a long training period and demanding strong identification with one's career goals. Certainly they are indicative of an unhappy state of affairs within the ministry. Also as before, we find that disenchantment with the ministerial profession is the greatest among the modernist clergy: 15 percent of the most modernist group said that they would probably or definitely not enter the ministry again, and 19 percent were not sure what they would do, if given another chance. Such doubts were far less commonly reported among the more traditionalist-oriented respondents.

We should be cautious in interpreting the responses to this question, since theological orientations had at least some effect on the manner in which the ministers replied. A number of the more traditionalist respondents indicated that they were "called" to the ministry by God, echoing the words of a Southern Baptist clergymen who said that he would "leave the church when I feel the Lord leading me." Thus the greater tendency of the traditionalist clergy to say that they would "definitely" enter the ministry again reflects, at least in part, this supernatural aspect of their theological convictions. Nevertheless, the differences between the modernist and traditionalist clergy are large and cannot be dismissed in these terms alone. We suggest that they are a product both of the problems encountered by modernist clergymen with their parishioners and of the ambiguity and uncertainty marking modernist theology. Again, we find a strong relationship between the level of lay conflict reported by our respondents and their disillusionment with the ministry. Even when we control for this factor, however, we find less certainty in the modernists' evaluations of their profession. The level of religious "satisfactions" enjoyed by these ministers, we suggest, is simply not as high as that experienced by the more orthodox clergy.

What about the new breed clergy? Are they disenchanted with the ministerial profession, and might we then expect the attrition rate to be especially high among the most outspoken of the parish clergy? Interestingly, the greatest level of dissatisfaction within the ministry seems to exist not among the most socially active ministers but among the modernist, ethically oriented ministers who had chosen not to become overly involved in controversial public issues (see Table 11.5). In the table, the respondents are divided according to whether they had ever engaged in an act of civil protest—an action that created great controversy at the time of our survey and is used here to classify the new breed activists. Modernist-oriented ministers who had not joined their colleagues in such actions, it appears, were the most unhappy with their parish situations and with their choice of careers. Half these ministers reported that they wanted to move to another position, and a surprisingly high 22 percent said that they probably or definitely would

Table 11.5.   Modernist but Socially Inactive ClergymenWere the Most Unhappy with the Ministry

| | Religious Orientation[a] | | | | | |
	1	2	3	4	5	Total
	WANT TO MOVE TO ANOTHER POSITION					
Engaged in civil protest[b]	40%	30%	30%	39%	38%	35%
(defined as among the new breed)	(162)	(114)	(70)	(36)	(8)	(400)
Did not engage in civil protest	50%	40%	31%	27%	24%	32%
	(135)	(198)	(239)	(257)	(300)	(1109)
	DEFINITELY OR PROBABLY WOULD NOT ENTER THE MINISTRY AGAIN					
Engaged in civil protest[b]	8%	5%	3%	3%	—	6%
	(168)	(116)	(69)	(35)	(7)	(395)
Did not engage in civil protest	22%	5%	3%	2%	3%	5%
	(141)	(203)	(244)	(269)	(314)	(1171)

[a] On this 5-point scale, 1 is most modernist; 5 is most traditionalist.
[b] Includes respondents who had engaged in a civil rights or antiwar protest march or act of civil disobedience.

not enter the ministry again if they had it to do over. The comparable figures for equally modernist but more socially active ministers were 40 and 8 percent, respectively.

Thus at the time of our survey it was not the new breed clergy who seemed to be most disappointed with their careers, but the ethically oriented clergymen who had chosen not to become involved in controversial acts of social activism. This most interesting finding can be interpreted in several ways. We might focus on the modernist "inactivists" and suggest that these clergymen have compromised their own ethical commitments because of lay pressures and are thus more unhappy with their situation than clergymen who followed their personal convictions. Alternatively, we might focus on the activists, concluding that these modernist ministers found in social activism a meaningful outlet for their worldly based theological convictions. In the latter case, we might say that an active involvement in social affairs indeed serves as a meaningful substitute for the loss in religious function due to modernist theology. A degree of truth most certainly exists in both interpretations, although other factors undoubtedly contribute to the unhappiness of modernist clergymen as well.

The Politicization of the Protestant Ministry.   It is fitting to conclude our study with some general observations about politics in the middle
and late 1960s and its impact on such professions as the Protestant ministry.
We hardly need add to what has already been said about the political developments that marked this period—surely one of the most politically in-
fused and divisive times in our history. Large numbers of Americans involved themselves in the political events of the sixties, often in militant and
unlawful ways.

Such periods of intense political concern and activism have, of course,
occurred before. They have contributed to major realignments among the
voting public and, to a lesser extent, to new public policies and programs.
It is through such periodic upheavals and realignments that many new ideas
have been introduced into the American political system. The late 1960s and
early 1970s exhibit many of the same characteristics of such periods of political change as the populist and progressive era and the New Deal. Politics
is now highly salient, strong challenges have been made to old public policies
and programs, and new forces are emerging among the nation's voters and
political leaders. Whether these developments will lead to some of the same
consequences is yet uncertain.

Along with such societal alterations, periods of intense political turmoil
also have an impact on the thinking of individuals and on the structure of
society. Many persons acquire a different understanding of the world around
them (their political consciousness is raised), and the groups to which they
belong become colored by external political events (they become politicized).
Clearly we have depicted in this study some of the individual and institutional consequences of this period of intense political concern and involvement. Protestant clergymen were well aware of the issues troubling American
society in the 1960s and were generally responsive to them. They involved
themselves in these issues to an extent that is uncommon, if not unprecedented, in American history. The church itself, furthermore, was rent with
the divisions and antagonisms caused by this rise in ethical and political
consciousness. The clerical response to the events of the period deepened
theological divisions that have existed among church leaders for the past
half-century or more, causing new conflicts between the modernist clergy
and their parishioners. Next to the university, it would appear that no other
institution in American society was so greatly affected by the political climate
of this period.

A great deal of attention has been given in this study and in other accounts
to the conflicts that social activism created between the ethically committed
clergy and the Protestant laity. It is sometimes argued that ethics may become the "death" of Christianity: that the ethical concerns of the modernist
clergy will drive conservative churchmen away from liberal denominations

and that the demythologizing of traditional religious formulations will weaken the laity's institutional ties to the church.[3] We have demonstrated here that there is a great deal of evidence to support these contentions. Most parish ministers report their congregational members to be opposed to clergy activism, and many parishioners have in fact left the church or withdrawn contributions as a result of ministerial activism. We cite once more the array of evidence mustered by Dean Kelley to show that liberal denominations are in poor organizational health.[4]

Such statistics have been used to justify a reduction in church involvement in public affairs. Our study leaves little doubt that the social activism of the 1960s contributed to the organizational difficulties of liberal churches. As we have suggested, however, the problems facing modernist religion are much more deep-seated and severe than those arising out of the activist controversy alone. In a general sense, Kelley is probably correct in suggesting that the failure of liberal churches to pursue strict, meaningful, and inspiring goals is responsible for their declining membership and influence. Modernist theology certainly lacks the rigid doctrinal structure and focused orientation of traditional Protestantism. It demands no strict standards of individual conduct and offers no prescribed solutions to life's problems. The modernist acceptance of the scientific approach to human problems seems to offer liberal churchmen no choice in this matter. The church may assist the individual to gain a "religious" understanding of the human predicament, but it has no "final" solutions; the individual himself remains responsible for working out his own answers to life's ultimate questions.[5]

In addition, religious certainty is often accompanied by disagreeable social consequences. As Kelley himself admits (but generally ignores), religious zeal is associated not only with a high religious commitment but also with close-mindedness, bigotry, xenophobia, and religious persecution. Thus a highly committed lay membership and a growing religious organization should not necessarily be taken as ends in themselves. Liberal clergymen may have lost members and contributions because of their active opposition to the Vietnam war. But in assessing the country's eventual extrication from this unhappy episode, it should be borne in mind that this was one of the few wars in American history that was not fought in God's name.

It would seem apparent, then, that the modernist demythologization of religion is an established fact; that American society is likely to become even more secularized in the future; and that the disunity in liberal churches over clergy activism is only one manifestation of the modernist trend in religion. Liberal churches face a difficult and uncertain future in their efforts to define new religious roles and functions. A concern with social ethics, however, is only one part of this process. Despite the ballyhoo surrounding the social activism of the 1960s, we should not forget that liberal churches survived the period without suffering extremely serious repercussions. Although the activism of the sixties resulted in the loss of some members and financial contributions, it might be argued that in the long run this development will strengthen liberal religion. Certainly it led to a recognition of the clergy as important leaders in public affairs and served to reestablish organized religion as a moral force in American society.

We suggest that social ethics may have much to do with the future growth or decline of modernist religion, but it is only one factor among many that will influence the viability of liberal churches in the "post-Reformation" era. If an ethically engaged church is not the panacea for liberal religion offered by some, neither does it seem to be the burden described by others.

What of the future of clergy activism? What kinds of relationship might we expect to develop between Protestant laymen and religious leaders over the churches' role in public affairs? If our analysis is correct, we would expect the answers to these questions to depend primarily on the intensity and direction of future political controversies in this country. Commitment to liberal politics and to ethical leadership appears to be an integral part of the belief systems of most modernist ministers, and we would expect to find them at the forefront of any future movements toward social reform. As our study shows, support for a critical, action-oriented church is widespread at the parish level, as well as among the denominational leadership of liberal churches.

The lay response to future political issues will be more variable and difficult to predict. Mass opinion at present is uncertain and contradictory; it seems to acknowledge the depth of the problems facing American society (thus to favor political reform) and at the same time to yearn for simpler days (thus to be uneasy with social change). How this contradiction is eventually resolved will have much to do with future political alignments in this country, as well as with future conflicts within Protestant churches. The last major realignment of political loyalties in the United States—that which developed between 1928 and the early days of the New Deal—intensified class divisions. It resulted in the wealthier segments of American society giving greater allegiance to the conservatism of the Republican party and the poorer segments embracing the welfare liberalism of the Democrats. If the issues raised in the late 1960s and early 1970s lead to further intensification of class differences, they are likely to cause severe ruptures between the modernist clergy and the Protestant laity. The former have been outspoken in support of liberal programs; the latter remain predominantly white, middle class, and affluent. We have seen, furthermore, that the modernist, new breed clergy serve disproportionately high-status, wealthy congregations.

We do not yet know whether new political alignments will result from the events of the past two decades—or, if they do, exactly what their dynamics will be. It appears, however, that the political issues that divided Americans in the late 1960s and continue to do so at this writing are not strongly related to class interests. They may yet emerge as such; but Vietnam, racism, pollution, governmental irresponsiveness, and a concern with the quality of American life all appear to be issues that cross-cut social classes. On many of these issues, in fact, the affluent, white, suburban population and their children seem to be the most heavily involved in these problems and the most supportive of major societal reforms to correct them. Thus it is not necessarily true that the political orientations of the new breed clergy will come to be diametrically opposed to those of their predominantly middle-class membership. As presidential candidates, both Eugene McCarthy and George McGovern appealed successfully to large sections of the suburban middle class on issues essentially the same as those espoused by the socially active clergy in the 1960s.

In addition, public opinion seems to be more open and receptive to political change and innovation today than in the recent past. Political activism may have been in the decline since the late sixties, and it is apparent that a mood of resignation and uncertainty has affected liberal politics during the past several years. At the same time, however, we find more Americans voicing opinions that were regarded as dangerously radical only a few years ago; in addition, a greater public tolerance exists for those who hold different values or practice different modes of living. Within the churches, by the same token, social activism remains controversial, and most laymen continue to reject the notion that the church should become critically involved in public affairs. At the same time, again, many of the positions espoused by the new breed activists of the sixties are viewed now with less apprehension and are being considered by broader elements within organized religion.

In conclusion, let us offer some evaluative comments on what it means for an institution such as the church to become politicized. In the value framework common to most religious observers—and indeed to many political analysts as well—this is not a respectable word. To be politicized means to inject private values, bias, and personal predilections into a "nonpolitical" situation. No doubt this may be true; there are certainly many areas in our lives that we wish to keep free from politics, and knotty questions are involved in the politicization of any institution. But it seems that the pendulum can swing too far in the other direction as well: that such determined efforts can be made to keep our institutions and thought processes free from "politics" that the important questions are defined away as being irrelevant and worthy of consideration only in a private context. In such a situation, important value issues may never receive adequate hearing. Furthermore, it is virtually impossible for a major value-creating and value-sanctifying institution such as the church to keep strict neutrality during a time of great political upheaval. To remain silent on such issues as Vietnam and racism is, in effect, to take sides. Nondecisions, as political scientists frequently remind us, are often in themselves acts of great political consequence.

Thus we conclude our analysis by suggesting that Protestant churches may be in for a period of continuing politicization, not only on the clerical level but perhaps among many laymen as well. Whether this happens will probably depend in large part on the political issues that emerge in the years ahead and the divisions they create in the greater society. Such a politicization is by no means unprecedented in the annals of organized religion or in the history of other major institutions in American society. It is an event, we would argue, that should be evaluated in terms of its positive as well as its negative effects. It has and will most certainly continue to upset existing conditions within Protestantism, leading to conflict between church conservatives and liberals. It will probably cause further losses in the traditional bases of support and financing of liberal churches. It may even result in a realignment of churchgoers along theological lines not unlike those found among the clergy. At the same time, however, the introduction of ethical questions into church affairs will bring new relevance to organized religion. It will make Protestant churches wrestle with new values, issues, and societal conditions, and keep them in communication with the problems of the poor and the dispossessed. In the long run, some politicization of the ministerial profession would seem to be necessary if Protestants are to stay in touch with their own tradition of Christian love and brotherhood. A church concerned exclusively with middle-class problems and values would cut itself off from fundamental questions of humanity, and deny the universality of its message.

Protestant churches may indeed become so directly embroiled in public issues that their more traditional religious functions are impaired. But the danger is at least as great that they will define their ethical concerns so narrowly as to become irrelevant to social values and to the difficult political decisions that lie in the future.

NOTES AND REFERENCES

1. Langdon Gilkey, "Social and Intellectual Sources of Contemporary Protestant Theology in America," *Daedalus*, **96** (Winter 1967), pp. 81–83.

2. *Ibid.*, pp. 85–92.

3. See, for example, Rodney Stark and Charles Y. Glock, "Will Ethics Be the Death of Christianity?" *Trans-Action*, **5** (June 1968), pp. 7–14.

4. Dean Kelley, *Why Conservative Churches Are Growing* (New York: Harper & Row, 1972).

5. See the discussion of these matters in Robert N. Bellah, "Religious Evolution," *American Sociological Review*, **29** (June 1964), pp. 373–374. This description, of course, is somewhat idealized. Our study shows that relatively few modernist ministers on the parish level have adopted a completely demythologized view of religion.

APPENDIX: METHODOLOGICAL NOTES

$A.$ This first appendix discusses some of the major decisions made during the course of this research and provides statistical information regarding the response rate and representativeness of those answering the mail questionnaire. Typically, such appendices are more concerned with questions of sample design and response reliability than with the more substantial questions that occupy the majority of the researcher's time. Once the decision is made to study a subject such as social activism among the clergy, however, a number of strategic questions are immediately raised. How, for example, should the universe be defined? Should all major religious groups—Protestants, Catholics, and Jews—be included in the sample? If only Protestants are to be studied, should the sample include all Protestant denominations, and how are they to be defined? How many individual respondents should be surveyed within each denomination? How are they to be selected? What research techniques should be used to reach these respondents—personal interviewing or a mail questionnaire? If the latter, how can a sufficient return rate be guaranteed? What types of response bias are likely to occur? How can they be reduced? How can they be measured?

Most research notes leave the impression that the answers to such questions were relatively easy and were known to the researcher all along. This, of course, is seldom the case. At each point in the research process a number of alternatives are available which could change the focus of the study in major respects; few studies end with a theoretical perspective and focus identical to that with which they were conceived. At the same time, the answers to the previous questions are by no means arbitrary; they follow from the theoretical purposes and conceptions that motivate the study. This appendix thus begins with a discussion of the two major theoretical commitments that

312

were brought to the study and influenced subsequent decisions concerning the sample universe, survey design, and methods of data collection.

The Professional Minister. The study was conceived as a means to link an individual's professional occupation with his politics. Ministers were selected because of their prominence as political actors and because their activism had received little attention from social scientists. Many of the theoretical notions and research decisions resulted from this commitment to the study of "the professions" rather than a particular set of professionals. This approach was useful because it served to differentiate the more generic aspects of the clerical profession and provided a comparative framework from which to draw hypotheses. However, it also meant that certain unique aspects of the ministerial position would be neglected. For example, someone with express interests in the clerical profession itself might have paid greater attention to doctrines concerning the separation of church and state, the theological belief system unique to those who deal in the supernatural, the effect of a "religious experience" on a person's mode of thinking, or the implications of certain theological beliefs to particular economic or political values. Instead primary emphasis was placed on the *occupation* itself—the daily tasks on which the clergyman spends his time, the rewards and sanctions he experiences in his work, his private need to provide for his family, and his desire to maintain calm and equanimity with those with whom he must interact.

A religious person might have approached the study in an entirely different manner. Thus a few respondents took offense at the implications underlying several of the questions included in the survey. "I personally don't think in terms of 'choice ministerial positions,' " wrote one minister. "The ministry is more than a vocation," agreed a second. "It should be a calling of God which I believe in for life." Another asserted: "You should have confined this survey to pastors having nothing better to do than reform and dress up society. I'm concerned with changing the whole man, from the heart out." And a fourth replied that the questionnaire did not deal with the "vital issues":

> The questionnaire, like much public opinion, did not deal with the more vital issues of: (1) Who is sovereign, God and His Christ, or men who govern? (2) Toward what kind of world and society do we aspire? What are our true goals and destinies? (3) What are really the basic problems of our world? (4) What is the only *sure workable remedy* of all human problems?

Three of these four respondents happened to be Southern Baptist ministers —which suggests to us certain tendencies in the religious orientations of the members of this church denomination. To consider the ministry as a "calling" and nothing else also ignores the Baptist minister who was leaving his church because he could not support his family, the Lutheran pastor who called for the unionization of his profession in an attempt to modernize it, the Methodist clergyman who moved to Delano and refused to discuss the farm unionization issue with his new parishioners because they "are still leaving the church three years later if a new minister indicates his support," as well as the Presbyterian minister who felt that success in his profession was dependent on ties of consanguinity: "The ministry is only for those whose fathers were in the profession and who inherited the worthwhile parishes and other ecclesiastical positions by virtue of their family connections."

Thus it was decided to treat the ministry as a professional occupation and to study largely the characteristics it shares with other such occupations. Role was chosen as the basic theoretical framework of the analysis because it gave us useful comparisons of individuals involved in similar interaction processes. The decision to treat the ministry as an occupational role system, however, meant that primary emphasis would be placed on individuals who occupied certain defined positions in relation to the minister. Thus the clergy's parishioners, colleagues, and organizational superiors were taken as basic reference groups instead of such potentially important role definers as the prominent theologian, the "great teacher," or the exemplary relative. (Eighteen percent of the respondents, in fact, reported that their fathers had served in the ministry and 22 percent that another close relative had done so.)

The selection of occupational role relations as primary explanatory variables also meant that it would be more fruitful to study one major religious group than all three—a decision dictated by the resources available to the author as well. Since clergymen in the Protestant, Catholic, and Jewish faiths often experience quite different role restraints, it would be impossible to use the same interview schedule for all three major religious groups. The church hierarchy in the Catholic Church, for example, plays a much more prominent role than does that in Protestant denominations—where the major role restraints are provided by the clergy's parishioners. For a similar reason we excluded from the survey the Protestant sects, which generally have little hierarchical organization, are largely composed of lower-class members, and represent a radically different religious tradition. In addition, the ministers of most sect churches are likely to have little formal training—often holding other full-time jobs—and thus fail to qualify as "professional" ministers. Jewish clergymen, finally, were likewise not included because of variations in organizational characteristics and theological tradition.

The mainline Protestant denominations were thus chosen for the study because of their easier access, the size of their constituencies, their participation in social and political activities, and limitations in time and financial resources.

Attitudes and Behavior. A second major decision was to focus on behavior as well as attitudes. Theoretically, it was felt that the ministers' three occupational role groups would have their greatest impact on a clergyman's behavior rather than his attitudes. Past studies had shown little correlation between the attitudes of clergymen and their parishioners,[1] and, paradoxically, liberalism among parish ministers appeared to be inversely related to the class composition of their churches.[2] Substantively, it was felt to be at least as important to study behavior as attitudes. Political events are affected, after all, only insofar as attitudes are translated into overt actions. The involvement of Protestant ministers in the issues of the day is generally of greater interest to the political scientist than their opinions about these issues.

For obvious reasons, most social surveys deal largely with attitudinal questions. Not only are behavioral questions difficult to ask, but the range of behavioral events that can be included in a general survey is also very limited. For a particular form of involvement to be included within a survey, it must be a live issue to all those within the universe of the sample. The problem is that few issues affect more than a small section of the population. Thus national surveys are usually confined to such general behavioral data as voting, giving money to a political party, discussing politics, and sending a letter to the editor of a newspaper.

Once the decision was made to place primary emphasis on the clergy's involvement in actual issues, the survey had to be limited to an area small enough to encompass common political issues and public events. Eventually it was decided to use a state as the sampling universe rather than a smaller area. The larger number of respondents, of course, made the state an attractive sampling unit. In addition, all three issues that had most embroiled the clergy during the past few years were at least statewide in scope: Proposition 14, the organization of migratory farm workers, and the Vietnam War.

Sample Design. The selection of specific denominations and individual ministers to be included within the sample was relatively easy. The largest of the mainline Protestant churches were conveniently distributed almost evenly along the liberal–conservative continuum; in addition, they represented each of the three major types of polity structures. The nine largest denominations were thus selected for the survey: American Baptist, American

Lutheran Church, Episcopal, Lutheran Church in America, Missouri Synod-Lutheran Church, Methodist, Presbyterian, Southern Baptist, and United Church of Christ. Each of these denominations publishes a list of the names and addresses of its own members; these were obtained from each church group and, when possible, brought up to date. All but two denominations had published new membership books just before the survey was taken. The Southern Baptist list was a year old and the Episcopal list about seven months old. As a result, a larger number of the ministers in these two denominations were eventually dropped from the survey because they had moved from their parish, retired, or left the ministry (see Table A-1). Once the membership books were obtained, each parish minister was assigned a number and a two-thirds sample was drawn from a table of random numbers.[3] This percentage of respondents was chosen because it provided enough respondents in the two smallest denominations to be statistically useful and satisfied the budgetary and time restrictions imposed on the study.

Response Rate. A total of 2830 parish ministers were included within the initial sample of clergymen—ranging from a high of 571 Methodists to a low of 144 within the Lutheran Church in America (see Table A-1). The turn-

Table A-1. Sample Size and Distribution of Returns

Denomination	Original Sample Size	Elimina- tions by Return	Elimina- tions by Follow-Up	Final Sample Size	Num- ber Re- turned	Percent- age Re- turned
American Baptist	283	15	2	264	147	56%
American Lutheran Church	180	6	0	174	118	68
Episcopal	378	50	6	316	207	66
Lutheran Church in America	144	3	0	141	87	62
Methodist	571	28	9	525	354	67
Missouri Synod- Lutheran Church	227	2	1	223	134	60
Presbyterian	340	12	1	326	226	69
Southern Baptist	489	150	3	333	170	51
United Church of Christ	218	15	2	199	137	69
Total	2830	281	24	2501	1580	63%

over rate among Protestant ministers is extremely high, however, and most such directories are dated before they can even be printed. During the course of the three regular mailings, therefore, 281 names were eliminated because the individuals had moved, left the ministry, were abroad, had retired, or were deceased. Most of these eliminations were made when the questionnaire itself was returned stamped as "not forwardable"; a few through new directory lists that subsequently became available for some of the denominations; others through personal letters from church secretaries, the ministers, or their wives. From the pattern of eliminations, however, it appeared that still more respondents were likely to have moved or to have left the ministry since the membership lists were prepared. Thus on a subsequent mailing sent to one-half the remaining nonrespondents (see below) the addressee was asked not to forward the letter but to return it to the sender. Twenty-four more eliminations were made in this manner; this number was doubled (since it represented one-half the remaining respondents), and the final sample size was set at 2501.

Table A-1 contains the relevant information concerning the rate of response. As expected, the return rate corresponded somewhat with the degree of liberalism within the nine denominations. Sixty-nine percent returned completed questionnaires in the Presbyterian and United Church of Christ denominations; these were followed in order by members of the American Lutheran Church, Methodists, Episcopalians, members of the Lutheran Church in America, the Missouri Synod-Lutheran Church, American Baptists, and Southern Baptists. Similar denominational differences have been found in other surveys of Protestant denominations.[4] All together, 1580 clergymen filled out usable questionnaires for a final response rate of 63 percent.

The final sample thus slightly underrepresents three of the more conservative denominations (American Baptist, Missouri Synod-Lutheran Church, and Southern Baptist); their members composed 33 percent of the total membership of the nine-denomination sample, but they comprised only 29 percent of the respondents. However, this difference in denominational return rate had little effect on the results of the survey. Weighting denominational responses to produce identical return rates did not change any of the major attitudinal measures in the study by more than 2 percent. Since this margin was negligible, no weighting was carried out to correct for differences in denominational response rate.

Representativeness. Response bias may occur because of differences within the denominations as well as between them. A major hazard in using a mail questionnaire is the possibility that those who take ,the time to aoswer may not be representative of the entire sample. Two kinds of response bias are often encountered. In the first place, such bias may result from the substantive concerns of the survey itself; those who are more concerned about a particular subject may be more likely to respond than those who are not. In this case, clergymen who feel that the church should assume a more active role in social and political affairs may be more likely to respond than those who feel that the church should stay out of these activities. For this reason special efforts were made throughout the data-collecting process to emphasize the importance of obtaining responses from individuals of all political persuasions and to appeal to those who did not see themselves as activist oriented. A second kind of bias often occurs simply because certain types of people are more likely to answer such inquiries—men, the highly educated, individuals of high occupational prestige, the socially gregarious, and the like. Of course the sampling of a single occupational group such as ministers minimizes some of these problems, since those included in the survey will share most of these attributes. Differences may still occur, however, between the old and the young, ministers serving large and small churches, and so on.

To test for the possibility of these two kinds of response bias, the sample of respondents was divided into halves. It was hypothesized that if certain types of people were more likely to respond to the survey, this difference should emerge between those who responded relatively quickly and those who required additional prompting to return their questionnaires. In addition, a one-page questionnaire was prepared and sent to one-half the nonrespondents. It contained a number of key questions to measure their attitudes toward clergy activism, their theological position, and their political views; they were also asked their age, education, present ministerial position, place of upbringing, size of church, and county in which their church was located. Fifty-four percent of the second sample returned either the short questionnaire or the original longer form. This group of ministers was then compared with the previous two. If a systematic response bias were occurring, it should have emerged from a comparison of the attitudes and backgrounds of the three groups of respondents.

Ten questions were asked of the "nonrespondents" concerning their approval of clergy activism, their political liberalism, and their theological position. The most important queries involved various forms of social activism: publicly taking a stand on a political issue, publicly supporting a political candidate, taking a stand from the pulpit on a political issue, participating in a civil rights protest march, and participating in civil rights civil disobedience. On the first three questions there were no statistically significant differences; on the two forms of civil rights protest, however, the "nonrespondent" sample had more conservative views than the respondents to the main survey. A similar pattern emerged on the questions involving the clergy's political views. On two of these questions, a statistically significant trend toward greater conservatism was found; on the remaining two, no such relationship existed. On the clergy's theological positions, finally, no significant differences were found between our various groups of respondents.

Thus the 10 attitudinal questions we used to test the representativeness of our respondents are somewhat inconsistent in the descriptions they provide of our respondents and nonrespondents. Taken together, however, they appear to indicate that some bias exists in our sample; on some attitudinal measures, at least, those who reported late or not at all were more conservative than those who answered the questionnaire quickly.

The background measures are less ambiguous. On the variables of age, education beyond the college or seminary level, place of upbringing, and church size, there is a clear and statistically significant difference among our three groups. Apparently the representativeness of the sample was most affected by these more general response attributes. The respondents were younger, slightly better educated, and less likely to have been raised in the West. Being younger, they were less likely to occupy positions in the larger churches, and they tended somewhat to be from the more rural sections of the state.

Thus there appears to be some bias in the response rate within the nine denominations. There is some—albeit ambiguous—evidence that those who answered the questionnaire were more liberally oriented than those who did not; there are clear differences in the background characteristics of the two groups. Neither difference, however, is large enough to cause great alarm. From a theoretical perspective, the differences are not overly important, since a large portion of the study is concerned with the actions or opinions of certain types of clergymen rather than with describing the attitudes or opinions of those within the original sampling universe. Most of the descriptive statements made during the course of the study, furthermore, concern attitudinal dimensions rather than background characteristics, and the bias on these dimensions did not appear to be substantial. At any rate, it is probably impossible to eliminate all such response bias from a survey of this kind. In deciding whether to use a mail technique to obtain data, one must consider the relative advantages and disadvantages. In this case, it was felt that the advantages clearly outweighed the disadvantages.

Procedures of Data Collection. The primary problem in using a mail questionnaire is to ensure that enough individuals will respond to the survey to make its results significant. Thus extreme caution must be taken in the wording of questions, an attractive format must be provided, and follow-ups must be planned. Protestant ministers, unfortunately, are one of the most surveyed groups in American society. Not only do social scientists and students flood them with questionnaires, they are literally besieged with information polls from their national churches, local officials, community agencies, and magazines. A large number of respondents complained about the number of requests made on their time, as well as the length of the questionnaire they received from us. The final form of the questionnaire was 31 pages in length and contained 100 numbered questions and 333 separate answers. The length of the questionnaire undoubtedly affected the return rate somewhat but probably not as much as one might expect. The thoroughness of the questionnaire itself was apparently an attractive feature to many respondents. Many praised the questionnaire for its "comprehensiveness" and said that they had learned much about their own attitudes while completing the form. Apparently the length of the questionnaire deterred some from completing it, but attracted others by its detailed probing into both the clergy's attitude and the problems they experienced with their parishioners.[5]

In addition, efforts were taken to design a professional-appearing, simple-to-answer format. The cover letter was printed on the front page of the questionnaire itself, and the respondent was able to return the completed form simply by folding the back flap over the front page and sealing the gummed edge. All the questions were closed-ended and precoded—except for the respondents' county of residence and father's occupation. The questionnaire was organized into a series of substantive sections, permitting the respondent to see the interrelationships among his answers. Finally, the ministers were instructed simply to check the box beside the answers chosen and to "please write your comments in the margin when you feel a question is unclear, or doesn't allow you to express exactly how you feel." Thus the ministers were enabled to express additional views about certain subjects and frustrations at having to reduce opinions to simple "agree" or "disagree" response categories; the procedure also provided valuable anecdotal material, which was used throughout the final report.

The initial cover letter was straightforward in its approach and appeals (see Appendix C). The recipient was told that a "crisis" exists among many Protestant churches—as witnessed in the decline in seminary enrollment, the number of men leaving the ministry, and the criticism of the church from both within and without. "One of the basic causes of these problems," according to the cover letter, "has been the controversy over the church's role in politics." Such a controversy was not only important to the church, it was argued, but to political scientists; hence this study. An identification number was stamped on the back page of each questionnaire to avoid sending follow-up letters to those who had already responded. This technique was chosen over the use of a separate postcard because it is simple and affords greater accuracy in eliminating respondents. It is impossible to know the effects of this means of identification on those who never responded to the survey. However, those who did return their questionnaires had few reservations about the identification procedure. Many wrote in their own names, explaining that they wished to be personally identified with their beliefs; only 10 of those who returned the questionnaire clipped the identification number from the corner of the back page.

The questionnaire was mailed to 2830 clergymen on March 13, 1968. The response pattern is depicted in Table A-2; the influence of follow-up appeals, public events, and periods of special religious concentration are all apparent. The sudden drop in returns during the fourth week of sampling, for example, represented not only the ministers' preparations for Easter but was probably also affected by the assassination of Dr. Martin Luther King, Jr. (One respondent apologized for the "slowness" of his response: "I have been going through a personal crisis with my conscience and congregation brought on by King's death. . . . I have taken an outspoken stand and have been so caught up on the issues . . . that I could not find an hour anywhere.") A second copy of the questionnaire was sent out on April 12; it contained an additional cover letter stressing the importance of obtaining responses from all clergymen to make the survey representative. A third follow-up—a single letter—was mailed on May 3. Because of different response rates between the conservative and liberal denominations, it was felt that a special appeal should be made to those who did not consider themselves to be activist oriented. Thus the letter noted that some ministers were not returning their questionnaires because they did not consider themselves to be as socially active as some others or because they did not participate in such activities at all. It was pointed out that to be successful, the survey had to receive "a similar proportion of responses from ministers of all political persuasions as well as from all denominations."

The Questionnaire.   A few final remarks should be made about the questionnaire used in the study. Considerations of time and money made the choice between a mail questionnaire and personal interviewing largely academic. Not only were the resources available to the investigator limited, but the increased costs of personal interviewing were so great that this technique was unfeasible in itself. In addition, it is difficult if not impossible to ask questions of a religious nature in a face-to-face interview. Some ministers are reluctant to discuss theological issues with strangers, while others are likely to expound their views at such great length that it becomes impossible to ask all the scheduled questions during the interview session. It was the author's experience in preliminary interviewing that few ministers could resist the temptation to inquire about the questioner's religious beliefs and affiliation.

Table A-2.   Returns by Week

Week			Number Returned
March	1	(initial questionnaire sent 3/13)	540
	2		222
April	3		90
	4		11
	5	(second questionnaire sent 4/12)	197
	6		125
May	7		46
	8	(follow-up letter sent 5/4)	111
	9		100
	10		53
	11		22
June	12	(one-page questionnaire sent to one-half of	
	13	remaining respondents 6/10)	12
	14		13
	15		14
July	16–19	(follow-up on second questionnaire sent 7/1)	24
	Total		1580

The initial questionnaire was constructed with the assistance of a number of sociologists and ministers and was pretested with a mail sample of 175 clergymen. It was decided to include all potentially relevant questions in the pretest to verify their significance and to eliminate possible ambiguities in wording. Surprisingly, more than 40 percent of this sample returned the questionnaire—which was 37 pages long, although less compactly organized than the final form. From this response rate it appeared that many ministers were highly concerned about the subject matter of the study and that the length of the questionnaire would not be a major cause of a reduced rate of return. Thus not only was the mail questionnaire less costly and more efficient than personal interviewing, but many more questions could be asked with this technique.

NOTES AND REFERENCES

1. Charles Y. Glock, Benjamin B. Ringer, and Earl R. Babbie, *To Comfort and To Challenge: A Dilemma of the Contemporary Church* (Berkeley: University of California Press, 1967), pp. 113–201; and Jeffrey K. Hadden, *The Gathering Storm in the Churches* (Garden City, N.Y.: Doubleday, 1969), pp. 69–159.

2.   Benton Johnson, "Theology and the Position of Pastors on Public Issues," *American Sociological Review*, **32** (June 1967), pp. 433–442; and Hadden, *op. cit.*, pp. 83–88.

3.   Most of the lists were arranged in some type of geographical order. For all but two denominations, as a result, the sample was stratified according to the location of the clergyman's church. For three denominations this involved a simple North–South division; the other four were arranged according to local associations, presbyteries, or dioceses.

4.   Hadden, *op. cit.*, and Rodney Stark and Charles Y. Glock, *American Piety: The Nature of Religious Commitment* (Berkeley: University of California Press, 1968).

5.   See the similar comments to this effect in Charles Y. Glock and Rodney Stark, *Christian Beliefs and Anti-Semitism* (New York, Harper & Row, 1966), Appendix A.

APPENDIX: SCALE CONSTRUCTION

B.

B. A number of methods can be used to construct attitudinal measures from survey data—the most common are Guttman scaling, factor analysis, and simple index construction. Each has some advantages and disadvantages. It became quickly apparent as the analysis unfolded, however, that the ministers in our study possessed highly interrelated beliefs about a wide variety of issues. Therefore, our primary objective in devising attitudinal measures became to find the underlying structure in the clergy's responses to religious, ethical, and political questions. Factor analysis is ideally suited for this purpose and was used to construct the seven attitudinal scales discussed in Chapter 2 and used in the subsequent analysis.*

As we noted in Chapter 2, a single factor accounted for most of the variance in the ministers' responses to the 10 items used to construct our religious modernism–traditionalism scale. The questions used and the factor loadings for this measure appear in Table B.1. The first six questions dealt with supernaturalism and orthodoxy and were taken from the work of Charles Y. Glock and Rodney Stark on Protestant laymen; the question on Biblical literalism was drawn from the national survey of Protestant ministers conducted by Jeffrey K. Hadden. In addition, we devised three questions dealing with religious worldliness—since we were particularly interested in the ministers' orientations toward life on earth or life after death. These questions loaded on the same factor as the others, which suggests that they are an integrated part of the clergy's religious belief systems. As a result, we used all 10 questions

*The method of principal factoring with iterations was followed as described in the SPSS manual. See Norman H. Nie, Dale H. Bent, and C. Hadlai Hull, *Statistical Package for the Social Sciences* (New York: McGraw-Hill, 1970), Chapter 17.

Table B.1. Factor Analysis of Ministers' Attitudes Toward Religious Issues

Attitude Statement	Loading
"I know God really exists and I have no doubts about it."[a]	.65
"Jesus is the Divine Son of God and I have no doubts about it."[a]	.75
"There is a life beyond death."[b]	.60
"Jesus was born of a Virgin."[b]	.87
"The Devil actually exists."[b]	.85
"Jesus walked on water."[b]	.86
"I believe in a literal or nearly literal interpretation of the Bible."[a]	.83
"If enough men were brought to Christ, social ills would take care of themselves."[a]	.57
"It is not as important to worry about life after death as about what one can do in this life."[a]	.63
"It would be better if the church were to place less emphasis on individual sanctification and more on bringing human conditions into conformity with Christian teachings."[a]	.68

[a] Respondents were asked whether they agreed or disagreed with each statement.
[b] Respondents were asked whether they believed these statements were literally true.

to construct our scale of religious beliefs. As we noted in the text, this measure was largely interchangeable with the ministers' own designations of their religious positions and thus possesses a high degree of validity.

Missing data were not a significant problem in this survey because only a few ministers failed to answer any of the questions used in our scale constructions. Accumulated over all 10 response items used to construct this religious scale, however, the proportion of missing responses rose to about 7 or 8 percent of the total number of respondents. Therefore, we assigned the mean response to any minister who failed to answer one of the items used in this measure—a technique that was followed for our other attitudinal scales as well.

We constructed our measure of ministerial attitudes toward clergy activism by asking our respondents whether they approved or disapproved of the 10 forms of activism discussed in Chapter 2 and shown in Table B.2. Obviously, the clergy's responses to these questions correlated highly with one another.

When subjected to factor analysis, however, three separate factors emerged and can be easily identified theoretically: we have called them protest, church, and public leadership (see Table B.2). (A factor analysis of the clergy's actual participation in these 10 forms of activism resulted in similar loadings and identical factors. This analysis is not shown here because it was not used in the text.)

Table B.2.   Factor Analysis of Ministers' Attitudes Toward Clergy Activism

Activist Behavior[a]	I	II	III
Civil rights protest marches	.78	.45	.17
Antiwar protest marches	.82	.40	.19
Civil rights civil disobedience (risk arrest to symbolize protest)	.88	.30	.18
Antiwar civil disobedience (risk arrest)	.90	.26	.18
Take a stand from the pulpit on some political issue	.29	.68	.33
Deliver a sermon on a controversial political or social topic	.33	.74	.20
Organize a study group within the church to discuss public affairs	.28	.77	.08
Organize a social action group within the church to accomplish directly some social or political goal	.41	.73	.13
Publicly (not from the pulpit) take a stand on some political issue	.17	.48	.72
Publicly (not from the pulpit) support a political candidate	.21	.07	.91

[a] Respondents were asked whether they approved or disapproved of clergymen who took each of these actions.

Our political measures were built by using factor analysis to select the questions that loaded most highly on each of the major factors initially extracted. The final items used and their factor loadings are given in Table B.3. We have named these three factors economic liberalism and civil rights, foreign policy, and civil protest and disobedience, respectively. Obviously we might have arrived at somewhat different factors if we had asked more political questions of one type or another. For example, we probably would

Table B.3. Factor Analysis of Ministers' Attitudes Toward Political Issues

Attitude Statement	I	II	III
"The federal government should do more about such social problems as poverty, unemployment, and housing."[a]	.66	.36	.21
A guaranteed minimum income for all families[b]	.53	.29	.36
A large-scale program, of Marshall Plan proportions, to deal with all urban problems[b]	.68	.26	.12
A national fair housing law to prohibit discrimination in the sale and rental of housing[b]	.63	.27	.18
Help for Negro-owned business and institutions[b]	.69	—.04	.06
"Red China should be admitted to the United Nations."[a]	.35	.67	.36
"Congressional investigations into un-American activities are essential to our nation's security."[a]	.15	.70	.31
"A larger proportion of United States foreign aid should be channeled through multilateral agencies such as the United Nations."[a]	.33	.67	.24
"The United States is spending too much money for military and defensive purposes."[a]	.12	.81	.05
"The black power movement is probably necessary in order for white society to realize the extent of Negro frustrations and deprivations."[a]	.39	.34	.56
"An individual should never deliberately disobey a law he considers wrong, but should work through the proper democratic channels to have that law changed."[a]	.14	.39	.61
"Black power groups such as the Student Non-Violent Coordinating Committee (SNCC) are doing the Negro cause a disservice in their emphasis upon racial conflict and violence."[a]	.15	.16	.74
Under certain circumstances militant procedures and even violence are legitimate means to bring about changes in the law."[a]	.12	.08	.77

[a] Respondents were asked whether they agreed or disagreed with the statement.
[b] Respondents were asked whether they approved or disapproved of the program.

have found a separate civil rights dimension if we had addressed more inquiries to the clergy about racial issues. Thus all we will say about these political dimensions is that they reflect the underlying structure of the ministers' positions on the questions we have asked them. It is significant, of course, that these dimensions are meaningful in political terms. It is also interesting to observe how some of these items load on these factors—for example, the black power question is related to the civil protest and disobedience dimension more strongly than to the economic liberalism and civil rights factor.

APPENDIX: THE QUESTIONNAIRE

C. The cover letter and the questionnaire described in the text are reproduced on the following pages.

STANFORD UNIVERSITY
STANFORD, CALIFORNIA 94305

INSTITUTE OF POLITICAL STUDIES
Studies in International Conflict and Integration
Studies of the Communist System
Studies in Comparative Politics
Studies in American Politics

550 Salvatierra St.

Spring, 1968

Dear Clergyman:

As you know, a crisis exists today among many Protestant churches. Seminary enrollment is down; more and more men are leaving the ministry; and the church is being strongly criticized from both within and without.

One of the basic causes of these problems has been the controversy over the church's role in politics. Some churchmen feel that it is the duty of the church to make judgments about human actions and to become directly involved in political issues. Others just as strongly feel that the church must stay out of politics if it is to maintain its traditional role in American society.

While there has been much discussion among churchmen on both sides of the issue, there is hardly any empirical information available about what clergymen think about public affairs. As political scientists, we feel that this subject is of such great importance that we are undertaking a full-scale study of the views and activities of parish ministers in California. We hope that you will agree with us about the value of this project.

The major source of data for this study will be the questionnaire which you have received. We would greatly appreciate your filling out the questionnaire and returning it to us at the earliest possible opportunity. The success of our project is dependent upon the degree of response we receive from you and your colleagues; it is important that all types of opinion are represented in our sample.

The information collected in these questionnaires, of course, will remain completely anonymous. An identification number is included on the back page only for administrative purposes, and your name will never be linked with your responses.

We hope that you will enjoy filling out the questionnaire and would greatly appreciate any comments you might have on the subjects explored in it. Space is provided on the last page for this purpose.

Sincerely yours,

Harold Quinley
Project Director

To Mail: No envelope or postage is required for returning this questionnaire. Fold back flap over this page and moisten gummed edge to seal.

1-4/
  5/1

THIS QUESTIONNAIRE FOCUSES UPON A NUMBER OF DIFFERENT AREAS IN THE CLERGYMAN'S LIFE.
IN THIS FIRST PART, WE ARE INTERESTED IN YOUR OPINIONS CONCERNING THE CHURCH'S IN-
VOLVEMENT IN PUBLIC AFFAIRS.

1. Disagreement exists among many church members concerning whether the church
   should speak out on social and political issues. In general, do you think
   that your <u>national church</u> should take an official position on the important
   issues of the day?

6-8/   1☐   Yes
                2☐   No
                3☐   Not sure

2. Do you think that your national church should take an official position on
   social and political issues even when a substantial portion of its members
   are in disagreement about the issue?

                1☐   Yes
                2☐   No
                3☐   Not sure

3. Are you yourself in general agreement with most of the positions taken by your
   national church--or do you think that it has gone too far on most issues or
   that it has not gone far enough?

                1☐   Generally agree with national church's positions
                2☐   Think that the national church has gone too far
                3☐   Think that the national church has not gone far enough
                4☐   Not sure

4. There are many ways by which clergymen can and do express their views on public
   issues. Not everyone agrees, however, that all of these forms of social action
   are appropriate for ministers. Please indicate for each of the following
   whether you approve or disapprove of clergymen who take that action. (Please
   check one box on each line.)

9-19/

		Strongly Approve	Ap-prove	No Opinion	Dis-approve	Strongly Disapprove
A.	Publicly (not from the pulpit) take a stand on some political <u>issue</u>	1 ☐	2 ☐	3 ☐	4 ☐	5 ☐
B.	Publicly (not from the pulpit) support a political <u>candidate</u> . .	☐	☐	☐	☐	☐
C.	Take a stand from the pulpit on some political <u>issue</u>	☐	☐	☐	☐	☐
D.	Deliver a sermon on a controversial political or social topic	☐	☐	☐	☐	☐
E.	Urge the members of their congregation to vote	1 ☐	2 ☐	3 ☐	4 ☐	5 ☐
F.	Organize a study group within their church to discuss public affairs	☐	☐	☐	☐	☐
G.	Organize a social action group within their church to accomplish directly some social or political goal	☐	☐	☐	☐	☐

5. A number of clergymen have recently become involved in public protests over
   certain controversial issues, such as civil rights and the Vietnam War.

   5a. Do you approve or disapprove of clergymen participating in any of the following activities?

		Strongly Approve	Ap-prove	No Opinion	Dis-approve	Strongly Disapprove
A.	Civil rights protest marches . .	1 ☐	2 ☐	3 ☐	4 ☐	5 ☐
B.	Anti-war protest marches	☐	☐	☐	☐	☐
C.	Civil rights civil disobedience (risk arrest to symbolize protest)	☐	☐	☐	☐	☐
D.	Anti-war civil disobedience (risk arrest)	☐	☐	☐	☐	☐

335

5b. Have you yourself--while serving in your present church or before entering your present church--engaged in such activities in support of civil rights protests? (Please check the one appropriate box in each line.)

20-32/

	Yes, while in present church	Yes, before present church	Yes, both present Ch. and before	No, never did this
	1	2	3	4
A. Attended protest meeting	☐	☐	☐	☐
B. Participated in protest march . .	☐	☐	☐	☐
C. Practiced civil disobedience (risked arrest to symbolize protest)	☐	☐	☐	☐

5c. Have you engaged in any such activities in support of anti-Vietnam War protests? (Please check the one appropriate box on each line.)

	Yes, while in present church	Yes, before present church	Yes, both present Ch. and before	No, have never done this
	1	2	3	4
A. Attended protest meeting	☐	☐	☐	☐
B. Participated in protest march . .	☐	☐	☐	☐
C. Practiced civil disobedience (risked arrest)	☐	☐	☐	☐

6. Have you made your views on public affairs known in any of the following ways? (Please check the one appropriate box in each line.)

	Yes, while in present church	Yes, before present church	Yes, both present Ch. and before	No, have never done this
	1	2	3	4
A. Wrote a letter to the editor of a newspaper	☐	☐	☐	☐
B. Signed or circulated a petition .	☐	☐	☐	☐
C. Wrote a public official	☐	☐	☐	☐
D. Personally contacted a public official	☐	☐	☐	☐
E. Publicly (not from the pulpit) took a stand on some public issue	1 ☐	2 ☐	3 ☐	4 ☐
F. Publicly (not from the pulpit) supported a political candidate .	☐	☐	☐	☐
G. Took a stand from the pulpit on some political issue	☐	☐	☐	☐

33-43/		Yes, while in pres-ent church	Yes, before present church	Yes, both present Ch. and before	No, have never done this
H.	Organized a study group within your church to discuss public affairs	1	2	3	4
I.	Organized a social action group within your church in order to accomplish directly some social or political goal				

7. There are many reasons why some clergymen participate in social action activities while others do not. Indicate for each of the factors listed below whether you feel it generally encourages or discourages your participation in such activities. Please answer in terms of your present situation.

		Generally Encourage	Generally Discourage	Neither
A.	The attitudes of the local denominational offi-cials in your immediate jurisdiction	1	2	3
B.	The attitudes of your local parishioners			
C.	The attitudes of your colleagues among the clergy			
D.	Your own political beliefs and attitudes			
E.	Your own theological views	1	2	3
F.	Your own goals as a parish minister			
G.	Your own personality			
H.	The community in which your church is located .			

8. Which of the following factors do you feel is most important in encouraging your participation in social action activities in your present situation?

(Please check only one.)

1 The attitudes of your local denominational officials
2 The attitudes of your local parishioners
3 The attitudes of your colleagues
4 Your own political beliefs and attitudes
5 Your own goals as a parish minister
6 Your own personality
7 The community in which your church is located
8 None of the above

9. Which of the following factors do you feel is most important in discouraging your participation in social action activities in your present situation?

(Please check only <u>one</u>.)

1☐ The attitudes of your local denominational officials
2☐ The attitudes of your local parishioners
3☐ The attitudes of your colleagues
4☐ Your own political beliefs and attitudes
5☐ Your own goals as a parish minister
6☐ Your own personality
7☐ The community in which your church is located
8☐ None of the above

10. If it were possible, would you like to be more or less involved in social action activities than you presently are?

1☐ More
2☐ Less
3☐ Continue present degree of involvement

THE FOLLOWING SET OF QUESTIONS DEALS WITH THREE MAJOR CONTROVERSIES WHICH HAVE INVOLVED MANY CLERGYMEN IN THIS AREA. WE'D LIKE TO KNOW YOUR VIEWS ON THESE ISSUES AND WHETHER YOU PARTICIPATED IN THEM IN ANY WAY.

11. Proposition 14 (the anti-fair housing referendum) was a major issue in California three years ago. Those favoring the referendum desired a repeal of certain sections of the state's fair housing legislation, while those against the referendum wanted to retain existing laws. What was your personal position on this issue?

1☐ Not in California at that time (PLEASE SKIP TO QUESTION 16)
2☐ Favored Proposition 14 (opposed to fair housing legislation)
3☐ Opposed Proposition 14 (favored fair housing legislation)
4☐ Undecided

12. At the time that Proposition 14 was an issue in 1964, were you serving in your present church assignment or in a different church or position?

1☐ Serving in present church
2☐ Serving in different church
3☐ Not serving as a parish minister (PLEASE SKIP TO QUESTION 16)

13. Did the majority of the members of the following groups favor or oppose Proposition 14?

	Favored Prop. 14 (opposed fair housing leg.)	Opposed Prop. 14 (favored fair housing leg.)	About Evenly Divided	Not Sure
A. The local denominational officials in your immediate jurisdiction	1 ☐	2 ☐	3 ☐	4 ☐
B. Your close colleagues among the clergy	☐	☐	☐	☐
C. Your local council of churches or ministerial association	☐	☐	☐	☐
D. The members of your congregation	☐	☐	☐	☐

14. Did you express your views on Proposition 14 in any of the following ways?

	Yes 1	No 2
A. Prayed privately	☐	☐
B. Signed a petition	☐	☐
C. Wrote a public official	☐	☐
D. Made a public statement	☐	☐
E. Served on a committee which campaigned for or against the proposition	☐	☐
F. Discussed it informally with some of the members of your congregation	☐	☐
G. Delivered a prayer before your congregation	☐	☐
H. Delivered a sermon or a section of a sermon on the subject	☐	☐
I. Organized a study group within your church to discuss the subject	☐	☐
J. Organized a social action group within your church in order to persuade others on the issue	☐	☐

If you expressed your view on Proposition 14 in any way, please answer questions 15a-c. If you did not, please skip to question 16.

IF YOU HAVE EXPRESSED YOUR VIEW ON PROPOSITION 14:

15a. Did any parishioners make their opposition to your participation known to you by taking the following actions?

	Yes 1	No 2
A. Privately expressed their opposition	☐	☐
B. Publicly expressed their opposition before the church board	☐	☐
C. Reduced their contributions to the church	☐	☐
D. Tried to have you removed from the church	☐	☐

15b. Did any parishioners make their approval of your participation known to you by taking the following actions?

	Yes 1	No 2
A. Privately expressed their approval	☐	☐
B. Publicly expressed their approval before the church board	☐	☐
C. Increased their contributions to the church	☐	☐
D. Joined you in some public expression or your views	☐	☐

15c. Do you feel that you gained or lost any church members because of your participation in this issue?

70-77/

- 1 ☐ Both gained some and lost some
- 2 ☐ Gained some
- 3 ☐ Lost some
- 4 ☐ Neither gained nor lost any

16a. A second major controversy in California centers around the participation of clergymen in the organization of migratory farm workers in the Delano area. Do you personally favor the organization of migratory farm workers in California?

1 ☐ Yes   2 ☐ No   3 ☐ Not sure

IF YES: ↓

16b. Do you personally favor the participation of clergymen in the organization of farm workers?

1 ☐ Yes   2 ☐ No   3 ☐ Not sure

17. At the time that the organization of migratory workers was a major issue, were you serving in your present church assignment or in a different church or position?

- 1 ☐ Serving in present church
- 2 ☐ Serving in different church
- 3 ☐ Not serving as a parish minister (PLEASE SKIP TO QUESTION 21)

18. Did the majority of the members of the following groups favor or oppose the participation of clergymen in the organization of migratory farm workers?

	Favored	Opposed	About Evenly Divided	Not Sure
	1	2	3	4
A. The local denominational officials in your immediate jurisdiction	☐	☐	☐	☐
B. Your close colleagues among the clergy .	☐	☐	☐	☐
C. Your local council of churches or ministerial association	☐	☐	☐	☐
D. The members of your congregation	☐	☐	☐	☐

340

1-4/
 5/2

19. Did you express your views on this issue in any of the following ways?

6-18/

		Yes 1	No 2
A.	Prayed privately	☐	☐
B.	Signed a petition	☐	☐
C.	Wrote a public official	☐	☐
D.	Made a public statement	☐	☐
E.	Marched or traveled to the Delano area	☐	☐
F.	Discussed it informally with some of the members of your congregation	☐	☐
G.	Delivered a prayer before your congregation	☐	☐
H.	Delivered a sermon or a section of a sermon on the subject	☐	☐
I.	Organized a study group within your church to discuss the subject	☐	☐

If you have expressed your views on the organization of migratory farm workers in _any way_, please answer questions 20a-c. If you have not, please skip to question 21.

IF YOU HAVE EXPRESSED YOUR VIEWS ON THIS ISSUE:

20a. Did any parishioners make their opposition to your participation known to you by taking the following actions?

		Yes 1	No 2
A.	Privately expressed their opposition	☐	☐
B.	Publicly expressed their opposition before the church board	☐	☐
C.	Reduced their contributions to the church	☐	☐
D.	Tried to have you removed from the church	☐	☐

20b. Did any parishioners make their <u>approval</u> of your participation known to you by taking the following actions?

	Yes 1	No 2
A. Privately expressed their approval	☐	☐
B. Publicly expressed their approval before the church board	☐	☐
C. Increased their contributions to the church	☐	☐
D. Joined you in some public expression of your views	☐	☐

20c. Do you feel that you gained or lost any church members because of your participation in this issue?

1 ☐ Both gained some and lost some
2 ☐ Gained some
3 ☐ Lost some
4 ☐ Neither gained nor lost any

21. The third controversy concerns the Vietnam War. Churchmen throughout the country have increasingly become concerned about the situation in Vietnam. Have the local denominational officials in your immediate jurisdiction made a formal statement on the Vietnam War?

1 ☐ Yes, in favor of greater efforts to negotiate
2 ☐ Yes, in support of present policies
3 ☐ No, they did not take a position
4 ☐ Not sure

22. The following list contains some of the major proposals which have been made in order to bring the war to a conclusion. How strongly do you agree or disagree with each of these alternatives? (Please check one on each line.)

	Strongly Agree	Agree	No Opinion	Dis- agree	Strongly Disagree
	1	2	3	4	5
A. Increase our military efforts in order to win the war	☐	☐	☐	☐	☐
B. Seek negotiations while continuing to exert military pressure on the enemy, including the bombing of North Vietnam	☐	☐	☐	☐	☐
C. Unilaterally stop the bombing of North Vietnam and offer to negotiate	☐	☐	☐	☐	☐
D. Unilaterally stop the bombing of North Vietnam and withdraw to the coastal areas and population centers	☐	☐	☐	☐	☐
E. Unilaterally stop the bombing and begin preparations for complete withdrawal .	☐	☐	☐	☐	☐

23. Do you think that the majority of your congregation would take a more hawkish or dovish position on the war than your own?

30-44/
    1☐ More hawkish
    2☐ More dovish
    3☐ About the same position
    4☐ Not sure

24. Do you think that the majority of your close colleagues among the clergy would take a more hawkish or dovish position on the war than your own?

    1☐ More hawkish
    2☐ More dovish
    3☐ About the same position
    4☐ Not sure

25. Have you expressed your views on the Vietnam War in any of the following ways?

	Yes	No
	1	2
A. Prayed privately	☐	☐
B. Signed a petition	☐	☐
C. Wrote a public official	☐	☐
D. Made a public statement	☐	☐
	1	2
E. Joined a peace organization of some kind	☐	☐
F. Discussed it informally with some of the members of your congregation	☐	☐
G. Delivered a prayer before your congregation	☐	☐
H. Delivered a sermon or a section of a sermon on the subject	☐	☐
I. Organized a study group within your church to discuss the subject	☐	☐

If you have expressed your views on the Vietnam War in any way, please answer questions 26a-c. If you have not, please skip to question 27.

IF YOU EXPRESSED YOUR VIEWS ON THE VIETNAM WAR:

26a. Did any parishioners make their opposition to your participation known to you by taking the following actions?

	Yes	No
	1	2
A. Privately expressed their opposition	☐	☐
B. Publicly expressed their opposition before the church board	☐	☐
C. Reduced their contributions to the church	☐	☐
D. Tried to have you removed from the church	☐	☐

26b. Did any parishioners make their <u>approval</u> of your participation known to you by taking the following actions?

	Yes 1	No 2
A. Privately expressed their approval	☐	☐
B. Publicly expressed their approval before the church board	☐	☐
C. Increased their contributions to the church	☐	☐
D. Joined you in some public expression of your views . .	☐	☐

26c. Do you feel that you gained or lost any church members because of your participation in this issue?

1☐ Both gained some and lost some
2☐ Gained some
3☐ Lost some
4☐ Neither gained nor lost any

NOW WE'D LIKE TO ASK SOME QUESTIONS ABOUT THOSE GROUPS YOU MOST OFTEN HAVE CONTACT WITH--YOUR CONGREGATION, YOUR LOCAL DENOMINATIONAL OFFICIALS, AND YOUR COLLEAGUES. FIRST, SOME QUESTIONS ABOUT YOUR CONGREGATION.

27. How many adult members are there presently in your congregation?

1☐ Less than 50
2☐ 50-149
3☐ 150-299
4☐ 300-499
5☐ 500-1,000
6☐ More than 1,000

28. Many people think of themselves as belonging to either the working class or the middle class. Do you think that your congregation is composed primarily of members of the working class, the lower middle class, or the upper middle class?

1☐ Primarily working class
2☐ Primarily lower middle class
3☐ Primarily upper middle class

29. On the average how often do you usually have social visits with your parishioners in their homes or in your own home?

1☐ Five or more times a week
2☐ 3-4 times a week
3☐ 1-2 times a week
4☐ Less than once a week

30. Have you had any serious differences of opinion with some of the members of your congregation over the following matters?

53-66/

	Many	Some	None
	1	2	3
A. The church budget	☐	☐	☐
B. Your theological views	☐	☐	☐
C. Church organization	☐	☐	☐
D. Your participation in social action activities	☐	☐	☐

31. Do you think that most members of your congregation would approve or disapprove if you were to do each of the following? (Please check one on each line.)

	Strongly Approve	Approve	Evenly Divided	Disapprove	Strongly Disapprove	No Opinion
A. Publicly (not from the pulpit) take a stand on some political issue	1 ☐	2 ☐	3 ☐	4 ☐	5 ☐	6 ☐
B. Publicly (not from pulpit) support a political candidate	☐	☐	☐	☐	☐	☐
C. Take a stand from the pulpit on some political issue	☐	☐	☐	☐	☐	☐
D. Participate in a civil rights protest march . .	☐	☐	☐	☐	☐	☐
E. Participate in an anti-war protest march	1 ☐	2 ☐	3 ☐	4 ☐	5 ☐	6 ☐
F. Be arrested to symbolize your civil rights protest	☐	☐	☐	☐	☐	☐
G. Be arrested to symbolize your anti-war protest . .	☐	☐	☐	☐	☐	☐
H. Deliver a sermon on a controversial political or social topic	1 ☐	2 ☐	3 ☐	4 ☐	5 ☐	6 ☐
I. Organize a study group within your church to discuss public affairs . . .	☐	☐	☐	☐	☐	☐
J. Organize a social action group within your church to accomplish directly some social or political goal	☐	☐	☐	☐	☐	☐

32. Some congregations supervise the activities of their ministers very closely while others generally let the clergymen run things. How closely do your parishioners supervise each of the following?

	Closely 1	Moderately 2	Little 3	Not At All 4
A. The church budget	☐	☐	☐	☐
B. The church's programs	☐	☐	☐	☐
C. Your salary	☐	☐	☐	☐
D. Your participation in social action activities	☐	☐	☐	☐

33. Do you use the pulpit or church bulletins in your present church to urge your parishioners to come out and vote?

	Yes 1	No 2
A. In national elections	☐	☐
B. In state elections	☐	☐
C. In local elections	☐	☐

34. How often do you discuss public affairs with members of your congregation?

1 ☐ Frequently
2 ☐ Occasionally
3 ☐ Never

35. During the past year, how often did you deliver sermons which dealt mainly with controversial social or political topics?

1 ☐ 8 or more times
2 ☐ 5-7 times
3 ☐ 3-4 times
4 ☐ Once or twice
5 ☐ Never

36. During the past year, how often did you deliver sermons which touched upon, but did not deal mainly with, controversial social or political topics?

1 ☐ 8 or more times
2 ☐ 5-7 times
3 ☐ 3-4 times
4 ☐ Once or twice
5 ☐ Never

NOTE: IF YOU ANSWERED "NEVER" FOR BOTH QUESTION 35 AND 36 PLEASE SKIP NOW TO QUESTION 38.

346

37. During the past year did you deliver a sermon which dealt mainly with, or touched upon, each of the following topics?

		Dealt mainly with topic	Touched upon topic but did not deal mainly with it	Did not deal with topic
		1	2	3
A.	The UN and world peace	☐	☐	☐
B.	Racial problems	☐	☐	☐
C.	Birth control	☐	☐	☐
D.	The use of drugs	☐	☐	☐
		1	2	3
E.	Crime, juvenile delinquency . . .	☐	☐	☐
F.	The conduct of public officials .	☐	☐	☐
G.	Black power	☐	☐	☐
H.	Abortion laws	☐	☐	☐
		1	2	3
I.	World poverty	☐	☐	☐
J.	National poverty	☐	☐	☐
K.	Alcoholism	☐	☐	☐
L.	Sexual conduct	☐	☐	☐
M.	Capital punishment	☐	☐	☐

38. How important do you feel it is that you accomplish each of the following purposes in your sermons?

		Very important	Fairly important	Somewhat important	Not important at all
		1	2	3	4
A.	Provide spiritual uplifting and moral comfort to those who are distressed	☐	☐	☐	☐
B.	Illustrate the type of life a Christian should follow	☐	☐	☐	☐
C.	Point out the existence of human sin	☐	☐	☐	☐
D.	Apply Christian standards to judge human institutions and behavior	☐	☐	☐	☐

347

QUESTIONS ABOUT YOUR LOCAL DENOMINATIONAL OFFICIALS (THOSE IN YOUR IMMEDIATE JURISDICTION)

39. Sometimes local denominational officials disagree with their national officials concerning the positions which the church should take. Do you feel that the local officials in your immediate jurisdiction would agree with your national church's positions on most social and political issues, think that the national church has gone too far, or think that it has not gone far enough?

23-31/

1☐ Generally agree with the national church's positions
2☐ Think that the national church has gone too far
3☐ Think that the national church has not gone far enough
4☐ Not sure

40. The amount of supervision which local denominational officials exercise over local clergymen often varies from one denomination to another. How closely do your local denominational officials supervise the following activities?

	Closely	Moderately	Little	Not At All
	1	2	3	4
A. The appointment of parish ministers . .	☐	☐	☐	☐
B. The programs of the local church . . .	☐	☐	☐	☐
C. The removal of parish ministers	☐	☐	☐	☐

41. If you were in conflict with your parishioners over the following issues, how much assistance would you expect from your local denominational officials?

	A Great Deal of Assistance	Some Assistance	Little Assistance	No Assistance
	1	2	3	4
A. Your theological views	☐	☐	☐	☐
B. The content of your sermons . . .	☐	☐	☐	☐
C. Your participation in social action activities	☐	☐	☐	☐

42. Do you think that your local denominational officials would approve or disapprove if you were to do each of the following? (Please check one on each line.)

	Strongly Approve	Approve	Evenly Divided	Disapprove	Strongly Disapprove	No Opinion
	1	2	3	4	5	6
A. Publicly (not from the pulpit) take a stand on some political issue . .	☐	☐	☐	☐	☐	☐
B. Publicly (not from the pulpit) support a political candidate	☐	☐	☐	☐	☐	☐

348

32-40/		Strongly Approve	Ap- prove	Evenly Divided	Dis- approve	Strongly Disapprove	No Opinion
C.	Take a stand from the pul- pit on some political issue	1 ☐	2 ☐	3 ☐	4 ☐	5 ☐	6 ☐
D.	Participate in a civil rights protest march . . .	☐	☐	☐	☐	☐	☐
E.	Participate in an anti-war protest march	☐	☐	☐	☐	☐	☐
F.	Be arrested to symbolize your civil rights protest	☐	☐	☐	☐	☐	☐
G.	Be arrested to symbolize your anti-war protest . .	1 ☐	2 ☐	3 ☐	4 ☐	5 ☐	6 ☐
H.	Deliver a sermon on a con- troversial political or social topic	☐	☐	☐	☐	☐	☐
I.	Organize a study group within your church to dis- cuss public affairs . . .	☐	☐	☐	☐	☐	☐
J.	Organize a social action group within your church to accomplish directly some social or political goal	☐	☐	☐	☐	☐	☐

43. In some denominations a minister who raises controversial social issues with his parishioners will have difficulty obtaining choice ministerial positions in the future, while in others a controversial minister will often receive the choice positions. Which of the following statements most closely describes the situa- tion in your denomination? (Please check only one.)

        1 ☐   The way to obtain a choice ministerial position in my denom- ination is to remain noncontroversial on social and political issues

        2 ☐   A minister's social activism has little relation to the type of ministerial position he receives in my denomination

        3 ☐   Controversial ministers in my denomination are often able to obtain suitable positions even though many do suffer because of their activism

        4 ☐   Ministers who are socially active in my denomination are more likely to receive choice ministerial positions than those who do not speak out on social issues

349

QUESTIONS ABOUT YOUR COLLEAGUES AMONG THE CLERGY

44. In which social group are <u>most</u> of your close friends located?

41-51/   1☐ Colleagues among the clergy
          2☐ Parishioners
          3☐ Other (please specify):_____

45. During the past year, approximately how many times a month did you visit informal-
    ly with clergymen of your own denomination? With clergymen of other denominations?

	Six or more times a month	3-5 times a month	1-2 times a month	Less than once a month
A. Clergy of your <u>own</u> denomination	1 ☐	2 ☐	3 ☐	4 ☐
B. Clergy of <u>other</u> denominations	☐	☐	☐	☐

46. Would most of your <u>close colleagues</u> among the clergy approve or disapprove if
    you were to do each of the following? (Please check one on each line.)

	Strongly Approve	Approve	Evenly Divided	Disapprove	Strongly Disapprove	No Opinion
A. Publicly (not from the pulpit) take a stand on some political <u>issue</u> . . .	1 ☐	2 ☐	3 ☐	4 ☐	5 ☐	6 ☐
B. Publicly (not from the pulpit) support a political <u>candidate</u>	☐	☐	☐	☐	☐	☐
C. Take a stand from the pulpit on some political issue	☐	☐	☐	☐	☐	☐
D. Participate in a civil rights protest march . . .	☐	☐	☐	☐	☐	☐
E. Participate in an anti-war protest march	1 ☐	2 ☐	3 ☐	4 ☐	5 ☐	6 ☐
F. Be arrested to symbolize your civil rights protest	☐	☐	☐	☐	☐	☐
G. Be arrested to symbolize your anti-war protest . .	☐	☐	☐	☐	☐	☐
H. Deliver a sermon on a controversial political or social topic	☐	☐	☐	☐	☐	☐

	Strongly Approve	Ap- prove	Evenly Divided	Dis- approve	Strongly Disapprove	No Opinion
52-55/

I. Organize a study group within your church to discuss public affairs . .

| | 1 | 2 | 3 | 4 | 5 | 6 |

J. Organize a social action group within your church to accomplish directly some social or political goal . . . .

IN THIS PART OF THE QUESTIONNAIRE, WE'D LIKE TO KNOW WHAT YOU THINK ABOUT A NUMBER OF AREAS OF CONCERN TO CLERGYMEN. THE FOLLOWING QUESTIONS, FIRST OF ALL, HAVE TO DO WITH RELIGIOUS BELIEF. THEY ARE BEING ASKED IN THE INTEREST OF ASSESSING THE EXTENT TO WHICH THERE IS PRESENTLY CONSENSUS AMONG THE CLERGY ABOUT TRADITIONAL ARTICLES OF CHRISTIAN FAITH.

47. Which of the following statements comes closest to expressing what you believe about God? (Please check only one.)

1 I know God really exists and I have no doubts about it

2 While I have doubts, I feel that I do believe in God

3 I find myself believing in God some of the time, but not at other times

4 I don't believe in a personal God, but I do believe in a higher power of some kind

5 I don't know whether there is a God and I don't believe there is any way to find out

6 I don't believe in God

7 None of the above represents what I believe. What I believe about God is _____

_____

48. Which of the following statements comes closest to expressing what you believe about Jesus? (Please check only one.)

1 Jesus is the Divine Son of God and I have no doubts about it

2 While I have some doubts, I feel basically that Jesus is Divine

3 I feel that Jesus was a great man and very holy, but I don't feel Him to be the Son of God any more than all of us are children of God

4 I think Jesus was only a man, although an extraordinary one

5 Frankly, I'm not entirely sure there really was such a person as Jesus

6 None of the above represents what I believe. What I believe about Jesus is _____

_____

351

49. Which group do you think was most responsible for crucifying Christ?

56-68/
1☐ The Romans
2☐ The Greeks
3☐ The Jews
4☐ The Christians
5☐ None of these rather _____
6☐ Don't know

50. Admittedly, there are difficulties associated with describing oneself in terms of broad theological positions. However, within the following categories, which of the following best describes your theological position? (Please check only one.)

1☐ Fundamentalist
2☐ Conservative
3☐ Neo-orthodox
4☐ Liberal
5☐ Other (please specify): _____

51. For each of the religious beliefs listed below, would you please indicate whether you personally believe them to be literally true, true in a symbolic sense, probably not true at all, or definitely not true?

	Literally True	Symbolically True	Probably Not True	Definitely Not True
	1	2	3	4
A. There is a life beyond death	☐	☐	☐	☐
B. Jesus was born of a virgin	☐	☐	☐	☐
C. The Devil actually exists	☐	☐	☐	☐
D. Jesus walked on water	☐	☐	☐	☐
E. Man cannot help doing evil	☐	☐	☐	☐
F. A child is born into the world already guilty of sin	☐	☐	☐	☐

52. Would you please read each of the items listed below and decide whether you think it is: (a) absolutely necessary for salvation
(b) probably would help in gaining salvation, or
(c) probably has no influence on salvation.

	Absolutely Necessary	Would Probably Help	Probably Has No Influence
	1	2	3
A. Belief in Jesus Christ as Savior	☐	☐	☐
B. Holy Baptism	☐	☐	☐
C. Membership in a Christian church	☐	☐	☐
D. Doing good for others	☐	☐	☐
E. Being a member of your particular religious faith	☐	☐	☐

53. We now turn to relations between Christians and Jews. There is a great deal of disagreement among Christians about what Jews are like. Here are some things that have been said at one time or another about Jews. For each statement, would you decide whether you think Jews are like this or not and check the appropriate answer.

69-77/

		Yes	Somewhat	No
		1	2	3
A.	Jews are particularly generous and give a great deal of money to charity	☐	☐	☐
B.	Jews like to be with other Jews and tend to avoid non-Jews	☐	☐	☐
C.	Jews are more likely than Christians to cheat in business	☐	☐	☐
D.	Jews are less likely than Christians to oppose Communism .	☐	☐	☐
		1	2	3
E.	Jews, in general, are inclined to be more loyal to Israel than to America	☐	☐	☐
F.	Because Jews are not bound by Christian ethics, they do things to get ahead that Christians generally will not do	☐	☐	☐
G.	Many Jews oppose allowing Christian holidays, such as Christmas and Easter, to be celebrated in the public schools	☐	☐	☐
H.	Jews want to remain different from other people, and yet they are touchy if people notice these differences	☐	☐	☐

54. All in all, as you assess your own feelings about Jews, which of the following statements comes closest to representing the way you feel about them? (Please check only one.)

1 ☐ Frankly, looking inside myself, I tend to feel somewhat hostile toward Jews

2 ☐ There are many individual Jews whom I admire but I feel that I do harbor some ill feelings toward Jews in a general way

3 ☐ I believe I can honestly say that I have no ill feelings about Jews at all though I am not disposed to favor them over other groups

4 ☐ Not only do I bear no resentment toward Jews, but I feel particularly drawn to them in a positive way

5 ☐ None of the above comes close to representing my feelings. I feel

_____

_____

353

55. The following statements have sometimes been made about religious issues. Please
indicate your agreement or disagreement with each of them by checking the appropriate response.

		Strongly Agree	Agree	No Opinion	Dis- agree	Strongly Disagree
A.	Organized religion is the one sure in- fallible foundation of life	1 ☐	2 ☐	3 ☐	4 ☐	5 ☐
B.	As long as the churches persist in re- garding the parish of the local congre- gation as their normative structure, they will not confront life at its most significant point	☐	☐	☐	☐	☐
C.	If enough men were brought to Christ, so- cial ills would take care of themselves	☐	☐	☐	☐	☐
D.	At the present time religion appears to be losing its influence on American life	☐	☐	☐	☐	☐
E.	I believe in a literal or nearly liter- al interpretation of the Bible	1 ☐	2 ☐	3 ☐	4 ☐	5 ☐
F.	It is not as important to worry about life after death as about what one can do in this life	☐	☐	☐	☐	☐
G.	It would be better if the church were to place less emphasis on individual sancti- fication and more on bringing human con- ditions into conformity with Christian teachings	☐	☐	☐	☐	☐
H.	By comforting those who are deprived, the church often deters such individuals from going to the political arena to solve their social grievances	☐	☐	☐	☐	☐
I.	The Jews can never be forgiven for what they did to Jesus until they accept Him as the True Savior	1 ☐	2 ☐	3 ☐	4 ☐	5 ☐
J.	It's probably better for Negroes and whites to have their own separate churches	☐	☐	☐	☐	☐
K.	The reason the Jews have so much trouble is because God is punishing them for re- jecting Jesus	☐	☐	☐	☐	☐

56. During the past two years, have you given a sermon from the pulpit of a church
other than your own?

        1 ☐   Yes   2 ☐   No

57. Would you approve of another minister delivering a sermon from the pulpit of your church?

18-27/   1☐ Yes   2☐ No   3☐ Not sure

58. If there were more churches in your area than the neighborhood could apparently support, would you favor the merger of your church with one of another denomination?

       1☐ Yes   2☐ No   3☐ Not sure

59. Do you favor the eventual union of all major Protestant denominations in a single church structure?

       1☐ Yes   2☐ No   3☐ Not sure

60. Do you favor the eventual union of the Protestant and Catholic churches in a single church structure?

       1☐ Yes   2☐ No   3☐ Not sure

WE NOW TURN FROM THEOLOGICAL ISSUES TO PUBLIC AFFAIRS. THESE QUESTIONS ARE BEING ASKED IN ORDER TO DETERMINE THE DEGREE TO WHICH CLERGYMEN DIFFER IN THEIR THINKING ABOUT GOVERNMENT AND PUBLIC ISSUES.

61. Please indicate how strongly you agree or disagree with each of the following statements.

	Strongly Agree	Agree	No Opinion	Dis-agree	Strongly Disagree
A. The black power movement is probably necessary in order for white society to realize the extent of Negro frustrations and deprivations	1 ☐	2 ☐	3 ☐	4 ☐	5 ☐
B. The federal government should do more about such social problems as poverty, unemployment, and housing	☐	☐	☐	☐	☐
C. Red China should be admitted to the United Nations	☐	☐	☐	☐	☐
D. Congressional investigations into un-American activities are essential to our nation's security	☐	☐	☐	☐	☐
E. An individual should never deliberately disobey a law he considers wrong, but should work through the proper democratic channels to have that law changed	1 ☐	2 ☐	3 ☐	4 ☐	5 ☐
F. It would be better if large corporations such as U.S. Steel were owned by the federal government	☐	☐	☐	☐	☐

28-36/

		Strongly Agree	Agree	No Opinion	Dis-agree	Strongly Disagree

G. The United States should use its military forces only when it is attacked or about to be attacked . . . .
   1 ☐   2 ☐   3 ☐   4 ☐   5 ☐

H. Black power groups such as the Student Non-Violent Coordinating Committee (SNCC) are doing the Negro cause a disservice in their emphasis upon racial conflict and violence . . . .
☐   ☐   ☐   ☐   ☐

I. Civil disobedience is permissible when an individual has carefully thought about the consequences of his actions and is willing to accept the penalties for breaking the law . . . .
☐   ☐   ☐   ☐   ☐

J. The government is providing too many services that should be left to private enterprise . . . .
☐   ☐   ☐   ☐   ☐

K. A larger proportion of United States foreign aid should be channeled through multilateral agencies such as the United Nations . . . .
   1 ☐   2 ☐   3 ☐   4 ☐   5 ☐

L. Under certain circumstances militant procedures and even violence are legitimate means to bring about changes in the law . . . .
☐   ☐   ☐   ☐   ☐

M. The United States is spending too much money for military and defensive purposes
☐   ☐   ☐   ☐   ☐

N. Communists should not be allowed the use of public buildings in order to give speeches about their ideology . . . . .
☐   ☐   ☐   ☐   ☐

62. An important issue today in the conduct of foreign policy is the extent to which the United States should use its military forces to intervene in unstable situations which communist elements might exploit. Which of the following statements comes closest to representing your view on this matter? (Please check only one.)

    1 ☐ The United States should not intervene militarily in such situations at all

    2 ☐ While the United States has recently been too quick to intervene militarily in such situations, it does have some responsibilities in this regard

    3 ☐ The United States should continue at its present level of military involvement in such situations

    4 ☐ The United States should react to such situations with greater military firmness and dispatch

63. The question of military intervention has come up many times in the past. The following is a list of such instances in which the United States had to make a decision of whether or not to send in troops. In each case please indicate whether you think the United States should or should not have used military force.

37-50/

	Should Have Intervened (1)	Should Not Have Intervened (2)	Not Sure (3)
A. North-South Korea conflict in 1950	☐	☐	☐
B. Hungarian Revolution in 1956	☐	☐	☐
C. Bay of Pigs Invasion in 1962	☐	☐	☐
D. Vietnam buildup in 1964-65	☐	☐	☐
E. Revolt in the Dominican Republic in 1965	☐	☐	☐
F. Overthrow of constitutional government in Greece in the summer of 1967	☐	☐	☐

64. Do you think that laws regulating each of the following types of social conduct should be made stronger, weaker, or kept as they are?

	Stronger (1)	Kept As They Are (2)	Weaker (3)
A. Gambling	☐	☐	☐
B. The sale of liquor to adults	☐	☐	☐
C. The use of marijuana	☐	☐	☐
D. The sale of "obscene" materials	☐	☐	☐

65. Do you agree or disagree with the Supreme Court decision ruling as unconstitutional the use of non-sectarian prayers in public schools?

1☐ Agree   2☐ Disagree   3☐ Not sure

66. Do you favor the elimination of the tax-free status of church properties and commercial income?

	Yes (1)	No (2)	Not Sure (3)
A. Church properties	☐	☐	☐
B. Commercial income of the church	☐	☐	☐

67. Do you favor laws punishing individuals who burn draft cards in protest of United States policies or actions?

1☐ Yes   2☐ No   3☐ Not sure

68. A number of policy suggestions have been made in reaction to the recent urban unrest. Would you approve or disapprove of the following such proposals?

51-60/

	Approve	Disapprove	Not Sure
	1	2	3
A. A guaranteed minimum income for all families . .	☐	☐	☐
B. Tougher police practices in riot areas	☐	☐	☐
C. A large-scale program, of Marshall Plan proportions, to deal with all urban problems	☐	☐	☐
D. A national fair housing law to prohibit discrimination in the sale and rental of housing	☐	☐	☐
	1	2	3
E. Help for Negro-owned businesses and institutions	☐	☐	☐
F. Tough legislation dealing with crime on the streets (including sniping, arson, and looting)	☐	☐	☐

69. Do you favor the busing of Negro students to white area schools and white students to Negro area schools in order to deal with de facto school segregation?

1☐ Favor busing of both Negro and white students
2☐ Favor busing of Negro students but not of white students
3☐ Favor busing of white students but not of Negro students
4☐ Not in favor of busing of either Negro or white students

70. A disagreement exists among some church members as to how the church should help poor people. Some people agree with Saul Alinsky that the church should help the poor to organize themselves, while others feel that the church should help these people but should not become involved in the politics of their problems. Which position is closest to your own?

1☐ Should help the poor to organize essentially as Alinsky suggests
2☐ Should help the poor to organize but not follow Alinsky tactics
3☐ Should help the poor as individuals but not become involved in their political problems
4☐ The church has no special duty to help the poor

71a. Do you think that your denomination should attempt to induce its local churches to adopt an "open church" policy with respect to the membership of individuals from minority racial and ethnic groups?

1☐ Yes   2☐ No   3☐ Not sure

IF YES:

> 71b. Do you think that your denomination should institute official sanctions (such as denying certification of pastoral assignments) against those local churches which refuse to open their membership to such individuals?
>
> 1☐ Yes   2☐ No   3☐ Not sure

72. There are many other ways by which the church can become directly involved in
public affairs. Would you approve or disapprove if your denomination were to
do the following?

61-72/

                                                       Approve Disapprove Not Sure

A. Use its economic powers (e.g., withdrawal of
patronage and trade) to force equal rights in
your community   1   2   3

B. Refuse to cooperate with the government's War on
Poverty unless the programs guaranteed power and
participation for the poor . . . .

C. Assist those who refuse induction into the military
forces because they conscientiously object to war
in general . . . .

D. Assist those who refuse induction into the military
forces because they conscientiously object to the
Vietnam War in particular . . . .

E. Sponsor a meeting in which draft cards are turned
in or burned . . . .

73. The following statements have frequently been made about clergymen, the church, and
politics. Please indicate whether you agree or disagree with each of them.

	Strongly Agree	Agree	No Opinion	Dis- agree	Strongly Disagree
A. It is difficult for clergymen to know the proper political channels through which to accomplish something which should be done	1	2	3	4	5
B. Because of their positions in society, clergymen have a special obligation to stay politically informed					
C. Protestant churches have become too aligned with the status quo in the United States to become major agents of social reform					
D. Clergymen have great potential to influence the political and social beliefs of their parishioners					
E. Clergymen should not criticize their political leaders when they cannot possibly know all the facts involved in the problems which must be faced	1	2	3	4	5
F. The Protestant emphasis on individual responsibility is a major deterrent to the development of social action programs by the church					
G. Sometimes politics and government seem so complicated that a clergyman cannot really understand what is going on					

FINALLY, WE WOULD LIKE SOME BACKGROUND INFORMATION.

74. Your age:

73-80/
1 ☐ 29 or under
2 ☐ 30-34
3 ☐ 35-39
4 ☐ 40-44
5 ☐ 45-49
6 ☐ 50-54
7 ☐ 55-59
8 ☐ 60-64
9 ☐ 65 or over

75. Your present position:

1 ☐ Minister
2 ☐ Assistant or associate minister
3 ☐ Other (please specify): _____

76. Your marital status:

1 ☐ Married
2 ☐ Single
3 ☐ Widowed, separated, divorced

77. In which part of the country were you raised?

1 ☐ East-Northeast
2 ☐ Midwest
3 ☐ South
4 ☐ West
5 ☐ Outside of U.S.

78. Your race:

1 ☐ White
2 ☐ Negro
3 ☐ Other (please specify): _____

79. Which of the following best describes the community you lived in during most of your childhood?

1 ☐ Small farming or rural community
2 ☐ Small town
3 ☐ Medium size town
4 ☐ Suburb
5 ☐ Small city
6 ☐ Large city

80a. During the time you were growing up, did your father serve as a clergyman at any time?

1 ☐ Yes   2 ☐ No

IF NO: ↓

80b. What was your father's principal occupation while you were growing up?

_____

360

81. During the time you were growing up did any of your close relatives (other than your father) serve as clergymen?

6-16/   1☐ Yes   2☐ No

82a. Did you attend college?

1☐ Yes   2☐ No

IF YES: ↓

82b. Did you graduate?

1☐ Yes
2☐ No

83a. Did you attend seminary school?

1☐ Yes   2☐ No

IF YES: ↓

83b. Did you graduate?

1☐ Yes   84c. What was the name of the seminary?
2☐ No

_____

84. Have you had any other higher education?

1☐ Yes   2☐ No

85. How many years have you been at your present church?

1☐ Less than one
2☐ One
3☐ Two
4☐ Three
5☐ Four
6☐ Five
7☐ 6-10
8☐ 11-15
9☐ 16 or more

86. In what county is your present church?

_____
(name of county)

87. Which of the following best describes the community in which your present church is located?

1☐ Small farming or rural community
2☐ Small town
3☐ Medium size town
4☐ Suburb
5☐ Small city
6☐ Large city

88. What is the total number of years you have been in the ministry?

17-34/
    1☐ 0-5
    2☐ 6-10
    3☐ 11-15
    4☐ 16-20
    5☐ 21-25
    6☐ 26-30
    7☐ 31 or more

89. How many churches have you served?

    1☐ One
    2☐ Two
    3☐ Three
    4☐ Four
    5☐ 5-6
    6☐ 7 or more

90. Have you served your denomination in any capacity other than that of parish minister?

    19/ ☐ No, no capacity other than parish minister
    20/ ☐ Yes, denominational office
    21/ ☐ Yes, campus minister
    22/ ☐ Yes, teaching position
    23/ ☐ Yes, other (please specify): _____

91. When do you expect to move from your church to another position?

    1☐ Fairly soon
    2☐ Not for a few years
    3☐ Not for a long time
    4☐ Never

92. Would you like to move to another position?

    25/ ☐ No
    26/ ☐ Yes, to another congregation
    27/ ☐ Yes, to a denominational office
    28/ ☐ Yes, to a teaching position
    29/ ☐ Yes, to something else (please specify): _____

93. Much of a clergyman's time is spent on activities other than preparing sermons and conducting services. About how many hours a week do you spend on the following activities?

	7 or More Hours	5-6	3-4	1-2	Less Than One Hour
	1	2	3	4	5
A. Educating the youth of the church	☐	☐	☐	☐	☐
B. Attending to administrative matters	☐	☐	☐	☐	☐
C. Participating in public affairs	☐	☐	☐	☐	☐
D. Counseling parishioners on their personal problems	☐	☐	☐	☐	☐
E. Counseling parishioners on religious matters	☐	☐	☐	☐	☐

94. To what extent do you participate in the activities of the following organizations?

35-42/

		Quite A Lot	Occa- sionally	Very Little	Never
		1	2	3	4
A.	Your national church organization	☐	☐	☐	☐
B.	Your regional church organization	☐	☐	☐	☐
C.	Community service groups	☐	☐	☐	☐
D.	A local council of churches or ministerial association	☐	☐	☐	☐

95. Generally speaking, do you think of yourself as a Republican, a Democrat, or an independent?

1 ☐ Republican
2 ☐ Democrat
3 ☐ Independent
4 ☐ Other (please specify):_____

96. When you were young, did your father think of himself mostly as a Democrat or Republican, or did he shift around?

1 ☐ Republican
2 ☐ Democrat
3 ☐ Shift around
4 ☐ Other
5 ☐ Don't know

97. It is sometimes said that not all ministers receive salaries and benefits sufficient to support themselves in suitable fashion. Compared with parish ministers in other denominations, how well, on the average, do ministers in your denomination do?

1 ☐ Much better than most other denominations
2 ☐ Somewhat better than most other denominations
3 ☐ About the same as most other denominations
4 ☐ Somewhat worse than most other denominations
5 ☐ Much worse than most other denominations

98. Compared with other parish ministers in your own denomination, how would you describe your salary and benefits?

1 ☐ Much above average
2 ☐ Somewhat above average
3 ☐ About average
4 ☐ Somewhat below average
5 ☐ Much below average

99. What is your present denomination?

43-44/
- 1[___] American Baptist
- 2[___] American Lutheran Church
- 3[___] Episcopal
- 4[___] Lutheran Church in America
- 5[___] Methodist
- 6[___] Missouri-Synod, Lutheran Church
- 7[___] Presbyterian
- 8[___] Southern Baptist
- 9[___] United Church of Christ
- 10[___] Other (please specify): _____

100. Looking back on things--if you had it to do over--how certain are you that you would enter the ministry?
- 1[___] Definitely would do it again
- 2[___] Probably would do it again
- 3[___] Not sure whether you would do it again or not
- 4[___] Probably would not enter the ministry
- 5[___] Definitely would not enter the ministry

THANK YOU FOR YOUR COOPERATION. If you have any additional opinions on the subjects explored in this questionnaire, we'd appreciate your comments.

INDEX